Boris Hirsch

Monopsonistic Labour Markets and the Gender Pay Gap

Theory and Empirical Evidence

Dr. Boris Hirsch
Friedrich-Alexander-Universität Erlangen-Nürnberg
Chair of Labour and Regional Economics
Lange Gasse 20
90403 Nürnberg
Germany
boris.hirsch@wiso.uni-erlangen.de

ISSN 0075-8442
ISBN 978-3-642-10408-4   e-ISBN 978-3-642-10409-1
DOI 10.1007/978-3-642-10409-1
Springer Heidelberg Dordrecht London New York

Library of Congress Control Number: 2010920969

© Springer-Verlag Berlin Heidelberg 2010
This work is subject to copyright. All rights are reserved, whether the whole or part of the material is concerned, specifically the rights of translation, reprinting, reuse of illustrations, recitation, broadcasting, reproduction on microfilm or in any other way, and storage in data banks. Duplication of this publication or parts thereof is permitted only under the provisions of the German Copyright Law of September 9, 1965, in its current version, and permissions for use must always be obtained from Springer. Violations are liable for prosecution under the German Copyright Law.
The use of general descriptive names, registered names, trademarks, etc. in this publication does not imply, even in the absence of a specific statement, that such names are exempt from the relevant protective laws and regulations and therefore free for general use.

Cover design: SPi Publisher Services

Printed on acid-free paper

Springer is part of Springer Science+Business Media (www.springer.com)

To my parents and grandparents

Lecture Notes in Economics and Mathematical Systems   639

Founding Editors:

M. Beckmann
H.P. Künzi

Managing Editors:

Prof. Dr. G. Fandel
Fachbereich Wirtschaftswissenschaften
Fernuniversität Hagen
Feithstr. 140/AVZ II, 58084 Hagen, Germany

Prof. Dr. W. Trockel
Institut für Mathematische Wirtschaftsforschung (IMW)
Universität Bielefeld
Universitätsstr. 25, 33615 Bielefeld, Germany

Editorial Board:

H. Dawid, D. Dimitrow, A. Gerber, C-J. Haake, C. Hofmann, T. Pfeiffer,
R. Slowiński, W.H.M. Zijm

For further volumes:
http://www.springer.com/series/300

Acknowledgements

I would like to thank all those people who have helped me in the course of my research that culminated in this Ph.D. thesis.

First and foremost, I am deeply indebted to my academic supervisors. My special thanks go to my principal academic supervisor Claus Schnabel for his perpetual guidance and encouragement and for the many insightful discussions that helped greatly in forming this work. I am also deeply grateful to my second supervisor Jürgen Jerger for valuable advice and many useful suggestions that contributed substantially to this thesis' completion.

Apart from my supervisors, I am particularly grateful to my co-authors Marion König, Joachim Möller, Thorsten Schank, and Claus Schnabel. Large parts of Chapters 6 and 9 are grounded on joint work with them, and I benefited a lot from their comments and suggestions.

Many thanks go to my colleagues at the Friedrich–Alexander–Universität Erlangen–Nürnberg and to the Bavarian Graduate Program in Economics and its members. The program's excellent courses and seminars proved to be instrumental in writing this thesis. The program's generosity also allowed me to spend half a year at the Centre for Economic Performance at the London School of Economics and Political Science, which has been a great stimulation in the course of writing this thesis. I would like to thank for the centre's warm hospitality and in particular Alan Manning for many fruitful conversations and helpful suggestions.

My very special thanks go to Jürgen Deinhard. He not only proof-read the whole thesis (including the technical appendices) and pointed me at several inaccuracies and obscurities in the exposition but also provided me with a lot of useful econometric comments and suggestions. Last but not least, I owe my deepest gratitude to my parents and grandparents, to whom I dedicate this work.

Contents

1	**Introduction**	1
	1.1 Wage Setting vs. Wage Taking	1
	1.2 'Classic' vs. 'New' Monopsony	3
	1.3 Plan of the Book	6

Part I Spatial Monopsony

2	**Simple Static Monopsony**	11
3	**Short-Run Spatial Monopsony**	15
	3.1 The Basic Assumptions	15
	3.2 The Elasticity of the Firm's Aggregate Labour Supply	19
	3.3 Convexity and Elasticity of Individual Labour Supply	21
	3.3.1 Convexity Relative to an Exponential	21
	3.3.2 Spatial Implications of Individual Labour Supply's Convexity	27
	3.4 Spatial vs. Spaceless Monopsony	28
	3.5 Firms' Interaction and Conjectural Variations	31
	3.6 The Short-Run Equilibrium	35
	3.7 Short-Run Comparative Statics	38
	3.8 Conclusions	46
4	**Long-Run Spatial Monopsony**	49
	4.1 The Zero-Profit Locus	50
	4.2 The Wage-Setting Curve	52
	4.3 The Long-Run Equilibrium	55
	4.4 Long-Run Comparative Statics	60
	4.4.1 Changes in the Position of the Zero-Profit Locus and the Wage-Setting Curve	61
	4.4.2 Comparative Statics in the Fixed Costs and the Worker Density	62
	4.4.3 Comparative Statics in the Marginal Revenue Product of Labour	65
	4.4.4 Comparative Statics in the Travel Cost	67

	4.5	Long-Run Spatial Monopsony under Linear Individual Labour Supply	70
		4.5.1 The Löschian Equilibrium	75
		4.5.2 The Greenhut–Ohta Equilibrium	78
		4.5.3 The Hotelling–Smithies Equilibrium	79
	4.6	Long-Run Spatial Monopsony with Constant Individual Labour Supply	82
		4.6.1 The Hotelling–Smithies and the Greenhut–Ohta Equilibrium	83
		4.6.2 Allowing for Varying Participation	87
		4.6.3 The Löschian Equilibrium	90
	4.7	Conclusions	92
5	**Spatial Monopsony and the Gender Pay Gap**	95
	5.1	The Gender Pay Gap and Beckerian vs. Robinsonian Discrimination	95
	5.2	The Model	98
		5.2.1 The Basic Assumptions	98
		5.2.2 Firm-Level Labour Supply and Firms' Wage-Setting Behaviour	100
		5.2.3 The Equilibrium and Its Properties	103
	5.3	Conclusions	108
6	**Spatial Monopsony and Regional Differences in the Gender Pay Gap**	113
	6.1	Theoretical Considerations	114
	6.2	Empirical Specification	116
	6.3	Data	119
	6.4	Descriptive Evidence	123
	6.5	Multivariate Evidence	125
	6.6	Conclusions	128

Part II Dynamic Monopsony

7	**Simple Dynamic Monopsony**	133
8	**A General Equilibrium Model of Dynamic Monopsony**	137
	8.1	Some Introductory Remarks	137
	8.2	The Model	139
		8.2.1 The Basic Assumptions	139
		8.2.2 Workers' Reservation Wage	141
		8.2.3 Firms' Steady-State Labour Supply	143
		8.2.4 The Steady-State Equilibrium and Its Properties	144
	8.3	Some Concluding Remarks	148

Contents   xi

9 Dynamic Monopsony and the Gender Pay Gap 151
   9.1   A Simple Measure of On-the-Job Search Frictions 153
   9.2   A Semi-Structural Estimation Approach to the
          Firm-Level Labour Supply Elasticity 155
        9.2.1   Combining Simple Dynamic Monopsony
               and the Burdett–Mortensen Model 155
        9.2.2   Introducing Stochastic Job-to-Job Transitions 157
        9.2.3   Introducing Elastic Transitions
               from and to Non-Employment 158
        9.2.4   Procedure for Identifying the Long-Run
               Labour Supply Elasticity at the Level of the Firm 160
        9.2.5   Empirical Specification 160
        9.2.6   Related Empirical Literature 163
   9.3   Data 164
   9.4   Gender Differences in Search Frictions 168
   9.5   Estimates of the Gender Difference in Long-Run
          Firm-Level Labour Supply Elasticities 173
        9.5.1   Transition to Employment 174
        9.5.2   Transition to Non-Employment 181
        9.5.3   Hiring from Employment 187
        9.5.4   Estimates of the Long-Run Firm-Level Labour
               Supply Elasticities 192
   9.6   Conclusions 199

10 Concluding Remarks 201

A Appendix: Spatial Monopsony 207
   A.1   Proof of Remark 3.2 207
   A.2   Proof of Example 3.5 208
   A.3   Proof of Proposition 3.3 210
   A.4   Proof of Proposition 3.5 217
   A.5   The Slope of the Zero-Profit Locus in the Löschian
          Long-Run Equilibrium 220
   A.6   Proof of Lemma 4.1 220
   A.7   Proof of Lemma 4.3 222
   A.8   Comparative Statics under Linear Spatial Monopsony 226
   A.9   The Implicit Solution for the Long-Run Hotelling–
          Smithies Equilibrium Wage in the Linear
          Model 227
   A.10   Proof of Corollary 5.3 228
   A.11   Appendix to Chapter 6 229

B Appendix: Dynamic Monopsony 231
   B.1   The Relation between the Firm's Short- and Long-Run
          Labour Supply Elasticity 231

B.2	Workers' Optimal Reservation Wage	232
B.3	Proof of Proposition 8.1: Workers' Expected Wage	233
B.4	Proof of Equation (9.1)	233
B.5	Proof of Equation (9.12)	235
B.6	Proof of Equation (9.17)	236
B.7	Appendix to Chapter 9	236

References 245

Index 257

List of Figures

2.1 Wage and employment chosen by a non-discriminating monopsonist..... 13
3.1 Wage reactions of the firm's rival under Löschian, Hotelling–Smithies, and Greenhut–Ohta competition and the associated changes in the firm's market radius......................... 32
3.2 Perceived labour supply curves for a labour market consisting of market areas of a given radius $0 < X < X_M$ under Löschian, Hotelling–Smithies, and Greenhut–Ohta competition ... 38
4.1 The zero-profit locus in the (X, w)-plane................................... 51
4.2 The wage-setting curves and a family of zero-profit loci for different levels of fixed costs under strictly log-concave individual labour supply.. 55
4.3 The existence and uniqueness of the long-run equilibrium under Greenhut–Ohta competition.. 57
4.4 The long-run equilibrium under strictly log-convex individual labour supply.. 58
4.5 The long-run equilibrium under strictly log-concave individual labour supply.. 58
4.6 The long-run equilibrium under log-linear individual labour supply 58
4.7 The impact of an increase in the fixed costs or a decrease in the worker density on the long-run equilibrium wage and market radius under Greenhut–Ohta competition........................... 63
4.8 The impact of an increase in the fixed costs or a decrease in the worker density on the long-run equilibrium wage and market radius under Hotelling–Smithies competition if individual labour supply is strictly log-concave and competition is fierce 63
4.9 The impact of an increase in the fixed costs or a decrease in the worker density on the long-run equilibrium wage and market radius under Löschian competition if individual labour supply is strictly log-concave 64

4.10 The impact of an increase in the fixed costs or a decrease in the worker density on the long-run equilibrium wage and market radius under Löschian competition if individual labour supply is log-linear 64
4.11 The impact of an increase in the marginal revenue product of labour on the long-run equilibrium wage and market radius under Greenhut–Ohta competition... 66
4.12 The impact of an increase in the marginal revenue product of labour on the long-run equilibrium wage and market radius under Löschian competition if individual labour supply is strictly log-concave 67
4.13 The impact of an increase in the travel cost on the long-run equilibrium wage and market radius under Greenhut–Ohta competition .. 68
4.14 The impact of an increase in the travel cost on the long-run equilibrium wage and market radius under Hotelling–Smithies competition if individual labour supply is strictly log-concave and competition is weak............................ 69
4.15 A family of zero-profit loci for different fixed costs $f^1 < f^2 < f^3 < f_{max}$ 72
4.16 A family of zero-profit loci for different fixed costs $f^1 < f^2 < f^3 < f_{max}$ and the wage-setting curves under Löschian, Hotelling–Smithies, and Greenhut–Ohta competition 75
4.17 The Löschian long-run equilibrium under linear individual labour supply for different levels of fixed costs $f^1 < f^2 < f^3 < f_{max}$ ... 76
4.18 The Greenhut–Ohta long-run equilibrium under linear individual labour supply for different levels of fixed costs $f^1 < f^2 < f^3 < f_{max}$ 79
4.19 The Hotelling–Smithies long-run equilibrium under linear individual labour supply for different levels of fixed costs $f^1 < f^2 < f^3 < f_{max}$ 80
4.20 The Löschian, the Hotelling–Smithies, and the Greenhut–Ohta long-run equilibrium under constant individual labour supply 86
4.21 The impact of an increase in the travel cost on the Hotelling–Smithies long-run equilibrium under constant individual labour supply... 86
4.22 The impact of an increase in the worker density (or a decrease in the fixed costs) on the Hotelling–Smithies long-run equilibrium under constant individual labour supply 86
4.23 The impact of an increase in the marginal revenue product of labour on the Hotelling–Smithies long-run equilibrium under constant individual labour supply..................................... 87

List of Figures

6.1	The gender wage differentials Δ_w^1 and Δ_w^0 for segmented female and male labour markets with worker densities D^1 and D^0 with $D^1 > D^0$	115
6.2	Hot spots and rural areas	122
6.3	Average wages and raw gender pay gaps at the NUTS 3 regional level by population density	123
6.4	Average raw gender pay gaps in hot spots and rural areas 1975–2004	124
6.5	Unexplained gender pay gaps in hot spots and rural areas 1975–2004 using nearest neighbour matching without replacement	126
6.6	Unexplained gender pay gaps in hot spots and rural areas 1975–2004 using kernel matching	126
6.7	Unexplained gender pay gaps in hot spots and rural areas 1975–2004 using the Oaxaca–Blinder decomposition	127
9.1	Transitions of men	167
9.2	Transitions of women	168
A.1	Unexplained gender pay gaps in hot spots and rural areas 1975–2004 using three-nearest neighbour matching with replacement	229
A.2	Unexplained gender pay gaps using only individuals without change of regional type of first appearance in the labour market and nearest neighbour matching without replacement	230

List of Tables

3.1	Wage and market radius responses under Löschian, Hotelling–Smithies, and Greenhut–Ohta competition	33
3.2	Comparative static effects on the short-run equilibrium wage	40
4.1	The impact of changes in the market conditions on the position of the zero-profit locus and the wage-setting curve	61
4.2	Comparative static effects on the long-run equilibrium wage	70
4.3	Comparative static effects on the long-run equilibrium wage under linear individual labour supply	81
4.4	Comparative static effects on the long-run equilibrium wage under constant individual labour supply	87
9.1	Determinants of the probability of being hired from non-employment	170
9.2	Determinants of males' instantaneous separation rate to employment	176
9.3	Determinants of females' instantaneous separation rate to employment	178
9.4	Determinants of males' instantaneous separation rate to non-employment	182
9.5	Determinants of females' instantaneous separation rate to non-employment	184
9.6	Determinants of males' probability of being hired from employment	188
9.7	Determinants of females' probability of being hired from employment	190
9.8	Estimates of the long-run firm-level elasticity of female and male labour supplies when tenure is not controlled for	194
9.9	Estimates of the long-run firm-level elasticity of female and male labour supplies when tenure is controlled for	196
B.1	Descriptive statistics for the whole sample	237
B.2	Descriptive statistics for the recruitment sample	239
B.3	Wage regressions	241
B.4	Estimates of the long-run firm-level elasticity of female and male labour supplies when tenure is not controlled for and downsizing establishments are excluded	243

xvii

List of Abbreviations

BBR	Federal Office for Building and Regional Planning (*Bundesamt für Bauwesen und Raumordnung*)
c.d.f.	cumulative distribution function
GO	Greenhut–Ohta
HS	Hotelling–Smithies
IAB	Institute for Employment Research (*Institut für Arbeitsmarkt- und Berufsforschung*) of the Federal Employment Agency (*Bundesagentur für Arbeit*)
IAB-REG	Regional File of the IAB Employment Samples (IABS)
LIAB	Linked Employer–Employee Data Set of the Institute for Employment Research (*Institut für Arbeitsmarkt- und Berufsforschung*)
Lö	Löschian
NUTS	nomenclature des unités territoriales statistiques
WSC	wage-setting curve
ZPL	zero-profit locus

List of Symbols

C	firm's production costs
D	worker density
E	percentage gap between workers' wages and their marginal revenue product of labour ('exploitation')
F	c.d.f. of wages across firms (wage offer distribution)
G	c.d.f. of wages across workers (wage distribution)
I	number of employment spells
I_R	number of transitions
J	number (mass) of firms
L	employment
L^d	firm's labour demand
L^s	firm's labour supply
$\mathcal{L}$	Lagrangean
M	number (mass) of workers
M_R	number of recruits
N	number (mass) of non-employed
R	number (mass) of recruits (hires)
$\mathcal{R}$	total number (mass) of recruits (hires) in an economy
S	support of covariates
V	value function
W	wage-setting condition
X	firm's market radius
Y	firm's revenue
Z	set of positive wage–distance pairs yielding incomes above workers' reservation income (or their reservation incomes' infimum, respectively) r and below their marginal revenue product ϕ, $Z := \{(w, x) \gg 0 \mid r < z(w, x) < \phi\}$
b	workers' opportunity cost of employment
c	number of cells containing a given combination of covariates

List of Symbols

d	female dummy (dummy variable taking on the value one if the individual under consideration is female and zero otherwise)
e	firm's aggregate labour supply elasticity
e_{Lw}	firm-level labour supply elasticity
e_{Rw}	wage elasticity of the firm's number (mass) of recruits
e_{sw}	wage elasticity of the firm's separation rate
e_{wL}	inverse firm-level labour supply elasticity
f	fixed costs
f_{max}	highest level of fixed costs that allows some firms to stay in the labour market, $f_{max} := (\phi - w_M) L(w_M, X_M)$
h	weighting function, $h(x) := l(w - tx) / (\int_0^X l(w - tx)\, dx)$
l	individual (market-level) labour supply
ℓ	logarithm of individual (market-level) labour supply, $\ell(z) := \ln l(z)$
n	non-employment rate
r	reservation income; infimum of workers' reservation incomes; reservation wage
r_{max}	supremum of workers' reservation incomes
$\bar{r}$	high reservation income
$\underline{r}$	low reservation income
s	separation rate
t	travel cost per unit distance; time; tenure
$\bar{t}$	high travel cost
$\underline{t}$	low travel cost
v	conjectural variations parameter, $v := \partial X / \partial w$
w	wage
$\tilde{w}$	direct competitor's wage
$\bar{w}$	supremum of the wage offer distribution's support
$\underline{w}$	infimum of the wage offer distribution's support
x	distance; vector of person-specific regressors
y	regressand
z	income; vector of establishment-specific regressors
Δ_e	gender firm-level labour supply elasticity differential, $\Delta_e := e^m - e^f$
Δ_w	gender wage differential, $\Delta_w := w^m - w^f$
$\Delta_{\%w}^\sigma$	gender pay gap with group σ as reference group, $\Delta_{\%w}^\sigma := (w^\varsigma - w^\sigma)/w^\sigma$ with $\sigma, \varsigma = f, m$ and $\varsigma \neq \sigma$
$\Gamma(w, t \mid F, r)$	number (mass) of workers employed at a wage no more than w at time t
Λ	c.d.f. of the standard logistic distribution
Π	firm's profits
Φ	c.d.f. of the standard normal distribution

List of Symbols

α	parameter
β	parameter; vector of person-specific regressors' coefficients
γ	parameter; vector of establishment-specific regressors' coefficients
δ	job destruction rate
ε	individual (market-level) labour supply elasticity
ζ	share of recruits hired from non-employment
η	share of female workers with high travel cost
θ_R	share of recruits from employment
θ_S	share of separations to employment
κ	share of workers with low reservation income
λ	job offer arrival rate
μ	density of male workers
ν	Lagrange multiplier
ξ	market friction parameter, $\xi := \delta/\lambda^e$
ρ	discount factor
ϱ	(instantaneous) discount rate
τ	equilibrium ratio of employed female to employed male workers
υ	frailty (random effect)
ϕ	marginal revenue product of labour
φ	workers' job-to-job transition probability function
ω	reaction function

Subscripts:

c	competitive
GO	Greenhut–Ohta
HS	Hotelling–Smithies
$Lö$	Löschian
M	spatial monopsony
m	spaceless monopsony

Superscripts:

e	employment
f	female
$\overline{f}$	high-travel-cost female
$\underline{f}$	low-travel-cost female
LR	long-run
SR	short-run
m	male
n	non-employment

Chapter 1
Introduction

1.1 Wage Setting vs. Wage Taking

In his ground-breaking monograph *Monopsony in Motion: Imperfect Competition in Labor Markets*, Manning (2003a, p. 3) starts his argument in favour of a monopsonistic approach to labour market phenomena with a compelling case against perfect competition: 'What happens if an employer cuts the wage it pays its workers by one cent? Much of labor economics is built on the assumption that all existing workers immediately leave the firm as that is the implication of the assumption of perfect competition in the labor market.' Taking the model literally, this would indeed be its prediction. Other than in a perfectly competitive labour market where employers are wage takers unable to deviate from the market wage, a monopsonistic approach assumes that employers possess significant wage-setting power and actually exercise their market power. Put differently, it argues that some of the workers stay with the firm, giving the firm some discretion in wage setting. Technically speaking, the main difference between the two models is that under perfect competition the labour supply faced by the firm is infinitely elastic, whereas this does not hold under monopsony.[1]

While Manning is right in stating that the model of a perfectly competitive labour market still dominates teaching and considerable parts of labour economics, there are of course notable exceptions, for instance, the efficiency wage (e.g., Schlicht, 1978; Salop, 1979a; Shapiro and Stiglitz, 1984; Yellen, 1984), the search and equilibrium unemployment (e.g., Mortensen and Pissarides, 1999; Pissarides, 2000; Rogerson *et al.*, 2005), the signalling and screening (e.g., Spence, 1973; Stiglitz,

---

[1] In the following, we will follow the common usage of the term 'monopsony' in labour economics today (cf., e.g., Boal and Ransom, 1997; Manning, 2003a; Hirsch and Schumacher, 2005) and refer to a situation where individual firms face an upward-sloping labour supply curve as monopsony, notwithstanding that monopsony literally refers to a situation with a single buyer of labour (for etymological details, see Section 1.2). There is astonishingly little evidence on the elasticity of firm-level labour supply which is mainly due to the substantial difficulties involved in identification (for an excellent overview, see Manning, 2003a, pp. 80–114). We shall turn to this point later in Section 9.2 when we will apply a semi-structural approach brought forward by Manning resting on methods of survival analysis to identify the firm-level labour supply elasticity.

B. Hirsch, *Monopsonistic Labour Markets and the Gender Pay Gap*, Lecture Notes in Economics and Mathematical Systems 639, DOI 10.1007/978-3-642-10409-1_1,
© Springer-Verlag Berlin Heidelberg 2010

1975; Weiss, 1995), or the theoretical literature on trade unions (e.g., Farber, 1986; Booth, 1995; Naylor, 2003) – just to name a few. Whereas it is certainly true that '[r]eal-world labor markets are far removed from the ideal model of perfect competition' (Samuelson, 1951, p. 597) and that in reality an infinitesimally small cut in its wage does not cause a firm to lose all its employees in the next instant, this needs not to undermine the usefulness of the competitive model. 'Truly important and significant hypotheses will be found to have "assumptions" that are wildly inaccurate descriptive representations of reality, and, in general, the more significant the theory, the more unrealistic the assumptions.... The relevant question to ask about the "assumptions" of a theory is not whether they are descriptively "realistic," for they never are, but whether they are sufficiently good approximations for the purpose in hand.' (Friedman, 1953, pp. 14/15) Thus, the question is whether a monopsonistic approach with wage setting or a competitive approach with wage taking or neither of them are best suited for explaining the labour market phenomenon at hand.[2] And, basically, Manning's argument 'is that, for many questions, the competitive model is not a tolerable approximation, and that our understanding of labor markets would be much improved by thinking in terms of a model where the labor supply curve facing the firm is not infinitely elastic'. (Manning, 2003a, p. 13) In a nutshell, Manning proposes a 'monopsonistic-competition revolution' similar to the 'monopolistic-competition revolution'. (Brakman and Heijdra, 2004) That is to say, he prompts the profession to follow the 'post-revolutionary' industrial organisation literature in shifting the standard assumption from saying that firms have no market power to one that states that all firms possess some market power, though some of them might have more market power than others (cf. Manning, 2003a, p.10).

While there are certainly convincing reasons for following Manning in his 'revolution' – in particular his substantial and thorough monograph itself[3] –, we will adopt a more agnostic approach in the spirit of Samuelson (1951, p. 598), who in an early edition of his famous principles textbook has put the state of affairs as follows:

'The fact that a firm of any size *must* have a wage policy is additional evidence of labor market imperfections. In a perfectly competitive market, a firm need not make decisions on its pay schedules; instead it would turn to the morning newspaper to learn what its wage policy would *have* to be. Any firm, by raising wages ever so little, could get all the extra

---

[2] At this point, it is important to stress that an alternative way of modelling the labour market neither relying on wage setting nor on wage taking would be a model of bilateral monopoly. Since the discussion of bilateral monopoly by Edgeworth (1881), however, the profession has been aware of the problem of indeterminacy of the outcome under bilateral monopoly (cf., e.g., Pigou, 1908; Bowley, 1928). Although there has been considerable progress in terms of identifying situations where a certain specification of the bargaining process yields a determinate equilibrium outcome (e.g., Nash, 1953; Rubinstein, 1982; Binmore *et al.*, 1986), the problem of indeterminacy is mainly tackled by imposing rules of the bargaining process that are essentially arbitrary themselves (cf. Manning, 2003a, p. 4). For a synthesis of collective bargaining and monopsony, see Falch and Strøm (2007).

[3] It has also been argued recently that the imbalance in bargaining power assumed by the monopsonistic approach makes it best suited to investigate today's 'post-union labour markets' (e.g., Erickson and Mitchell, 2007).

help it wanted. If, on the other hand, it cut the wage ever so little, it would find no labor to hire at all.

But just because competition is not 100 per cent perfect does not mean that it must be zero. The world is gray, not black or white – it is a blend of (1) competition and (2) some degree of monopoly power over the wage to be paid. If you try to set your wage too low, you will soon learn this. At first nothing much need happen, but eventually you will find your workers quitting a little more rapidly than would otherwise be the case. Recruitment of new people of the same quality will begin to get harder and harder, and you will begin to notice slackening off in the performance and productivity of the people who remain on the job.'

To retain with Samuelson's metaphor, we are concerned with a high-contrast picture in gray, some parts of it containing more black and others containing more white. In the following, our aim will be to advance the monopsonistic approach theoretically and to apply it to a particular topic, namely gender discrimination in the labour market. While we will keep an agnostic attitude towards the applicability of the monopsonistic approach to the whole picture and other labour market phenomena, we shall argue that it substantially contributes to the understanding of the gender pay gap, both theoretically and empirically. Likewise, its potential to the understanding of other labour market phenomena (as well as the broad picture) is an empirical question – not one to be settled by black-and-white *ex ante* reasoning alone, but by carefully investigating the grayness of the topic of interest.

1.2 'Classic' vs. 'New' Monopsony

The origins of the monopsonistic approach lay in Robinson's (1933; 1969) influential *Economics of Imperfect Competition*, 'a book ... presented to the analytical economist as a box of tools. It is an essay in the technique of economic analysis, and can make only an indirect contribution to our knowledge of the actual world.' (Robinson, 1969, p. 1) It has been called, together with Chamberlin's (1933; 1962) *Theory of Monopolistic Competition*, the initiator of 'the first monopolistic competition revolution' (Brakman and Heijdra, 2004, p. 2) – the second revolution being identified with Dixit and Stiglitz's (1977) seminal work.[4] Similar to Manning's case for a monopsonistic approach, Robinson (1969, p. 307) argues in her 27th chapter 'A World of Monopolies' in favour of a monopolistic approach:

'It is customary, in setting out the principles of economic theory, to open with the analysis of a perfectly competitive world, and to treat monopoly as a special case. It has been the purpose of the foregoing argument to show that this process can with advantage be reversed and that it is more proper to set out the analysis of monopoly, treating perfect competition as a special case.'

---

[4] For a historical account, see the volume edited by Brakman and Heijdra (2004). Before the pathbreaking works by Robinson and Chamberlin, issues of imperfect competition were traditionally discussed within the standard model of monopoly (e.g., Marshall, 1920). Pioneering precursors of their work include, among others, Cournot (1838), Sraffa (1926), and Hotelling (1929).

In this sense, it is particularly appropriate to refer to Manning's *Monopsony in Motion: Imperfect Competition in Labor Markets* as a direct successor – an intellectual heir – of Robinson, concerned with a world of monopsonies.

While the theory of monopolistic competition is at the heart of Robinson's book, one of the tools it offers is a simple model of monopsony (see pp. 211–231), the insights of which are applied to the labour market in general and to gender discrimination at the labour market in particular (see pp. 292–304). Though Robinson was not the first to think about labour market phenomena in a monopsonistic way (cf. Manning, 2003a, pp. 5/6), she was the first to do it in a coherent analytical framework; and she was the first to propose the term 'monopsony' for a market with a single buyer (cf. Robinson, 1969, p. 215), derived from combining the Greek verb ὀψωνέω ('buy fish and other dainties,' e.g., Liddell *et al.*, 1996) and the prefix μονο ('single').[5]

Following Hirsch and Schumacher's (2005) terminology, this 'classic' approach to monopsony based on the simple monopsony model or on a standard Cournot-type multi-employer oligopsony model gives rise to monopsonistic wage-setting power if and only if there is concentration on the demand side of the labour market. While there are some cases where this sort of concentration is regarded as plausible – examples include the labour market for professional athletes (e.g., Scully, 1974; Brown, 1993; McCormick and Tollison, 2001), registered nurses (e.g., Link and Landon, 1976; Sullivan, 1989; Hirsch and Schumacher, 1995), public school teachers (e.g., Luizer and Thornton, 1986; Beck, 1993; Falch, 2008), and the labour markets in (coal-mining) company towns (e.g., Boyd, 1993; Boal, 1995) – 'classic' monopsony is typically regarded as a theoretical peculiarity of little general interest:

> 'Monopsony models of labor market behavior seem like an idea whose time has passed. Textbook treatments of monopsony ... leave little doubt that monopsony power is not an important characteristic of (at least) U.S. labor markets, except possibly for some public sector jobs in non-metropolitan areas and perhaps in some areas of professional sports. A crude summary of the prevailing perception in labor economics is that the opening up of the interstate highway system and the decline of company towns eliminated essentially all elements of monopsony power that might have existed previously.'
>
> (Kiefer and Neumann, 1993, p. 57)

Other than models of 'classic' monopsony which give rise to wage-setting power due to demand-side concentration or collusion in the labour market, models of 'new' monopsony – again we follow Hirsch and Schumacher's (2005) terminology – do not require labour markets to be 'thin' in the literal sense (cf. Manning, 2003b). Within this class of models, employers face upward-sloping labour supply curves

---

[5] The actual genesis of the term by Joan V. Robinson and classicist Bertrand L. Hallward is described by Thornton (2004). Interestingly, both Manning (2003a, p. 3) and Thornton (2004) report that the more natural candidate ὠνέομαι ('buy, purchase,' e.g., Liddell *et al.*, 1996) was rejected in favour of ὀψωνέω, for Hallward both wanted to avoid a deponent and argued that the resulting 'monoöny' would not 'produce an attractive (in rhythm or sound) word' (Thornton, 2004, p. 259).

1.2 'Classic' vs. 'New' Monopsony

because labour markets are 'thin' in a broader sense. As Robinson (1969, p. 296) already noted,

> '[m]onopsonistic exploitation can also arise where firms are not acting in concert, but where the supply of labour to each firm is less than perfectly elastic, just as monopolistic arises where the market for selling the commodity is imperfect. We have seen in what circumstances the supply of a factor to an industry may be less than perfectly elastic. The supply of labour to an individual firm might be limited for the same sort of reasons. For instance, there may be a certain number of workers in the immediate neighbourhood and to attract those from further afield it may be necessary to pay a wage equal to what they can earn near home *plus* their fares to and fro; or there may be workers attached to the firm by preference or custom and to attract others it may be necessary to pay a higher wage. Or ignorance may prevent workers from moving from one firm to another in response to differences in the wages offered by the different firm.'

In recent technical terms, monopsony power may arise because of

(1) mobility costs,
(2) heterogenous preferences, or
(3) incomplete information (search frictions).

Put differently, labour markets may be 'thin' in a wider sense: Firstly, they might be 'thin' in geographical space because employers do not exist everywhere. Second, they might be 'thin' in job characteristics space because existing employers and the jobs they offer differ, as do workers in terms of their preferences. And, third, they might appear 'thin' to workers because they only know a small detail of the whole picture.

Unsurprisingly, the 'new' monopsony literature has made use of all these three channels. While its first systematic exposition and application to nearly all traditional topics of labour economics given by Manning (2003*a*) focusses on the impact of search frictions in models of equilibrium search theory with wage posting – or models of dynamic monopsony to follow Boal and Ransom's (1997) terminology –, the impact of heterogenous preferences among workers and mobility costs is analysed by Bhaskar and To (1999; 2003) and Bhaskar *et al.* (2002) within models of horizontal job differentiation or spatial monopsony.[6,7] Though Bhaskar *et al.* (2002)

---

[6] Unlike vertical job differentiation, utilised by the theory of compensating wage differentials (cf., e.g., Rosen, 1974; 1986; Cahuc and Zylberberg, 2004, pp. 248–256, 276–280) that distinguishes 'good' from 'bad' jobs, horizontal job differentiation just assumes different preferences over non-wage characteristics, so that some jobs are 'good' for some workers and 'bad' for others. This is formalised by considering economic space (or the job characteristics space), where otherwise identical workers are located at different places, while employers do not exist at each potential location. Workers commute and face travel cost to do so, so that workers consider jobs nearby as 'better' than jobs far away. Of course, one might think of travelling literally in a geographical way or, more generally, one might think of different preferences over non-wage job characteristics that demand 'travelling,' i.e., the abdication of some preferred job characteristics. We will, however, in the following stick to the case where employers are horizontally differentiated due to their locations.

[7] An alternative way of modelling monopsonistic wage-setting power due to heterogenous preferences over non-wage job characteristics is to follow Dixit and Stiglitz's (1977) model of monopolistic competition, as is done by To (2009).

give a convincing overview of spatial monopsony's usefulness to address several labour market phenomena, there has been – contrary to the search-theoretic strand of the 'new' monopsony literature – little interest in exploring potential generalisations of the spatial strand theoretically or to investigate potential applications in more detail hitherto, notable exceptions being Nakagome (1986), Staiger *et al.* (1999), Booth and Coles (2007), and Kaas and Madden (2008). Apart from applying the monopsonistic approach both in its spatial and its dynamic variant to the gender pay gap, we shall in the following try to fill this gap. Fortunately, we will be able to build on results gained in the 'post-revolutionary' industrial organisation literature, in particular on Greenhut *et al.*'s (1987) monograph *Economics of Imperfect Competition: A Spatial Approach* which provides a convenient analytical framework for our task. But before plunging *in medias res*, we shall first give a detailed outline of the things to follow.

1.3 Plan of the Book

This book is split into two parts: Part I deals with models of spatial monopsony. While Chapters 2–4 are devoted to the theoretical discussion of spatial monopsony alone, Chapters 5 and 6 apply the insights gained to the gender pay gap, both theoretically and empirically. The framework employed in Chapters 3 and 4 is analogous to the one used by Greenhut *et al.* (1987) to analyse spatial oligopoly. While the framework chosen in Part I stresses mobility costs and/or heterogenous preferences as sources of firms' monopsony power, Part II focusses on search frictions. It places emphasis on models of dynamic monopsony and how they can be used to help understanding the gender pay gap empirically.

Part I starts with Chapter 2, *Simple Static Monopsony*. A simple static model of monopsony, similar to the standard monopsony model proposed by Robinson (1969, pp. 218–228), with a single buyer of labour is laid out, which serves as a benchmark for the following more sophisticated models of spatial monopsony. Absent from this model are issues of (spatial) competition which will play an important role in the remainder of Part I.

Chapter 3, *Short-Run Spatial Monopsony*, builds on Chapter 2 by setting up a spatial monopsony model, more precisely both a model of spatial monopsony with a single employer and a model of spatial oligopsony with many employers. In this setting, workers are located at different places, while employers do not exist at each potential location. Therefore, workers have to commute, facing some travel cost. Since employers and the jobs they offer are for this reason not perfect substitutes to workers, competition among employers is imperfect and employers possess some monopsony power. We refer to this as short-run spatial monopsony because the number of employers is fixed. While this approach stresses the role of mobility costs as a source of firms' monopsony power, it is easily relabelled to embrace the case of heterogenous preferences among workers over non-wage job characteristics.

1.3 Plan of the Book

Chapter 4, *Long-Run Spatial Monopsony*, considers the model from Chapter 3 allowing for free entry and exit of firms, i.e., by looking at the long-run zero-profit equilibrium of the model. Since there are some fixed setup costs involved, firms indeed do not exist at each potential location, for this would not allow them to break even, so that the level of the fixed costs is intimately related to the degree of competition in the labour market. Moreover, we investigate some special cases of long-run spatial monopsony where the labour supply of individuals takes on a particularly simple functional form, leading, among others, to the models of Nakagome (1986) and Bhaskar and To (1999).

Chapter 5, *Spatial Monopsony and the Gender Pay Gap*, then moves on to utilise a simplified version of the short-run spatial monopsony model from Chapter 3, viz. a simple dyopsony[8] model, to present a 'new' monopsony re-formulation of Robinson's (1969, pp. 302–304) explanation of gender discrimination in the labour market. This explanation stresses that some women have higher travel cost than men, e.g., due to more domestic responsibilities. Being aware of this, employers can then increase their profits by offering lower wages to women than men, i.e., by exploiting that women are less inclined to commute and to offer their labour to competing firms. Put differently, employers pay women lower wages because they supply labour less elastically at the level of the firm than men. Finally, we discuss what happens to this Robinsonian explanation of the gender pay gap when relaxing some of the assumptions involved.

Chapter 6, *Spatial Monopsony and Regional Differences in the Gender Gap*, closes Part I. We deduce four hypotheses applying the theoretical explanation of the gender pay gap presented in Chapter 5 and test them with German social security data. In particular, we investigate whether the gender pay gap is less pronounced in agglomerations, which is the prediction of the theory, and how the difference in the gap between cities and rural areas evolved between 1975–2004. We find (1) that the gender pay gap is larger in rural areas, (2) that it decreased over time both in cities and rural areas, and (3) that the regional difference in the gap remained remarkably stable over time. All these findings affirm the model's predictions. Since there has been made no attempt – both theoretically and empirically – to investigate

---

[8] In the English-speaking world, it is more common to use the spelling 'duopsony' instead of 'dyopsony,' although the former is a Greek–Latin mishmash, while the latter is more clearly Greek as the term 'monopsony' itself (see the discussion in Section 1.2). The same holds for the term 'duopoly.' However, like the term 'monopsony' the roots of the term 'monopoly' stem from combining a Greek verb, the verb πωλέω ('sell or offer to sell,' e.g., Liddell *et al.*, 1996), with the prefix μονο. Interchanging prefixes, we arrive at situations where there is a single (μονο) or where there are some (ὀλίγο) or even many (πολυ) sellers. Coherently, a situation with two sellers would be described by combining πωλέω and the prefix δύω ('two,' ibid.) to arrive at 'dyopoly,' as is done, for instance, in German by von Stackelberg (1934; 1943) and Eucken (1950). For some unclear reasons the spelling 'duopoly,' combining the Greek πωλέω with the Latin prefix 'duo,' however, 'has been generally accepted and has held its ground against the linguistically preferable term dyopoly' (Machlup, 1952, p. 348). The same holds for the term 'duopsony.' Though the spelling 'dyopoly' and the spelling 'dyopsony' may seem a little alien to some readers – for an example, see Leontief's (1936) review of von Stackelberg (1934) –, we shall stick to this, in our eyes, more coherent spelling.

systematically regional differences in the gender pay gap, we conclude from this that spatial monopsony provides a promising framework to think about the regional dimension of the gap.

Chapter 7, *Simple Dynamic Monopsony*, starts Part II by laying out a simple model of dynamic monopsony, which will serve as the starting point for the following analysis of dynamic monopsony. In particular, a simple specification of it relating the firm's dynamic labour supply to its in- and outflow of workers will turn out to be helpful. Similar to the simple static monopsony model in Chapter 2, this model does not address issues of competition.

Competition is added in Chapter 8, *A General Equilibrium Model of Dynamic Monopsony*, by means of Burdett and Mortensen's (1998) model of equilibrium search with wage posting, which can be thought of as a general equilibrium version of simple dynamic monopsony. In this model, workers are confronted with incomplete information on available job offers and search for jobs both on and off the job. By chance, some non-employed workers initially end up with low-paying and some with high-paying firms and try to work their way up the wage distribution through job-to-job moves. Due to the search frictions, both low- and high-pay firms are able to survive in the labour market, and therefore firms possess some wage-setting power.

Chapter 9, *Dynamic Monopsony and the Gender Pay Gap*, then demonstrates how dynamic monopsony can be used to set up a semi-structural approach to identify the labour supply elasticity at the level of the firm based on methods of survival analysis. Putting this approach into practice and utilising German linked employer–employee data, we find that firm-level labour supply elasticities are small (1.9–3.7) and that women's labour supply is less elastic than men's (which is the reverse of gender differences in labour supply usually found at the level of the market). Our results imply that a substantial part of the gender pay gap might be explained by Robinsonian discrimination. Moreover, a simple measure of on-the-job search frictions indicates that women also face more on-the-job search frictions than men. So women's lower ability to work their way up the wage distribution might be the reason for both differences in elasticities and differences in outcomes.

Chapter 10 draws some conclusions. Two appendices contain many of the more complex proofs, descriptive statistics of the samples used, and results from various robustness checks carried out in the empirical analyses: Appendix A those from Part I and Appendix B those from Part II.

Part I
Spatial Monopsony

Chapter 2
Simple Static Monopsony

A good starting point for the discussion of spatial monopsony is a simple static monopsony model in the fashion of Robinson (1969, pp. 211–231), i.e., considering a spaceless market for homogenous labour with a single non-discriminating firm producing a homogenous commodity from its labour input.[1] This single firm has not to bother with other firms' decisions and is unable to pay different wages to its employees. Let

$$L^s := L(w) \qquad (2.1)$$

denote the firm's labour supply. Assume that the wage w is the firm's only instrument to affect the quantity of labour supplied to it and that L is twice continuously differentiable with $L'(w) > 0$ for all $w > 0$.[2] Since the firm is the single buyer in this labour market, the firm's labour supply is identical to market labour supply, so that we have both upward-sloping labour supply at the level of the firm and the market. Let in the following $w(L)$ denote the inverse of $L(w)$.

We assume that labour is the firm's only factor of production. Let C denote the firm's production costs which are

$$C(L) := wL + f, \qquad (2.2)$$

where f denotes the firm's fixed costs and wL its labour costs. Hence, there are economies of scale because of strictly decreasing average costs. The firm is assumed to produce a homogenous single commodity from its labour input L with a constant marginal revenue product of labour ϕ.[3] Thus, its revenue is given by

---

[1] For a textbook treatment of simple static monopsony, see Blair and Harrison (1993, pp. 36–42), Manning (2003a, pp. 30/31), or Cahuc and Zylberberg (2004, pp. 257–261).

[2] Manning (2006) considers the more general case where the monopsonist is also able to raise her labour supply by increasing her expenditures on recruitment.

[3] It is straightforward to generalise this setting to the case with a second factor of production, say capital, and a constant returns to scale production technology. In this case, we get a constant marginal revenue product of labour for each ratio of the output price and the capital rental rate due to the firm's optimal adjustment of the capital stock employed (e.g., Bhaskar and To, 1999;

$$Y(L) := \phi L. \tag{2.3}$$

Next, the firm is assumed to maximise its profits by choosing the amount of labour employed.[4] The firm's profits are its revenue net of production costs

$$\Pi(L) := Y(L) - C(L) = [\phi - w(L)]L - f, \tag{2.4}$$

where the firm's labour input decision is constrained by market-level inverse labour supply $w(L)$. Since the firm gains a profit of $\phi - w$ from every unit of labour employed, its labour demand L^d is infinite if $\phi - w > 0$, zero if $\phi - w < 0$, and indefinite if $\phi - w = 0$, i.e.,

$$L^d = \begin{cases} \infty & \text{if } \phi > w \\ [0, \infty) & \text{if } \phi = w \\ 0 & \text{if } \phi < w.^5 \end{cases} \tag{2.5}$$

Maximising profits as given by (2.4) yields the first-order condition $\Pi'(L) \stackrel{!}{=} 0$. In the optimum, firm's labour demand behaviour is described by

$$Y'(L_m) = C'(L_m) \Leftrightarrow \phi = w(L_m) + w'(L_m)L_m.^6 \tag{2.6}$$

This condition says that the marginal revenue product has to be equal to the marginal cost of labour, where a diagrammatic representation – with linear market-level labour supply for expositional convenience – is given by Figure 2.1 on the following page. Since the non-discriminating monopsonist has to increase her wage paid to all her existing employees in order to raise her labour supply, she does not hire additional workers until the wage equals the marginal revenue product of labour. But instead, she stops hiring at a lower level L_m, so that this – other than under perfect competition – yields a monopsony wage w_m below workers' marginal revenue

---

2003). Moreover, Bradfield (1990) shows that the (long-run) marginal revenue product of labour is constant if the firm's production technology inhibits constant returns of scale and if there is perfect competition as well on all other factor markets than the labour market as on the monopsonist's output market (see also Hicks, 1963, pp. 242–246). Hence, we can think of labour as one of the factors of production, where the other factors are thought of as set at values that maximise the firm's profits given its labour input.

[4] Of course, this is equivalent to maximising profits by choosing the wage offered to workers. Using employment as the choice variable, however, leads to intuitively more appealing results.

[5] Note that, though the fixed costs f affect overall profits Π, they do not affect marginal decision-making and therefore are irrelevant for the firm's labour demand behaviour.

[6] We assume that $\phi > w(L) + w'(L)L$ for some $L > 0$ in order to avoid a corner solution with $L_m = 0$. Furthermore, we assume that this unique global maximum of profits actually exists. This is guaranteed if $\Pi'(L) > 0$ for all $L < L_m$ and $\Pi'(L) < 0$ for all $L > L_m$. This holds, for example, if profits are strictly concave in w, which in turn is implied if, for instance, market-level labour supply is concave in w.

2 Simple Static Monopsony

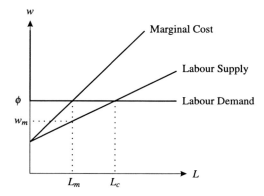

Fig. 2.1 Wage and employment chosen by a non-discriminating monopsonist

product. Some minor algebraic manipulations on (2.6) reveal that the monopsonist's wage is implicitly given by

$$w_m = \frac{e(w_m)}{1 + e(w_m)} \phi, \qquad (2.7)$$

where $e(w) := L'(w)w/L(w)$ is the elasticity of the firm's labour supply at wage w. Hence, the percentage gap between workers' marginal revenue product and the monopsony wage is represented by

$$E_m := \frac{\phi - w_m}{w_m} = \frac{1}{e(w_m)}. \qquad (2.8)$$

E_m represents the classic measure of 'exploitation' introduced by Pigou (1932, pp. 813/814) and is an analogue to the Lerner index utilised in the industrial organisation literature (e.g., Tirole, 1988, p. 66; Blair and Harrison, 1993, pp. 48/49). In our case with a constant marginal revenue product of labour (and thus a horizontal labour demand curve), E_m also gives the percentage gap between the competitive wage $w_c = \phi$ and the monopsony wage w_m – Pigou's (1932, ibid.) 'unfairness.' It therefore serves as a direct measure of the welfare loss caused by the monopsonist which is given by $(\phi - w_m)(L_c - L_m)$.[7]

Obviously, the case of perfect competition is nested in this model. If labour supply becomes infinitely elastic, i.e., $e(w_m) \to \infty$, the monopsonist pays the workers their marginal revenue product. We have $w_m \to \phi$ and, equivalently, $E_m \to 0$ as

---

[7] This does not hold if labour demand is not horizontal but decreasing. In this case, $w_c = Y'(L_c) < Y'(L_m)$ holds, so that E_m overstates the departure of the monopsony wage from the competitive wage and the associated welfare loss (e.g., Boal and Ransom, 1997).

can be seen from (2.7) and (2.8). Moreover, (2.7) shows that the more elastic is the firm's labour supply the higher is the monopsony wage chosen.[8]

It is straightforward to extend this framework by considering more than one employer (though we shall not do so here). For instance, one could consider a Cournot model or a collusive model with more than just one employer. In the collusive model, things are virtually the same as under simple monopsony (cf. Blair and Harison, 1993, pp. 42–46), while the general message of the Cournot model is that, other things being equal, employers' market power decreases with the number of firms competing for workers (cf. Boal and Ransom, 1997). In these models of 'classic' monopsony, labour markets therefore have to be 'thin' in the literal sense of consisting of few employers on the demand side to generate substantial monopsony power.

Things work differently in models of 'new' monopsony. One strand of these models, which we refer to as spatial monopsony and the discussion of which we will begin in the next chapter, gives rise to monopsony power due to mobility costs and/or workers' heterogenous preferences over non-wage job characteristics. The implication of economic space – which can be thought of as geographical space or as job characteristics space – is that agents incur significant travel/transportation cost, for 'costless space is *not economic space*'. (Ohta, 1988, p. 5) On account of the fixed costs, however, firms are not set up at any location possible, so that labour markets are 'thin' to some extent even if there are many employers in economic space.

---

[8] This follows at once from (2.7) because $\partial w_m / \partial e(w_m) = \phi/[1 + e(w_m)]^2 > 0$ for all $w_m > 0$.

Chapter 3
Short-Run Spatial Monopsony

In this chapter economic space comes into play. This is done in a framework analogous to the flexible one used by Greenhut *et al.* (1987) to investigate spatial oligopoly in commodity markets. The main implication of economic space is that agents face significant travel/transportation cost. First, we will discuss the basic assumptions employed by this framework.

3.1 The Basic Assumptions

The model which we will set up in the following is defined by the following basic assumptions:

(A1) Each firm is located at a point on an unbounded line market.
(A2) All firms produce a homogenous product from their homogenous labour input with the same cost function C and a constant marginal revenue product ϕ.
(A3) Firms are local monopsonists. When firms are in competition, there is no market overlap, and workers supply labour to the firm offering the highest income (wage net of travel cost).
(A4) Workers with identical abilities are continuously distributed over the market at a uniform density D.
(A5) The travel cost is proportional to distance and is paid by the worker.
(A6) Workers' labour supply behaviour is the same at any point in space and is summarised by an individual labour supply function l. The individual labour supply function depends on the worker's income (wage net of travel cost) and is strictly increasing on the relevant domain.
(A7) In the short run, equidistant firms are immobile and the distance between them is fixed. In the long run, firms are free to relocate and continue to enter (leave) the market till profits are driven to zero.

We shall now discuss these assumptions in some detail. Assumption (A1) tells us that we are dealing with one-dimensional unbounded economic space. Hence, economic space is represented simply by the real line. This is not restrictive as it is straightforward to extend the following analysis to the case of two-dimensional economic space by considering circular or hexagonal market areas (e.g., Greenhut and Ohta, 1973; Capozza and Attaran, 1976). However, while this would complicate the mathematical analysis considerably, no generality is lost by considering a line market instead (cf. Greenhut et al., 1987, p. 374).

Assumption (A2) excludes any sort of firm heterogeneity by assuming that firms use the same production technology. To be more concrete, we will employ the same assumptions as in Chapter 2. Because of the constant marginal revenue product of labour and firms' homogeneity, each firm's revenue is given by

$$Y(L) := \phi L. \tag{3.1}$$

Each firm's cost function again contains fixed and variable costs,

$$C(L) := wL + f. \tag{3.2}$$

Due to the fixed costs component, this cost function implies economies of scale as average costs are strictly decreasing in the output produced (or, equivalently, in the input used). Finally, each firm's profits are again given by

$$\Pi(L) := Y(L) - C(L) = (\phi - w)L - f. \tag{3.3}$$

Assumption (A3) states that at any place workers are working for exactly one employer, if working at all. This holds because they always choose the employer offering the highest income. For this reason, firms are always monopsonists within their market areas, although they may face competitors if their market areas adjoin another firm's market area.[1]

Assumptions (A4)–(A6) make clear that we consider homogenous economic space, in the sense that the impact of travel cost is everywhere the same and that there are identical workers in terms of ability and number at any place in space. Workers' labour supply behaviour, i.e., their preferences relevant for their leisure–consumption choice, is summarised by an individual labour supply function l. There are two ways of thinking of the individual labour supply function. The first is to assume that it represents workers' common labour supply curve. Individual labour supply of a worker located at distance x to his or her employer is assumed to be given by

$$l(w, x) := l[z(w, x)] \begin{cases} > 0 \text{ if } z > r \\ = 0 \text{ if } z \leqslant r \end{cases} \tag{3.4}$$

---

[1] Of course, there are places where workers receive the same income from two firms and are therefore indifferent between working for the one firm or the other. For instance, this holds at the border of the adjoint market areas of two firms. However, since we are considering the real line as economic space, the set of these places is a null set with mass zero, and so all workers indeed work for only one employer in a well-defined sense.

3.1 The Basic Assumptions

with $l'(z) > 0$ for all $r < z < \phi$. Here z denotes the income received by the worker, i.e., the wage net of the travel cost he or she faces when travelling to the firm, w the wage paid by the firm, and r workers' common reservation income. In the following, we will additionally assume that the restriction of l on (r, ϕ) is a smooth function, i.e., $l|_{(r,\phi)} \in C^\infty$.[2] According to assumption (A5), the income of a worker at distance x from an employer offering the wage w is given by

$$z(w, x) = w - tx \tag{3.5}$$

with the travel cost per unit distance denoted by t. Next, turn to workers' reservation income. Mathematically, workers' reservation income is defined as $r := \inf\{z | l(z) > 0\}$, where we require $r < \phi$.[3] Verbally, workers do not supply any work if their income does not exceed their reservation income, whereas they supply a positive amount of labour as soon as this happens to be the case. Furthermore, their individual labour supply is strictly increasing in the income and the wage offered, implying that the substitution effect of a wage change outweighs the income effect for all individuals over the whole range of possible wages.

What is meant by 'possible wages?' In the definitions above, we restricted attention to cases with $r < z < \phi$. In particular, the worker's income and thus his or her wage is no larger than workers' marginal revenue product. This must be the case, for otherwise firms would not want to employ any workers as they would incur (variable) losses from doing so. Furthermore, when offering workers their marginal revenue product, firms are indifferent between employing some workers and not employing any workers. Hence, considering cases with $z \geq \phi$ is not particularly interesting. Of course, individual labour supply might also be strictly increasing even for $z \geq \phi$, but this is simply irrelevant for the following analysis because no firm's wage offer yields such an income.

There are several reasons why one might consider it implausible that workers vary the hours worked in a way described by l above. Firstly, it does not allow for hump-shaped labour supply, where labour supply is increasing in the wage for low wages but decreasing for high wages. This follows from the global dominance of the substitution effect over the income effect. Hump-shaped (or backward-bending) labour supply, however, has great appeal because it seems reasonable to believe that the income effect is dominating if the wage is sufficiently high, which is also in line with empirical observation (e.g., Cahuc and Zylberberg, 2004, pp. 12, 38/39). Second, complete flexibility in hours worked is clearly at odds with empirical

---

[2] Note that all the following results do not hinge on $l|_{(r,\phi)}$'s smoothness. They also hold if $l|_{(r,\phi)}$ is just twice continuously differentiable, i.e., $l|_{(r,\phi)} \in C^2$, where C^k with $k \geq 1$ denotes the set of functions with k continuous derivatives. For analytical convenience, though, we will regard $l|_{(r,\phi)}$ as smooth below. In the following, we shall also not bother with explicitly distinguishing the individual labour supply function from its restriction on (r, ϕ) whenever there is no danger of confusion or no need for such rigour but just sloppily refer to both as individual labour supply.

[3] If otherwise $r > \phi$, there would be no gains from trade and both firms and workers would not be willing to participate in the labour market, preferring inactivity instead.

observation (e.g., Nakagome, 1986; Cahuc and Zylberberg, 2004, p. 12). Third, interpreting individual labour supply as the upward-sloping labour supply curve of a single individual would imply that workers farther away from their employers would supply less labour, *ceteris paribus*, and that their labour supply reduces gradually with the distance from their employer. There is, however, no broad empirical evidence supportive to this pattern. Fourth and most importantly, '[a] consensus is emerging around the idea that movements in labour supply are principally owing to variations in the participation rate'. (Cahuc and Zylberberg, 2004, p. 38) Hence, empirical observation indicates that most of the variation in labour supply is along the extensive margin, while our way of modelling individual labour supply would put much more weight on variation along the intensive margin. Put differently, participation decisions appear to be much more important than 'amount' decisions.

In the light of these criticisms, interpreting the individual labour supply function as individual workers' common labour supply curve may seem inappropriate. Nevertheless, we can overcome these objections when we consider a second way of thinking of individual labour supply and why it is increasing. Assume that there is at every point of space a continuum of workers with different reservation incomes, where reservation incomes are continuously distributed on the interval (r, r_{max}) with $r_{max} > \phi$. Now, let l denote the cumulative distribution function (c.d.f.) of workers' reservation incomes and assume the following: If offered their reservation income, workers supply a single unit of labour. Otherwise, they do not offer any labour at all. From above we know that (r, r_{max}) gives l's support. Furthermore, l's derivative l' is the density function of workers' reservation incomes and is thus positive on $(r, \phi) \subset (r, r_{max})$. Again, $r = \inf\{z | l(z) > 0\}$ holds because r is the infimum of l's support. Therefore, telling this different story in terms of workers having different reservation incomes and deciding whether to participate by supplying a single unit of labour yields the same labour supply behaviour as described in equation (3.4) – apart from the detail that now $0 < l(z) < 1$ for all $r < z < \phi$.

Of course, both interpretations of the individual labour supply function have their virtues and shortcomings. For instance, the second way of interpreting it as the c.d.f. of workers' reservation incomes does not allow workers to vary the hours worked in response to a change in the wage – apart from their participation decision. Consequently, all variation in their labour supply is along the extensive margin. For this reason, we will adopt a pragmatic approach and use both interpretations below depending on their usefulness in the particular context to be discussed.

Finally, assumption (A7) pins down two different concepts of time. In the short run, we consider a fixed number of equidistant firms with a fixed market radius which may be subject to profits or losses.[4] In the long run, however, incumbent firms are free to leave the market, and newcomers are free to enter it. Hence, ultimately

---

[4] In equilibrium, firms indeed choose the same wage and thus have the same market radius due to the symmetry of the framework. This will be discussed in some detail in Section 3.6.

firms enter or leave the market till profits are driven to zero, so that the number of firms is such that every firm exactly covers its fixed costs. Furthermore, costless relocation of firms ensures that symmetric market areas are also maintained after firms' entry or exit.[5]

3.2 The Elasticity of the Firm's Aggregate Labour Supply

Abstract for the moment from competition and consider a single firm with some market radius $X > 0$ offering some wage w. Making use of equations (3.4) and (3.5), aggregate spatial labour supply of this firm is

$$L^s := L(w, X) = 2D \int_0^X l(w - tx)\, dx.^6 \qquad (3.6)$$

Note that $\partial L(w, X)/\partial w > 0$ for all $(w, X) \in Z := \{(w, X) \gg \mathbf{0} | r < z(w, X) < \phi\}$ follows at once from $l'(z) = l'(w - tx) > 0$ for all $r < z < \phi$, so that the firm's aggregate labour supply is strictly increasing in its wage.[7] The firm's profits are given by

$$\Pi(w, X) = (\phi - w)L(w, X) - f. \qquad (3.7)$$

Maximising profits with respect to the wage offered gives the first-order condition

$$\frac{\partial \Pi(w, X)}{\partial w} = (\phi - w)\frac{\partial L(w, X)}{\partial w} - L(w, X) \stackrel{!}{=} 0.^8 \qquad (3.8)$$

---

[5] It should be noted though that this equilibrium concept is static by nature. We will discuss this point later in some detail when dealing with the long-run equilibrium's stability in Section 4.4.

[6] Note that the Riemann integral given on the right-hand side of (3.6) exists because l is smooth and therefore continuous, which implies l's Riemann integrability. Note further that for circular markets, the firm's aggregate spatial labour supply would be given by

$$L(w, X) = D \int_0^{2\pi}\!\!\int_0^X l(w - tx)x\, dx\, d\vartheta = 2\pi D \int_0^X l(w - tx)x\, dx.$$

(For a derivation of this result, see Ohta, 1988, pp. 16–19.) As already stated in Section 3.1, considering two-dimensional economic space is therefore both straightforward and messy, so that, for simplicity, we shall stick to one-dimensional economic space instead.

[7] Obviously, individual labour supply and market areas must be positive, while wages must be no more than workers' marginal revenue product in economically relevant situations, so that we will restrict attention to cases with $r < z(w, X) < \phi$ or $(w, X) \in Z = \{(w, X) \gg \mathbf{0} | r < z(w, X) < \phi\}$, respectively, where $(w, X) \gg \mathbf{0} :\Leftrightarrow (w, X) \in \{(w, X) | w > 0, X > 0\} = \mathbb{R}^2_+$.

[8] First of all, note that Π as given by (3.7) is smooth and therefore differentiable because l is smooth, so that the standard approach to profit maximisation is viable. Next, similar to our discussion of simple spaceless monopsony in Chapter 2 (see footnote 6 on page 11), assume that there exists a unique positive solution of (3.8). This is, for instance, satisfied if $\partial \Pi(w, X)/\partial w > 0$ for

From this it is straightforward to derive a spatial analogue to (2.7)

$$w_M = \frac{e(w_M, X)}{1 + e(w_M, X)}\phi, \tag{3.9}$$

where $e(w, X) := [\partial L(w, X)/\partial w]w/L(w, X)$ is now the wage elasticity of the firm's aggregate spatial labour supply for some market radius X at wage w. Similar to the results above, we find that the more elastic is aggregate labour supply the higher is the wage offered by the firm. And again we have $w_M \to \phi$ if $e(w_M, X) \to \infty$.

However, because of spatial aggregation (and, as we shall see in Section 3.5, spatial competition), the aggregate labour supply elasticity differs conceptually from the wage elasticity of individual labour supply in a fundamental way. The individual labour supply elasticity of a worker distanced x from the firm is defined as $\varepsilon(w, x) := l'(w - tx)w/l(w - tx)$. Applying the Leibniz rule[9], the elasticity of aggregate labour supply is given by

$$e(w, X) = \int_0^X \frac{wl'(w-tx)}{\int_0^X l(w-tx)\,dx}\,dx + \frac{\partial X}{\partial w}\frac{wl(w-tX)}{\int_0^X l(w-tx)\,dx}, \tag{3.10}$$

where $\partial X/\partial w$ is the change in the firm's market radius due to an increase in the wage offered. In a next step, define a weighting function h by

$$h(x) := \frac{l(w-tx)}{\int_0^X l(w-tx)\,dx}, \tag{3.11}$$

where obviously $\int_0^X h(x)\,dx = 1$ holds. Intuitively, $h(x)$ gives the share of the firm's labour that is supplied by workers distanced x from the firm. Making use of this weighting function and defining $v := \partial X/\partial w$, the aggregate labour supply elasticity becomes

$$e(w, X) = \int_0^X \varepsilon(w, x)h(x)\,dx + vwh(X). \tag{3.12}$$

---

all w smaller than the wage solving (3.8) and $\partial \Pi(w, X)/\partial w < 0$ for all w larger than this wage. In particular, this is implied by strict concavity of Π with respect to w. Besides, by drawing attention to $(w, X) \in Z$ we also avoid dealing with corner solutions.

[9] The Leibniz rule for differentiation under the integral sign states that

$$\frac{\partial}{\partial y}\int_{a(y)}^{b(y)} z(x, y)\,dx = \int_{a(y)}^{b(y)} \frac{\partial z(x, y)}{\partial y}\,dx + b'(y)z[b(y), y] - a'(y)z[a(y), y]$$

under certain conditions; in particular, this holds if z, a, and b are continuously differentiable real functions.

Ignore for the moment the second term on the right-hand side of (3.12), that is, assume that changing the wage has no impact on the firm's market radius. For a given market radius X, the elasticity of aggregate labour supply to the firm is just a weighted average of the wage elasticities of individual labour supply in the firm's market area, where the weights are given by $h(x)$. Accordingly, the weight applied to the individual labour supply elasticity of workers distanced x from the firm is just the share of the firm's labour that is supplied by these workers. Furthermore, the weight given to workers farther away is lower than that of workers nearby, because h (like l) is strictly decreasing in distance x. All this seems intuitively appealing. Before taking a closer look at the second term on the right-hand side of (3.12), which will be crucial when discussing the impact of spatial competition, we shall investigate the first term in detail, i.e., the behaviour of the individual labour supply elasticity $\varepsilon(w, x)$.

3.3 Convexity and Elasticity of Individual Labour Supply

3.3.1 Convexity Relative to an Exponential

For the analyses to follow, it will be useful to introduce the following classification of individual labour supply functions (e.g., Löfgren, 1985; 1986), which is an analogue to the demand classification introduced by Stevens and Rydell (1966). But first define $\ell(z) := \ln l(z)$ to be able to state the following definitions more concisely.

Definition 3.1 (Log-Linearity). An individual labour supply function l is log-linear if $\ell''(z) = 0$ for all $r < z < \phi$.

Definition 3.2 (Strict Log-Concavity). An individual labour supply function l is strictly log-concave if $\ell''(z) < 0$ for all $r < z < \phi$.

Definition 3.3 (Strict Log-Convexity). An individual labour supply function l is strictly log-convex if $\ell''(z) > 0$ for all $r < z < \phi$.

Before discussing these definitions in more detail, it will be helpful to state the following remark (cf. Löfgren, 1985, p. 285; 1986, p. 723):[10]

---

[10] Note that Definitions 3.1–3.3 only make sense if l is at least twice differentiable, so that $\ell''(z)$ actually exists for all $r < z < \phi$. Since we assumed in Section 3.1 that l is smooth, it is convenient to work with these definitions. One can, however, state more general definitions of log-linearity, -concavity, and -convexity that do not require the function under consideration to be twice differentiable. For example, using Prékopa's (1973) definitions, an individual labour supply function is strictly log-concave (log-convex) if $l[\vartheta z_1 + (1-\vartheta)z_2] < l(z_1)^\vartheta l(z_2)^{1-\vartheta}$ ($l[\vartheta z_1 + (1-\vartheta)z_2] > l(z_1)^\vartheta l(z_2)^{1-\vartheta}$) for all $r < z_1, z_2 < \phi$ with $z_1 \neq z_2$ and all $0 < \vartheta < 1$; and log-linear if $l[\vartheta z_1 + (1-\vartheta)z_2] = l(z_1)^\vartheta l(z_2)^{1-\vartheta}$. If l is twice differentiable, these definitions are equivalent to those given by us in Definitions 3.1–3.3, which should not be surprising given the analogy to the well-known concept of a function's concavity, convexity, and linearity.

Remark 3.1 (Convexity Relative to an Exponential). If and only if an individual labour supply function is log-linear, then it is as convex as an exponential; if and only if it is strictly log-convex (log-concave), then it is more (less) convex than an exponential.

Proof. Note that

$$\ell''(z) = \frac{d^2 \ln l(z)}{dz^2} = \frac{l''(z)l(z) - l'(z)^2}{l(z)^2} \gtreqless 0 \qquad (3.13)$$

if and only if $l''(z) \gtreqless l'(z)^2/l(z)$. Hence,

$$\forall r < z < \phi : \ell''(z) \gtreqless 0 \Leftrightarrow \forall r < z < \phi : l''(z) \gtreqless \frac{l'(z)^2}{l(z)}. \qquad (3.14)$$

In the case of exponential individual labour supply $l(z) = \alpha \exp(\beta z)$ with parameters $\alpha, \beta > 0$, $\ell''(z) = 0$ and thus $l''(z) = l'(z)^2/l(z)$ holds (see Example 3.1 on the following page). Consider now individual labour supply functions l_1 and l_2 that are strictly log-convex and strictly log-concave, respectively. Obviously, $l_1''(z) > l_1'(z)^2/l_1(z)$ and $l_2''(z) < l_2'(z)^2/l_2(z)$ hold, so that l_1 is more and l_2 less convex than an exponential individual labour supply function. ∎

Remark 3.1 helps to build up an intuition what is meant by an individual labour supply function's log-linearity, -convexity, or -concavity. Intuitively, the standard notion of strict convexity, linearity, and strict concavity can be thought of as 'convexity relative to an affine function.' Strictly convex functions are therefore functions that are 'more convex than an affine function,' whereas strictly concave functions are 'less convex than an affine function.' On the other hand, whether the logarithm of a function is less, more, or as convex as an affine function, i.e., whether the function is strictly log-concave, strictly log-convex, or log-linear depends on the function's convexity relative to an exponential. If a function is more (less) convex than an exponential, then it is strictly log-convex (log-concave); and if a function is as convex as an exponential, then it is log-linear.[11]

Note also that, depending on the interpretation of l as workers' common individual labour supply function or as the c.d.f. of workers' reservation incomes, its convexity relative to an exponential refers to the curvature of individual workers' labour supply curve or to the shape of the distribution of workers' reservation incomes at any point in space. In both cases, however, its curvature is of interest only

---

[11] This will perhaps become even clearer if one considers Prékopa's (1973) less restrictive definition of a function's log-linearity (that does not require l to be twice differentiable) and compares it to the definition of a function's linearity. While a function l_1 is log-linear if $l_1[\vartheta z_1 + (1-\vartheta)z_2] = l_1(z_1)^\vartheta l_1(z_2)^{1-\vartheta}$ for all $r < z_1, z_2 < \phi$ with $z_1 \neq z_2$ and all $0 < \vartheta < 1$, a function l_2 is linear if $l_2[\vartheta z_1 + (1-\vartheta)z_2] = \vartheta l_2(z_1) + (1-\vartheta)l_2(z_2)$. Consider now l_1. Taking the logarithm of l_1, we see at once that $\ell_1[\vartheta z_1 + (1-\vartheta)z_2] = \vartheta \ell_1(z_1) + (1-\vartheta)\ell_1(z_2)$ holds. Hence, ℓ_1 is linear, while $l_1 = \exp \ell_1$ is log-linear and therefore as convex as an exponential.

3.3 Convexity and Elasticity of Individual Labour Supply

up to an upper ceiling given by workers' marginal revenue product. Moreover, when interpreting l as workers' individual labour supply curve, it is evident that workers' labour supply will finally become (log-)concave as labour supply must be bounded above by some real value, so that restricting to cases with $z < \phi$ is necessary for Definitions 3.1 and 3.3 to make sense.

While we shall see that by means of this classification we will be able to present general results holding for every member of these three groups of individual labour supply functions, it is important to stress that these mutually exclusive definitions are not exhaustive (cf. Stevens and Rydell, 1966; Löfgren, 1986):

Remark 3.2 (Definitions 3.1–3.3 Are Not Exhaustive.). There exist labour supply functions in the sense of (3.4) that do not fit into the classification given by Definitions 3.1–3.3.

Proof. The proof of this claim is quite straightforward, for we just have to find an example. For instance, $l(z) := \exp[\tan(z - \pi/2)]$ with $r = 0$ and $\phi = \pi$, the appropriateness of which is demonstrated in Appendix A.1, will do the job.[12] ∎

Remark 3.3 (Definitions 3.1–3.3 Are Mutually Exclusive.). An individual labour supply function is either strictly log-concave, log-linear, strictly log-convex, or neither of these possibilities.[13] ∎

Equipped with the result from Remark 3.1, it is now helpful to consider some examples:

Example 3.1 (Exponential Individual Labour Supply). The exponential individual labour supply function

$$l(z) := \alpha \exp(\beta z) \equiv \alpha e^{\beta z} \tag{3.15}$$

with constants $\alpha, \beta > 0$ is log-linear and thus as convex as an exponential. The reservation income implied is given by $r = -\infty$.[14]

---

[12] By the way, $\exp[\tan(z - \pi/2)]$ is an example of a convex function with strictly log-convex parts (for $\pi/2 < z < \phi = \pi$) and strictly log-concave parts (for $r = 0 < z < \pi/2$).

[13] Contrary to Remark 3.3, Greenhut et al. (1987, p. 25) claim that Definitions 3.1–3.3 are not mutually exclusive. Hence, there should be functions that fit to more than just one of these definitions. Actually, it is clear that there exist functions that do not fit either of Definitions 3.1–3.3. However, it is impossible for a function to fit two or even all of them, for (restrictions of) functions and their logarithms can be either strictly convex, linear, strictly concave, or neither of these three possibilities. The reason for Greenhut et al.'s claim might be Stevens and Rydell's (1966, p. 197) remark that Definitions 1–7 in their paper are not mutually exclusive. Their Definitions 1–3, however, are the standard definitions of strict convexity, strict concavity, and linearity, whilst Definitions 4–6 correspond to convexity relative to an exponential. As shown above, upward-sloping affine functions are always less convex than an exponential, so that Definitions 2 and 4 in Stevens and Rydell (1966, p. 196) are indeed not mutually exclusive, whereas our Definitions 1–3 on their own certainly are.

[14] Note that we shall speak of r as *the* reservation income in the following. However, as noted above in Section 3.1, r can also be thought of as the lower bound of the support of workers' reservation incomes depending on the interpretation of the individual labour supply function as either workers' individual labour supply curve or as the c.d.f. of their reservation incomes.

Proof. Since $\ell(z) = \ln \alpha + \beta z$, $\ell''(z) = 0$ holds for all $r < z < \phi$. Furthermore, $r = -\infty$ holds because $l(z) \to 0$ if $z \to -\infty$ and $l(z) > 0$ for all $z \in \mathbb{R}$. ∎

Example 3.2 (Generalised Exponential Individual Labour Supply). The generalised exponential individual labour supply function

$$l(z) := \alpha \exp_\gamma(\beta z) \equiv \alpha \gamma^{\beta z} \tag{3.16}$$

with constants $\alpha, \beta > 0$ and $\gamma > 1$ is log-linear and therefore as convex as an exponential. The reservation income implied is given by $r = -\infty$. Exponential labour supply, as presented in Example 3.1, is gained if $\gamma = e$.

Proof. The restriction $\gamma > 1$ is needed to generate strictly increasing individual labour supply. Since $\ell(z) = \ln \alpha + \beta z \ln \gamma$, we get $\ell''(z) = 0$ for all $r < z < \phi$. Finally, $r = -\infty$ follows from $l(z) \to 0$ if $z \to -\infty$ and $l(z) > 0$ for all $z \in \mathbb{R}$. ∎

Example 3.3 (Linear Individual Labour Supply). The linear individual labour supply function

$$l(z) := \alpha + \beta z \tag{3.17}$$

with constants $\alpha \leq 0$ and $\beta > 0$ is strictly log-concave and therefore less convex than an exponential. The reservation income implied is $r = -\alpha/\beta$.

Proof. The restriction $\alpha \leq 0$ is needed to get $r = \inf\{z | l(z) > 0\} = -\alpha/\beta \geq 0$. From $\ell(z) = \ln(\alpha + \beta z)$ it follows immediately that $\ell''(z) = -\beta^2/(\alpha + \beta z)^2 < 0$ for all $r < z < \phi$. ∎

Example 3.4 (Iso-Elastic Individual Labour Supply). The iso-elastic individual labour supply function

$$l(z) := \alpha z^\beta \tag{3.18}$$

with constants $\alpha, \beta > 0$ and implied reservation income $r = 0$ is

(a) strictly log-concave and thus less convex than an exponential;
(b) strictly convex if $\beta > 1$, linear if $\beta = 1$, and strictly concave if $\beta < 1$.

Proof. For iso-elastic labour supply we have $l''(z) = \alpha\beta(\beta-1)z^{\beta-2}$, so that $l''(z) \gtreqless 0$ for all $r < z < \phi$ if $\beta \gtreqless 1$. Furthermore, from $\ell(z) = \ln \alpha + \beta \ln z$ it follows that $\ell''(z) = -\beta/z^2 < 0$ for all $r < z < \phi$. Eventually, $l(0) = 0$ and $l(z) > 0$ for all $z > 0$ imply $r = 0$. ∎

Example 3.5 (A General Individual Labour Supply Function). The individual labour supply function

$$l(z) := \left(\frac{\gamma}{\beta}(z - \alpha)\right)^{1/\gamma} \tag{3.19}$$

with constants $\alpha, \beta > 0$ and $-1 < \gamma \neq 0$

3.3 Convexity and Elasticity of Individual Labour Supply

(a) has an implied reservation income $r = \alpha > 0$ if $\gamma > 0$ and $r = -\infty$ if $-1 < \gamma < 0$;
(b) is strictly log-convex and therefore more convex than an exponential if $\gamma < 0$;
(c) is strictly log-concave and thus less convex than an exponential if $\gamma > 0$;
(d) converges to log-linear exponential individual labour supply if $\gamma \to 0$;[15]
(e) is strictly convex if $\gamma < 1$, linear if $\gamma = 1$, and strictly concave if $\gamma > 1$;
(f) converges to iso-elastic individual labour supply with elasticity $1/\gamma$ if $\alpha \to 0$;
(g) converges to constant individual labour supply if $\gamma \to \infty$.

Proof. See Appendix A.2. ∎

Functional forms similar to this quite flexible one, in which all examples considered above are nested, are discussed by several authors, among them Greenhut and Greenhut (1975; 1977), Greenhut *et al.* (1975; 1987), and Benson (1980; 1984). While the functional form (3.19) may seem a little complicated at first sight, considering the indirect individual labour supply function

$$z(l) = \alpha + \frac{\beta l^\gamma}{\gamma} \tag{3.20}$$

with $l > 0$ reveals the underlying simplicity in structure.

Example 3.6 (Constant Individual Labour Supply). Consider the constant individual labour supply function

$$l(z) := \begin{cases} 1 & \text{if } z > r \\ 0 & \text{if } z \leqslant r \end{cases} \tag{3.21}$$

with some reservation income $r \geqslant 0$. Its restriction $l|_{(r,\phi)}$ is log-linear and therefore inhibits similar properties to (generalised) exponential individual labour supply.[16] ∎

Not surprisingly, (generalised) exponential individual labour supply is log-linear and therefore as convex as an exponential. Using the classification of convexity relative to an exponential given by Definitions 3.1–3.3 in combination with Remark 3.1, we find that both linear and iso-elastic individual labour supply are members of the set of strictly log-concave individual labour supply functions, though iso-elastic individual labour supply is strictly convex if its elasticity exceeds one. Therefore,

---

[15] To be precise, (3.19) does not converge pointwise to exponential individual labour supply if $\gamma \to 0$ because this limit is not defined. It is defined, however, if we add a one to the term in parentheses. Then (3.19) indeed converges pointwise to exponential individual labour supply, which is shown in Appendix A.2. For expositional convenience, however, we shall not bother with this detail here.

[16] This claim follows immediately from $\ell(z) = 0$ for all $r < z < \phi$, so that $\ell''(z) = 0$ for all $r < z < \phi$.

strictly log-convex, i.e., more convex than an exponential, individual labour supply functions are very convex, whilst strictly log-concave individual labour supply functions may be concave, linear, or even convex. This can be seen best from Example 3.5 which presents a quite general individual labour supply function which may be more, less, or even as convex as an exponential depending on its parameter γ. Furthermore, both linear and iso-elastic individual labour supply are nested in this general functional form.

That more convex than an exponential or strictly log-convex individual labour supply indeed refers to 'extremely convex' supply in a well-defined sense can be seen readily from the following remark:

Remark 3.4 (Elasticity and Convexity Relative to an Exponential). If an individual labour supply function is more (less) convex than an exponential, then its elasticity increases more (less) than proportionately to the related increase in the income. If it is log-linear, then its elasticity increases proportionately to the related income.

Proof. The proportionate change in the individual labour supply elasticity $\varepsilon(z) := l'(z)z/l(z)$ to an increase in the income is given by

$$\frac{\varepsilon'(z)z}{\varepsilon(z)} = 1 + \frac{[l''(z)l(z) - l(z)^2]z^2}{l'(z)l(z)}. \qquad (3.22)$$

According to the proof of Remark 3.1, (3.22) is larger (smaller) than one if individual labour supply is strictly log-convex (log-concave) and equals one if individual labour supply is log-linear. ∎

Hence, strictly log-convex individual labour supply is indeed 'extremely convex' in the sense that not only it increases more than proportionately to the income, but also its percentage change does so. On the other hand, the latter increases proportionately to the income if individual labour supply is log-linear or less than proportionately to the income if it is strictly log-concave. We will see later in Lemma 3.1 that individual labour supply's convexity relative to an exponential has important spatial consequences that are intimately related to the result presented in Remark 3.4 (cf., e.g., Greenhut and Greenhut, 1975; Greenhut et al., 1995).

In the following, it will be particularly useful that linear individual labour supply is strictly log-concave: 'As a consequence, the assumption of linear demand [i.e., supply in the present context, BH] that is often necessary to facilitate mathematical analysis is not, in fact, a special case. Qualitative results that hold for the linear case will also hold for a wide range of convex and concave demand functions.' (Greenhut et al., 1987, p. 25) The case of linear individual labour supply is also particularly interesting for another reason: If the linear individual labour supply function gained from Example 3.5 by letting $\gamma = 1$

$$l(z) = \frac{1}{\beta}(z - \alpha) \qquad (3.23)$$

3.3 Convexity and Elasticity of Individual Labour Supply

is interpreted as the c.d.f. of workers' reservation incomes, it corresponds to the case of uniformly distributed reservation incomes on the interval (r, r_{max}) with $\alpha = r$ and $\beta = 1/(r_{max} - r)$.[17]

It should also be noted that the c.d.f.s of a lot of commonly-used distributions fit in either of Definitions 3.1–3.3, most of them being strictly log-concave (cf. Bagnoli and Bergstrom, 2005). For example, the c.d.f.s of the uniform, normal, lognormal, logistic, and the Pareto distribution are all strictly log-concave (on their entire support). Eventually, it is interesting to mention that (equilibrium) search theory with wage posting has also employed the assumption of log-concavely distributed reservation incomes to facilitate analyses when dealing with heterogeneity in reservation incomes (e.g., Flinn and Heckman, 1983; Manning, 2003a, pp. 64/65; 2003b). In this respect, it will be particularly interesting to investigate the case with strictly log-concave individual labour supply.

3.3.2 Spatial Implications of Individual Labour Supply's Convexity

After all, one might ask now: What is the reason for using this clumsy classification? In a nutshell, the reason is that if distance is varying the behaviour of the individual labour supply elasticity differs among the three groups formed by Definitions 3.1–3.3, while it is the same for all functions within each of these groups. And this, in turn, has significant consequences on wage determination. To see the prior point, differentiation of the individual labour supply elasticity with respect to x yields

$$\frac{\partial \varepsilon(w, x)}{\partial x} = \frac{\partial}{\partial x} \frac{l'(w - tx)w}{l(w - tx)} \qquad (3.24)$$

$$= \frac{\partial}{\partial z(w, x)} \frac{l'[z(w, x)]w}{l[z(w, x)]} \frac{\partial z(w, x)}{\partial x} \qquad (3.25)$$

$$= -wt \frac{l''[z(w, x)]l[z(w, x)] - l'[z(w, x)]^2}{l[z(w, x)]^2} \qquad (3.26)$$

$$= -wt \ell''[z(w, x)], \qquad (3.27)$$

where the last equality follows from (3.13). From this it follows at once that

$$\operatorname{sgn} \frac{\partial \varepsilon(w, x)}{\partial x} = -\operatorname{sgn} \ell''[z(w, x)]. \qquad (3.28)$$

---

[17] Furthermore, one should stress that the linear case can also serve as an approximation for the more general case with arbitrary individual labour supply functions as given by (3.4). For instance, Beckmann (1976, p. 619) states that '[l]inearity is not much of a restriction as long as the range of prices considered is small. This will be true, in turn, when transportation costs per unit distance are small relative to mill prices.'

Hence, we have proven the following extraordinarily useful lemma:

Lemma 3.1 (The Sign of $\partial \varepsilon(w, x)/\partial x$). *The individual labour supply elasticity is constant with respect to distance if the individual labour supply is log-linear; and it is strictly increasing (decreasing) in distance if individual labour supply is strictly log-concave (log-convex):*

$$\forall r < z < \phi : \ell''(z) \lesseqqgtr 0 \Rightarrow \forall (w, x) \in Z : \frac{\partial \varepsilon(w, x)}{\partial x} \gtreqqless 0$$

with $Z = \{(w, x) \gg 0 | r < z(w, x) < \phi\}$. ∎

Lemma 3.1 thus tells us that with strictly log-concave individual labour supply workers more distanced from their employer supply labour more elastically than workers nearby. This, in turn, affects the firm's aggregate labour supply elasticity because, according to equation (3.12), the aggregate labour supply elasticity is a weighted average of the individual labour supply elasticities at distance $0 \leqslant x \leqslant X$ plus some term depending on the increase in the market area following from a rise in the wage. On the other hand, with strictly log-convex individual labour supply, more distanced workers supply labour less elastically. Eventually, with log-linear individual labour supply, all workers of the firm supply labour with the same individual labour supply elasticity.

Given Remark 3.4, these results should not surprise. Remark 3.4 tells us that the individual labour supply elasticity is less than proportionately increasing in the income if individual labour supply is strictly log-concave. Since the travel cost is proportionate to distance, the income resulting from some wage is proportionately decreasing in distance. Thus, with strictly log-concave individual labour supply, the elasticity increases in distance. Things are the other way round if individual labour supply is strictly log-convex. Finally, with exponential labour supply, the income decreases proportionately to distance, while the elasticity increases proportionately to the income. Hence, the individual labour supply elasticity is constant in distance. This is an interesting case since the aggregate labour supply elasticity is then, according to equation (3.12), the common individual labour supply elasticity plus something. Anticipating later discussion, if $\partial X/\partial w = 0$ with log-linear individual labour supply, then we have a spatial model of oligopsony which bears a lot of similarities with simple static monopsony as presented in Chapter 2. And this is the only (generic) case where aggregate and individual labour supply elasticities coincide.

3.4 Spatial vs. Spaceless Monopsony

With Lemma 3.1 in place, we are now able to discuss the difference between spaceless and spatial monopsony.[18] The spatial monopsonist employs every worker left and right to her who receives an income larger than his or her reservation income

---

[18] For an analysis of spatial monopsony with stochastic individual (labour) supply, see Löfgren (1992).

3.4 Spatial vs. Spaceless Monopsony

with individual labour supply of workers located at distance x from the monopsonist given by (3.4). Since the spatial monopsonist demands labour to that market boundary at which individual labour supply falls to zero, her market radius given some wage $w > r$ is represented by $X_M = \sup\{x > 0 | z(w, x) > r\}$. This holds because no worker offered an income no larger than r is willing to work for her. Therefore, her market radius is implicitly given by $w - tX_M = r$, so that

$$X_M = \frac{w-r}{t} \tag{3.29}$$

with $v_M := \partial X_M / \partial w = 1/t > 0$. Not surprisingly, by raising her wage the monopsonist's labour supply increases. This holds for two reasons: On the one hand, her existing employees supply more labour, i.e., individual labour supply at any point in space rises. On the other hand, new workers farther away from her are attracted and decide to supply labour to her, i.e., her market radius X_M increases.

Since $l(w - tx) = 0$ for all $x \geq X_M$, $h(x) = l(w - tx)/\int_0^x l(w - t\vartheta)\,d\vartheta = 0$ for all $x \geq X_M$ as well, and the spatial monopsonist's aggregate labour supply elasticity becomes

$$e_M(w, X_M) = \int_0^{X_M} \varepsilon(w, x) h(x)\, dx, \tag{3.30}$$

which follows directly from equation (3.12). To get the labour supply elasticity of the spaceless monopsonist, we have to abstract from space by just looking at individual labour supply at $x = 0$. Hence, the spaceless monopsonist's aggregate labour supply elasticity is given by

$$e_m(w, X_M) = \varepsilon(w, 0) = \int_0^{X_M} \varepsilon(w, 0) h(x)\, dx, \tag{3.31}$$

where the second equality holds due to $\int_0^{X_M} h(x)\, dx = 1$. Combining (3.30) and (3.31), the difference in elasticities of the spacial and the spaceless monopsonist is

$$e_M(w, X_M) - e_m(w, X_M) = \int_0^{X_M} [\varepsilon(w, x) - \varepsilon(w, 0)] h(x)\, dx. \tag{3.32}$$

By virtue of Lemma 3.1, we know that $\varepsilon(w, x)$ is larger than $\varepsilon(w, 0)$ if individual labour supply is strictly log-concave because then $\partial \varepsilon(w, x)/\partial x > 0$ for all $(w, x) \in Z$, whereas it is smaller if individual labour supply is strictly log-convex. Moreover, the individual labour supply elasticity is constant with respect to difference, i.e., $\varepsilon(w, x) = \varepsilon(w, 0)$ for all $(w, x) \in Z$, if individual labour supply is log-linear. Making use of the optimal wage-setting rule (3.9), the following proposition follows immediately:

Proposition 3.1 (Spatial vs. Spaceless Monopsony). *If individual labour supply is strictly log-concave (log-convex), then the spatial monopsonist's aggregate labour* supply is more (less) elastic than the spaceless monopsonist's and her wage is thus higher (lower). If individual labour supply is log-linear, then both elasticities and wages are the same:

$$\forall r < z < \phi : \ell''(z) \lesseqgtr 0 \Rightarrow \forall (w, X_M) \in Z_M : e_M(w, X_M) \gtreqless e_m(w, X_M)$$
$$\Rightarrow w_M \gtreqless w_m$$

with $Z_M = \{(w, X_M) \gg 0 | r < z(w, X_M) < \phi\}$. ∎

Proposition 3.1 makes clear that individual labour supply's convexity relative to an exponential has immediate consequences on a spatial monopsonist's wage-setting power over her workers as opposed to the wage-setting power of a spaceless monopsonist. If individual labour supply is strictly log-concave, space effectively inhibits the spatial monopsonist's market power: Since more distant workers' labour supply adds elasticity to the monopsonist's aggregate labour supply elasticity – as shown in Lemma 3.1, the individual labour supply elasticity is strictly increasing in distance in this case –, the spatial monopsonist's aggregate labour supply is more elastic than the supply of her spaceless counterpart. And this causes her to set a higher wage in the optimum. In this sense, workers are made better off under spatial than under spaceless monopsony. Things work in the opposite direction if individual labour supply is strictly log-convex. Then the aggregate labour supply elasticity is lower than the individual labour supply elasticity at the monopsonist's location because the individual elasticity is strictly decreasing in distance. Finally, with log-linear individual labour supply wages of both the spatial and the spaceless monopsonist do not differ.

A last thing to note is that spaceless monopsony is nested in spatial monopsony. Suppose the spatial monopsonist's market radius approaches zero. Then it is appropriate to think of aggregate labour supply as individual labour supply at distance zero from the spatial monopsonist, i.e., $L^s := Dl(w, 0)$, so that the aggregate labour supply elasticity is given by $\varepsilon(w, 0)$. Hence, application of the optimal wage-setting rule (3.9) yields $w_M = w_m$.[19] Now that we have investigated the spatial monopsonist's problem, it is time to consider the impact of competition, a task which we will address ourselves to in the next sections.

---

[19] More formally, this can be established by using equation (3.10) to arrive at

$$\lim_{X_M \to 0} e_M(w, X_M) = \lim_{X_M \to 0} \frac{w \int_0^{X_M} l'(w - tx) \, dx}{\int_0^{X_M} l(w - tx) \, dx}$$
$$= \lim_{X_M \to 0} \frac{wl'(w - tX_M)}{l(w - tX_M)}$$
$$= \varepsilon(w, 0),$$

where the second equality follows after applying both de l'Hôpital's and the Leibniz rule.

3.5 Firms' Interaction and Conjectural Variations

While the only constraint on the spatial monopsonist's market radius is given by the shape of the individual labour supply function, this does not hold for firms under spatial competition. Under competition, firms' market areas are constrained by their neighbours' market areas. Workers' labour supply behaviour has now two dimensions: (1) to whom and (2) how much. On account of assumption (A3), workers always supply labour to the firm which offers them the highest income, so that there is no market area overlap. Consider now some firm. If this firm changes its wage, this will not only be likely to change its market radius, but also to change its neighbours' wage-setting decisions. For optimal decision-making, the firm obviously has to take these impacts into account. It does so by forming conjectures about its neighbours' likely responses. In the following, we will utilise the 'conjectural variations' approach to model how the firm's conjectures about its neighbours' likely responses enter the firm's decision problem.[20]

In particular, there are three assumptions concerning the wage reaction of a firm to a change in its competitor's wage which have been extensively employed in spatial price theory (e.g., Capozza and Van Order, 1978; Greenhut *et al.*, 1987, pp. 19–56; Ohta, 1988, pp. 113–126):

(Lö) *Löschian competition*: Under Löschian (Lö) competition, each firm presumes its competitors to react identically to any proposed wage change.

(HS) *Hotelling–Smithies competition*: Under Hotelling–Smithies (HS) competition, each firm presumes its competitors not to react to a proposed wage change.

(GO) *Greenhut–Ohta competition*: Under Greenhut–Ohta (GO) competition, each firm presumes its wage on the market boundary to be fixed.

Obviously, HS competition, the roots of which stem from the influential contributions of Hotelling (1929) and Smithies (1941) to the theory of spatial dyopoly, is equivalent to the standard Bertrand–Nash assumption employed in spaceless oligopoly theory (e.g., Greenhut and Norman, 1992). Although this assumption seems to be the 'natural' way of modelling spatial monopsonistic competition (or competitive spatial oligopsony), the spatial economics literature has traditionally used the assumption of Löschian competition, which originates from Lösch's (1944) seminal contribution and its formalisation by Mills and Lav (1964), when investigating spatial monopolistic competition. Löschian competition, however, refers to a situation where (tacit) collusion takes place. Since we are agnostic regarding the reasons for firms' conjectural variations, we allow firms to collude in an explicit fashion or just tacitly, i.e., without formal agreement or explicit coordination.[21] In

---

[20] For a survey on the conjectural variations approach, which originates from the work of Bowley (1924, p. 38), see Greenhut and Norman (1992) and Figuières *et al.* (2004). An interesting historical account is given by Giocoli (2003; 2005).

[21] As Ivaldi *et al.* (2007, p. 4) put the state of affairs: 'Tacit collusion refers to a group of oligopolists' ability to coordinate, even in the absence of explicit agreement, to raise price or

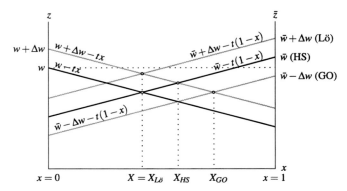

Fig. 3.1 Wage reactions of the firm's rival under Löschian, Hotelling–Smithies, and Greenhut–Ohta competition and the associated changes in the firm's market radius

this respect, it is legitimate to refer to Löschian competition as collusive spatial oligopsony. Thus, we will follow Capozza and Van Order's (1978) terminology and refer to HS competition as spatial monopsonistic competition and to Löschian competition as spatial collusive competition. Eventually, GO competition – introduced by Greenhut and Ohta (1973; 1975) – may seem as an odd thing to assume for the moment; nonetheless, it will turn out to serve as a very useful extreme case later on.

These three different competitive assumptions translate into conjectural variations held by spatial competitors about their rivals' wage reactions. Consider without loss of generality two firms at the ends of the unit interval, as shown in Figure 3.1. Assume that the firm located at 0 offers some wage w, while its competitor offers some (possibly different) wage $\bar{w}$. Assume further that wages are such that every worker on the unit interval receives an income above his or her reservation income, i.e., $w + \bar{w} > t + r$, and that wages do not differ too much between the firms, so that both firm 0 and firm 1 are able to attract some workers, i.e., $|w - \bar{w}| < t$. The income a worker receives when working for firm 0 decreases as the distance to firm 0 x rises, whereas the income received when working for firm 1 increases. Due to assumption (A3), the worker prefers to work for firm 0 if $w - tx > \bar{w} - t(1-x)$, while he or she prefers to work for firm 1 if $w - tx < \bar{w} - t(1-x)$. If the incomes received from firm 0 and firm 1 are the same, then the worker is indifferent between working for firm 0 and working for firm 1. So firm 0's market radius is given by

$$X = \frac{w - \bar{w} + t}{2t}, \qquad (3.33)$$

---

more generally increase profit at the detriment of consumers. ... "Tacit collusion" need not to involve any "collusion" in the legal sense, and in particular need involve no communication between the parties.' By using the term 'tacit collusion,' it is just emphasised that the outcome (e.g., parallel wage-setting behaviour of spatial competitors) resembles the pattern that would have been observed had there been explicit collusion.

3.5 Firms' Interaction and Conjectural Variations

Table 3.1 Wage and market radius responses under Löschian, Hotelling–Smithies, and Greenhut–Ohta competition

	Conjectural variation for the market radius $v := \partial X/\partial w$	Conjectural variation for the wage $\partial \bar{w}/\partial w$
Löschian competition	0	1
HS competition	$1/2t$	0
GO competition	$1/t$	-1
Spatial monopsony	$1/t$	—

from which it follows at once that $X = 1/2$ if $w = \bar{w}$. That is to say, if both firms offer the same wage, then firm 0's and 1's market boundary exactly lies in the middle of them.

Now, what will happen if firm 0 increases its wage by some Δw? Making use of (3.33), we get

$$v := \frac{\partial X}{\partial w} = \frac{1}{2t}\left(1 - \frac{\partial \bar{w}}{\partial w}\right), \qquad (3.34)$$

so that the change in firm 0's market radius from a unit change in its wage depends both on the wage reaction of firm 1 and the magnitude of travel cost. Under Löschian competition, firm 0 presumes its competitor to react identically to any proposed wage change, i.e., $\partial \bar{w}/\partial w = 1$. Hence, it conjectures its market radius to be fixed, so that $X_{L_ö} = X$ with $v_{L_ö} = 0$ holds. Things are different under HS competition: Here firm 0 presumes its competitor not to react to its wage change at all, i.e., $\partial \bar{w}/\partial w = 0$. Therefore, firm 0 is able to expand its market radius by increasing its wage, its market boundary moves rightwards to X_{HS}. According to (3.34), the rise in the firm's market radius per unit increase in the wage is given by $v_{HS} = 1/2t$. Finally, under GO competition, firm 0 presumes the wage at its market boundary to be constant. Taking a look at Figure 3.1, this requires that firm 1 reduces its wage by the same amount Δw by which firm 0 has increased its wage, i.e., $\partial \bar{w}/\partial w = -1$, and therefore implies that firm 0's market boundary moves more rightwards than under HS competition, viz. to X_{GO}. Thus, under GO competition, the rise in the firm's market radius per unit increase in the wage is $v_{GO} = 1/t$, which is the same as for the spatial monopsonist in Section 3.4. Intuitively, GO competition refers to a situation that is more competitive than HS competition. If an employer exerts wage cutting, then its rival will react by raising his wage, so that it will even lose more workers than in a situation where his rival would not have changed his wage.[22] Table 3.1 summarises these relationships.

As we have seen, the conjectural variations approach enables us to model dynamic features of strategic interaction between employers within a purely static framework, which facilitates analyses vitally. However, it has been argued, among

---

[22] It is interesting to note that in a spaceless dyopoly setting GO conjectures give rise to perfectly competitive outcomes (e.g., Giocoli, 2005). This also holds in a spaceless oligopsony setting (e.g., Naylor, 1996). Therefore, it seems particularly appropriate to refer to GO conjectures as representing a more competitive environment than HS conjectures.

others, by Friedman (1983, pp. 109/110) and Tirole (1988, pp. 244/245) that conjectural variations cannot be regarded as an actual expectation of future strategic interactions, for they arise in a static ('one-shot') model. It is instructive to quote Tirole's objections extensively:

> 'However, this methodology suffers from one major drawback: A static game is, by definition, a game in which each firm's choice is independent of its rivals' choices. By the very timing and information structure of the game, firms cannot react to one another. Thus, any conjecture about one's opponents' reaction that differs from no reaction [i.e., from HS conjectures, BH] is irrational. We conclude that this methodology is not theoretically satisfactory, as it does not subject itself to the discipline imposed by game theory.'

(Tirole, 1988, pp. 244/245)

Accordingly, the main points of criticism are given as follows: (1) The conjectural variations approach derives dynamic conclusions from a static framework (2) where firms' expectations about their rivals reactions need not to be correct.[23] Hence, '[a]t best it is some sort of static approximation to the real-time action and reaction that arises in a dynamic setting.' (Brandner and Zhang, 1990, p. 569) Though it may be preferred, from a game-theoretic point of view, to use the supergame framework, we follow Brandner and Zhang in arguing that the appropriateness of using the conjectural variations approach is a question of how useful an approximation of strategic reactions it gives.

> '[T]he conjectural variation is simply a useful and intuitive summary measure of market conduct. ... We prefer to think of the conjectural variation as an indicator of the strategy variable, or as an indicator of the degree of collusion, and therefore refer to [it] simply as a "conduct parameter"....'

(Brandner and Zhang, 1990, p. 569)

While it is hard for us to figure out how a *rigorous* way of doing the following analysis that avoids the objections made by Tirole should look like, the core of

---

[23] To deal with the second criticism several authors have worked out the concept of consistent conjectural variations, which was first introduced by Harrod (1934b), influential contributions including Bresnahan (1981), Perry (1982), Boyer and Moreaux (1983a; 1983b), and Kamien and Schwartz (1983). For instance, Capozza and Van Order (1989) investigate consistent conjectural variations within a linear oligopoly model completely analogous to the linear oligopsony model to be presented in Section 4.5. Another related problem consistent conjectural variations aim to alleviate is that imposing arbitrary conjectures may yield a theory of economic behaviour that is not refutable in the Popperian (2005) sense. This may be the case as it allows for (almost) any observed behaviour to be 'explained' by a suitable choice of the conjectural variations (cf. Figuières et al., 2004, p. ix). Furthermore, one should add that the first criticism – vigorously stated for the first time by Harrod (1934a), Kahn (1937), Stigler (1940), and Fellner (1949) – has not to be lethal at all. For example, Dockner (1992), Cabral (1995), and Figuières et al. (2004, pp. 33–64) discuss under which conditions the conjectural variations approach gives a reduced form of the equilibrium of an (unmodelled) dynamic game. In particular, it is well-known that collusive behaviour or tacit collusion, i.e., Löschian conjectures, can be in some cases supported even in noncooperative dynamic settings by trigger strategies (cf., e.g., Friedman, 1971; 1983, pp. 123–134). An interesting historical account of the conjectural variations approach and the problem of imposing consistency conditions on firms' conjectures is given by Giocoli (2005).

our attitude towards his objections has been stated unequivocally elsewhere: 'This approach is subject to the criticism that static conjectures, consistent or otherwise, cannot be rigorously justified. The usual defense of analytical convenience and the absence of a superior alternative applies.' (Dixit, 1988, pp. 57/58)

3.6 The Short-Run Equilibrium

Now that we have formed conjectural variations as a powerful and simple means of incorporating firms' strategic interaction in the spatial competitors' decision problem, we are able to derive the short-run equilibrium of the labour market. What is meant by *short run*? According to assumption (A7), equidistant firms' locations in the short run are fixed, and so are their market radii. Due to the symmetry of the framework, firms' market radii and wages in the short-run equilibrium are the same, e.g., $X = 1/2$ in Figure 3.1 on page 32, or, more generally, half the distance between firms. Of course, this reasoning is quite heuristic. It would be more rigorous to model the short-run dynamics explicitly. For example, this could be done along the lines of Capozza and Van Order (1978, p. 907). Since this is a straightforward task that does not yield any additional insights, we shall not bother to do so here. Instead, we just assume that the short-run equilibrium with equidistant firms offering the same wage is obtained instantaneously in order to suppress the dynamics of short-run adjustments, as is done by Capozza and Van Order.

According to equation (3.9), the firms' optimal wage satisfies

$$w_i = \frac{e_i(w_i, X)}{1 + e_i(w_i, X)} \phi \qquad (3.35)$$

for all $0 < X < X_M$, where $i \in \{Lö, HS, GO\}$ depending on the conjectural variations held by spatial competitors. By virtue of (3.12), we know that for a labour market consisting of market areas of a given radius smaller than the market radius chosen by a spatial monopsonist, i.e., for a labour market with the distance between (equidistant) firms being less than $2X_M$, the Löschian competitor faces the lowest aggregate labour supply elasticity and therefore offers the lowest wage. On the other hand, both the elasticity and the wage are higher for the HS competitor and highest for the GO competitor. This follows directly from $0 = v_{Lö} < v_{HS} < v_{GO}$ and the fact that the right-hand side of (3.35) is strictly increasing in $e_i(w_i, X)$, for

$$\frac{\partial}{\partial e_i(w_i, X)} \left(\frac{e_i(w_i, X)}{1 + e_i(w_i, X)} \phi \right) = \frac{\phi}{[1 + e_i(w_i, X)]^2} > 0 \qquad (3.36)$$

for all $e_i(w_i, X)$ with $(w_i, X) \in Z$. More generally, we find that the aggregate labour supply elasticity is strictly increasing in firms' conjectural variations, as can be seen from partially differentiating (3.12) with respect to v, which gives

$$\frac{\partial e(w, X)}{\partial v} = wh(X) > 0 \tag{3.37}$$

for all $(w, X) \in Z$. Hence, we have proven the following proposition:

Proposition 3.2 (The Short-Run Equilibrium for $0 < X < X_M$). *In a labour market consisting of market areas of a given radius $0 < X < X_M$, both the aggregate labour supply elasticity and the short-run equilibrium wage are strictly increasing in the conjectural variations held by spatial competitors about the expected rise in the market radius that will follow from an increase in the wage offered:*

$$\forall (w, X) \in Z \; \forall j \neq i :$$
$$v_j > v_i \;\Rightarrow\; e_j(w, X) > e_i(w, X) \;\Rightarrow\; w_j(X) > w_i(X).$$

In particular,
$$e_{Lö}(w, X) < e_{HS}(w, X) < e_{GO}(w, X)$$
for all $(w, X) \in Z$ and thus
$$w_{Lö}(X) < w_{HS}(X) < w_{GO}(X)$$
for all $0 < X < X_M$. ∎

Of course, Proposition 3.2 is a short-run result. In the long-run equilibrium with free market entry, not only the wage but also the market radius differs for the three modes of competition. This holds because free entry causes the labour market to head for a zero-profit equilibrium, so that the market radius is determined endogenously. In the short run, however, the market radius is fixed to some X regardless of firms' conjectural variations. Thus, we are able to state the following corollary:

Corollary 3.1 (Short-Run Equilibrium Employment). *In a labour market consisting of market areas of a given radius $0 < X < X_M$, firms' employment is strictly increasing in the conjectural variations held by spatial competitors about the expected rise in the market radius that will follow from an increase in the wage offered:*

$$\forall 0 < X < X_M \; \forall j \neq i : v_j > v_i \;\Rightarrow\; L_j(X) > L_i(X).$$

In particular, firms' employment under Löschian, HS, and GO competition satisfies

$$L_{Lö}(X) < L_{HS}(X) < L_{GO}(X)$$

for all $0 < X < X_M$.

Proof. According to Proposition 3.2, the short-run equilibrium wage is strictly increasing in the conjectural variations. Since each firm's aggregate labour supply is also strictly increasing in the wage if $0 < X < X_M$ holds, Corollary 3.1 follows immediately. ∎

3.6 The Short-Run Equilibrium

Before discussing these results in more detail, we want to consider cases where $X \geqslant X_M$, i.e., cases where firms are distanced at least $2X_M$ from each other. Intuition tells us that this yields (spatial) monopsonistic outcomes, so that firms' conjectural variations do not play any role in wage determination. And intuition is right: From the discussion in Section 3.4 we know that without competitors the firm's profits are maximised by setting $w = w_M$ and thus $X = X_M$, so that the firm does not want to increase w and X further. This also holds if there is more than just one firm in the market. Firms do not increase w beyond w_M and thus X beyond X_M. That is, if firms are distanced more than $2X_M$ from each other, their market areas are not adjoint and firms behave like spatial monopsonists. Formally, this is shown by the following corollary:

Corollary 3.2 (The Short-Run Equilibrium for $X \geqslant X_M$). *In a labour market consisting of market areas of a given radius $X \geqslant X_M$, firms offer the spatial monopsonist's wage irrespectively of their conjectural variations about the expected rise in their market radius that will follow from an increase in the wage offered.*

Proof. Since $l(w, x) = 0$ for all $x \geqslant X_M$, equation (3.11) gives $h(x) = 0$ for all $x \geqslant X_M$. Furthermore, from equation (3.37) it follows that $\partial e(w, X)/\partial v = 0$ for all $X \geqslant X_M$, so that the aggregate labour supply elasticity is a constant. From equation (3.12) it thus follows that $e(w, X) = e_M(w, X_M)$ for all $X \geqslant X_M$. Hence, (3.35) yields $w = w_M$ for all $X \geqslant X_M$ independently of v. ∎

Now, it is time to discuss these results in some detail. When determining its wage, the spatial competitor faces two forces: (1) a *supply effect* that is related to the fact that individual labour supply is increasing in the income received by the workers and (2) a *competition effect* that is related to the wage conjectural variations held by spatial competitors. Since the Löschian firm presumes its competitors to exactly match its wage and therefore assumes a market area of fixed size, its decisions are only driven by the supply effect. Within its market area, it sets wage and employment in exactly the same way as the spatial monopsonist, whose behaviour we discussed in Section 3.4. Things are different for HS and GO firms: They also face the supply effect, but additionally their conjectural variations about their competitors' wage reactions make them believe that they can expand their market area at the expense of their rivals by raising their wages. Therefore, the competition effect adds elasticity to their aggregate labour supply.

Diagrammatically, this translates into different *perceived* labour supply curves for Löschian, HS, and GO employers (cf. Ohta, 1980), which are illustrated by Figure 3.2 on the following page. The higher are their conjectural variations, the less steep is the spatial competitors' *perceived* labour supply curve. And this, in turn, gives rise as well to a higher wage as to higher firm- and market-level employment. Hence, the strength of the competition effect is directly determined by the magnitude of the conjectural variations. Put differently, the more likely firms are to collude (tacitly), i.e., the lower are their conjectural variations, the lower are both the wage and the employment in the short-run equilibrium. Finally, Corollary 3.2 makes clear that the competition effect can only occur if any competition takes place in a

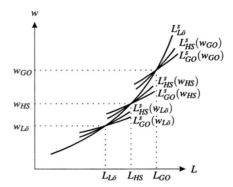

Fig. 3.2 Perceived labour supply curves for a labour market consisting of market areas of a given radius $0 < X < X_M$ under Löschian, Hotelling–Smithies, and Greenhut–Ohta competition

well-defined sense: Firms have to be rivalling neighbours with their market radius being smaller than under spatial monopsony. Otherwise, firms just were isolated regional monopsonists and their conjectural variations would not play any role in wage determination.

3.7 Short-Run Comparative Statics

From the discussion in Section 3.6 we know that equation (3.35) implicitly defines the short-run equilibrium wage under spatial competition. We are now interested in answering the question how changes in the underlying exogenous parameters affect the equilibrium outcome. That is to say, we are interested in the comparative static change of the equilibrium wage in response to a *ceteris paribus* change in the fixed costs, the density of workers, the marginal revenue product of labour, the travel cost, or the distance between firms, which corresponds to a change in the firms' market radius. We restrict attention to cases where Proposition 3.2 applies, i.e., cases with a market radius $0 < X < X_M$, for we are interested in the comparative static effects under spatial competition and not in those occurring under a situation of isolated firms behaving like spatial monopsonists. Since the fixed costs and the worker density affect overall profits but do not impact marginal productivity and marginal costs, they do not have any effect on marginal decision-making and thus do not affect wages.

Things, however, are different for changes in the travel cost, the marginal revenue product, and the market radius. From spaceless economic theory, one would expect the equilibrium wage to depend positively on workers' marginal revenue product. Under spaceless monopsony, for example, the workers' wage is given by some mark-down on workers' marginal revenue product, so that both of them move in the same direction (see our discussion in Chapter 2). We will see that this intuition stemming from spaceless theory carries over to the short-run spatial equilibrium.

3.7 Short-Run Comparative Statics

Next, consider changes in the travel cost and the distance between firms. Arguably, increases in the travel cost and the market radius have similar economic connotations: They both imply that space's economic significance rises. This is obviously true if firms' market radius increases because firms are then less densely distributed in space. Similarly, higher travel cost, though they do not affect the distance between firms directly, make the same distance more distant in an economic sense: So to speak, firms are now less densely distributed in *economic* space. The other way round, lower travel cost or less distanced firms cause space to matter less in an economic sense. Given these intuitive remarks, we would expect that changes in the travel cost and the firms' market radius have the same qualitative impact on wages and employment levels. Moreover, we are inclined to conjecture that an increase in any of these parameters reduces competitive forces and should therefore reduce wages.

While we shall discuss changes in firms' market radius, i.e., competitive entry, in greater detail later on, the following proposition shows how a change in the fixed costs, the worker density, the marginal revenue product, or the travel cost affects firms' wage and employment in the short-run equilibrium, *ceteris paribus*:

Proposition 3.3 (Comparative Statics in f, D, ϕ, and t). *Consider a short-run spatial equilibrium in a labour market consisting of market areas of a given radius $0 < X < X_M$. Then the following holds:*

(a) *A change in the fixed costs or the worker density does neither affect firms' wage nor their employment in the short-run equilibrium no matter the convexity of individual labour supply and the mode of competition.*

(b) *An increase in the marginal revenue product of labour raises firms' wage and employment in the short-run equilibrium no matter the convexity of individual labour supply and the mode of competition.*

(c) *Under GO competition, an increase in the travel cost reduces firms' wage and employment in the short-run equilibrium no matter the convexity of individual labour supply.*

(d) *Under Löschian competition, an increase in the travel cost raises (reduces) firms' wage and employment in the short-run equilibrium if individual labour supply is strictly log-concave (log-convex) and does not affect them if it is log-linear.*

(e) *Under HS competition, an increase in the travel cost reduces firms' wage and employment in the short-run equilibrium if individual labour supply is strictly log-convex or log-linear and reduces (raises) them if it is strictly log-concave and firms' market radius is sufficiently small (large) initially.*

Proof. For the comparative static effects on the short-run equilibrium wage, see Appendix A.3. From the wage effect the comparative static effect on firms' employment follows at once because firms' aggregate labour supply is strictly increasing in the wage paid by them. ∎

Table 3.2 on the next page summarises these (and the forthcoming) results. Firstly, we can conclude that intuition is affirmed when considering changes in

Table 3.2 Comparative static effects on the short-run equilibrium wage

	Lö competition			HS competition[a]			GO competition		
Increase:	log-concave	log-linear	log-convex	log-concave	log-linear	log-convex	log-concave	log-linear	log-convex
Fixed costs (f)	0	0	0	0	0	0	0	0	0
Worker density (D)	0	0	0	0	0	0	0	0	0
Productivity (ϕ)	+	+	+	+	+	+	+	+	+
Travel cost (t)	+	0	−	$\mp^b$	−	−	−	−	−
Market radius (X)	+	0	−	$\mp^b$	−	−	−	−	−

[a] The same results hold for every mode of competition i with conjectural variations $0 < v_i < 1/t$.
[b] − if competition is strong (small market areas); + if it is weak (large market areas).

the fixed costs, the worker density, and the marginal revenue product. Second, it is interesting to note that there is quite a range of different comparative static results for changes in the travel cost. The equilibrium wage does not necessarily respond in the direction suggested by intuition: If individual labour supply is strictly log-convex, then the wage always decreases in response to a rise in the travel cost. That is to say, if economic space matters more, workers get harmed because competitive forces are weakened. Things, however, are less clear-cut if individual labour supply is strictly log-concave: Under Löschian competition, i.e., under collusive spatial oligopsony, things are the other way round; and under HS competition, i.e., under competitive spatial oligopsony, things depend on the magnitude of competitive forces in the initial equilibrium. Our first intuition obviously failed to grasp that the impact of changes in the travel cost crucially depends on the mode of competition if individual labour supply is strictly log-concave. Nevertheless, this can be explained intuitively when considering market entry, i.e., changes in firms' market radius, which will be done next.

As we argued above, an increase in the travel cost and an increase in the market radius are equivalent in an economic sense. Therefore, we would expect them to have the same qualitative comparative static effect on the short-run equilibrium wage. Plausibly, a decreasing market radius can be interpreted as competitive entry.[24] So what are the consequences of competitive entry on firms' equilibrium aggregate labour supply elasticity, wage, and employment? These questions are answered quite easily under Löschian competition, whereas the answer becomes

---

[24] Of course, for this interpretation of a decreasing market radius as competitive entry to hold, we have to impose a costless relocation assumption like the one imposed in the long run (see basic assumption (A7) in Section 3.1). Then competitive entry actually yields a symmetric reduction in firms' market radius (see the discussion of the short-run dynamics in Section 3.6 and the discussion of free entry and costless relocation in Section 4.4).

3.7 Short-Run Comparative Statics

quite intricate under HS and GO competition. It is not hard to prove the following proposition:

Proposition 3.4 (Competitive Entry under Löschian Competition). *Consider a short-run spatial equilibrium in a labour market consisting of market areas of a given radius $0 < X < X_M$. If individual labour supply is strictly log-concave (log-convex), then competitive entry reduces (raises) Löschian firms' aggregate labour supply elasticity, wage, and employment in the equilibrium. If individual labour supply function is log-linear, then competitive entry does not affect their aggregate labour supply elasticity, wage, and employment.*

Proof. The main result to be proven is

$$\forall r < z < \phi : \ell''(z) \lesseqqgtr 0 \Rightarrow \forall (w, X) \in Z : \frac{\partial e_{Lö}(w, X)}{\partial X} \gtreqqless 0, \quad (3.38)$$

where

$$e_{Lö}(w, X) = \int_0^X \varepsilon(w, x) h(x) \, dx \quad (3.39)$$

according to (3.12) with $v_{Lö} = 0$. Applying the Leibniz rule, we get

$$\frac{\partial e_{Lö}(w, X)}{\partial X} = \int_0^X \varepsilon(w, x) \frac{\partial h(x)}{\partial X} \, dx + \varepsilon(w, X) h(X) \quad (3.40)$$

$$= \int_0^X \varepsilon(w, x) \frac{\partial h(x)}{\partial X} \, dx - \varepsilon(w, X) \int_0^X \frac{\partial h(x)}{\partial X} \, dx \quad (3.41)$$

$$= \int_0^X [\varepsilon(w, x) - \varepsilon(w, X)] \frac{\partial h(x)}{\partial X} \, dx \quad (3.42)$$

with

$$\frac{\partial h(x)}{\partial X} = -\frac{l(w - tx) l(w - tX)}{\left(\int_0^X l(w - tx) \, dx\right)^2} < 0 \quad (3.43)$$

for all $(w, X) \in Z$. Note that the equality in (3.41) follows from partial differentiation of $\int_0^X h(x) \, dx = 1$ with respect to X which gives $h(X) = -\int_0^X [\partial h(x)/\partial X] \, dx$. Since $0 \leqslant x \leqslant X$ and $\partial h(x)/\partial X < 0$ under the integration sign in (3.42), Lemma 3.1 tells us that the integrand is positive (negative) if individual labour supply is strictly log-concave (log-convex) and zero if it is log-linear because then $\varepsilon(w, x) = \varepsilon(w, X)$ for all $0 \leqslant x \leqslant X$. Hence, we have proven (3.38). As competitive entry reduces X, Proposition 3.4 follows now immediately from applying the optimal wage-setting rule (3.35). ∎

The intuition behind this result is quite straightforward. The Löschian competitor's aggregate labour supply elasticity is just an employment share-weighted average of the individual labour supply elasticities at $0 \leqslant x \leqslant X$. If individual labour supply is strictly log-concave, then workers far away from the firm react more elastically to wage changes than workers nearby. Due to competitive entry, the firm's market area reduces, so that it loses its most elastic workers. This, in turn, decreases the aggregate labour supply elasticity, which translates into a lower wage and thus lower employment by the firm. The opposite holds if individual labour supply is strictly log-convex. Basically, the same story can be told when the travel cost rises under Löschian competition, so that we also get an intuition for the comparative static impact of changes in the travel cost from Proposition 3.3.

This intuition is also helpful when comparing spatial monopsony and collusive spatial oligopsony, i.e., Löschian competition. Doing this gives one result that has been intensively analysed in the spatial economics literature (e.g., Greenhut and Ohta, 1973; Greenhut et al., 1975; Capozza and Van Order, 1977a): Spatial competition may lead to a lower equilibrium wage than spatial or spaceless monopsony. Proposition 3.1 tells us that the spatial monopsonist faces more (less) elastic aggregate labour supply and thus offers a higher (lower) wage than its spaceless counterpart if individual labour supply is strictly log-concave (log-convex). Since Löschian competitors' market radius lies between the spaceless and the spatial monopsonist's market radius, i.e., $0 < X < X_M$, in all cases of interest, we know from Lemma 3.1 that the aggregate elasticity and thus the wage paid in the Löschian short-run equilibrium must lie in between, too. This holds because the individual labour supply elasticity is strictly decreasing in distance if individual labour supply is strictly log-concave and strictly increasing in distance if it strictly log-convex. Finally, applying the wage-setting rule (3.35), we get the following corollary:

Corollary 3.3 (Löschian Competition vs. Monopsony). *Consider a short-run spatial equilibrium in a labour market consisting of market areas of a given radius $0 < X < X_M$. If individual labour supply is strictly log-concave (log-convex), then Löschian competitors' aggregate labour supply elasticity and wage are lower (higher) than the spatial monopsonist's and higher (lower) than the spaceless monopsonist's aggregate labour supply elasticity and wage. They are the same under Löschian competition, spatial, and spaceless monopsony if individual labour supply is log-linear:*

$$\forall r < z < \phi : \ell''(z) \lesseqqgtr 0$$
$$\Rightarrow \forall (w, X) \in Z : e_M(w, X_M) \gtreqqless e_{L\ddot{o}}(w, X) \gtreqqless e_m(w, X_M)$$
$$\Rightarrow \forall 0 < X < X_M : w_M \gtreqqless w_{L\ddot{o}}(X) \gtreqqless w_m$$

with $e_m(w, X_M) := \varepsilon(w, 0)$. ∎

Paralleling the discussion in Section 3.4, we know that under strictly log-concave individual labour supply space puts a constraint on the spatial monopsonist's wage-setting power compared to the spaceless monopsonist's because workers more distanced from her supply labour more elastically. Löschian competitors, in turn, behave like spatial monopsonists within their market areas. Since their market areas are smaller than the spatial monopsonist's, space inhibits their wage-setting power less than the spatial monopsonist's, and therefore they pay a lower wage

3.7 Short-Run Comparative Statics

than the spatial and a higher wage than the spaceless monopsonist. On the other hand, things work the other way round if individual labour supply is strictly log-convex.

When investigating the impact of competitive entry under GO and HS competition, things get more complicated. While under Löschian competition only the supply effect matters, so that the aggregate labour supply elasticity is simply an employment share-weighted average of individual labour supply elasticities, under HS and GO competition also the competition effect is of importance. The reason for this is that spatial competitors now hold conjectures about their rivals wage reactions to a proposed wage change that make them think they could expand their market radius via raising their wage, i.e., $v = \partial X/\partial w > 0$. Since $v_{GO} = 1/t$ and $v_{HS} = 1/2t$, equation (3.12) gives the respective aggregate labour supply elasticity as

$$e_{GO}(w, X) = e_{L\ddot{o}}(w, X) + \frac{wh(X)}{t} \quad (3.44)$$

and

$$e_{HS}(w, X) = e_{L\ddot{o}}(w, X) + \frac{wh(X)}{2t} \quad (3.45)$$

for all $(w, X) \in Z$. While the supply effect affects the Löschian part of these elasticities, the competition effect is related to the non-Löschian part and unambiguously raises the aggregate labour supply elasticity under both competitive assumptions because $h(X) > 0$ for all $0 < X < X_M$. Furthermore, since

$$\frac{\partial h(X)}{\partial X} = \frac{-l'(w - tX)t \int_0^X l(w - tx)\,dx - l(w - tX)^2}{\left(\int_0^X l(w - tx)\,dx\right)^2} < 0 \quad (3.46)$$

for all $0 < X < X_M$, the second term in both (3.44) and (3.45) is strictly decreasing in the market radius. As we saw in the proof of Proposition 3.4, the Löschian aggregate elasticity is also strictly decreasing in it if individual labour supply is strictly log-convex, while it is constant in it if individual labour supply is log-linear. Hence, in both cases, the aggregate labour supply elasticity and the wage in the short-run equilibrium rise if competitive entry takes place, i.e., if the market radius falls. Moreover, one can show that under GO competition the aggregate elasticity is always strictly decreasing in the market radius, so that competitive entry unambiguously raises the wage paid by GO competitors.[25] Under HS competition, however, it is unclear *ex ante* whether competitive entry increases or decreases the aggregate elasticity and the wage. This depends on the extent of competition in the initial equilibrium. Nonetheless, it holds that substantial entry causes the wage to

---

[25] This is shown in Appendix A.4.

rise (cf. Greenhut et al., 1987, p. 34). The following proposition summarises these findings:

Proposition 3.5 (Competitive Entry under HS and GO Competition). *Consider a short-run spatial equilibrium in a labour market consisting of market areas of a given radius $0 < X < X_M$. Then the following holds:*

(a) Under GO competition, competitive entry unambiguously raises firms' aggregate labour supply elasticity, wage, and employment in the short-run equilibrium no matter the convexity of individual labour supply.

(b) Under HS competition, competitive entry raises firms' aggregate labour supply elasticity, wage, and employment in the short-run equilibrium if individual labour supply is strictly log-convex or log-linear. If individual labour supply is strictly log-concave, then the impact of competitive entry on their aggregate elasticity, wage, and employment is positive (negative) if the market radius is larger (smaller) than some unique X^* with $0 < X^* < X_M$.

Proof. For the impact of competitive entry on the aggregate labour supply elasticity, see Appendix A.4. Application of the wage-setting rule (3.35) then yields the impact on firms' wage. Finally, taking into account that firms' aggregate labour supply is strictly increasing in the wage gives the effect on firms' employment levels. ∎

Again, Table 3.2 on page 40 summarises the comparative static effect of competitive entry (or a decrease in the market radius) on the short-run equilibrium wage. But before discussing these results in some detail, we would like to know what the consequences of massive competitive entry or zero travel cost are. Or, put differently, what are the equilibrium outcomes of the model if space ceases to matter because firms are at any possible location or space becomes costless and thus *economically irrelevant*? The answer is given by the following corollary:

Corollary 3.4 (The Short-Run Equilibrium for $X \to 0$ or $t \to 0$). *Consider a short-run spatial equilibrium in a labour market consisting of market areas of a given radius $0 < X < X_M$. If firms' market radius or the travel cost approaches zero, then Löschian competition yields the (spaceless) monopsony solution, i.e., the wage is given by w_m, while both HS and GO competition yield the competitive solution, i.e., the wage is given by $w_c = \phi$, no matter the convexity of individual labour supply.*

Proof. Firstly, consider the case $X \to 0$. Since Löschian competitors act like spatial monopsonists within their market areas, so that the result from footnote 19 on page 30 applies, we have $e_{L\ddot{o}}(w, X) \to \varepsilon(w, 0)$ if $X \to 0$. Next, consider equation (3.10). For all $0 < v_i \leqslant 1/t$ we have

$$\lim_{X \to 0} e_i(w, X) = \lim_{X \to 0} \frac{w\left(\int_0^X l'(w - tx)\,dx + v_i l(w - tX)\right)}{\int_0^X l(w - tx)\,dx} = \infty. \quad (3.47)$$

3.7 Short-Run Comparative Statics

In particular, $e_{HS}(w, X) \to \infty$ and $e_{GO}(w, X) \to \infty$ hold if $X \to 0$. Thus, application of the wage-setting rule (3.35) yields $w_{Lö}(X) \to w_m$ and $w_{HS}(X), w_{GO}(X) \to \phi$ if $X \to 0$. Second, consider the case $t \to 0$. Taking the limit of equation (3.10) gives

$$\lim_{t \to 0} e_i(w, X) = \lim_{t \to 0} \frac{w\left(\int_0^X l'(w - tx)\,dx + v_i l(w - tX)\right)}{\int_0^X l(w - tx)\,dx} \quad (3.48)$$

$$= \begin{cases} \varepsilon(w, 0) & \text{if } i = Lö \\ \infty & \text{if } i = HS, GO \end{cases} \quad (3.49)$$

because $v_{Lö} = 0$, $v_{HS} = 1/2t$, and $v_{GO} = 1/t$. Hence, application of the wage-setting rule (3.35) yields $w_{Lö}(X) \to w_m$ and $w_{HS}(X), w_{GO}(X) \to \phi$ for all $0 < X < X_M$ if $t \to 0$. ∎

Corollary 3.4 makes clear why it is particularly sensible to refer to Löschian competition as collusive spatial oligopsony. Löschian competitors not only behave like spatial monopsonists within their market areas, but they also offer the same wage as the spaceless monopsonist if firms' market radius becomes infinitesimally small or space becomes costless and the labour market therefore becomes atomistic in a strict or in an economic sense, respectively. Other than GO and HS competition, Löschian competition thus fails to behave like perfect competition when space becomes economically irrelevant.

Since changes in the travel cost and the market radius have the same qualitative comparative static effects on the short-run equilibrium wage, it is now evident that both indeed play the same (short-run) role from an economic point of view. But as the discussion stressed, stronger competitive forces due to more densely distributed employers in economic space need not to cause the short-run equilibrium wage to rise. While this is at odds with *spaceless* economic intuition, we demonstrated above that these outcomes can be explained intuitively using a *spatial* reasoning (cf. Benson, 1988; 1989).

A last thing to note is that HS competition apparently shares some properties with Löschian or GO competition depending on the economic relevance of space. If space matters a lot, i.e., if firms' market radius or the travel cost is sufficiently high, it behaves in a way similar to Löschian competition, whereas it is similar to GO competition if space does not. In particular, if economic space ceases to be relevant because the labour market becomes atomistic or the travel cost approaches zero, both HS and GO competition behave like perfect competition, whilst Löschian competitors offer the same wage as a spaceless monopsonist. While these comments may seem a little arbitrary at the moment, it will be shown in the following analysis of the long-run equilibrium that HS competition indeed has this characteristic in a more general way.

3.8 Conclusions

In this chapter, we have dealt with a short-run model of spatial competition in the labour market. After stating the basic assumptions of the model, in particular the assumption of costly or economic homogenous space populated by homogenous firms and workers, we considered the problem of a single spatial monopsonist in an unbounded line market. We found that the spatial monopsonist may pay a higher or a lower wage than her spaceless counterpart depending on the convexity of individual labour supply relative to an exponential, where individual labour supply can be regarded either as the labour supply curve of a single worker or as the c.d.f. of workers' reservation incomes. In particular, under strictly log-concave individual labour supply, which encloses a large variety of concave and convex individual labour supply functions, space inhibits the wage-setting power of a spatial monopsonist, so that she offers a higher wage than her spaceless counterpart.

Next, we introduced spatial competition by means of the conjectural variations approach. We distinguished three different conjectures, viz. Löschian, HS, and GO competition, that can be held by firms about their rivals' wage reaction to a proposed wage change and which therefore differ in the conjectured expansion in the market radius due to a rise in the wage. When setting its wage, each firm is confronted with (finitely) elastic spatially aggregated labour supply due to two forces: Individual labour supply at each point of space is elastic (*supply effect*) and raising its wage allows the firm to increase its market area at the expense of neighbouring firms (*competition effect*). Under Löschian competition, firms regard their market areas as fixed, so that the supply effect is the only source of elasticity and the Löschian competitors behave like spatial monopsonists within their market areas. Under HS and GO competition, however, firms conjecture that their market radius will rise in response to an increase in their wage, so that the competition effect adds elasticity to their *perceived* labour supply. Hence, the short-run equilibrium wage is lowest under Löschian competition and highest under GO competition where the competition effect is more pronounced than under HS competition. Put differently, the more firms collude, the lower is the equilibrium wage.

Standard comparative static analyses showed that spaceless economic intuition will do in some cases, but will fail to grasp others. While changes in the fixed costs, the worker density, and the marginal revenue product of labour did show the expected impact on the short-run equilibrium wage, viz. no impact for the first two and a positive for the latter, things turned out to be different when considering changes in the travel cost and competitive entry. Somewhat surprisingly, the equilibrium wage will not necessarily rise if employers populate economic space more densely. Again, individual labour supply's convexity relative to an exponential and the mode of competition turned out to be crucial. Under GO competition and with strictly log-convex individual labour supply, the wage will always rise. It will fall, however, under Löschian competition if labour supply is strictly log-concave. Eventually, under HS competition with strictly log-concave individual labour supply, it will rise (fall) if economic space's relevance is sufficiently low (high). While these 'perverse' results are at odds with spaceless economic intuition, we showed that they

3.8 Conclusions

make intuitively sense when spatial considerations come into play and can thus be considered 'normal' within a spatial framework (e.g., Benson, 1988; 1989). Finally, we showed that both HS and GO competition behave like perfect competition if economic space becomes irrelevant, whereas Löschian competitors pay the same wage as a spaceless monopsonist.

Our next task will be to consider the long-run equilibrium – in the sense given by assumption (A7), i.e., the equilibrium arising in a situation where free entry of firms drives profits to zero. Accordingly, firms' market radius will become another endogenous variable to be determined by the model. And the fixed costs will turn out to be another driving force behind imperfect competition; for they limit the number of employers and therefore are crucial in determining how densely employers actually populate economic space. Put differently, the fixed costs and the implied economies of scale will turn out to be the reason why employers do not exist at any possible location in space, so that commuting takes place and space is economically relevant.

Chapter 4
Long-Run Spatial Monopsony

In the following, we will deal with long-run spatial monopsony. As stated in assumption (A7), we consider the model's outcomes – discussed for fixed market areas in Chapter 3 – when free entry of firms drives profits to zero. In other words, we solve the model for the zero-profit equilibrium. Hence, firms' market radius becomes an endogenous outcome of the model. Nevertheless, we already have the central building blocks of the long-run model at hand: The results gained from the analysis carried out in Chapter 3 still determine firms' optimal wage-setting behaviour within a market area of a given radius. To close the model, we just have to impose a zero-profit condition. Together, optimal (short-run) wage setting and the zero-profit condition then determine the long-run equilibrium wage–market radius pair.

The algebraic analysis of the long-run model will be very difficult at some instances. Therefore, we will repeatedly employ a diagrammatical representation, which – to our knowledge – was first used by Capozza and Van Order (1977a; 1978). The idea is to represent both optimal wage setting for a given market radius and given conjectural variations as well as wage–market radius pairs that give rise to zero profits diagrammatically in the (X, w)-plane. This yields a zero-profit locus and three wage-setting curves – one for each mode of competition. The intersection point of a wage-setting curve and the zero-profit locus then gives us the respective equilibrium where firms choose wages optimally and earn zero profits at the same time. In a next step, the standard comparative static analysis can be done by just shifting curves instead of doing the messy algebra, which would be far too intricate to gain unambiguous results without imposing additional structure on the model.

Hence, our next tasks are clear: We will derive the zero-profit locus and the three wage-setting curves under Löschian, HS, and GO competition. After that, we shall look for the corresponding equilibria and will analyse the comparative statics of the model. Eventually, we shall show how the model solves algebraically in the special case with linear or constant individual labour supply.

4.1 The Zero-Profit Locus

The first step is to derive the zero-profit locus. From Section 3.2 we know that firms' profits are given by equation (3.7). Therefore, the zero-profit condition is represented by

$$\Pi(w, X) = 2D(\phi - w) \int_0^X l(w - tx)\, dx - f \stackrel{!}{=} 0. \tag{4.1}$$

Applying the implicit function theorem, the zero-profit condition (4.1) defines a function $X(\cdot)$ of w with

$$X'(w) = -\frac{\partial \Pi(w, X)/\partial w}{\partial \Pi(w, X)/\partial X} \tag{4.2}$$

$$= \frac{\int_0^X l(w - tx)\, dx - (\phi - w) \int_0^X l'(w - tx)\, dx}{(\phi - w) l(w - tX)}, \tag{4.3}$$

where $X'(w) \gtreqless 0$ if and only if $\partial \Pi(w, X)/\partial w \lesseqgtr 0$.[1] This holds because the denominator in (4.3) is positive for all $(w, X) \in Z$, while the nominator can take every sign. Since Löschian competitors set their wage as if they were monopsonists in their market areas, $\partial \Pi(w, X_{Lö})/\partial w = 0$ must hold in the Löschian zero-profit equilibrium. So the slope of the zero-profit locus (ZPL) in the (X, w)-plane is infinity at Löschian competitors' market radius $X_{Lö}$.[2] Next, consider the case $X \to X_M$. From taking another look at equation (4.3) we see that the denominator approaches zero because $l(w - tX) \to 0$. Hence, the absolute value of (4.3) tends to infinity and thus the ZPL's slope in the (X, w)-plane to zero if $X \to X_M$.

To derive the ZPL diagrammatically in the (X, w)-plane consider Figure 4.1 on the facing page. The Löschian zero-profit equilibrium is characterised by a wage $w_{Lö}$ and a market radius $X_{Lö}$. As argued in the previous paragraph, the ZPL's slope in the (X, w)-plane is infinity in the Löschian equilibrium. Furthermore, Löschian competition involves the largest profits for any given market size, so that any other wage than $w_{Lö}$ yields negative profits at market radius $X_{Lö}$. Therefore, the ZPL must

---

[1] Just note that application of the Leibniz rule yields

$$\frac{\partial \Pi(w, X)}{\partial X} = 2D(\phi - w) l(w - tX) > 0$$

for all $(w, X) \in Z$, so that we are indeed allowed to apply the implicit function theorem, and

$$\frac{\partial \Pi(w, X)}{\partial w} = -2D \int_0^X l(w - tx)\, dx + 2D(\phi - w) \int_0^X l'(w - tx)\, dx \gtreqless 0$$

depending on the $(w, X) \in Z$ at which this partial derivative is evaluated.

[2] This is shown more rigorously in Appendix A.5.

4.1 The Zero-Profit Locus

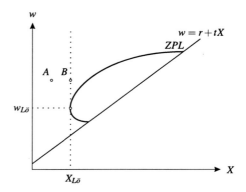

Fig. 4.1 The zero-profit locus in the (X, w)-plane

go vertically through the point $(X_{L\ddot{o}}, w_{L\ddot{o}})$ and lie to the right or to the left of $X_{L\ddot{o}}$ for any other possible wage. Next, note that profits are strictly increasing in the market radius as long as it is less than the spatial monopsonist's, i.e., $\partial \Pi(w, X)/\partial X > 0$ for all $(w, X) \in Z$. Hence, the ZPL must lie to the right of $X_{L\ddot{o}}$ for all wages $w \neq w_{L\ddot{o}}$. Furthermore, the more the wage departs from the collusive Löschian solution $w_{L\ddot{o}}$, the lower are profits, *ceteris paribus*; and the higher must be firms' market radius X to attain zero profits.

To make the point of the last paragraph more rigorously, suppose that the ZPL passed through point A in Figure 4.1. Since $\partial \Pi(w, X)/\partial X > 0$ for all $(w, X) \in Z$, the firm would earn positive profits in point B. This, however, is a contradiction because the Löschian wage $w_{L\ddot{o}}$ – chosen to maximise *actual* profits within spatial competitors' market areas – is the only wage at market radius $X_{L\ddot{o}}$ that involves nonnegative profits. Hence, the ZPL must lie to the right of $X_{L\ddot{o}}$ for wages other than $w_{L\ddot{o}}$, where we have to assume that the individual labour supply function l is such that this unique global maximum of profits exists. One way to achieve this, is to assume that $\partial \Pi(w, X_{L\ddot{o}})/\partial w > 0$ for all $w < w_{L\ddot{o}}$ and $\partial \Pi(w, X_{L\ddot{o}})/\partial w < 0$ for all $w > w_{L\ddot{o}}$, which even implies that profits are lower the more wages deviate from $w_{L\ddot{o}}$. An even stronger condition would be strict concavity of profits with respect to w, i.e., $\partial^2 \Pi(w, X_{L\ddot{o}})/\partial w^2 < 0$ for all $r < w < \phi$.[3] If the latter condition holds, then we obtain the rotated U-shape of the ZPL in the (X, w)-plane as shown in Figure 4.1, which we will assume from now on for expositional convenience. It should be noted though that this condition is much stronger than needed; the prior condition totally suffices to gain all the results to follow.

As already noted above, the slope of the ZPL in the (X, w)-plane approaches zero if the income at the market area boundary $w - tX$ approaches workers' reservation income r, that is, if $X \to X_M$. Since the straight line $w = r + tX$ in Figure 4.1

---

[3] From
$$\frac{\partial^2 \Pi(w, X)}{\partial w^2} = 2D(\phi - w) \int_0^X l''(w - tx)\,dx - 4D \int_0^X l'(w - tx)\,dx$$
we see at once that strict concavity of profits with respect to w follows, in particular, from concave individual labour supply (with $l''(w - tx) \leqslant 0$ for all $r < w - tx < \phi$).

gives all wage–market radius pairs that yield incomes that exactly meet workers' reservation income (or the lowest reservation income among workers if individual labour supply refers to the c.d.f. of workers' reservation incomes), the ZPL becomes horizontal at the two intersection points with this line.

Finally, what happens if $X \geqslant X_M$ or $w-tX \leqslant r$, respectively? From Corollary 3.2 we know that firms then behave like spatial monopsonists, i.e., they choose the wage w_M. This holds irrespectively of the level of X. Furthermore, we know that w_M yields an X_M such that individual labour supply drops to zero at firms' market boundaries. Thus, firms choose a wage–market radius pair on the straight line $w = r + tX$. For this reason, wage–market radius pairs right to this straight line are irrelevant and we shall thus ignore the ZPL's shape right to it.

What have we shown so far? Since we are looking for a zero-profit long-run equilibrium, we now know that this equilibrium will lie on the ZPL. Furthermore, we know from the discussion above that the Löschian equilibrium will be at the leftmost point of the ZPL as Löschian competitors maximise *actual* (and not *perceived*) profits within their market areas. To find the other equilibria, however, we have to take firms' optimal wage-setting behaviour for different conjectural variations into account. This will be done in the next section.

4.2 The Wage-Setting Curve

Now that we have derived the ZPL's shape in the relevant part of the (X, w)-plane, it is time to consider firms' wage-setting behaviour under the alternative competitive assumptions. As derived in Chapter 3, firms' wage-setting behaviour for a given market radius X with $0 < X < X_M$ is described by equation (3.35), where the elasticity of aggregate labour supply depends on the conjectural variations held by spatial competitors, i.e., on the conjectured change in the market radius in response to a proposed change in the wage. Rearranging (3.35), we get the following wage-setting condition

$$W_i(w, X) := (\phi - w)e_i(w, X) - w \stackrel{!}{=} 0 \qquad (4.4)$$

with $i \in \{Lö, HS, GO\}$ depending on competitors' conjectural variations. Applying the implicit function theorem yields a function $w_i(\cdot)$ of X, which gives the profit-maximising wage chosen by a firm given some market radius $0 < X < X_M$, with

$$w_i'(X) = -\frac{\partial W_i(w, X)/\partial X}{\partial W_i(w, X)/\partial w}.\qquad (4.5)$$

[4]

---

[4] That $\partial W_i(w, X)/\partial w < 0$ for all $(w, X) \in Z$ that satisfy (4.4) and all $i \in \{Lö, HS, GO\}$, which justifies the application of the implicit function theorem, will be shown in Lemma 4.1.

4.2 The Wage-Setting Curve

To be able to give a diagrammatic representation of $w_i(\cdot)$ in the (X, w)-plane, to which we will refer as the wage-setting curve (WSC) below, we have to take a closer look at the sign of (4.5). It should be clear from the discussion in Sections 3.6 and 3.7 that $w_i(X)$ is the short-run equilibrium wage for some market radius X and that the slope of $w_i(\cdot)$ is the comparative static change in the short-run equilibrium wage in response to an increase in the market radius. So if competitive entry, i.e., a decrease in the market radius, causes the wage to rise, then the WSC is downward-sloping, while it is upward-sloping if competitive entry causes the wage to fall. Therefore, the following lemma, which investigates the signs of both the nominator and the denominator of (4.5), follows directly from Propositions 3.4 and 3.5:

Lemma 4.1 (The Signs of $\partial W_i(w, X)/\partial w$ and $\partial W_i(w, X)/\partial X$). *Consider wage–market radius pairs $(w, X) \in Z$ where the wage is chosen to maximise firms' perceived profits given some market radius X and where the corresponding second-order condition is assumed to hold. Then the following holds:*

(a) $\partial W_i(w, X)/\partial w < 0$ *for all* $(w, X) \in Z$ *that satisfy (4.4) and all* $i \in \{Lö, HS, GO\}$ *no matter the convexity of individual labour supply.*
(b) *If individual labour supply is strictly log-convex, then* $\partial W_i(w, X)/\partial X < 0$ *holds for all* $(w, X) \in Z$ *that satisfy (4.4) and all* $i \in \{Lö, HS, GO\}$.
(c) *If individual labour supply is strictly log-concave, then* $\partial W_{Lö}(w, X)/\partial X > 0$ *and* $\partial W_{GO}(w, X)/\partial X < 0$ *hold for all* $(w, X) \in Z$ *that satisfy (4.4); furthermore,* $\partial W_{HS}(w, X)/\partial X < 0$ *holds for all* $X < X^*$ *and* $\partial W_{HS}(w, X)/\partial X > 0$ *for all* $X > X^*$ *for some unique* X^* *with* $0 < X^* < X_M$; *the same holds for every mode of competition i with conjectural variations* $0 < v_i < 1/t$.
(d) *If individual labour supply is log-linear,* $\partial W_{GO}(w, X)/\partial X < \partial W_{HS}(w, X)/\partial X < \partial W_{Lö}(w, X)/\partial X = 0$ *holds for all* $(w, X) \in Z$ *that satisfy (4.4).*

Proof. That $\partial W_i(w, X)/\partial w < 0$ for all $(w, X) \in Z$ that satisfy (4.4) and all $i \in \{Lö, HS, GO\}$ is an immediate consequence of firms' profit maximisation. Gaining the other results parallels the proofs of Propositions 3.4 and 3.5. All these proofs are found in Appendix A.6. ∎

With Lemma 4.1 in place, we know that the slope of the WSC in the (X, w)-plane solely depends on the sign of the partial derivative of the wage-setting condition (4.4) with respect to the market radius. Therefore, combining the results from Lemma 4.1 and Proposition 3.2 yields the following lemma:

Lemma 4.2 (Curvature of the Wage-Setting Curves). *Consider wage–market radius pairs $(w, X) \in Z$ where the wage is chosen to maximise firms' perceived profits given some market radius X and where the corresponding second-order condition is assumed to hold. Then the following holds:*

(a) *If individual labour supply is strictly log-convex, then the WSCs are downward-sloping in the (X, w)-plane with $w_{GO}(X) > w_{HS}(X) > w_{Lö}(X)$ for all $0 < X < X_M$.*
(b) *If individual labour supply is strictly log-concave, then the WSC under Löschian competition is upward-sloping, while the WSC under GO competition is downward-sloping; the WSC under HS competition is downward-sloping*

for all $X < X^*$ and upward-sloping for all $X > X^*$ for some unique X^* with $0 < X^* < X_M$; the same also holds for every mode of competition i with conjectural variations $0 < v_i < 1/t$. Furthermore, $w_{GO}(X) > w_{HS}(X) > w_{Lö}(X)$ holds for all $0 < X < X_M$.

(c) If individual labour supply is log-linear, then the WSC under Löschian competition is a horizontal line in the (X, w)-plane, while the WSCs under HS and GO competition are downward-sloping, where the curve under GO competition is steeper than its HS competition counterpart. Finally, $w_{GO}(X) > w_{HS}(X) > w_{Lö}(X)$ holds for all $0 < X < X_M$.

Proof. By virtue of Lemma 4.1, we know that $\partial W_i(w, X)/\partial w < 0$ for all $(w, X) \in Z$ that maximise firms' perceived profits and all i with $0 \leqslant v_i \leqslant 1/t$. Since

$$w_i'(X) = -\frac{\partial W_i(w, X)/\partial X}{\partial W_i(w, X)/\partial w} \tag{4.6}$$

holds for all $0 < X < X_M$, we have

$$\operatorname{sgn} w_i'(X) = \operatorname{sgn} \frac{\partial W_i(w, X)}{\partial X} \tag{4.7}$$

for all $0 < X < X_M$ or $(w, X) \in Z$ that satisfy (4.4), respectively. Making again use of the results from Lemma 4.1 and noting that Proposition 3.2 implies $w_{GO}(X) > w_{HS}(X) > w_{Lö}(X)$ for all $0 < X < X_M$, (a)–(c) follow immediately. ∎

Figure 4.2 on the next page adds the Löschian, HS, and GO WSC to Figure 4.1 for strictly log-concave individual labour supply, where a number of ZPLs for different levels of fixed costs $f^3 > f^2 > f^1$ are drawn. In the next section, we shall also draw figures for log-linear and strictly log-convex individual labour supply. Nonetheless, some general properties can be seen from Figure 4.2 that do not depend on the convexity of individual labour supply and are worth mentioning: Firstly, both the intercept of the GO and the HS WSC is the spaceless competitive wage, i.e., workers' marginal revenue product of labour, while, second, the Löschian WSC's intercept is the spaceless monopsony wage. Both properties follow directly from Corollary 3.4, which states $w_{GO}(X), w_{HS}(X) \to \phi$ and $w_{Lö}(X) \to w_m$ if $X \to 0$. Third, if $X \to X_M$, then all WSCs approach the point $M = (X_M, w_M)$, i.e., the wage–market radius pair chosen by a spatial monopsonist, which stems from Corollary 3.2. Fourth, higher fixed costs cause the ZPL to contract because a higher market radius is needed to gain zero profits, *ceteris paribus*.[5] Fifth, since the fixed costs must not exceed the highest profits achievable, i.e., the profits gained by a spatial monopsonist without any fixed costs, for otherwise no firm is able survive in the

---

[5] This will be shown more rigorously in Section 4.4.1.

4.3 The Long-Run Equilibrium

Fig. 4.2 The wage-setting curves and a family of zero-profit loci for different levels of fixed costs under strictly log-concave individual labour supply

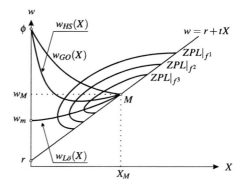

labour market, the ZPL collapses around the point M. In the following discussion, we will refer to this level of fixed costs as f_{max}.[6]

Now that we have derived both the ZPL and the WSCs for Löschian, HS, and GO competition, we are ready to derive the long-run equilibrium of the model and to discuss its properties. From the discussion so far we know, firstly, that the ZPL does not depend on the mode of competition, while, second, the curvature of the WSC does. Third, the curvature of the WSC also depends on individual labour supply's convexity relative to an exponential. Therefore, the equilibrium – the intersection point of the respective WSC and the ZPL – will crucially depend on the mode of competition and the convexity of individual labour supply.

4.3 The Long-Run Equilibrium

With the WSC and the ZPL at hand, we are now able to derive the long-run equilibrium conveniently in a diagrammatical way. The long-run equilibrium refers to a situation where both the wage-setting condition (4.4) and the zero-profit condition (4.1) hold. That is to say, firms both behave optimally by choosing a profit-maximising wage given their conjectures about their rivals' reactions to a proposed wage change and enter the market as long as there is an opportunity of earning a profit. Diagrammatically, the wage-setting condition for Löschian, HS, and GO conjectures is represented by the corresponding WSC, while the ZPL reflects the zero-profit condition. Together, the WSC and the ZPL determine the long-run equilibrium under the respective mode of competition: The ZPL represents all wage–market radius pairs consistent with zero profits, while the respective WSC determine which point on the ZPL is actually achieved in equilibrium, viz. the zero-profit wage–market radius pair consistent with firms' optimal wage-setting. Or, put

---

[6] More formally, f_{max} is the single level of fixed costs that solves $\Pi(w_M, X_M) = (\phi - w_M) L(w_M, X_M) - f \stackrel{!}{=} 0$, i.e., $f_{max} := (\phi - w_M) L(w_M, X_M)$.

the other way round, the respective WSC gives all (short-run) wage–market radius pairs consistent with firms' optimal wage-setting behaviour, while the ZPL tells us which pair is actually achieved in the long run where free entry drives profits to zero.

To find the long-run equilibrium under the respective mode of competition diagrammatically, we simply look for the intersection point of the ZPL and the respective WSC. If there is a unique intersection point, then the equilibrium is also unique. The following proposition establishes the existence and uniqueness of the long-run equilibrium:

Proposition 4.1 (The Long-Run Equilibrium's Existence and Uniqueness). *Suppose the fixed costs are smaller than f_{max}. Then there exists a unique long-run equilibrium where firms set wages optimally, so that equation (4.4) holds, and free entry drives profits to zero, so that (4.1) holds, no matter individual labour supply's convexity nor the mode of competition i with conjectural variations $0 \leqslant v_i \leqslant 1/t$.*

Proof. Under Löschian competition, we know from the discussion in Section 4.1 and Appendix A.5 that the long-run Löschian equilibrium is given by the leftmost point of the ZPL which exists and is unique for all $f < f_{max}$. Now, consider GO competition. Combining the results from Corollaries 3.2 and 3.4 and Proposition 3.5, we have $w_M < w_{GO}(X) < \phi$ with $w'_{GO}(X) < 0$ for all $0 < X < X_M$, $w_{GO}(X) \to \phi$ if $X \to 0$, and $w_{GO}(X) \to w_M$ if $X \to X_M$. From the discussion in Section 4.1 we know further that $X(w_M) < X_M = (w_M - r)/t$ for all $f < f_{max}$ and $X'(w) > 0$ for all $w > w_M$ as long as $X(w) < (w-r)/t$. Hence, there obviously exists a unique intersection point of $w_{GO}(\cdot)$ and $X(\cdot)$ for all $f < f_{max}$, which gives the unique long-run GO equilibrium and which can readily be seen from Figure 4.3 on the facing page. Finally, there exists a unique intersection point of $w_i(\cdot)$ with conjectural variations $0 < v_i < 1/t$ and $X(\cdot)$. This follows immediately from $w_{Lö}(X) < w_i(X) < w_{GO}(X)$ for all $0 < X < X_M$, $w_i(X) \to \phi$ if $X \to 0$, $w_i(X) \to w_M$ if $X \to X_M$, and the curvature of the WSC and the ZPL.[7] ∎

After having established the existence and uniqueness of the long-run equilibrium for conjectural variations $0 \leqslant v_i \leqslant 1/t$, it is interesting to have a closer look at the long-run equilibrium's properties, a depiction of which, depending on individual labour supply's convexity relative to an exponential, is found in Figures 4.4– 4.6 on page 58.

---

[7] Note that multiple intersection points of $w_i(\cdot)$ and $X(\cdot)$ are ruled out because the WSC cannot intersect the ZPL from below in the (X, w)-plane. If this were the case, this would imply that (infinitesimally) reducing the wage and the market radius at the same time gives an increase in actual but a decrease in perceived profits. Since the partial derivative of perceived profits with respect to the wage is always larger than its actual profits counterpart (due to the competition effect) and the partial derivative of perceived and actual profits with respect to the market radius is the same, this cannot happen and therefore rules out that the ZPL is intersected by the WSC from below. And this, in turn, rules out multiple intersection points, so that we indeed arrive at a unique long-run equilibrium for all conjectural variations $0 \leqslant v_i \leqslant 1/t$.

4.3 The Long-Run Equilibrium

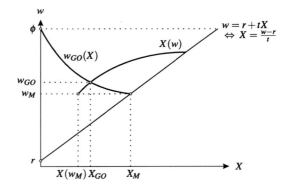

Fig. 4.3 The existence and uniqueness of the long-run equilibrium under Greenhut–Ohta competition

Proposition 4.2 (The Long-Run Equilibrium's Properties). *Consider a long-run equilibrium where firms set wages optimally according to equation (4.4), free entry drives profits to zero according to equation (4.1), and the fixed costs are smaller than f_{max}. Then the long-run equilibrium market radius and wage are strictly increasing functions of the conjectural variations held by spatial competitors about the expected rise in the market area that will follow from a proposed increase in the wage offered with $0 \leqslant v_i \leqslant 1/t$ no matter the convexity of individual labour supply. In particular,*

$$X_{Lö} < X_{HS} < X_{GO}$$

and

$$w_{Lö} < w_{HS} < w_{GO}.$$

Proof. Bearing in mind the discussion of the shape of the ZPL in Section 4.1, which is upward-sloping in the (X, w)-plane for all $w > w_{Lö}$ as long as $X(w) < (w - r)/t$, the claim follows at once from the short-run result from Proposition 3.2 that the wage optimally chosen for a given market radius $0 < X < X_M$ is strictly increasing in the conjectural variations with $0 \leqslant v_i \leqslant 1/t$. ∎

The idea behind Proposition 4.2 is best understood by looking carefully at the diagrams: The curvature of the WSC for the different modes of competition and depending on the convexity of individual labour supply relative to an exponential are shown in Figures 4.4–4.6. As said above, the intersection of the ZPL and the respective WSC gives the long-run equilibrium. Firstly, note that the higher are the conjectural variations held by competitors about the expected rise in their market radius in response to an increase in their wage the higher is the short-run equilibrium wage (i.e., the equilibrium wage for a given market radius $0 < X < X_M$, see Proposition 3.2). Since the ZPL is upward-sloping for all $w > w_{Lö}$, the intersection point of the ZPL and the non-Löschian WSC must lie northeast of the Löschian equilibrium point $(X_{Lö}, w_{Lö})$. By repeated application of this argument, the long-run equilibrium wage and market radius must be higher, the higher are conjectural variations. Since $v_{GO} > v_{HS} > v_{Lö}$ holds, we get $w_{GO} > w_{HS} > w_{Lö}$ and $X_{GO} > X_{HS} > X_{Lö}$.

Fig. 4.4 The long-run equilibrium under strictly log-convex individual labour supply

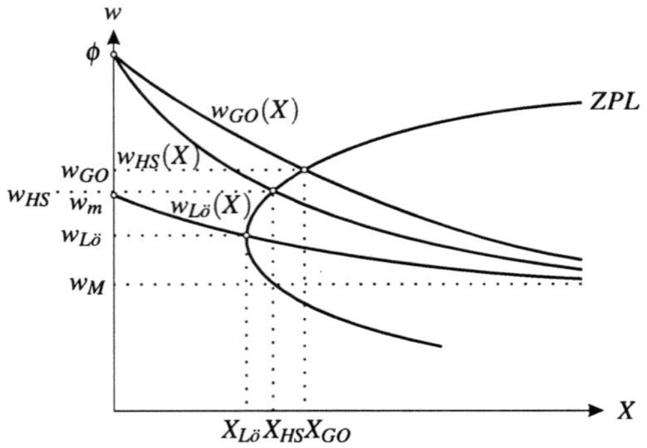

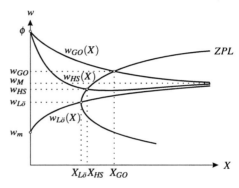

Fig. 4.5 The long-run equilibrium under strictly log-concave individual labour supply

Fig. 4.6 The long-run equilibrium under log-linear individual labour supply

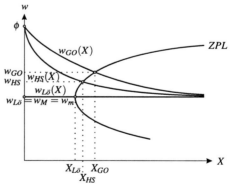

The intuition behind this result is straightforward: Think of an initial zero-profit equilibrium under Löschian competition with the lowest conjectural variations $v_{Lö} = 0$. Higher conjectural variations result in more elastic perceived aggregate labour supply and therefore in a higher short-run equilibrium wage. Hence, the higher are conjectural variations, the more firms deviate from the Löschian wage. Since this decreases firms' profitability, they would incur losses for a given market radius. Hence, some of them must leave the market, which, in turn, raises the market radius of the remaining firms. Clearly, the amount of competitive exit needed

4.3 The Long-Run Equilibrium

to guarantee zero profits is increasing in the conjectural variations because they pin down how much the *perceived optimal* wage deviates from the profit-maximising Löschian one. Although larger market areas may allow the firms to reduce their wage compared to the initial situation, all in all, both their market radius and wage increase in the conjectural variations – irrespectively of the shape of individual labour supply.

It is interesting to note that both in the short-run and the long-run equilibrium the wage depends positively on the conjectural variations. In particular, this translates into the same ordering of equilibrium wages under Löschian, HS, and GO competition. What differs in general, however, are the gaps between the short-run wages under the different competitive assumptions and those between the long-run wages. This stems from endogenous and thus different market radii for the different competitive assumptions in the long run that result from the varying efficacy of firms in extracting profits under different conjectural variations.

In a next step, it is interesting to compare spatial monopsony to long-run spatial oligopsony, which is done by the following corollary:

Corollary 4.1 (Spatial Monopsony vs. Long-Run Spatial Oligopsony). *Consider a long-run equilibrium where firms set wages optimally according to equation (4.4), free entry drives profits to zero according to equation (4.1), and the fixed costs are smaller than f_{max}. Then the following holds:*

(a) If individual labour supply is strictly log-convex, then the spatial monopsonist offers the lowest wage compared to Löschian, HS, and GO competitors:

$$\forall r < z < \phi : \ell''(z) > 0 \Rightarrow w_M < w_{L\ddot{o}} < w_{HS} < w_{GO}.$$

(b) If individual labour supply is log-linear, then the spatial monopsonist offers the same wage as Löschian competitors, but a lower one than HS and GO competitors:

$$\forall r < z < \phi : \ell''(z) = 0 \Rightarrow w_M = w_{L\ddot{o}} < w_{HS} < w_{GO}.$$

(c) If individual labour supply is strictly log-concave, then the spatial monopsonist offers a higher wage than Löschian competitors and a lower wage than GO competitors. Whether the spatial monopsonist offers a higher or a lower wage than HS competitors depends on the strength of competition (the level of fixed costs f). If competition is strong (f low), then the ranking of the wage offers is

$$w_{L\ddot{o}} < w_M < w_{HS} < w_{GO}.$$

On the other hand, if competition is weak (f high), then the ranking is

$$w_{L\ddot{o}} < w_{HS} < w_M < w_{GO}.$$

Finally, there exists some unique critical strength of competition (and level of fixed costs $f^* < f_{max}$) such that

$$w_{L\ddot{o}} < w_{HS} = w_M < w_{GO}.$$

Proof. (a) and (b) follow immediately from combining the results from Corollary 3.3 and Proposition 4.2. To prove (c), note that for strictly log-concave individual labour supply we have $w_{L\ddot{o}}(X) < w_M$ for all $0 < X < X_M$ (see Corollary 3.3) and $w_{GO}(X) > w_M$ for all $0 < X < X_M$ because $w_{GO}(X) \to w_M$ if $X \to X_M$ (see Corollary 3.2) and $w'_{GO}(X) < 0$ for all $0 < X < X_M$ (see Proposition 3.5). Thus, $w_{L\ddot{o}} < w_M < w_{GO}$ holds whenever $f < f_{max}$. Further, if the fixed costs are sufficiently low, so that competition is sufficiently fierce, then $w_{L\ddot{o}} < w_M < w_{HS} < w_{GO}$ holds in the long-run equilibrium because $w_{HS}(X) \to w_{GO}(X)$ if $X \to 0$ (see Corollary 3.4). The remaining claims follow at once from the shape of the WSC under HS conjectures (see Lemma 4.2 and Figure 4.2). ∎

Hence, we find that even in the long-run zero-profit equilibrium Löschian competitors pay a lower wage than the spatial monopsonist if individual labour supply is strictly log-concave and that the same may also hold under HS competition if the fixed costs are such high that competition is sufficiently weak. Intuitively, the latter causes the market areas to grow very large, so that workers near the market boundary supply only negligible amounts of labour and competition among firms for these workers is very weak (cf. Capozza and Van Order, 1978).[8] These results correspond to the 'perverse results found in spatial price theory' (Capozza and Van Order, 1978, p. 896) observed by several authors (e.g., Greenhut *et al.*, 1975; Benson, 1980; Nakagome, 1986). This will become clearer when discussing the comparative statics of the model, which we will do next and which will give rise to further results that have attracted the label 'perverse' in the literature.

4.4 Long-Run Comparative Statics

Before investigating the model's comparative statics, we first have to discuss whether the zero-profit equilibrium under consideration is stable. Assumption (A7) tells us that firms are free to relocate and enter or leave the market until profits are driven to zero. Consequently, they enter or leave the market till *symmetric* market areas result that satisfy the zero-profit condition (see also the discussion of the short-run dynamics in the beginning of Section 3.6). By imposing assumption (A7), which includes a costless relocation assumption, we guarantee the zero-profit equilibrium's stability and suppress the whole adjustment process following competitive entry or exit. As Salop (1979b, p. 145) puts it: 'This equilibrium concept is static. In

---

[8] This corresponds to our observation in Section 3.7 that the supply effect under strictly log-concave individual labour supply tends to lower the wage in response to competitive entry, while the competition effect works the other way round and is increasing in the conjectural variations. If workers near the market boundary supply only little amounts of labour because both fixed costs and market areas are large, extending one's market area (and thus competitive forces) becomes less important.

4.4 Long-Run Comparative Statics

a dynamic context, it assumes that firms may costlessly relocate in response to entry and, in fact, do relocate. Thus, equal spacing is maintained.'[9] Since we indeed have a stable zero-profit equilibrium, we can move on to investigating the comparative statics of the model.

4.4.1 Changes in the Position of the Zero-Profit Locus and the Wage-Setting Curve

As we shall see, it is quite hard to derive unambiguous comparative static results. This is due to the fact that changes in the market conditions in some cases affect the position of both the ZPL and the respective WSC. The following lemma presents the impact of a *ceteris paribus* change in the fixed costs, the worker density, the marginal revenue product of labour, or the travel cost on the position of the ZPL and the WSC, a summary of which is given in Table 4.1.

Table 4.1 The impact of changes in the market conditions on the position of the zero-profit locus and the wage-setting curve[a]

Increase:	Zero-profit locus		Wage-setting curve					
			Lö competition			HS competition[b]		GO comp.
			log-concave	log-linear	log-convex	log-concave	log-linear	log-convex
Fixed costs (f)	→		0	0	0	0	0	0	0
Worker density (D)	←		0	0	0	0	0	0	0
Productivity (ϕ)	←		↑	↑	↑	↑	↑	↑	↑
Travel cost (t)	→		↑	0	↓	↓↑[c]	↓	↓	↓

[a] → (←) indicates a shift rightwards (leftwards); ↑ (↓) indicates a shift upwards (downwards); and 0 indicates no change in position.
[b] The same results hold for every mode of competition i with conjectural variations $0 < v_i < 1/t$.
[c] ↓ if competition is strong (i.e., the fixed costs are low, and thus firms' market areas are small); ↑ if competition is weak (i.e., the fixed costs are high, and thus firms' market areas are large).

---

[9] A similar reasoning is used by Mills and Lav (1964, p. 283) in their formalisation of Lösch's (1944) contribution, the so-called Lösch–Mills–Lav model: 'It should be emphasized that we consider only static industry equilibriums in this paper. We do not consider adjustment processes, and we make no attempt to ascertain whether any adjustment process will converge to industry equilibrium from any particular arbitrary initial arrangement of firms and market areas. One way to envisage the adjustment is to assume a *tâtonnement* process in which no plants are actually built until equilibrium is reached.'

Lemma 4.3 (Changes in the Position of the ZPL and the WSC). *Suppose the fixed costs are smaller than f_{max}. Then the following holds:*

(a) An increase in the fixed costs shifts the ZPL to the right and does not affect the WSC.

(b) An increase in the worker density shifts the ZPL to the left and does not affect the WSC.

(c) An increase in the marginal revenue product of labour shifts the ZPL to the left and the WSC upwards.

(d) An increase in the travel cost shifts the ZPL to the right. The impact on the WSC's position depends on the mode of competition and individual labour supply's convexity relative to an exponential. Under GO competition, the WSC is shifted downwards no matter the convexity of individual labour supply. Under Löschian competition, the WSC is shifted upwards (downwards) if individual labour supply is strictly log-concave (log-convex), while its position is unaltered if individual labour supply is log-linear. Under HS competition, the WSC is shifted upwards if individual labour supply is strictly log-concave and competition is sufficiently weak (the fixed costs are sufficiently high), while it is shifted downwards if individual labour supply is strictly log-convex, log-linear, or strictly log-concave with sufficiently fierce competition (low fixed costs).

Proof. See Appendix A.7. ∎

Lemma 4.3 will enable us to do the comparative static analysis diagrammatically. Actually, it will enable us to do it at all. This holds because the two conditions that have to be met by a long-run equilibrium, i.e., the wage-setting condition (4.4) and the zero-profit condition (4.1), are highly non-linear in the wage and the market radius, so that solving explicitly for their equilibrium values is not a feasible strategy. Nonetheless, explicit solutions can be obtained when imposing further simplifying assumptions on individual labour supply – e.g., by considering linear or constant individual labour supply – as will be demonstrated in Sections 4.5 and 4.6.

4.4.2 Comparative Statics in the Fixed Costs and the Worker Density

From the results of Lemma 4.3 we know that an increase in the fixed costs or a decrease in the worker density moves the ZPL to the right, whereas the WSC's position is unaffected. Therefore, we can see the comparative static results diagrammatically in a very convenient way, see Figures 4.7 and 4.8 on the next page and Figures 4.9 and 4.10 on page 64. As the ZPL contracts, the labour market moves along the respective WSC. Obviously, the consequences of a change in the fixed costs or the worker density depends on the slope of the WSC under consideration.

We know from Lemma 4.2 that the WSC is downward-sloping in the following instances: (1) under GO competition no matter the convexity of individual labour

4.4 Long-Run Comparative Statics

Fig. 4.7 The impact of an increase in the fixed costs or a decrease in the worker density on the long-run equilibrium wage and market radius under Greenhut–Ohta competition

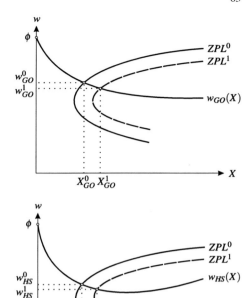

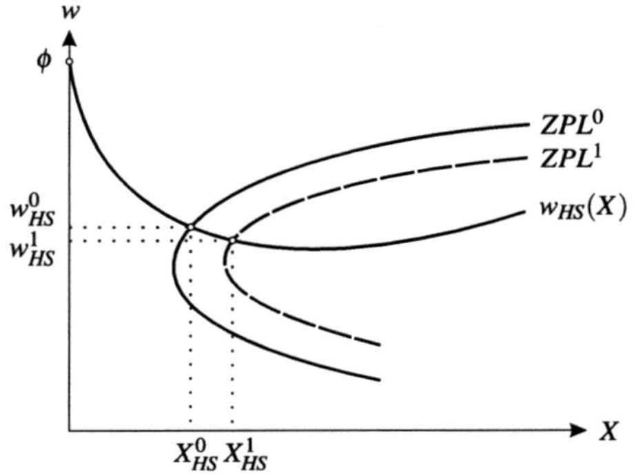

Fig. 4.8 The impact of an increase in the fixed costs or a decrease in the worker density on the long-run equilibrium wage and market radius under Hotelling–Smithies competition if individual labour supply is strictly log-concave and competition is fierce

supply, (2) under Löschian competition if individual labour supply is strictly log-convex, (3) under HS competition if individual labour supply is strictly log-convex or log-linear, or (4) under HS competition if individual labour supply is strictly log-concave and competition is sufficiently fierce (i.e., the fixed costs and thus firms' market areas are sufficiently small). Figure 4.7, which shows the comparative static effects for case (1), and Figure 4.8, which shows them for case (4), therefore tell us that in all these cases an increase in the fixed costs or a decrease in the worker density causes the long-run equilibrium wage to fall, while the long-run equilibrium market radius rises. This seems to be intuitively appealing: Higher fixed costs or a lower density of workers reduces the labour market's profitability, *ceteris paribus*, so that some firms are forced to leave the less profitable labour market until profits are zero again. This, in turn, enlarges market areas and thus reduces competition among firms which are now more distantly distributed in economic space, so that the long-run equilibrium wage is driven downwards.

Clearly, the comparative static effect on the wage is the other way round if the WSC under consideration is upward-sloping. According to Lemma 4.2 this can only happen if individual labour supply is strictly log-concave: (1) under Löschian competition or (2) under HS competition with weak competition (high fixed costs and thus large market areas). Case (2) is shown in Figure 4.8. Suppose the economy starts in a long-run equilibrium on the upward-sloping part of HS competitors' WSC

Fig. 4.9 The impact of an increase in the fixed costs or a decrease in the worker density on the long-run equilibrium wage and market radius under Löschian competition if individual labour supply is strictly log-concave

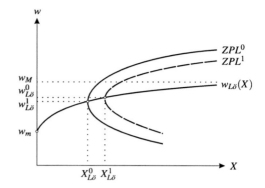

Fig. 4.10 The impact of an increase in the fixed costs or a decrease in the worker density on the long-run equilibrium wage and market radius under Löschian competition if individual labour supply is log-linear

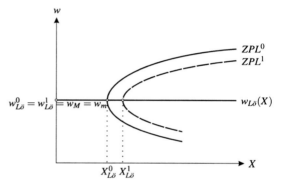

where market areas are relatively large and competition among firms is relatively low. If the fixed costs increase (or the worker density decreases), then the ZPL shifts to the right and we move along the WSC, so that both the long-run equilibrium wage and market radius rise. Case (1), on the other hand, is shown in Figure 4.9.

These latter results seem to be at odds with intuition because competitive forces seem to work in the 'wrong' direction. It is interesting to note that Löschian competition gives 'perverse' results only if individual labour supply is not convex enough – in the sense that it is not more convex than an exponential (cf. Benson, 1980). Otherwise, Löschian competition gives 'normal' results that are in line with intuition. As HS competition refers to conjectural variations in between those of GO and Löschian competition, it seems plausible that it can also give rise to 'perverse' results under certain conditions. In line with this, 'perverse' results are obtained under HS competition only if individual labour supply is less convex than an exponential and the labour market's initial long-run equilibrium is on the upward-sloping part of the WSC, that is to say, if competition is sufficiently weak initially because of high fixed costs. Nevertheless, these results should not appear too stunning in the light of our discussion of competitive entry in Section 3.7. If market areas are very large initially, the competition effect matters only little because workers at the market boundary supply only small amounts of labour. Therefore, the supply effect and thus the Löschian component of HS competitors' aggregate labour supply elasticity dominates over the competition effect, giving rise to Löschian results under HS conjectures.

Finally, the WSC may also be constant in the market radius which holds under Löschian competition if individual labour supply is log-linear. Then an increase in the fixed costs or a decrease in the worker density does not affect the long-run equilibrium wage, whereas firms' market radius grows larger. This can be seen at once from Figure 4.10 on the preceding page. Besides, the wage is the same as under spatial and spaceless monopsony. This is the case anticipated at the end of Section 3.3: With log-linear individual labour supply, Löschian competitors behave like spaceless monopsonists. In other words, space does not have any impact on their wage-setting behaviour in this particular case. Of course, it has one on workers' average incomes and thus on their overall labour supply; both of them fall as firms populate economic space less densely.

The following proposition summarises the discussion so far:

Proposition 4.3 (Long-Run Comparative Statics in f and D). *Consider a long-run equilibrium where firms set wages optimally according to equation (4.4), free entry drives profits to zero according to equation (4.1), and the fixed costs are smaller than f_{max}. Then an increase in the fixed costs or a decrease in the worker density*

(a) raises the long-run equilibrium market radius no matter the convexity of individual labour supply and the mode of competition;

(b) reduces the long-run equilibrium wage under GO competition no matter the convexity of individual labour supply;

(c) reduces the long-run equilibrium wage under HS competition if individual labour supply is strictly log-convex or log-linear;

(d) reduces (raises) the long-run equilibrium wage under HS competition if individual labour supply is strictly log-concave and the fixed costs are sufficiently low (high);

(e) reduces (raises) the long-run equilibrium wage under Löschian competition if individual labour supply is strictly log-convex (log-concave), whereas it is left unaltered if individual labour supply is log-linear. ∎

4.4.3 Comparative Statics in the Marginal Revenue Product of Labour

A change in the travel cost or the marginal revenue product of labour, however, affects both the ZPL's and the WSC's position, so that clear-cut comparative static results can be gained only in some cases. Consider an increase in the marginal revenue product first. According to Lemma 4.3, such an increase shifts the WSC upwards and the ZPL to the left. To identify the comparative static effect, the crucial thing to look at is again the slope of the WSC under consideration.

Fig. 4.11 The impact of an increase in the marginal revenue product of labour on the long-run equilibrium wage and market radius under Greenhut–Ohta competition

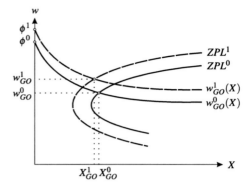

Remember again that Lemma 4.2 tells us that the WSC is downward-sloping in the following instances: (1) under GO competition no matter the convexity of individual labour supply, (2) under Löschian competition if individual labour supply is strictly log-convex, (3) under HS competition if individual labour supply is strictly log-convex or log-linear, or (4) under HS competition if individual labour supply is strictly log-concave and competition is sufficiently fierce (i.e., the fixed costs and thus firms' market areas are sufficiently small). Figure 4.11, which shows case (1), tells us that for a downward-sloping WSC the long-run equilibrium wage unambiguously rises, for both the shift of the ZPL to the left and the shift of the WSC upwards in isolation cause the long-run equilibrium wage to increase. On the other hand, the impact on the equilibrium market radius is ambiguous because the two shifts work in different directions. Under Löschian competition, however, we know that the effect on the equilibrium market radius is negative because the Löschian equilibrium must occur in the leftmost point of the ZPL, which shifts to the left.

Things get a little more complicated if the WSC is upward-sloping, i.e., if we consider (1) Löschian competition with strictly log-concave individual labour supply or (2) HS competition with strictly log-concave individual labour supply and weak competition (high fixed costs and thus large market areas). Case (1) is illustrated by Figure 4.12 on the next page. It is obvious from Figure 4.12 that the two shifts work in different directions when considering the long-run equilibrium wage: While the WSC's shift upwards tends to raise the wage (which is the familiar short-run result from Section 3.7), the ZPL's shift to the left tends to lower it because competitive entry puts downwards pressure on the short-run Löschian wage. Hence, the overall effect on the wage is unclear *ex ante*, whereas the market radius definitely falls.

Moreover, it should be clear from this discussion that with a horizontal WSC, i.e., under Löschian competition with log-linear individual labour supply, the long-run equilibrium wage rises and the long-run equilibrium market radius falls. Hence, we have shown that the following proposition holds:

Proposition 4.4 (Long-Run Comparative Statics in ϕ). *Consider a long-run equilibrium where firms set wages optimally according to equation (4.4), free entry*

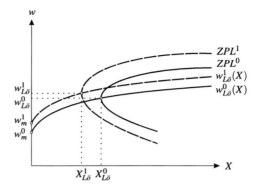

Fig. 4.12 The impact of an increase in the marginal revenue product of labour on the long-run equilibrium wage and market radius under Löschian competition if individual labour supply is strictly log-concave

drives profits to zero according to equation (4.1), and the fixed costs are smaller than f_{max}. Then an increase in the marginal revenue product of labour

(a) raises the long-run equilibrium wage under GO competition no matter the convexity of individual labour supply, while the impact on the market radius is unclear ex ante;

(b) raises the long-run equilibrium wage under Löschian competition if individual labour supply is strictly log-convex or log-linear, while the impact on the market radius is negative;

(c) has no clear-cut effect ex ante *on the long-run equilibrium wage under Löschian competition if individual labour supply is strictly log-concave, while the market radius falls;*

(d) raises the long-run equilibrium wage under HS competition if individual labour supply is (1) strictly log-convex, (2) log-linear, or (3) strictly log-concave with sufficiently low fixed costs, while the impact on the market radius is unclear ex ante;

(e) has no clear-cut effect ex ante *on the long-run equilibrium wage under HS competition if individual labour supply is strictly log-concave and the fixed costs are sufficiently high, while the market radius falls.* ∎

4.4.4 Comparative Statics in the Travel Cost

Eventually, consider a change in the travel cost. According to Lemma 4.3, an increase in the travel cost causes the ZPL to shift to the right, while the impact on the WSC depends on the mode of competition and the convexity of individual labour supply relative to an exponential.[10] Consider GO competition first. Under GO

---

[10] One should note at this stage that this finding is at odds with Greenhut *et al.*'s (1987) analysis of this model's comparative statics for the case of spatial oligopoly. In Section 3.2 (pp. 41–43), they state that an increase in the travel cost has the same impact on the long-run equilibrium price

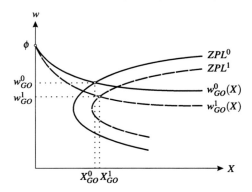

Fig. 4.13 The impact of an increase in the travel cost on the long-run equilibrium wage and market radius under Greenhut–Ohta competition

competition, a higher travel cost causes the short-run equilibrium wage to fall no matter the convexity of individual labour supply, so that the WSC is shifted downwards. Furthermore, the ZPL is shifted to the right. This corresponds to a reduction in the labour market's profitability, forces some firms to leave the market, and thus puts additional downwards pressure on the wage. Therefore, Figure 4.13 tells us that both shifts in isolation have a negative impact on the long-run equilibrium wage, so that the overall effect on the wage is unambiguously negative. On the other hand, the effect on the long-run equilibrium market radius is unclear *ex ante* because here the two shifts work in different directions.

The same argument holds (1) under Löschian competition if individual labour supply is strictly log-convex and (2) under HS competition if (a) individual labour supply is strictly log-convex, (b) log-linear, or (c) strictly log-concave and competition is strong (i.e., the fixed costs and thus firms' market areas are small); for in these cases the WSC under consideration is downward-sloping and shifted downwards if the travel cost rises. Hence, in all these instances, the long-run equilibrium wage falls if economic space becomes more costly, which is intuitively appealing. Under Löschian competition, we additionally know that the impact on the long-run equilibrium market radius is unambiguously positive due to the ZPL's shift to the right.

Things are again the other way round if the WSC under consideration is upward-sloping. This is the case (1) under Löschian competition if individual labour supply is strictly log-concave and (2) under HS competition if individual labour supply is strictly log-concave and competition is weak (i.e., the fixed costs and thus firms' market areas are large). Figure 4.14 on the next page gives a diagrammatic representation of case (2). In both cases, Lemma 4.3 tells us that the WSC is shifted

---

as an increase in the fixed costs, which (by analogy) we will be able to show for the model with strictly log-concave linear individual labour supply in Section 4.5. This stems from their claim that a change in the travel cost only affects the ZPL's and not the WSC's position, whereas it definitely has an impact also on the position of the WSC, as we have shown in Lemma 4.3. Hence, their clear-cut comparative static result of a change in the travel cost on the zero-profit equilibrium price need not to hold.

4.4 Long-Run Comparative Statics

Fig. 4.14 The impact of an increase in the travel cost on the long-run equilibrium wage and market radius under Hotelling–Smithies competition if individual labour supply is strictly log-concave and competition is weak

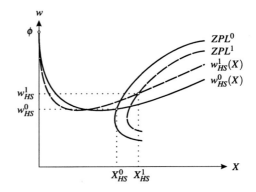

upwards because the optimal short-run wage chosen by firms is strictly increasing in the travel cost. Moreover, the ZPL's shift to the right and the corresponding reduced profitability of the labour market force some firms to exit the market, which also boosts the short-run wage chosen by firms. Since both the ZPL's shift to the right and the WSC's shift upwards in isolation cause both the long-run equilibrium wage and market radius to rise, the overall effect on both of them is positive, too. Thus, the impact on the equilibrium wage is 'counterintuitive' in both cases, which is in line with the 'perverse' results found in the short run and in the long-run comparative static analysis for changes in the fixed costs and the worker density.

Finally, consider a Löschian long-run equilibrium with log-linear individual labour supply. Since the WSC is horizontal in this case and does not change its position due to a change in the travel cost (see Lemma 4.3), the long-run equilibrium wage does not change, either. What does change, however, is the long-run equilibrium market radius. Since the ZPL contracts if the travel cost increases, market areas become larger (see Figure 4.10 on page 64 by analogy). Again, we find that the Löschian model with (generalised) exponential individual labour supply is a spatial analogue to spaceless monopsony where a change in the travel cost obviously has no consequence on the spaceless monopsonist's wage. The discussion so far is summarised by the following proposition:

Proposition 4.5 (Long-Run Comparative Statics in t). *Consider a long-run equilibrium where firms set wages optimally according to equation (4.4), free entry drives profits to zero according to equation (4.1), and the fixed costs are smaller than f_{max}. Then an increase in the travel cost*

(a) *reduces the long-run equilibrium wage under GO competition no matter the convexity of individual labour supply, while the impact on the market radius is unclear ex ante;*
(b) *reduces the long-run equilibrium wage under Löschian competition if individual labour supply is strictly log-convex and leaves it unaltered if individual labour supply is log-linear, while the market radius rises in both cases;*

Table 4.2 Comparative static effects on the long-run equilibrium wage

Increase:	Lö competition			HS competition[a]			GO competition		
	log-concave	log-linear	log-convex	log-concave	log-linear	log-convex	log-concave	log-linear	log-convex
Fixed costs (f)	+	0	−	$\mp^b$	−	−	−	−	−
Worker density (D)	−	0	+	$\pm^c$	+	+	+	+	+
Productivity (ϕ)	?	+	+	$+/?^d$	+	+	+	+	+
Travel cost (t)	+	0	−	$\mp^b$	−	−	−	−	−

[a] The same results hold for every mode of competition i with conjectural variations $0 < v_i < 1/t$.
[b] − if competition is strong (low fixed costs and thus small market areas); + if competition is weak (high fixed costs and thus large market areas).
[c] + if competition is strong (low fixed costs and thus small market areas); − if competition is weak (high fixed costs and thus large market areas).
[d] + if competition is strong (low fixed costs and thus small market areas); ? if competition is weak (high fixed costs and thus large market areas).

(c) *raises both the long-run equilibrium wage and market radius under Löschian competition if individual labour supply is strictly log-concave;*

(d) *raises the long-run equilibrium wage under HS competition if individual labour supply is (1) strictly log-convex, (2) log-linear, or (3) strictly log-concave with sufficiently low fixed costs, while the impact on the market radius is unclear ex ante;*

(e) *raises both the long-run equilibrium wage and market radius under HS competition if individual labour supply is strictly log-concave and the fixed costs are sufficiently high.* ∎

Table 4.2 summarises the findings presented in Propositions 4.3–4.5. As already stated, the lack of some clear-cut comparative static results with strictly log-concave individual labour supply is owed to the generality of our approach. Nevertheless, we can overcome this problem by considering the special case of strictly log-concave linear individual labour supply. In this case, we will be able to solve for the equilibrium wage implicitly, so that we will also be able to do the comparative statics of the model algebraically rather than diagrammatically.

4.5 Long-Run Spatial Monopsony under Linear Individual Labour Supply

We will now employ a linear individual labour supply function to analyse the given model framework with strictly log-concave individual labour supply more concretely. Note that this linear model is the one-dimensional analogue to the analyses

4.5 Long-Run Spatial Monopsony under Linear Individual Labour Supply

by Greenhut et al. (1975) and Capozza and Van Order (1977a; 1978).[11] The analysis will be done in much detail because the case of less convex than an exponential individual labour supply is the most interesting one: It not only allows for 'perverse' results in the sense discussed above, but it also bears the chance of identifying additional comparative static effects which we were unable to derive in the more general case considered hitherto. As already mentioned in Section 3.3, when interpreted as the c.d.f. of worker's reservation incomes, a linear individual labour supply function refers to the case of a uniform distribution of reservation incomes. For this special case, we will be able to fill in the gaps in Table 4.2 for strictly log-concave *linear* individual labour supply and to qualify what is meant by 'strong' and 'weak' competition under HS conjectures. Of course, the results to be obtained will not necessarily hold under strictly log-concave individual labour supply in general. Notwithstanding, our best guess is that things will work in a similar fashion in more general situations.

Linear individual labour supply is obtained if we consider the general individual labour supply function from Example 3.5 for $\gamma = 1$. Therefore,

$$l(w, x) := \frac{1}{\beta}(w - tx - \alpha). \tag{4.8}$$

Note that under linear individual labour supply $l(w, x) = 0$ holds if and only if the worker's income drops to α or below, i.e., $z(w, x) = w - tx \leq \alpha$. Hence, $r = \alpha$ and α represents, respectively, workers' common reservation income or the infimum of the support of their reservation income distribution depending on the interpretation of individual labour supply in mind. Applying the latter interpretation, $\beta := r_{max} - r$ refers to the range of workers' reservation income distribution, the support of which is given by the open interval (r, r_{max}) with some $r_{max} > \phi$. We will therefore refer to β below as the 'income range.' Since $r = \alpha$, firms' market radius for some wage $\alpha < w < \phi$ cannot exceed $(w - \alpha)/t$.

Aggregation of individual labour supply $l(w, x)$ over space yields aggregate firm-level labour supply as

$$L(w, X) = 2D \int_0^X \frac{1}{\beta}(w - tx - \alpha) \, dx = \frac{2DX}{\beta}\left(w - \frac{tX}{2} - \alpha\right). \tag{4.9}$$

Firms' profits are thus given by

---

[11] Other than these analyses, we restrict to the case of one-dimensional economic space (i.e., economic space is – according to assumption (A1) – given by the real line). Note, however, that only Capozza and Van Order (1978) actually incorporate two-dimensional space into their analysis of spatial competition. Greenhut et al. (1975) and Capozza and Van Order (1977a), on the other hand, introduce the notion of competition in n directions (where aggregate labour supply on the real line is just multiplied by n) but essentially stick to the one-dimensional case. As Capozza and Van Order (1977a, p. 1330) put it: 'This topology assumed ... is actually one-dimensional. That is, the space with competition in n directions is isomorphic to the real line not to the plane.'

Fig. 4.15 A family of zero-profit loci for different fixed costs $f^1 < f^2 < f^3 < f_{max}$

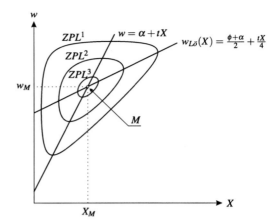

$$\Pi(w, X) = \frac{2DX}{\beta}\left(w - \frac{tX}{2} - \alpha\right)(\phi - w) - f. \qquad (4.10)$$

Hence, the ZPL $X(\cdot)$ is implicitly defined by

$$\Pi(w, X) = \frac{2DX}{\beta}\left(w - \frac{tX}{2} - \alpha\right)(\phi - w) - f \stackrel{!}{=} 0 \qquad (4.11)$$

and obviously contracts as the fixed costs increase.[12] Besides, as already noted in Section 4.1, neither the ZPL's shape nor its position depend on the mode of competition.

Figure 4.15 shows a family of ZPLs for different fixed costs $f^1 < f^2 < f^3 < f_{max}$. The relevant part of the ZPLs is left to the line $w = \alpha + tX$ because firms' market radius cannot exceed $(w - \alpha)/t$. Note that the ZPL collapses around the point M as the fixed costs rise, where $M = (X_M, w_M)$ gives the wage–market radius pair chosen by a spatial monopsonist. Since the spatial monopsonist's market radius is given by the distance from her at which individual labour supply drops to zero (see the discussion in Section 3.4), i.e., $w - tX - \alpha = 0$ and thus $X = (w - \alpha)/t$, her profits only depend on the wage chosen, i.e.,

$$\Pi(w) = \frac{D}{\beta t}(w - \alpha)^2(\phi - w) - f. \qquad (4.12)$$

---

[12] Algebraically, this follows at once from

$$\frac{\partial X(w)}{\partial f} = -\frac{\partial \Pi(w, X)/\partial f}{\partial \Pi(w, X)/\partial X} = \left(\frac{\partial \Pi(w, X)}{\partial X}\right)^{-1} = \left(\frac{2D}{\beta}(w - tX - \alpha)(\phi - w)\right)^{-1} > 0$$

because $(w - tX - \alpha)/\beta = l(w, X) > 0$ and $\phi > w$ for all $(w, X) \in Z$. For this reason, we also have $\partial \Pi(w, X)/\partial X > 0$ for all $(w, X) \in Z$, and we are therefore allowed to apply the implicit function theorem.

4.5 Long-Run Spatial Monopsony under Linear Individual Labour Supply

Profit maximisation requires

$$\Pi'(w) = \frac{D}{\beta t}[2(w-\alpha)(\phi-w) - (w-\alpha)^2] \stackrel{!}{=} 0 \qquad (4.13)$$

which holds if and only if $w_M = (2\phi+\alpha)/3$ because $w > \alpha$ must hold in all relevant cases.[13] This immediately gives $X_M = 2(\phi-\alpha)/3t$. Furthermore, the ZPL in coincidence with M corresponds to the highest amount of fixed costs f_{max} that can be afforded by the highest profits attainable, i.e., the spatial monopsonist's profits Π_M following from w_M and X_M.[14] For all $f > f_{max}$ profits are necessarily negative, and no firm stays in the market.

Now, turn to firms' optimal wage-setting behaviour. They want to maximise their perceived profits which gives the first-order condition

$$\frac{\partial \Pi(w,X)}{\partial w} = \frac{2D}{\beta}\left[X\left(\phi - 2w + \frac{tX}{2} + \alpha\right) + v(w - tX - \alpha)(\phi - w)\right] \stackrel{!}{=} 0, \qquad (4.14)$$

where $v := \partial X/\partial w$ again represents the conjectural variations held by spatial competitors about the increase in their market radius in response to a rise in their wage. Hence, (4.14) implicitly defines the profit-maximising wage for a given market radius and for given conjectural variations.

Under Löschian competition with $v_{Lö} = 0$, the optimal wage for a given market radius becomes

$$w_{Lö}(X) = \frac{\phi+\alpha}{2} + \frac{tX}{4} \qquad (4.15)$$

which is strictly increasing in the market radius due to $w'_{Lö}(X) = t/4 > 0$ for all relevant X. In the (X,w)-plane, the WSC under Löschian competition is thus an upward-sloping straight line with intercept $(\phi+\alpha)/2$, where the intercept is the wage chosen by a spaceless monopsonist.[15]

---

[13] Obviously, the corresponding second-order condition is satisfied because $\Pi''(w) = 2D(\phi-3w+2\alpha)/\beta t < 0$ if and only if $w > (\phi+2\alpha)/3$ and $w_M = (2\phi+\alpha)/3 > (\phi+2\alpha)/3$, where $\phi > \alpha = r$ holds by assumption (see also footnote 3 on page 17).

[14] To show this note that profit maximisation with respect to the wage for a given market radius X requires

$$\frac{\partial \Pi(w,X)}{\partial w} = \frac{2DX}{\beta}\left(\phi - 2w + \frac{tX}{2} + \alpha\right) \stackrel{!}{=} 0,$$

so that $w = (\phi+\alpha)/2 + tX/4$ must hold in the optimum. Since the firm's profits are strictly increasing in X, which follows from $\partial \Pi(w,X)/\partial X > 0$ for all $(w,X) \in Z$ as shown in footnote 12 on the facing page, they are only maximised if X is as large as possible, i.e., $X = (w-\alpha)/t$. Taken together, these two conditions imply that the firm's profits are maximised if and only if $w = w_M = (2\phi+\alpha)/3$ and $X = X_M = 2(\phi-\alpha)/3t$, which is the wage-market radius pair chosen by the spatial monopsonist.

[15] To see the latter point, consider the spaceless monopsonist's profits, which are

$$\Pi_m(w) = Dl(w,0)(\phi-w) - f = \frac{D}{\beta}(w-\alpha)(\phi-w) - f.$$

For conjectural variations $0 < v_i \leq 1/t$ the optimal wage for a given market radius is implicitly defined by

$$w_i(X) = \phi - \frac{X(w_i(X) - tX/2 - \alpha)}{v_i(w_i(X) - (t - 1/v_i)X - \alpha)}. \quad (4.16)$$

One obvious difference between non-Löschian and Löschian conjectural variations is that under excessive entry, which causes firms' market radius to tend to zero, the Löschian wage approaches the wage chosen by a spaceless monopsonist, whereas for all $0 < v_i \leq 1/t$ the wage converges to workers' marginal revenue product. This can be seen readily from (4.16) by noting that the second term on the right-hand side approaches zero if $X \to 0$, so that $w_i(X) \to \phi$.

Under HS competition with $v_{HS} = 1/2t$, the optimal wage for a given market radius is implicitly given by

$$w_{HS}(X) = \phi - \frac{2tX(w_{HS}(X) - tX/2 - \alpha)}{w_{HS}(X) + tX - \alpha}. \quad (4.17)$$

Implicit differentiation of (4.17) yields

$$w'_{HS}(X) = \frac{2t[tX(w_{HS}(X) + tX/2 - \alpha) - (w_{HS}(X) - \alpha)^2]}{(w_{HS}(X) + 2tX - \alpha)^2 - 2(w_{HS}(X) - \alpha)tX} \quad (4.18)$$

with nulls $\alpha + (1/2 \pm \sqrt{3/4})tX$. Since $w > \alpha$ must hold in all relevant cases, only the root $\alpha + (1/2 + \sqrt{3/4})tX$ is admissible. And since w'_{HS} is continuous with $w'_{HS}(0) = -2t < 0$ and $w'_{HS}(X_M) = t/7 > 0$, the WSC under HS competition is strictly decreasing left to the straight line $w = \alpha + (1/2 + \sqrt{3/4})tX$ and strictly increasing right to it.

Finally, under GO competition with $v_{GO} = 1/t$, the optimal wage for a given market radius is implicitly given by

$$w_{GO}(X) = \phi - \frac{tX(w_{GO}(X) - tX/2 - \alpha)}{w_{GO}(X) - \alpha}. \quad (4.19)$$

The WSC under GO competition is strictly decreasing in the market radius because implicit differentiation of (4.19) gives

---

Hence, her profits are maximised if and only if the first-order condition

$$\Pi'_m(w) = \frac{D}{\beta}[(\phi - w) - (w - \alpha)] \stackrel{!}{=} 0$$

is satisfied because Π_m is strictly concave (which follows from $\Pi''_m(w) = -2D/\beta < 0$ for all $w > 0$), and this implies $w_m = (\phi + \alpha)/2$.

4.5 Long-Run Spatial Monopsony under Linear Individual Labour Supply 75

Fig. 4.16 A family of zero-profit loci for different fixed costs $f^1 < f^2 < f^3 < f_{max}$ and the wage-setting curves under Löschian, Hotelling–Smithies, and Greenhut–Ohta competition

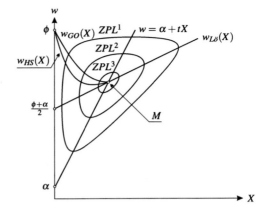

$$w'_{GO}(X) = -\frac{2t[(w_{GO}(X) - \alpha)^2 - tX(w_{GO}(X) - \alpha)]}{2(w_{GO}(X) - \alpha)^2 + t^2 X^2} < 0 \qquad (4.20)$$

for all $0 < X < X_M$ with $w'_{GO}(0) = -2t < 0$ and $w'_{GO}(X_M) = 0$.[16]

Figure 4.16 adds the three WSCs under Löschian, HS, and GO competition to the ZPLs from Figure 4.15. The intersection point of the corresponding WSC and ZPL gives the long-run equilibrium wage–market radius pair chosen by spatial competitors under the respective mode of competition and level of fixed costs. We shall now take a closer look at the equilibria under the different modes of competition.

4.5.1 The Löschian Equilibrium

Combining the zero-profit condition (4.11) and the wage-setting condition (4.15), we obtain after some straightforward algebraic manipulations

$$(2w_{Lö} - \phi - \alpha)(\phi - w_{Lö})^2 = \frac{f\beta t}{4D}, \qquad (4.21)$$

which implicitly determines the long-run equilibrium wage under Löschian competition. To get the equilibrium market radius, we only have to insert $w_{Lö}$ into the zero-profit condition (4.11). Figure 4.17 on the following page gives a diagrammatic representation of the Löschian equilibrium. While explicit solution of (4.21) is quite

---

[16] This holds because the nominator on the right-hand side of (4.20) is positive for all $0 < X < X_M$. To see this, note that

$$(w - \alpha)^2 - tX(w - \alpha) > (w - \alpha)^2 - (w - \alpha)^2 = 0,$$

for $X < (w - \alpha)/t$ and $w > \alpha$ hold in all relevant cases.

Fig. 4.17 The Löschian long-run equilibrium under linear individual labour supply for different levels of fixed costs $f^1 < f^2 < f^3 < f_{max}$

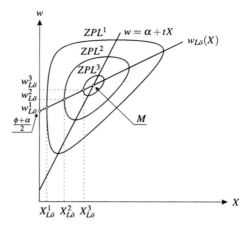

annoying, it is not needed to gain the key insights. Nevertheless, it can be shown that there are one real and two complex roots of (4.21), so that there is a unique Löschian wage in equilibrium as labour market phenomena are real but not complex.[17]

We can outline now some interesting properties of the Löschian equilibrium (which are familiar from the discussion in Sections 3.7 and 4.4). Firstly, note that there are two different ways of thinking of perfect competition in this modelling framework: the travel cost approaches zero since then space between firms does not matter anymore in an economic sense as commuting is costless or the fixed costs tend to zero because then economies of scale are absent and firms exist at any possible location, so that no commuting takes place anymore. In both cases, Löschian competition yields the wage chosen by a spaceless monopsonist, i.e., $w_{Lö} \to w_m = (\phi + \alpha)/2$, which can be seen both from (4.15) and (4.21). On the other hand, the highest possible wage under Löschian competition is $w_{Lö} \to w_M = (2\phi + \alpha)/3$, the wage chosen by a spatial monopsonist, gained if $f \to f_{max}$.

Now, turn to the model's comparative statics: An increase in the fixed costs causes the ZPL to contract, while the WSC is not affected. Hence, both the long-run equilibrium wage and market radius rise as the labour market moves northeast on the WSC. From the fact that the fixed costs, the worker density, the travel cost, and the 'income range' enter (4.21) as $f\beta t/D$, it is evident that an increase in the travel cost or the 'income range' has the same qualitative effect on the equilibrium

---

[17] The roots of (4.21) are

$$\underbrace{\frac{5}{6}\phi + \frac{1}{6}\alpha + \frac{\Theta}{12D} + \frac{D(\phi-\alpha)^2}{3\Theta}}_{= w_{Lö} \in \mathbb{R}} \pm \Psi i \in \mathbb{C}$$

with $\Theta := (D^2[108f\beta t + \sqrt{432f\beta t(27f\beta t - 4D(\phi-\alpha)^3)} - 8D(\phi-\alpha)^3])^{1/3} < 0$ and $\Psi := \sqrt{3/4}[\Theta/(12D) - D(\phi-\alpha)^2/(3\Theta)]$.

4.5 Long-Run Spatial Monopsony under Linear Individual Labour Supply

wage as a rise in the fixed costs, whilst an increase in the worker density has the opposite impact.[18] This holds, even though a change in the travel cost both affects the position of the ZPL and that of the WSC (see Lemma 4.3 and the discussion in Section 4.4). Note that, when interpreting the individual labour supply function as the c.d.f. of workers' reservation incomes, an increase in the 'income range' refers to a rise in the supremum of workers' reservation incomes r_{max}. That is, the support of workers' reservation income distribution is spread out with its infimum $r = \alpha$ being unaltered.[19]

Things are a little more intricate, though, if the reservation income or the marginal revenue product changes. As is shown in Appendix A.8, an increase in the reservation income raises the Löschian equilibrium wage, whereas the impact of an increase in the marginal revenue product depends on the initial strength of competition. If competition is strong (i.e., the fixed costs are low, and thus market areas are small), the equilibrium wage rises in response to an increase in the marginal revenue product. On the other hand, it falls if competition is weak (i.e., if the fixed costs are high, and thus market areas are large).[20] In this respect, the long-run Löschian model, i.e., long-run collusive spatial oligopsony, differs not only from spatial and spaceless monopsony (see the discussion in Chapter 2 and Section 3.4) but also from the short-run Löschian model (see Section 3.7), another 'perverse' result of spatial monopsony: There is not necessarily a positive relationship between workers' marginal revenue product and their equilibrium wage; and under certain conditions there may be even a negative one.

It is very important to note that the impact of a change in the reservation income discussed so far hinges on the interpretation of the individual labour supply function as workers' common labour supply curve. Accordingly, α denotes workers' common reservation income. However, we should also make clear what is meant by α if we interpret the individual labour supply function as the linear c.d.f. of workers' reservation incomes. Since then $\alpha = r$ and $\beta = r_{max} - r$ hold, a change in α would also affect the 'income range.' Since the interpretation of individual labour supply as workers' labour supply curve with $l[z(w, x)] > 0$ if $r < z(w, x) < \phi$ and $l[z(w, x)] = 0$ otherwise corresponds to a degenerated one-point distribution of reservation incomes at $\alpha = r$, an increase of α is in fact a shift of the entire probability mass and thus the entire distribution of reservation incomes to the right. Now, consider the case where reservation incomes are uniformly distributed on the interval (r, r_{max}). Then the proper analogue to a shift in workers' common reservation

---

[18] Appendix A.8 shows this more rigorously by means of implicit differentiation of (4.21) with respect to the parameter of interest.

[19] Note that changes in r_{max} must be such that $r_{max} > w_{Lö}$ is still satisfied, for otherwise we had to explicitly take account of $l[z(w, x)] = 1$ for all $z(w, x) > r_{max}$ in the derivation of the equilibrium wage. Since we assume $r_{max} > \phi$ throughout, $r_{max} > w_{Lö}$ is always met.

[20] More precisely,
$$\frac{\partial w_{Lö}}{\partial \phi} \gtreqless 0 \Leftrightarrow X \lesseqgtr X^* := \frac{2(\phi - \alpha)}{5t}$$
with $0 < X^* < X_M = 2(\phi - \alpha)/3t$. For a derivation of this result, see Appendix A.8.

income is a shift of the entire support of workers' reservation income distribution (r, r_{max}) to the right, i.e., all workers' reservation incomes rise at the same time by some amount. Since this does not change the 'income range' $\beta = r_{max} - r$ but raises $\alpha = r$, our results are the same as before. Hence, an increase in the reservation income refers either to a rise in workers' common reservation income or to a shift of the entire reservation income distribution to the right depending on the interpretation of individual labour supply in mind. Next, we want to discuss the GO equilibrium, which will yield results antipodal to the Löschian equilibrium.

4.5.2 The Greenhut–Ohta Equilibrium

Combining the zero-profit condition (4.11) and the wage-setting condition (4.19), we obtain after some simple algebraic manipulations

$$(w_{GO} - \alpha)(\phi - w_{GO})^2 = \frac{f\beta t}{2D}, \qquad (4.22)$$

which implicitly determines the long-run equilibrium wage under GO competition. To get the equilibrium market radius, we only have to insert w_{GO} into the zero-profit condition (4.11). Figure 4.18 on the next page gives a diagrammatic representation of the GO equilibrium. Again, we do not want to explicitly solve equation (4.22) for the equilibrium wage but just note that there are two complex and one real root, so that we have a unique solution for the zero-profit equilibrium wage under GO competition.[21]

We will now see that the properties of the GO equilibrium diametrically differ from those of the Löschian one. This stems from the fact that under GO competition the WSC is downward- instead of upward-sloping, giving rise to antipodal comparative static results and behaviour in the limiting cases of 'perfect' competition with firms' market radius approaching zero and 'pure' monopsony with firms' market radius approaching X_M. Firstly, note that if the fixed costs approach zero, causing firms to be at any possible location, or if the travel cost tends to zero, so that space loses its economic relevance, workers' equilibrium wage is given by their marginal revenue product. This is readily seen from both (4.19) and (4.22). On the other hand, the only equilibrium wage–market radius pair shared by GO and Löschian competitors is (w_M, X_M), which is plausible as competitive forces are negligible in this

---

[21] The roots of (4.22) are

$$\underbrace{\frac{2}{3}\phi + \frac{1}{3}\alpha + \frac{\Theta}{6D} + \frac{2D(\phi - \alpha)^2}{3\Theta}}_{= w_{GO} \in \mathbb{R}} \pm \Psi i \in \mathbb{C}$$

with $\Theta := (D^2[54f\beta t + \sqrt{108f\beta t(27f\beta t - 8D(\phi - \alpha)^3)} - 8D(\phi - \alpha)^3])^{1/3} > 0$ and $\Psi := \sqrt{3/4}[\Theta/(6D) - 2D(\phi - \alpha)^2/(3\Theta)]$.

4.5 Long-Run Spatial Monopsony under Linear Individual Labour Supply

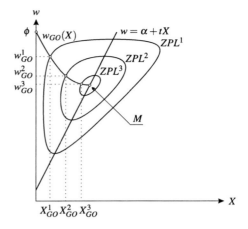

Fig. 4.18 The Greenhut–Ohta long-run equilibrium under linear individual labour supply for different levels of fixed costs $f^1 < f^2 < f^3 < f_{max}$

situation, so that the competition effect following from the GO conjectures does not play any role. Second, the model's comparative statics differ substantially, too: An increase in the fixed costs again causes the ZPL to shrink and does not affect the WSC. But since the WSC is now downward-sloping for all $0 < X < X_M$, the equilibrium wage falls as the labour market moves southeast on the WSC. Since the fixed costs, the worker density, the travel cost, and the 'income range' enter (4.22) as $f\beta t/D$, an increase in the fixed costs, the 'income range,' or the travel cost causes the equilibrium wage to fall, whereas an increase in the worker density has the opposite impact.[22] Furthermore, in Appendix A.8 it is shown that an increase in the marginal revenue product of labour raises the equilibrium wage, while an increase in the reservation income (or a shift of the entire distribution of workers' reservation incomes to the right, see the discussion in Section 4.5.1) causes the equilibrium wage to fall.

In the next step, it will become once more evident why we have focussed so much on GO competition. We shall demonstrate that HS competition – generated by the standard Bertrand–Nash assumption – is a hybrid case, showing Löschian results if competition is weak and GO results if competition is strong. Therefore, Löschian as well as GO competition are two limiting cases with HS competition in between.

4.5.3 The Hotelling–Smithies Equilibrium

Combining the zero-profit condition (4.11) and the wage-setting condition (4.24) and some tedious algebraic manipulations (for the details, see appendix A.9) yield the implicit solution of the HS long-run equilibrium wage as

---

[22] This is shown more rigorously by means of implicit differentiation of (4.22) with respect to the parameter of interest in Appendix A.8.

Fig. 4.19 The Hotelling–Smithies long-run equilibrium under linear individual supply for different levels of fixed costs $f^1 < f^2 < f^3 < f_{max}$

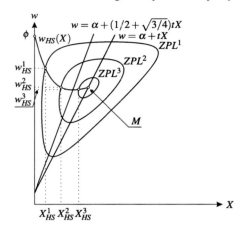

$$(2(w_{HS} - \alpha) + \Theta)(\phi - w_{HS})^2 = \frac{f\beta t}{D} \quad (4.23)$$

with $\Theta := w_{HS} - \phi \pm \sqrt{(\phi + 2\alpha - 3w_{HS})^2 - 4(\phi - w_{HS})(w_{HS} - \alpha)}$. Explicit solution of (4.23) for w_{HS}, which requires finding the roots of a sixth-order polynomial, is quite difficult but fortunately not needed to find the comparative static effects of interest. Figure 4.19 gives a diagrammatic representation of the HS equilibrium.

Remember that the WSC under HS competition is implicitly given by

$$w_{HS}(X) = \phi - \frac{2tX(w_{HS}(X) - tX/2 - \alpha)}{w_{HS}(X) + tX - \alpha}, \quad (4.24)$$

which is strictly decreasing left to the straight line

$$w = \alpha + (1/2 + \sqrt{3/4})tX \quad (4.25)$$

and strictly increasing right to it. Under HS competition, the properties of the long-run equilibrium crucially depend on whether it happens to occur on the downward-sloping part of the WSC where it has properties similar to the GO equilibrium or on the upward-sloping part where it has properties similar to the Löschian equilibrium. In Figure 4.19 for instance, we have an equilibrium left to $w = \alpha + (1/2 + \sqrt{3/4})tX$ for fixed costs f^1 or f^2 and one right to it for fixed costs f^3.[23]

As under GO and Löschian competition, an increase in the fixed costs causes the ZPL to contract, while it does not affect the WSC. Therefore, it causes the equilibrium wage to fall on the downward-sloping part of the WSC, i.e., if competition

---

[23] Note that $w = \alpha + (1/2 + \sqrt{3/4})tX$ always lies left to $w = \alpha + tX$ in the (X, w)-plane, so that under HS competition there is always an upward-sloping and a downward-sloping part of the WSC in the relevant part of the (X, w)-plane.

4.5 Long-Run Spatial Monopsony under Linear Individual Labour Supply

Table 4.3 Comparative static effects on the long-run equilibrium wage under linear individual labour supply

Increase:	Löschian competition	Hotelling–Smithies competition		Greenhut–Ohta competition
		$w_{HS} < \alpha +$ $(1/2 + \sqrt{3/4})tX_{HS}$	$w_{HS} > \alpha +$ $(1/2 + \sqrt{3/4})tX_{HS}$	
Fixed costs (f)	+	+	−	−
Worker density (D)	−	−	+	+
Productivity (ϕ)	±[b]	±[b]	+	+
Travel cost (t)	+	+	−	−
Reservation income[a] (α)	+	+	−	−
Income range (β)	+	+	−	−

[a] If the individual labour supply function is interpreted as workers' common labour supply curve, an increase in α refers to a rise in their common reservation income. If it is interpreted as the c.d.f. of workers' reservation incomes, an increase in α refers to a shift of the entire distribution to the right (see the discussion in Section 4.5.1).
[b] + if competition is strong (i.e., market areas are small with $X < 2(\phi - \alpha)/5t$); − if competition is weak (i.e., market areas are large with $X > 2(\phi - \alpha)/5t$).

is strong initially with $w_{HS} > \alpha + (1/2 + \sqrt{3/4})tX_{HS}$, and to rise on the upward-sloping part of the WSC, i.e., if competition is weak initially with $w_{HS} < \alpha + (1/2 + \sqrt{3/4})tX_{HS}$. Since the HS equilibrium has the same qualitative comparative static effects as the GO equilibrium on the downward-sloping part of the WSC, an increase in the travel cost, the 'income range,' or the reservation income (or a shift of the entire distribution of workers' reservation incomes to the right, see the discussion in Section 4.5.1) causes the equilibrium wage to fall, whereas an increase in the marginal revenue product or the worker density causes the equilibrium wage to rise. Things, however, are the other way round for the travel cost, the 'income range,' the reservation income, and the worker density on the upward-sloping part of the WSC. The impact of an increase in workers' marginal revenue product on the equilibrium wage on the upward-sloping part of the WSC again depends on the degree of competition in the initial equilibrium: It is positive if competition is sufficiently strong and negative if it is sufficiently weak.[24] Hence, under certain conditions there is no positive relationship between workers' equilibrium wage and their marginal revenue product even under competitive spatial oligopsony. In this respect, the long-run HS model may give the same 'perverse' result as collusive spatial oligopsony.

Table 4.3 summarises the comparative statics of the linear long-run spatial monopsony model. Unsurprisingly, the results do not differ qualitatively from those reported in Table 4.2 on page 70, while we have been successful in stating more

---

[24] All these results can be readily verified by implicit differentiation of (4.23) with respect to the parameter of interest. Since the resulting terms are exceptionally cumbersome, this task is left to the courageous reader, and we shall not bother with doing so here.

explicitly what is meant by strong or weak competition in the HS case. Furthermore, we have been able to fill in the gap of Table 4.2 for the comparative static effect of an increase in the marginal revenue product of labour on the equilibrium wage in the special case of linear strictly log-concave individual labour supply. Eventually, we have added comparative static effects of changes in the reservation income (distribution). Next, we shall investigate an even simpler specification than the linear long-run spatial monopsony model, viz. long-run spatial monopsony under constant individual labour supply.

4.6 Long-Run Spatial Monopsony with Constant Individual Labour Supply

Now that we have discussed the linear spatial monopsony model in detail, we shall also investigate what happens when considering the limiting case of log-linear constant individual labour supply. This can be best understood in terms of entirely homogenous workers: As individual labour supply can be interpreted as the c.d.f. of workers' reservation incomes (see the discussion in Section 3.1), constant individual labour supply just refers to the case where we have a degenerated one-point distribution concentrated at some reservation income r. On the other hand, if we refer to individual labour supply as workers' common labour supply curve, then we can think of, firstly, workers being constrained to supply exactly one unit of labour due to fixed working hours or, second, of globally balancing substitution and income effects, so that workers' labour supply is unaffected by wage changes.[25]

The constant spatial monopsony model, which is the one-dimensional analogue to the analysis by Capozza and Van Order (1977b) and which is, as shown by Greenhut *et al.* (1987, pp. 95/96), equivalent to the well-known Salop (1979b) model, is by far the most tractable specification of the spatial monopsony model considered.[26] Hence, it is particularly interesting to know whether this restrictive yet very tractable setting yields results qualitatively the same as those gained from more intricate settings with elastic individual labour supply. Of course, our best guess is

---

[25] Admittedly, the latter case refers to a quite knife-edged argument. Nonetheless, it is generally found that most of the variation in workers' labour supply is at the extensive instead of the intensive margin (cf., e.g., Cahuc and Zylberberg, 2004, p. 38).

[26] Salop (1979b) uses a model very similar in setting to our model in order to investigate the impact of market entry in differentiated-product markets. In this setting, geographic space refers to the characteristic space of the product under consideration. The producer's location is the variety being produced by her, while the consumer's location gives the variety preferred by him. The travel cost, eventually, refers to the utility loss induced by the fact that not every possible variety is actually produced because of the fixed setup costs involved. By complete analogy to our reasoning, the fact that some varieties are 'nearer' in characteristic space to the variety most preferred by the consumer constitutes market power on the supply side resulting in a higher equilibrium price than under perfect competition.

that it will differ substantially because with constant individual labour supply only the competition effect is at work, while the potentially countervailing supply effect is missing. Hence, we conjecture that the model will behave similarly to the case of log-linear individual labour supply, which is also characterised by the absence of any supply effect. Besides, finding the model's solution under Löschian competition will require a different approach than the one used under GO and HS conjectures, which is due to the absence of any competition effect (cf., e.g., Nakagome, 1986). We will thus first deal with the GO and the HS case, i.e., conjectural variations are $0 < v \leqslant 1/t$. After that we will consider a simple extension of the constant spatial monopsony model allowing for variation in workers' participation in such a way following Bhaskar and To (1999), who arrive at the same model restricting themselves to HS conjectural variations. Finally, we will turn to the Löschian case. We will then find that the Löschian model under constant individual labour supply bears a lot of similarity to the general model under strictly log-concave individual labour supply, although constant individual labour supply is log-linear. Again, this is due to the absence of any supply effect.[27]

4.6.1 The Hotelling–Smithies and the Greenhut–Ohta Equilibrium

Consider constant individual labour supply, where

$$l(w, x) := \begin{cases} 1 \text{ if } w - tx > r \\ 0 \text{ if } w - tx \leqslant r \end{cases} \quad (4.26)$$

with some $0 < r < \phi$ and l log-linear.[28] By the way, constant individual labour supply is obtained from the general individual supply function from Example 3.5 by letting $\gamma \to \infty$. With constant individual labour supply, aggregate firm-level labour supply is given by

$$L(w, X) = 2D \int_0^X l(w, x)\, dx = 2DX \quad (4.27)$$

---

[27] We conjecture that for this reason the Löschian model (of a commodity market) is usually discussed under linear individual demand (e.g., Mills and Lav, 1964; Capozza and Attaran, 1976; Capozza and Van Order, 1977b), which simplifies the algebraic analysis considerably. For a discussion of the Löschian model with alternative elastic individual demand functions, see Stern (1972). For an analysis of the Löschian model with linear individual demand and an arbitrary distribution of consumers in economic space, see Beckmann (1976).

[28] Note that the log-linearity of constant individual labour supply follows at once from $l|_{(r,\phi)} = \widehat{1}|_{(r,\phi)}$ implying $\ell|_{(r,\phi)} = \ell'|_{(r,\phi)} = \ell''|_{(r,\phi)} = \widehat{0}|_{(r,\phi)}$, where $\widehat{1}$ ($\widehat{0}$) is the constant function with value 1 (0).

with $0 < X < X_M = (w-r)/t$.[29] Consequently, firms' profits are

$$\Pi(w, X) = 2DX(\phi - w) - f. \qquad (4.28)$$

Maximisation of firms' perceived profits requires

$$\frac{\partial \Pi(w, X)}{\partial w} = 2D(\phi - w)v - 2DX \stackrel{!}{=} 0.^{30} \qquad (4.29)$$

Hence, with conjectural variations $0 < v_i \leqslant 1/t$, the WSC becomes

$$w_i(X) = \phi - \frac{X}{v_i} \qquad (4.30)$$

with $v_{GO} = 1/t$ and $v_{HS} = 1/2t$. In the (X, w)-plane, the WSC is therefore a downward-sloping straight line with w-intercept ϕ and slope $-1/v_i$. Accordingly, it is steeper for HS conjectures, its slope being $-2t$, than for GO competition, where its slope is just $-t$.[31] Three things are noteworthy: Firstly, if competition becomes fierce in the sense that there are many employers competing for workers, so that firms' market radius tends to zero, we approach the competitive solution where workers get paid their marginal revenue product. Second, if economic space becomes less densely populated by firms, so that firms' market radius increases, the wage chosen by firms falls, which is the consequence of weakening competitive forces. Third, the absence of any supply effect causes the WSC to be downward-sloping even under HS competition no matter firms' market radius (as is the case with non-constant log-linear individual labour supply in the generalised model, see the discussion in Section 4.2).

In the long run, profits have to be zero, i.e., $\Pi(w, X) \stackrel{!}{=} 0$. Rearranging (4.28) gives the ZPL

$$X(w) = \frac{f}{2D(\phi - w)}, \qquad (4.31)$$

which is strictly increasing in the wage, i.e., $X'(w) > 0$ for all $r < w < \phi$. Moreover, $X(w) \to \infty$ if $w \to \phi$. In the (X, w)-plane, the ZPL therefore is an upward-sloping curve with X-intercept $f/(2D\phi)$ and a w-asymptote at ϕ. The higher is firms' wage, the higher must be their market radius to guarantee zero profits to them. Furthermore, we get a vertical line at $X = 0$ if the fixed costs approach zero. So we also

---

[29] As we shall see later, this restriction is satisfied in equilibrium if competition is sufficiently strong.

[30] The corresponding second-order condition holds because $\partial^2 \Pi(w, X)/\partial w^2 = -4Dv < 0$ for all $(w, X) \in Z$ and $0 < v \leqslant 1/t$, so that perceived profits are strictly concave in the wage.

[31] One should add that market areas must be such that in equilibrium workers at firms' market boundaries get an income larger than their reservation income, for otherwise firms are local monopsonists and the logic employed to solve the model breaks down. Put differently, $0 < X_i < X_M$ has to hold in equilibrium.

4.6 Long-Run Spatial Monopsony with Constant Individual Labour Supply

arrive at the competitive solution if the fixed costs disappear and firms are therefore set up costlessly yielding an atomistic labour market with employers everywhere in space.

To solve for the long-run equilibrium wage, we combine the wage-setting condition (4.30) and the zero-profit condition (4.31). Taking economic admissibility into account, we get

$$w_i = \phi - \sqrt{\frac{f}{2Dv_i}}.\text{[32]} \qquad (4.32)$$

Therefore, the long-run equilibrium wage under GO competition with $v_{GO} = 1/t$ and HS competition with $v_{HS} = 1/2t$ is given by, respectively,

$$w_{GO} = \phi - \sqrt{\frac{ft}{2D}} \qquad (4.33)$$

and

$$w_{HS} = \phi - \sqrt{\frac{ft}{D}}. \qquad (4.34)$$

As before, the resulting equilibrium wage–market radius pair can be depicted in the (X, w)-plane as the intersection point of both the ZPL and the respective WSC (see Figure 4.20 on the next page). Partial differentiation of (4.33) or (4.34), respectively, with respect to the parameter of interest reveals immediately that our conjecture at the begin of this section was right: The model's comparative statics are the same as under exponential (log-linear) individual labour supply. An increase in the fixed costs or the travel cost reduces the long-run equilibrium wage, while an increase in the worker density or the marginal revenue product of labour has the opposite impact.

Diagrammatically, an increase in the travel cost causes the WSC both under GO and HS competition to become steeper, while the ZPL is – other than in the less restrictive cases discussed earlier on – unaffected due to the absence of any supply effect (see Figure 4.21 on the following page). Hence, a rise in the travel cost just raises the wage-setting power of employers as economic space – the source of firms' monopsony power – becomes more relevant. This reduces the equilibrium wage and, in turn, allows more firms to enter the more profitable labour market. Consequently, both the long-run equilibrium wage and market radius fall. As before, an increase

---

[32] There are actually two roots that simultaneously solve (4.30) and (4.31), viz.

$$\phi \pm \sqrt{\frac{f}{2Dv_i}},$$

but nonnegativity of profits requires $w_i < \phi$, so that (4.32) is the only economically relevant root. Besides, note that (4.32) and (4.31) can be used to impose a restriction on the fixed costs that guarantees $w_i - tX_i > r$ to hold, so that every worker participates and the derived equilibrium actually exists.

Fig. 4.20 The Löschian, the Hotelling–Smithies, and the Greenhut–Ohta long-run equilibrium under constant individual labour supply

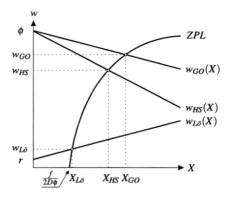

Fig. 4.21 The impact of an increase in the travel cost on the Hotelling–Smithies long-run equilibrium under constant individual labour supply

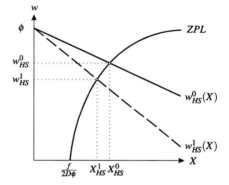

Fig. 4.22 The impact of an increase in the worker density (or a decrease in the fixed costs) on the Hotelling–Smithies long-run equilibrium under constant individual labour supply

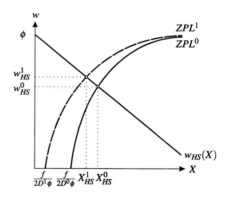

in the worker density or a decrease in the fixed costs affects only the ZPL, which moves to the left (see Figure 4.22). This raises the labour market's profitability, causes competitive entry, and by enhancing competition increases the equilibrium wage, while the market radius falls. Eventually, an increase in the marginal revenue product of labour affects both the WSC and the ZPL: While the WSC is shifted upwards in a parallel way, the ZPL moves to the left. For this reason, the effect on the equilibrium market radius is ambiguous in the diagrammatic analysis, whereas the

4.6 Long-Run Spatial Monopsony with Constant Individual Labour Supply

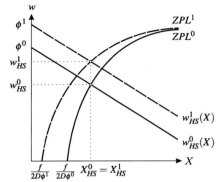

Fig. 4.23 The impact of an increase in the marginal revenue product of labour on the Hotelling–Smithies long-run equilibrium under constant individual labour supply

Table 4.4 Comparative static effects on the long-run equilibrium wage under constant individual labour supply

Increase:	Löschian competition	Hotelling–Smithies competition	Greenhut–Ohta competition
Fixed costs (f)	+	−	−
Worker density (D)	−	+	+
Productivity (ϕ)	−	+	+
Travel cost (t)	+	−	−

wage unambiguously increases (see Figure 4.23). Nevertheless, one can show algebraically that the two effects on the equilibrium market radius just offset each other, so that it remains unaltered.[33] The comparative statics of the model are summarised in Table 4.4.

4.6.2 Allowing for Varying Participation

The model with constant individual labour supply presented so far has been very restrictive in some respects. For instance, workers' labour supply behaviour has been modelled simplistically just as a '1–0 decision' with all workers having a reservation income of r. Therefore, every worker chooses to participate provided that the income obtained is larger than r everywhere in economic space. One way to allow for varying participation of workers is to add some worker heterogeneity in reservation incomes. To keep things simple, we follow Bhaskar and To (1999; 2003) and assume that at every location in space there are two groups of workers, where a

---

[33] Inserting the equilibrium wage (4.32) into the ZPL (4.31) yields the equilibrium market radius

$$X_i = \sqrt{\frac{f v_i}{2D}},$$

so that X_i is constant in ϕ, strictly increasing in f, and strictly decreasing in both t and D for all $0 < v_i \leq 1/t$.

share κ of workers has some low reservation income $\underline{r}$, while the remaining share $1-\kappa$ has some high reservation income $\bar{r}$.[34] The individual labour supply function thus becomes

$$l(w, x) := \begin{cases} 0 & \text{if } w - tx \leq \underline{r} \\ \kappa & \text{if } \underline{r} < w - tx \leq \bar{r} \\ 1 & \text{if } w - tx > \bar{r} \end{cases} \quad (4.35)$$

with $0 < \kappa < 1$ and $\bar{r} > \underline{r}$. Note that individual labour supply can also be interpreted as workers' common labour supply curve, where workers either choose non-participation or work either part-time (supplying $0 < \kappa < 1$ units of labour) or full-time (supplying a whole unit of labour).

Let us restrict attention to the interesting case where $\bar{r} < \phi$ is such high that only some high-reservation-income workers decide to work, while $\underline{r}$ is such low that all low-reservation-income workers want to work. Hence, assume $\underline{r} < w - tX < \bar{r}$ and $w > \bar{r}$. So to speak, we have a situation where the labour supply of high-reservation-income workers is locally segregated; provided participation, only one firm (i.e., the nearest) offers some of them an acceptable income larger than their reservation income. The labour supply of low-reservation-income workers to a firm offering some wage w is $2D\kappa X$, whereas the supply of high-reservation-income workers is given by $2D(1-\kappa)(w-\bar{r})/t$ because every high-reservation-income worker within distance $(w-\bar{r})/t$ wants to work for the firm. The labour supply of high-reservation-income workers thus is independent from the neighbouring firm's wage offer because of local segregation. Therefore, aggregate labour supply becomes

$$L(w, X) = 2D\left(\kappa X + (1-\kappa)\frac{w-\bar{r}}{t}\right). \quad (4.36)$$

From this we get firms' profits as

$$\Pi(w, X) = 2D\left(\kappa X + (1-\kappa)\frac{w-\bar{r}}{t}\right)(\phi - w) - f. \quad (4.37)$$

Since optimal wage setting requires $\partial \Pi(w, X)/\partial w \stackrel{!}{=} 0$, we get a modified WSC

$$w_i(X) = \frac{1-\kappa(1-v_i t)}{2-\kappa(2-v_i t)}\phi + \frac{1-\kappa}{2-\kappa(2-v_i t)}\bar{r} - \frac{\kappa t}{2-\kappa(2-v_i t)}X.[35] \quad (4.38)$$

Equation (4.38) defines a straight line in the (X, w)-plane, where the slope is given by $w'_i(X) = -\kappa t/[2-\kappa(2-v_i t)] < 0$ for all relevant X, while the w-intercept

---

[34] The following argument readily extends to the more general setting where we have any finite number of groups with different reservation incomes (cf. Bhaskar and To, 1999; 2003). If we considered a continuum of groups of workers, however, we would again get a continuous individual labour supply function as before.

[35] Note that firms' perceived profits Π_i are again strictly concave in w, so that (4.38) indeed yields the unique maximand we are looking for.

4.6 Long-Run Spatial Monopsony with Constant Individual Labour Supply

is a weighted average of workers' marginal revenue product and the reservation income of high-reservation-income workers.[36]

Next, we are interested in the long run where profits are driven to zero. From $\Pi(w, X) \stackrel{!}{=} 0$ the modified ZPL is

$$X(w) = \frac{f}{2D\kappa(\phi - w)} - \frac{1-\kappa}{\kappa}\frac{w - \bar{r}}{t} \qquad (4.39)$$

with $X'(w) > 0$ for all relevant w.[37] We therefore again get an upward-sloping curve in the relevant part of the (X, w)-plane describing all wage–market radius pairs that yield zero profits for firms.

Combining the wage-setting condition (4.38) and the zero-profit condition (4.39) yields the long-run equilibrium wage

$$w_i = \phi - \sqrt{\frac{ft}{2D[1 - \kappa(1 - v_i t)]}} \qquad (4.40)$$

with $v_{GO} = 1/t$ and $v_{HS} = 1/2t$.[38] A depiction of the equilibrium in the (X, w)-plane would yield a diagram qualitatively similar to the one from Figure 4.20, where the equilibrium wage–market radius pair is the intersection point of the WSC defined by (4.38) and the ZPL defined by (4.39). Note further that (4.40) can be used to specify parameter restrictions that guarantee $\underline{r} < w_i + tX_i < \bar{r}$ and $w_i > \bar{r}$ for $i \in \{GO, HS\}$ to hold in the equilibrium, so that indeed only some high- and all low-reservation-income workers participate in equilibrium.

From (4.40) it is obvious that the comparative statics are qualitatively the same as those gained for the basic specification presented in Section 4.6.1 and summarised

---

[36] Note that $w_i(X) \not\to \phi$ if $X \to 0$, so that the competitive solution is not achieved in the limiting case of irrelevant economic space. This holds because firms do not compete for high-reservation-income workers due to our assumption of local segregation and thus do not pay them their marginal revenue product even if market areas become infinitesimally small.

[37] We have

$$X'(w) = \frac{ft - 2D(1 - \kappa)(\phi - w)^2}{2Dt\kappa(\phi - w)^2}$$

which is positive for all

$$w < \phi - \sqrt{\frac{ft}{2D(1-\kappa)}},$$

and this will be shown to hold in every equilibrium, see equation (4.40).

[38] Again, there are two roots which simultaneously solve (4.38) and (4.39), viz.

$$\phi \pm \sqrt{\frac{ft}{2D[1 - \kappa(1 - v_i t)]}},$$

where nonnegativity of profits rules out the larger one, so that (4.40) follows.

in Table 4.4 on page 87.[39] Besides, we find that an increase in the share of high-reservation-income workers reduces the equilibrium wage. Diagrammatically, the comparative statics work in the same way as in Figures 4.21–4.23. Other than before, a variation in the equilibrium wage also gives rise to varying participation, which is increasing in the wage paid to workers. Note also that if worker heterogeneity disappears, i.e., $\kappa \to 1$, all the equations (4.38)–(4.40) approach their counterparts from Section 4.6.1, so that this simpler model is a nested limiting case. Finally, we should emphasise that the HS spatial monopsony model described in this section is the model pioneered by Bhaskar and To (1999).

4.6.3 The Löschian Equilibrium

Now that we have discussed the GO and HS model and one possible extension to allow for varying participation of workers, we shall turn to the Löschian model with constant individual labour supply. In particular, we want to demonstrate that it has similar properties under constant and linear individual labour supply, although constant supply is clearly log-linear, while linear supply is strictly log-concave. To derive the Löschian solution, we have to solve the profit maximisation problem of Löschian firms. Since Löschian competitors set their wage like monopsonists within their market areas, i.e., such that workers on the market boundary receive an income no more than their reservation wage, $r \leqslant w \leqslant r + tX$, their problem is

$$\max_{r \leqslant w \leqslant r+tX} \Pi(w, X) = 2DX(\phi - w) - f. \qquad (4.41)$$

To solve problem (4.41), we set up the Lagrangean as

$$\mathcal{L}(w, \nu_1, \nu_2) := 2DX(\phi - w) - f + \nu_1(r + tX - w) + \nu_2(w - r) \qquad (4.42)$$

with Lagrange multipliers ν_1 and ν_2. In the optimum, the following first-order Karush–Kuhn–Tucker conditions have to hold (cf., e.g., Boyd and Vandenberghe, 2004, p. 244):

$$\frac{\partial \mathcal{L}(w, \nu_1, \nu_2)}{\partial w} = 2D[(\phi - w)\nu_M - X] - \nu_1 + \nu_2 \stackrel{!}{=} 0 \qquad (4.43)$$

$$\nu_1(r + tX - w) \stackrel{!}{=} 0 \qquad (4.44)$$

$$\nu_2(w - r) \stackrel{!}{=} 0 \qquad (4.45)$$

$$\nu_1, \nu_2 \stackrel{!}{\geqslant} 0 \qquad (4.46)$$

---

[39] This and the following claim are easily verified by partial differentiation of (4.40) with respect to the parameter of interest.

4.6 Long-Run Spatial Monopsony with Constant Individual Labour Supply

Note that $v_M = 1/t$ enters condition (4.43) because Löschian firms pay a wage $w \leq tX + r$ and behave like spatial monopsonists within their market radius $0 < X \leq X_{Lö}$. Since Π is strictly concave in the wage, conditions (4.43)–(4.46) are sufficient for a unique global optimum. To solve for the wage optimally chosen by the firm, firstly note that $\partial \Pi(0, X)/\partial w = 2D(\phi/t - X) > 0$, so that $w_{Lö}(X)$ must be positive.[40] Second, by basically the same reasoning as before, $\partial \Pi(r, X)/\partial w = 2D[(\phi - r)/t - X] > 0$ holds, so that we have $v_2 = 0$ by virtue of the complementary-slackness condition (4.45). From condition (4.43) it follows that $v_1 = 2D([\phi - w_{Lö}(X)]/t - X) > 0$ because $w_{Lö}(X) < \phi - tX = w_{GO}(X)$ for all $0 < X < X_M$. So the complementary-slackness condition (4.44) implies

$$w_{Lö}(X) = r + tX. \qquad (4.47)$$

Hence, in the (X, w)-plane, the Löschian WSC is an upward-sloping straight line with slope t and w-intercept r.

Combining the wage-setting condition (4.47) and the zero-profit condition (4.31) and some straightforward algebraic manipulations yield

$$w_{Lö} = \frac{\phi + r - \sqrt{(\phi - r)^2 - 2ft/D}}{2}.^{41} \qquad (4.48)$$

Inspection of (4.48) shows that the Löschian model with constant individual labour supply indeed has similar qualitative properties as its counterpart under linear individual labour supply.[42] An increase in the fixed costs or the travel cost or a decrease in the worker density leads to the 'perverse' result of a higher equilibrium wage. Since the supply effect is absent, the effect of a rise in the marginal revenue product on the equilibrium wage becomes unambiguously negative, which is the only respect in which this simple model differs from the more general settings discussed

---

[40] This follows from

$$\frac{\phi}{t} > \frac{\phi - r}{t} > \frac{w - r}{t} = X_M > X_{Lö} \geq X,$$

which must hold in equilibrium due to $\phi > r$ and $\phi > w$.

[41] There are actually two roots that simultaneously solve (4.31) and (4.47), viz.

$$\frac{\phi + r \pm \sqrt{(\phi - r)^2 - 2ft/D}}{2},$$

but nonnegativity of profits requires $w_{Lö} < \phi$ and thus rules out the larger one, so that (4.48) follows.

[42] Note that it would be uninteresting to consider the extension of constant spatial monopsony presented in Section 4.6.2 under Löschian competition on account of the absence of any competition effect. Since Löschian firms set their wage such that either all workers participate, so that $w_{Lö}(X) = \bar{r} + tX$, or only low-reservation-income workers, so that $w_{Lö}(X) = \underline{r} + tX$, there is no comparative static variation in workers' participation.

above.[43] Diagrammatically, all these effects critically hinge on the upward-sloping Löschian WSC (see Figure 4.20 on page 86), which reverses all the results gained under HS and GO competition (see Table 4.4 on page 87).

To sum up, considering constant individual labour supply facilitates the analysis immensely under HS and GO competition but also yields a rather special case bearing much similarity with the general model under log-linear individual labour supply and not allowing for variation in workers' participation (labour supply). While the latter point is easily dealt with by allowing for some heterogeneity in reservation incomes by considering groups of workers with different reservation incomes (or part-time work when interpreting the individual labour supply function as workers' common labour supply curve), the absence of any supply effect leaves us with a model the results of which are entirely driven by the competition effect. Thus, when arguing within the simple Salop-style oligopsony model (with the standard Bertrand–Nash assumption at place), that is, when arguing within Bhaskar and To's (1999) model of spatial monopsony, one has to bear in mind that some of the results critically hinge on the absence of any supply effect. As soon as one considers strictly log-concave individual labour supply, the model yields less clear-cut results that depend on the strength of competition as we have seen in the linear HS model above. Under Löschian competition, results are similar to those gained from more general settings with strictly log-concave individual labour supply. Furthermore, the comparative static effects have now the opposite sign for all parameters compared to those under GO and HS competition. In particular, we find that workers' equilibrium wage and their marginal revenue product generally move in opposite directions, independently of the strength of spatial competition. Due to the absence of any supply effect, this 'perverse' result cannot be found in the HS model the properties of which are solely driven by the competition effect.

4.7 Conclusions

In this chapter, we have extended the short-run spatial monopsony model presented in Chapter 3 to the long run by allowing for free entry and costless relocation of firms. This drives profits to zero and thus endogenises the distance between equidistant firms, whilst firms' market radius was considered to be exogenous in the short run. Hence, the long-run monopsony model is gained from the short-run monopsony model by additionally imposing a zero-profit condition. Since there are some fixed costs, however, firms do not enter excessively but only exist at some places.

---

[43] Algebraically, the latter effect follows from

$$\frac{\partial w_{L\ddot{o}}}{\partial \phi} = \frac{1}{2}\left(1 - \frac{\phi - r}{\sqrt{(\phi - r)^2 - 2ft/D}}\right) < 0$$

because the denominator of the second term in parentheses is smaller than $\phi - r$.

4.7 Conclusions

The level of the fixed costs and the level of the travel cost thus represent the two obstacles to competition: The fixed costs prevent firms from being set up at any place, and the travel cost causes the distance between firms to matter in an economic sense. Firms thus are not perfect substitutes to workers who – other things being equal – prefer an employer nearby because travelling is costly. And this, in turn, equips firms with some monopsony power over their workers.

Both the zero-profit and the wage-setting condition together determine the wage–market radius pair in the long-run equilibrium. While the algebraic analysis of the equilibrium turned out to be a very tough task, we showed how to depict the equilibrium diagrammatically in the wage–market radius plain as the intersection point of a zero-profit locus and a wage-setting curve. The (relevant part of the) zero-profit locus gave us a positive relationship between wages and market radii: The higher is the wage paid by firms, the larger must be their market areas for them to break even. The wage-setting curve, on the other hand, represents the optimal wage chosen for a given market radius and thus the short-run equilibrium wages for different market radii. Since the slope of the wage-setting curve represents the impact of competitive entry on the short-run equilibrium, it differed depending on the mode of competition and individual labour supply's convexity relative to an exponential, as shown in Chapter 3.

In the long-run equilibrium, we found that the wage is again strictly increasing in the conjectural variations held by spatial competitors about their rivals' wage reaction to a proposed wage increase no matter individual labour supply's convexity. Put differently, the wage is higher, the less firms collude. Again the reason is that firms' maximisation of *perceived* profits leaves them with more elastic perceived aggregate labour supply on account of the competition effect embodied in the conjectural variations parameter. Furthermore, we found that the equilibrium market radius is strictly increasing in the conjectural variations because the higher wage paid by firms with higher conjectural variations decreases their profitability, so that they need larger market areas to break even.

Imposing the zero-profit condition, however, substantially changed the model's comparative statics. Other than in the short run, a change in the fixed costs or the worker density now has an impact on the equilibrium wage because both influence the labour market's overall profitability and thus the size of the zero-profit market areas. Again, the model generates 'perverse' results in the same instances as in Chapter 3, that is, basically, if competitive forces are weak. If individual labour supply is strictly log-concave, an increase in the fixed costs or the travel cost or a decrease in the worker density raises the long-run equilibrium wage both under Löschian competition and under HS competition with weak competition (large market areas). Since the fixed costs and the travel cost are intimately related to the degree of competition, spaceless intuition would suggest the opposite. The model's comparative statics become 'normal,' however, (1) if we consider GO competition, (2) if we consider HS competition with small market areas or log-linear individual labour supply, or (3) if individual labour supply is very elastic, i.e., more convex than an exponential. Moreover, if one of these conditions holds, we also have a positive relationship between workers' marginal revenue product and their equilibrium wage. Eventually, we found that the Löschian model with log-linear individual labour supply has the same comparative static properties as spaceless monopsony, which is driven by the absence of the competition effect and the constancy of the individual labour supply elasticity over space.

Next, we investigated the model under simple special individual labour supply functions, viz. strictly log-concave linear and log-linear constant individual labour supply. While all the results of the more general approach carried over to the linear model, it turned out to be much more tractable (especially when looking for algebraic solutions and when investigating the model's comparative statics). Moreover, we gained additional insights: We found that under Löschian and HS competition there may be a negative relationship between workers' marginal revenue product of labour and their equilibrium wage. Furthermore, we were able to quantify what is actually meant by 'sufficiently small' or 'sufficiently large' market areas.

Finally, when considering constant individual labour supply, tractability was increased further, although we arrived at a model that behaves rather special in some respects. While it turned out to be quite easy to incorporate the possibility of varying participation (labour supply) of workers, the absence of any supply effect causes the model under HS and GO competition to behave in the same way as the general model with GO conjectures and log-linear individual labour supply. Whereas this result is driven by the competition effect present in both cases, the absence of any competition effect under Löschian competition caused the Löschian model to behave diametrically different from the HS and the GO model. Hence, we found that it bears a lot of similarity to the model with strictly log-concave individual labour supply and weak competition.

Bearing these *caveats* in mind, we will in the following make use of the simple model with constant individual labour supply to analyse the gender pay gap. In Chapter 5, we shall utilise the short-run model with constant individual labour supply, restricting attention to a dyopsonistic labour market consisting only of two employers, to present an alternative explanation of the gender pay gap in line with firms' profit maximisation behaviour. In Chapter 6, we will extend this story to the long-run model with constant individual labour supply and deduce some regional implications for the gender pay gap that will also be investigated empirically.

Chapter 5
Spatial Monopsony and the Gender Pay Gap[1]

In the following, we shall apply the reasoning from the short-run model in Chapter 3 to investigate the gender pay gap. We will employ the simplest model possible by considering a situation of dyopsony with constant individual labour supply. Furthermore, we will exclusively focus on the solution under the Bertrand–Nash assumption, i.e., under HS conjectures. Since we will allow for heterogeneity among firms and workers, we will derive the solution within a more explicitly game-theoretic approach – in terms of finding a Nash equilibrium to the wage-setting game played by the two firms – as the short cut via conjectural variations used hitherto loses its analytical convenience. But before setting up the model, we shall first say something about the gender pay gap and the standard explanations brought forward to deal with this empirical regularity.

5.1 The Gender Pay Gap and Beckerian vs. Robinsonian Discrimination

One of the stylised facts of labour markets is that on average women earn substantially less than men. For example, the European Commission (2006) reports an average raw wage differential of about 25 per cent for the EU-25 countries and 26 per cent for Germany in 2002. While part of the gender pay gap can be explained by introducing controls for individual characteristics (such as education, occupation, and experience), a substantial part of it remains unexplained in all EU-25 countries.[2] Although still of considerable size, the gender pay gap has narrowed in most

---

[1] This chapter is an extended version of Hirsch (2009).

[2] For a comprehensive review of the huge empirical literature on the gender pay gap, its determinants, and its evolution over time, see Altonji and Blank (1999). Blau and Kahn (2003) investigate international differences in the gender pay gap for 22 countries between 1985–1994. Moreover, Weichselbaumer and Winter-Ebmer (2005) provide a large meta-analysis of more than 260 international studies between the 1960s and the 1990s. For additional surveys on the gender pay gap, see Blau and Kahn (2000), OECD (2002), and Cahuc and Zylberberg (2004, pp. 280–295). Finally, Maier (2007) provides a survey on the German literature.

countries as in Germany over the last decades.[3] In addition to reflecting differences in human capital or occupational segregation not controlled for, this unexplained part of the gap may also reflect discrimination against women.

Theoretical attempts of explaining discrimination often follow Becker's (1971) concept of discrimination due to distaste. Since some employers dislike employing women, which is modelled by means of a distaste parameter in those employers' utility function, they offer lower wages to women, *ceteris paribus*.[4] However, this kind of reasoning suffers from two severe shortcomings: On the one hand, it is difficult to interpret the gender pay gap as a long-run equilibrium outcome using Becker's concept of discrimination without assuming some market power on the demand side because under perfect competition discrimination due to distaste should be competed away in the long run. On the other hand, even if firms had some market power, the firm that engages in Beckerian discrimination would earn less profits than its non-discriminating competitors (e.g., Bhaskar *et al.*, 2002; Bowlus and Eckstein, 2002). These criticisms, however, are far from new to the profession. For instance, Madden (1977*b*, p. 370) states:

> 'There are three main objection to this approach: (1) By shifting the motivations of producers from profit maximization to utility maximization, a vague qualitative relation between wages and productivity is substituted for a specific quantifiable one. (2) The attitudes which produce discriminatory behavior are taken as given. There is no consideration of whether the economic system fosters these attitudes. (3) The dynamic implication of this static model is that discrimination must decrease over time and ultimately be alleviated. If markets are competitive and if employers pay for discrimination through a decrease in profits, then nondiscriminators will be more efficient producers and will expand relative to discriminators. This result has been seriously questioned by empirical research.'

Therefore, it may be promising to look at an alternative explanation of discrimination given by Robinson (1969) where firms do profit from engaging in discrimination, so that discrimination is more likely to sustain in the long run.[5] Robinson was the first to apply Pigou's (1932) concept of third-degree price discrimination at a commodity market to the labour market. She argued that if groups of workers can be distinguished that differ in their labour supply elasticities at the firm level the firm will profit from paying different wages to these groups. More elastic groups

---

[3] For Germany Maier (2007) arrives at the conclusion that the gap has remained rather stable during the last decade, while Blau and Kahn (2000) report a decreasing gap for West Germany and for almost all OECD countries up to the mid 1990s. Taking account of changes in the wage distributions as well as cohort and life cycle effects, Fitzenberger and Wunderlich (2002) find that the German gap has narrowed substantially at the bottom of the wage distribution but to a lesser extent at the top. Using linked employer–employee data for Germany, Hinz and Gartner (2005) arrive at the conclusion that within-job pay gaps have shrunk as well.

[4] Within an imperfect competition framework this is, for example, done by Gordon and Morton (1974), Naylor (1994), Black (1995), Bhaskar *et al.* (2002), and Bowlus and Eckstein (2002).

[5] Madden (1973) provides a detailed exposition and discussion of Robinsonian discrimination and contrasts it with other (competitive) theories of gender discrimination. An early non-Beckerian approach to discrimination is presented by Krueger (1963), who demonstrates that majorities may profit economically from discriminating against minorities without having a taste for discrimination in the Beckerian sense.

5.1 The Gender Pay Gap and Beckerian vs. Robinsonian Discrimination

will get higher wages than less elastic groups, *ceteris paribus*. 'Just as we have price discrimination for a monopolist, so we may have price discrimination for a monopsonist.' (Robinson, 1969, p. 224) Hence, if women's labour supply at the level of the firm is less elastic than men's, women will earn lower wages, other things being equal.

While there is broad empirical evidence that women's labour supply is even more elastic than men's at the level of the market (cf., e.g., Killingsworth and Heckman, 1986; Pencavel, 1986; Heckman, 1993; Blundell and MaCurdy, 1999) where the decision is whether to supply labour or not, this needs not to hold at the level of the firm. The latter, however, is the relevant perspective to look at because from the single firm's point of view it matters only whether an individual supplies labour to this firm or not, so that both non-employed and employed workers are potential suppliers of labour to this firm. Put differently in our spatial monopsony terminology, it is the elasticity of the firm's aggregate labour supply with respect to the wage that matters, not the elasticity of individual labour supply.[6] As Boal and Ransom (1997, p. 99) put the state of affairs: 'Empirical studies usually find that women's labor supply is more elastic than men's at the level of the market, but some researchers argue *informally* that this relation reverses at the level of the individual firm.' (emphasis added) In the following, our aim will be to offer a *formal* spatial monopsony explanation why women's labour supply elasticity at the level of the firm may be lower than men's, although their labour supply elasticity at the level of the market may be not.[7] As we shall discuss in more detail in Chapter 9, there is also empirical evidence for women's labour supply at the firm level being indeed substantially less elastic than men's, so that Robinsonian discrimination is not rejected by the data and might be one explanation of the persistent empirical regularity of the gender pay gap.

While Robinsonian discrimination gives a simple and intuitively appealing explanation of the gender pay gap, it differs fundamentally from Beckerian discrimination. Under Robinsonian discrimination, firms' actions are not governed by (costly) prejudices, for their only motive for engaging in discrimination is that they

---

[6] Since Robinson's (1969) original argument was given within the standard static model of monopsony with a single employer (see Chapter 2), there was no room for distinguishing firm- from market-level labour supply. Perhaps this is the main reason why the argument usually raised against Robinsonian discrimination – that women supply labour more elastically than men at the level of the market – still seems so convincing, while '[t]he problem may be that we are not considering the proper labor supply curves'. (Madden, 1973, p. 81)

[7] Of course, there are alternative ways of modelling Robinsonian discrimination than spatial monopsony. For an analysis of Robinsonian discrimination within a search model, see Schlicht (1982), Bowlus (1997), and Barth and Dale-Olsen (1999). Employing a framework similar in spirit to Burdett and Mortensen (1998, see Chapter 8), Bowlus demonstrates that a significant part of the gender pay gap can be explained in terms of women facing higher search frictions in the labour market. Furthermore, Madden (1977*b*) investigates Robinsonian discrimination for segmented local labour markets. Also within an imperfect competition framework, Naylor (1996) argues that differences in employers' wage conjectural variations (i.e., differences in their beliefs about the likeliness of collusive outcomes for male and female workers) may lead to wage discrimination against women, even if women supply labour more elastically at the level of the market.

can increase their profits by doing so. Nevertheless, in spite of its intuitive appeal, not much tribute is paid to Robinsonian discrimination. For instance, Altonji and Blank's (1999) comprehensive summary of race and gender in the labour market does not refer to it at all.[8] Hence, Robinsonian discrimination might seem as an idea whose time has passed, which parallels to some extent the little interest paid to monopsony in general.[9] Since Robinson's (1969) analysis assumes monopsony power in the 'classic' sense of a single employer, one might indeed doubt its relevance. Nonetheless, the 'new' monopsony literature in general and models of spatial monopsony, as laid out in Chapters 3 and 4, in particular highlight that monopsony power may even arise if there are many firms competing for workers.

Below, we will utilise a simple dyopsony model of the labour market in the spirit of the short-run model presented in Chapter 3 to analyse the link between gender differences in mobility patterns, the gender pay gap, and Robinsonian discrimination.[10] By doing so, we aim at giving a re-formulation of Robinsonian discrimination by means of a spatial monopsony model. On the one hand, the model employed will be more general than the model from Chapter 3 inasmuch as firms are allowed to be heterogenous. On the other hand, it will be more restrictive in the sense that we consider the special case of a dyopsony market with constant individual labour supply under HS competition.

5.2 The Model

5.2.1 The Basic Assumptions

In the following, the basic assumptions (A1)–(A7) from Section 3.1 will be slightly modified to give the following list:

(A1′) There are two firms located at 0 and 1 on the unit interval [0, 1].
(A2′) All firms produce a homogenous product from their total labour input with potentially different constant marginal revenue products ϕ_0 and ϕ_1.
(A3′) Firms are local monopsonists. When firms are in competition, there is no market overlap, and workers supply labour to the firm offering the highest income (wage net of travel cost).

---

[8] Another current survey not mentioning Robinsonian discrimination is Blau and Kahn (2000). Note that this frosty attitude towards Robinsonian discrimination is not an entirely new phenomenon as can be seen from two more dated summaries of discrimination models, viz. Arrow (1972) and Stiglitz (1973), which do not mention it either.
[9] An interesting discussion of this is given by Manning (2003a, pp. 6–10).
[10] To our knowledge, the first presentation of this Hotelling-style dyopsony model is due to Veendorp (1981). Further applications include, for instance, Bhaskar *et al.* (2002) and Kaas and Madden (2008).

5.2 The Model

(A4′) Female and male workers with identical abilities are continuously distributed over the market at uniform densities 1 and μ, respectively.

(A5′) The travel cost is proportional to distance and is paid by the worker. A share η with $0 < \eta \leqslant 1$ of female workers faces travel cost $\bar{t}$ per unit distance, while male workers and the remaining share $1 - \eta$ of female workers have travel cost $\underline{t}$ per unit distance with $0 < \underline{t} < \bar{t}$.

(A6′) Workers' labour supply behaviour is the same at any point in space and is summarised by the constant individual labour supply function l with

$$l(w, x) := \begin{cases} 1 \text{ if } w - tx > r \\ 0 \text{ if } w - tx \leqslant r, \end{cases} \quad (5.1)$$

where workers' common reservation income is assumed to be some $r \geqslant 0$.

(A7′) Firms are immobile and the distance between them is fixed.

Several of these assumptions call for some discussion. Consider assumption (A5′) first. What might be reasons for different travel cost among women? A reason for this might be that high-travel-cost women have higher indirect travel cost because they play a more exposed role in household production, particularly in rearing children, than the other women and men, so that they attach a higher disutility to the time loss due to commuting. In short, they face higher opportunity cost of travelling. This is also in line with empirical evidence. For instance, Hersch and Stratton (1997) show that for the U.S. married women's housework time is, on average, three times that of married men's and that women's more dominant role in housework is able to explain part of the gender pay gap in wage regressions. Furthermore, Manning (2003a, pp. 203/204) presents some evidence for the UK that travel-to-work times are lower for women than men, especially for those with more domestic responsibilities, while an older study by Madden (1977a) finds the same for women in the U.S.[11] Finally, the Statistisches Bundesamt (2005, Appendix Table 29) reports a similar pattern for Germany.

Assumption (A2′) introduces heterogeneity among firms by allowing firms' marginal revenue products of labour ϕ_0 and ϕ_1 to differ.[12] There are two potential reasons for that: firms may simply employ different production technologies or they may face different degrees of market power on their output markets translating into different output prices.[13] In both instances, the (constant) marginal revenue products of labour faced by firms ϕ_0 and ϕ_1 will differ. However, we do not allow

---

[11] Note that Madden also finds lower (spatial) labour supply elasticities for women than men, the prerequisite for Robinsonian discrimination to occur. Cardwell and Rosenzweig (1980) is another early study in this line.

[12] See footnote 3 on page 11 for a detailed discussion of the assumption of constant marginal revenue products.

[13] For an explicit derivation of this result with a second factor of production, see Bhaskar and To (1999; 2003). For an analysis of firms' behaviour explicitly taking account of both firms' wage-setting power in the labour market and their price-setting power in the output market, see Kaas and Madden (2004).

for the marginal revenue product to differ among workers. Thus, women and men are assumed to be perfect substitutes in production, which reflects our assumptions that men and women are equally productive and supply the same amount of labour whenever they receive an income larger than their common reservation income from working. Admittedly, this assumption is a strong one and abstracts from the problem that some women may be less than perfect substitutes to men for the very same reasons why they face higher travel cost. For example, those women may be less willing to work overtime due to domestic responsibilities or more likely to be absent when their children are sick. Nevertheless, we argue that it is sensible to rely on this assumption if one is concerned with wage differentials *ceteris paribus* caused by differences in travel costs. This is also plausible insofar as women's labour market outcomes would arguably be worsened further if they were less than perfect substitutes to men. Together with the remaining assumptions, we see that we consider a simplified dyopsony version of the short-run model from Chapter 3 with constant individual labour supply, heterogeneity of firms in productivity characteristics, and heterogeneity of workers' travel cost by gender.[14]

5.2.2 Firm-Level Labour Supply and Firms' Wage-Setting Behaviour

Firms are assumed to offer wages independently of workers' location separately to female and male workers.[15] Let the corresponding offers be w_0^f and w_0^m for firm 0 and w_1^f and w_1^m for firm 1. If $w_0^m + w_1^m > r + \underline{t}$ and $w_0^f + w_1^f > r + \bar{t}$, all female and male workers participate in the labour market as they gain an income larger than their reservation income from doing so. This will be assumed to hold from now on. As we shall see later, this indeed holds in equilibrium if firms are sufficiently productive. By this and the assumption that men and women supply a unit of labour inelastically provided participation, we disregard the problem of potential differences in participation rates. Since we are interested in the impact of differences in travel costs on group-specific wages *ceteris paribus*, we are interested

---

[14] Note that we will in the following abstract from any fixed costs in firms' cost functions as these are irrelevant for marginal decision-making and thus for the outcomes of spatial monopsony in the short run (see Section 3.6 and 3.7).

[15] Note that firms do not distinguish low- from high-travel-cost women by assumption. Allowing them to do so would leave us with a model in which firms engage in first-degree wage discrimination. This clearly would require firms to observe the types of women (e.g., because women signal their type credibly, thus yielding a separating equilibrium in a signalling game). Since we are interested in third-degree Robinsonian discrimination where firms use *easily observable* worker characteristics, such as sex, to distinguish groups of workers, we will not bother with discussing this case any further.

5.2 The Model

in comparing working men and women who *only* differ in travel costs. Therefore, we argue that these assumptions are reasonable.[16]

Next, assume in the following that both $|w_0^m - w_1^m| < \underline{t}$ and $|w_0^f - w_1^f| < \underline{t}$, so that both firms employ some workers from all three groups. Clearly, this requires that neither of the firms finds it profitable to oust its competitor by overbidding its wage offer by more than $\underline{t}$. We shall show later under which conditions this necessarily holds in equilibrium. To derive the firms' aggregate male labour supply denoted by $L_0^m(w_0^m, w_1^m)$ and $L_1^m(w_1^m, w_0^m)$, respectively, we take up the argument from Section 3.5 and calculate the location at which male workers are indifferent between working for firm 0 and 1. This coincides with firm 0's market radius for male workers X_0^m, while firm 1's X_1^m is just $1 - X_0^m$. Hence, we have

$$X_i^m(w_i^m, w_j^m) = \frac{w_i^m - w_j^m + \underline{t}}{2\underline{t}} \tag{5.2}$$

with $i, j = 0, 1$ and $j \neq i$. By virtue of assumption (A3), all male workers distanced $x < X_i^m$ ($x > X_i^m$) from firm i decide to work for firm i (j) because this earns them a higher income. Similarly, firm i's market radii for high- and low-travel-cost women are

$$X_i^{\overline{f}}(w_i^f, w_j^f) = \frac{w_i^f - w_j^f + \overline{t}}{2\overline{t}} \tag{5.3}$$

$$X_i^{\underline{f}}(w_i^f, w_j^f) = \frac{w_i^f - w_j^f + \underline{t}}{2\underline{t}}, \tag{5.4}$$

where again each high- or low-travel-cost woman located within (without) firm i's respective market radius prefers working for firm i (j).

Making use of the reasoning in the last paragraph, we get firm i's aggregate labour supply of men as the mass of male workers within its male market radius X_i^m, so that

$$L_i^m(w_i^m, w_j^m) = \frac{\mu(w_i^m - w_j^m + \underline{t})}{2\underline{t}}. \tag{5.5}$$

By complete analogy, women's labour supply to firm i is

$$L_i^f(w_i^f, w_j^f) = \frac{[\eta\underline{t} + (1-\eta)\overline{t}](w_i^f - w_j^f) + \overline{t}\underline{t}}{2\overline{t}\underline{t}}. \tag{5.6}$$

---

[16] Note, however, that the model easily extends to the modified constant spatial monopsony model from Section 4.6.2 in which workers' participation varies with the equilibrium wage, so that a gender pay gap would also imply a gender gap in participation rates.

Finally, assume that $\partial w_j^m/\partial w_i^m = \partial w_j^f/\partial w_i^f = 0$, that is, assume that firm i presumes its rival j not to react to a proposed wage change. From the discussion in Section 3.5 we know that this means we are assuming HS conjectures. So spatial competitors presume they are able to expand their market areas at the expense of their rival's via a wage increase with $\partial X_i^m/\partial w_i^m = \partial X_i^f/\partial w_i^f = 1/2t$. Under HS conjectures, both male and female aggregate labour supplies are therefore strictly increasing in firm i's own wage and strictly decreasing in its competitor's wage. As a consequence, this simple dyopsony model generates upward-sloping firm-level labour supply curves both for women and men as long as the travel costs are not very small and the offered wages are not too different, although both groups supply labour inelastically at the level of the market (provided participation).[17]

We now turn to firms' decisions. Firms are considered to behave as profit maximisers and are assumed to produce their output with a constant marginal revenue product ϕ_i from their total labour input $L_i^m + L_i^f$. Therefore, firm i's problem is to find a pair of wage offers (w_i^m, w_i^f) that maximises its profits Π_i given firm j's wage offers, where

$$\Pi_i(w_i^m, w_i^f, w_j^m, w_j^f) = \phi_i[L_i^m(w_i^m, w_j^m) + L_i^f(w_i^f, w_j^f)] \\ - w_i^m L_i^m(w_i^m, w_j^m) - w_i^f L_i^f(w_i^f, w_j^f). \quad (5.7)$$

In a next step, it is possible to split up this problem of finding a pair of wage offers (w_i^m, w_i^f) that maximises overall profits as given by (5.7) into two independent problems, namely of finding a wage offer w_i^m that maximises the profits from the employment of men given firm j's wage offer w_j^m and finding a wage offer w_i^f that maximises the profits from the employment of women given firm j's wage offer w_j^f. This is possible because women and men are perfect substitutes in production and firms are supposed to set wages separately for women and men and to produce with constant marginal revenue products of labour. Thus, we get

$$\max_{w_i^m, w_i^f} \Pi_i(w_i^m, w_i^f, w_j^m, w_j^f) \\ = \max_{w_i^m}(\phi_i - w_i^m)L_i^m(w_i^m, w_j^m) + \max_{w_i^f}(\phi_i - w_i^f)L_i^f(w_i^f, w_j^f). \quad (5.8)$$

---

[17] Of course, we could also have assumed GO conjectures with $\partial w_j^m/\partial w_i^m = \partial w_j^f/\partial w_i^f = -1$ and $\partial X_i^m/\partial w_i^m = \partial X_i^f/\partial w_i^f = 1/t$ or Löschian conjectures with $\partial w_j^m/\partial w_i^m = \partial w_j^f/\partial w_i^f = 1$ and $\partial X_i^m/\partial w_i^m = \partial X_i^f/\partial w_i^f = 0$ (see the discussion in Section 3.5). But as we have seen in Section 4.6.1, the conclusions drawn from the HS and the GO model do not differ qualitatively, so that there is no reason to overdo the analysis by also discussing the case of GO conjectures. Besides, we have seen in Section 4.6.3 that the model is not easily solved under Löschian conjectures. More importantly, we shall see later that the following Robinsonian explanation of the gender pay gap would not work under collusive spatial dyopsony, either, because of the model's 'perverse' comparative statics in this case.

5.2 The Model

Inserting equations (5.5) and (5.6) for firm i's female and male aggregate labour supplies into (5.7) yields

$$\Pi_i(w_i^m, w_i^f, w_j^m, w_j^f) = (\phi_i - w_i^m)\frac{\mu(w_i^m - w_j^m + \underline{t})}{2\underline{t}} \\ + (\phi_i - w_i^f)\frac{[\eta\underline{t} + (1-\eta)\bar{t}](w_i^f - w_j^f) + \bar{t}\underline{t}}{2\bar{t}\underline{t}}. \quad (5.9)$$

We now assume that firms simultaneously determine the wages they offer to women and men. Furthermore, we assume that the share η of high-travel-cost women is common knowledge. By this, we get two independent static wage-setting games of complete information, where we are interested in finding Nash equilibria for both games.[18] Maximisation of (5.9) with respect to w_i^m and w_i^f and rearranging of the respective first-order condition give firm i's reaction functions, i.e., the optimally chosen wage for men and women given firm j's respective wage offer.[19] The reaction function for male workers is given by

$$\omega_i^m(w_j^m) = \frac{1}{2}\left(\phi_i + w_j^m - \underline{t}\right), \quad (5.10)$$

whereas the reaction function for female workers is

$$\omega_i^f(w_j^f) = \frac{1}{2}\left(\phi_i + w_j^f - \frac{\bar{t}\underline{t}}{\eta\underline{t} + (1-\eta)\bar{t}}\right). \quad (5.11)$$

Since both ω_i^m and ω_i^f are strictly increasing in w_j^m and w_j^f, respectively, we have strategic complementarity in wage setting.

5.2.3 The Equilibrium and Its Properties

Mutually best responses yield unique, globally stable Nash equilibria in pure strategies with equilibrium wage offers $\widehat{w}_0^m$, $\widehat{w}_1^m$, $\widehat{w}_0^f$, and $\widehat{w}_1^f$ as is stated by the following proposition:

Proposition 5.1 (Equilibrium Wage Offers). *If $|\phi_0 - \phi_1| < 3\underline{t}$ and $\phi_0 + \phi_1 > r + \bar{t} + 2\bar{t}\underline{t}/[\eta\underline{t} + (1-\eta)\bar{t}]$, then there exists a unique, globally stable Nash equilibrium in pure strategies for both female and male workers. It yields wage offers*

---

[18] The alternative of introducing imperfect information to the model would aggravate the analysis by requiring to look for Bayesian Nash equilibria of the games without any additional gain of insights.

[19] Note that the corresponding second-order conditions are satisfied, so that we indeed find the respective maximand by considering the first-order condition.

$$\widehat{w}_i^m = \frac{2}{3}\phi_i + \frac{1}{3}\phi_j - \underline{t} \qquad (5.12)$$

and

$$\widehat{w}_i^f = \frac{2}{3}\phi_i + \frac{1}{3}\phi_j - \frac{\bar{t}\underline{t}}{\eta\underline{t} + (1-\eta)\bar{t}}, \qquad (5.13)$$

respectively, where $i, j = 0, 1$ and $j \neq i$.

Proof. (5.12) and (5.13) follow immediately from $\widehat{w}_i^m = \omega_i^m[\omega_j^m(\widehat{w}_i^m)]$ and $\widehat{w}_i^f = \omega_i^f[\omega_j^f(\widehat{w}_i^f)]$. The pure-strategy Nash equilibria are unique and globally stable due to the linearity of the reaction functions (5.10) and (5.11). Eventually, if $|\phi_0 - \phi_1| < 3\underline{t}$, then $|\widehat{w}_0^m - \widehat{w}_1^m| < \underline{t}$ and $|\widehat{w}_0^f - \widehat{w}_1^f| < \underline{t}$, and if $\phi_0 + \phi_1 > r + \bar{t} + 2\bar{t}\underline{t}/[\eta\underline{t} + (1-\eta)\bar{t}]$, then $\widehat{w}_0^f + \widehat{w}_1^f > r + \bar{t}$ and $\widehat{w}_0^m + \widehat{w}_1^m > r + \underline{t}$, so that the derived equilibria actually exist. ∎

Note that if firms are sufficiently productive all workers participate in the labour market. If this were not the case, the equilibria derived would fail to exist because we would have the trivial situation of local monopsonists without strategic interaction for (at least some) workers. Furthermore, if firms' productivity levels do no differ too much, i.e., by less than $3\underline{t}$, then in equilibrium no firm finds it profitable to overbid its competitor's wage offer by more than $\underline{t}$, and therefore each employs some workers from all groups.

According to (5.12) and (5.13), workers' equilibrium wages are weighted averages of their marginal revenue products at firms 0 and 1 net of a term related to the (group-specific) travel cost.[20] Thus, all workers receive (and accept) wage offers that are below their respective marginal revenue products. Interestingly, firm i's wage not only depends on i's own productivity but also on j's, even though to a lesser extent. The latter effect reflects the impact of wage competition among employers which is, however, not complete because firm i's own characteristics partly determine the wages paid by i in equilibrium. Another interesting point to mention is the link between productivity, firm size, profitability, and wages.[21] From (5.12) and (5.13) it follows immediately that the more productive firm in terms of a higher marginal revenue product of labour offers higher wages both to men and women. And this, in turn, implies according to (5.5) and (5.6) that the more productive firm is also the larger one in terms of employment. Therefore, this model is consistent with two stylised facts of labour markets, viz. the employer size–wage effect and the positive correlation between firms' productivity and wages (e.g., Brown and

---

[20] Note that under GO competition very similar equilibria would result. Only the weights attached to the respective components would differ, i.e., $3/4$ to ϕ_i, $1/4$ to ϕ_j, and $1/2$ to the travel-cost-related term. In the following, we shall therefore see that the gender pay gap would be less pronounced under GO competition, which is intuitively appealing as we regarded higher conjectural variations as representing stronger competitive forces.

[21] These properties of our Hotelling-style dyopsony model are discussed in detail by Bhaskar *et al.* (2002).

Medoff, 1989; Groshen, 1991; Oi and Idson, 1999). In particular, workers' marginal revenue product remains an important — but unlike perfect competition not the exclusive — determinant of workers' wages. Besides, the model also predicts that the more productive firm is also the more profitable one, so that there is a positive correlation between profitability and wages (e.g., Blanchflower et al., 1996; Hildreth and Oswald, 1997). Eventually, note that if firms are symmetric they offer the same wage and employ both half of the men and the women in the market, which parallels the discussion in Chapter 3.

Next, we are interested in differences in the labour market outcomes of men and women. Therefore, we consider the equilibrium wage differential $\Delta_w := \widehat{w}_i^m - \widehat{w}_i^f$ between male and female workers working for firm i.

Corollary 5.1 (Equilibrium Wage Differential). *The equilibrium wage differential between male and female workers is given by*

$$\Delta_w = \frac{\eta \underline{t}(\overline{t} - \underline{t})}{\eta \underline{t} + (1-\eta)\overline{t}}. \tag{5.14}$$

It is the same in firms 0 and 1. Moreover, it is positive and strictly increasing both in the travel cost of high-travel-cost women and the share of them among female workers.

Proof. Subtracting (5.13) from (5.12) yields (5.14), which is clearly positive. It is also independent of firms' characteristics. Furthermore, the wage differential is strictly increasing both in $\overline{t}$ and η, which follows immediately from partial differentiation of (5.14) with respect to the parameter of interest, where

$$\frac{\partial \Delta_w}{\partial \overline{t}} = \frac{\eta \underline{t}^2}{[\eta \underline{t} + (1-\eta)\overline{t}]^2} > 0 \tag{5.15}$$

and

$$\frac{\partial \Delta_w}{\partial \eta} = \frac{\overline{t}\underline{t}(\overline{t} - \underline{t})}{[\eta \underline{t} + (1-\eta)\overline{t}]^2} > 0, \tag{5.16}$$

respectively. ■

The consequence of Corollary 5.1 is that women earn less than men in equilibrium even though men and women are equally productive and perfect substitutes in production just because a share of women faces higher travel cost. The reasoning is as follows: Since firms do not distinguish low- from high-travel-cost women, all women receive lower wage offers. This holds because firms know that women face higher travel cost than men on average, so that the average woman is less inclined to change employers for wage-related reasons, which reduces competition among employers for female workers. Hence, even low-travel-cost women who do not differ from men in terms of productivity and travel cost are affected as they receive and accept lower wage offers than men due to statistical discrimination by the firms. In line with intuition, the extent of wage discrimination erodes as the share of high-travel-cost women declines and as their travel cost decreases.[22]

Next, we consider the equilibrium wage elasticity of firms' female and male labour supplies. As Robinsonian discrimination arises if and only if women's firm-level labour supply is less elastic than men's, it is of particular interest to investigate whether gender-specific labour supply elasticities differ and whether the difference goes in the same direction as it would if Robinsonian discrimination occurred. If this were the case, another point of interest would be the link between differences in elasticities and the wage differential. The following Corollary 5.2 shows not only that women's firm-level labour supply is less elastic than men's, but also that there is a direct link between the elasticity and the wage differential.

Corollary 5.2 (Equilibrium Firm-Level Labour Supply Elasticities). *In equilibrium, the elasticity of male labour supply to firm i $\widehat{e}_i^m$ is higher than the female labour supply elasticity $\widehat{e}_i^f$. The equilibrium differential in male and female labour supply elasticities to firm i $\Delta_{e,i} := \widehat{e}_i^m - \widehat{e}_i^f$ is given by*

$$\Delta_{e,i} = \frac{\phi_i}{\left(\frac{1}{3}\phi_i - \frac{1}{3}\phi_j + \underline{t}\right)\left(\frac{1}{3}\phi_i - \frac{1}{3}\phi_j + \frac{\overline{t}\underline{t}}{\eta \underline{t} + (1-\eta)\overline{t}}\right)} \Delta_w > 0 \qquad (5.17)$$

and differs among firms if and only if $\phi_0 \neq \phi_1$, where $i, j = 0, 1$ and $j \neq i$. It is proportional to the wage differential and strictly increasing both in the travel cost of high-travel-cost women and their share among female workers.

Proof. See Appendix A.10. ∎

First of all, it is interesting to note that women's labour supply to the firm is less elastic than men's even though both women and men supply labour inelastically at the level of the market (provided participation). This affirms theoretically the importance of distinguishing market- from firm-level labour supply when investigating firms' potential to engage in wage discrimination due to monopsonistic wage-setting power. Furthermore, the proportionality of the wage and the elasticity differential has an important consequence: In this model, the wage and the

---

[22] One might ask whether this sort of wage discrimination is a long-run equilibrium outcome. If firms choose wages once-for-all, an assumption typically made in search-theoretic models used to analyse oligopsonistic labour markets, such as the model by Burdett and Mortensen (1998), and quite reasonable an assumption in a steady-state environment (cf. Coles, 2001), the gender pay gap from Corollary 5.1 obviously is a long-run outcome. Things get more complicated if we allow for (infinitely) repeated interaction between employers. Analogously to the large tacit collusion literature (e.g., Friedman, 1971; 1983, pp. 123–134; Ivaldi et al., 2007), there might be feasible collusive wage offers in this case, where women whose reservation incomes are higher than men's (in terms of the wage offered plus the travel cost for high-travel-cost women) get a higher wage than men in order to guarantee their participation. We do not want to go into details, but note the following: If tacit collusion does not work, then the gender pay gap from Corollary 5.1 appears every period and is therefore again a long-run outcome.

5.2 The Model

elasticity differential are two sides of the same coin, which is clearly in line with Robinsonian discrimination. Moreover, we get an explanation why elasticities of men and women might differ, namely due to differences in mobility arising from differences in travel costs, which are the underlying force of both the wage and the elasticity differences.[23]

Eventually, one might also ask which firm employs more women relative to men. Let τ_i denote the number of firm i's female workers relative to its male workers in equilibrium. That is, $\tau_i := L_i^f(\widehat{w}_i^f, \widehat{w}_j^f)/L_i^m(\widehat{w}_i^m, \widehat{w}_j^m)$. The following corollary answers this question.

Corollary 5.3 (Equilibrium Job Location of Female Workers). *The higher is firm i's marginal revenue product of labour ϕ_i, the lower is its number of female relative to male workers in equilibrium τ_i, where $i = 0, 1$. In particular, this means that the more productive firm employs less women relative to men than its less productive competitor.*

Proof. Inserting (5.12) and (5.13) into (5.5) and (5.6) we have

$$\tau_i = \frac{[\eta \underline{t} + (1-\eta)\bar{t}]\left(\frac{1}{3}\phi_i - \frac{1}{3}\phi_j + \frac{\bar{t}\underline{t}}{\eta \underline{t} + (1-\eta)\bar{t}}\right)}{\mu \bar{t}\left(\frac{1}{3}\phi_i - \frac{1}{3}\phi_j + \underline{t}\right)}, \tag{5.18}$$

where $i, j = 0, 1$ and $j \neq i$. The partial derivative of τ_i with respect to ϕ_i is given by

$$\frac{\partial \tau_i}{\partial \phi_i} = -\frac{\eta \underline{t}(\bar{t} - \underline{t})}{3\mu \bar{t}\left(\frac{1}{3}\phi_i - \frac{1}{3}\phi_j + \underline{t}\right)^2} < 0, \tag{5.19}$$

so that τ_i decreases as ϕ_i increases. Since $\tau_0 = \tau_1$ holds if and only if $\phi_0 = \phi_1$, this implies that $\tau_i < \tau_j$ if and only if $\phi_i > \phi_j$. ∎

The intuition behind this result is rather straightforward. From Proposition 5.1 we know that the more productive firm pays higher wages to both men and women and therefore employs more workers from both groups, which reflects the aforementioned employer size–wage effect. Moreover, we know from Corollary 5.2 that women's (average) labour supply to the firm is less elastic than men's, so that the employer size–wage effect is more pronounced for male workers. Hence, the higher

---

[23] One objection that could be raised against our reasoning is that in the long run women may move, so that their firm-level labour supply becomes more elastic and discrimination cannot prevail. The dynamic analyses presented by Schlicht (1982), Boal and Ransom (1997), and Manning (2003a), however, make clear that this argument is invalid. In Chapter 7, for instance, we will demonstrate that in a dynamic model of monopsony the proportionate gap between workers' marginal revenue product and their wage is a weighted average of the inverse short-run and long-run firm-level labour supply elasticities, where the former's weight is the firm's discount factor (see Proposition 7.1). If thus workers, both men and women, move in the long run, so that the long-run elasticity tends to infinity for both groups, and firms discount future profits, women still get lower wages. The reason for this is simply their lower short-run elasticity which stems from their lower average short-term mobility.

wages paid by the more productive firm raise men's labour supply to this firm to a greater extent than women's. And this, in turn, translates into a lower share of women among the more productive firm's workers. The results from Corollary 5.3 add another hypothesis that can be tested empirically: We would expect that more productive firms have a lower share of women in their workforce.

5.3 Conclusions

The model derived presents a Robinsonian explanation of the gender pay gap based on a simplified dyopsony version of the short-run model from Chapter 3 allowing for firm and worker heterogeneity. Equally productive women and men are located at different places and supply labour inelastically at the level of the market (provided participation), while employers with potentially different productivity levels exist only at two locations. Therefore, female and male workers commute and face travel cost to do so, where we assume that a share of the female workers faces higher travel cost than men. Employers who offer wages separately to men and women exploit the fact that on average women are less inclined to commute than men (that is, that the wage competition among employers for female workers is less fierce) and pay lower wages to women than to men in equilibrium. Since employers do not distinguish low- from high-travel-cost women, even low-travel-cost women who do not differ from men in their behaviour are affected and earn lower wages due to statistical (i.e., third-degree) discrimination. Furthermore, both men and women earn less than their marginal revenue products because firms' different locations give rise to some monopsony power.

That women are less inclined to commute than men is reflected in their lower firm-level aggregate labour supply elasticity. Therefore, gender differences in wages and in firm-level aggregate labour supply elasticities are two sides of the same coin, viz. women's higher average travel cost. This, in turn, means that the difference in travel cost and thus in mobility represents the driving force of Robinsonian discrimination in this model.[24] This Robinsonian approach to the gender pay gap has the virtue of explaining it in lines of firms' profit maximisation. Hence, this reasoning does not suffer from the need to relax the assumption of firms' profit-maximising behaviour because there are no assumptions like a Beckerian distaste parameter involved. As firms do profit from paying lower wages to women, they behave like

---

[24] We thus have given a spatial 'new' monopsony re-formulation of Robinsonian discrimination in line with earlier contributions by Madden (1977*a*; 1977*b*): 'Women workers' shorter average length work trips are due to their household responsibilities and to their occupational structure (which is also chosen relative to family constraints). It is conceivable that the same household responsibilities which account for married women's shorter work trips also make them less sensitive to wage differentials between near and more distant employers, resulting in women workers having a relatively less wage-elastic spatial labor supply curve than men workers.' (Madden, 1977*a*, p. 162)

5.3 Conclusions

perfectly rational profit maximisers when discriminating against women. Since such a kind of (statistical) discrimination is not costly, we argue that it also is more likely to survive in the long run.[25]

Additionally, the model generates several hypotheses that can be tested empirically: Firstly, the more productive firm pays higher wages to both men and women and therefore employs more workers from both groups and earns higher profits. The model is thus consistent with the empirical regularity of an employer size–wage effect and a positive correlation between firms' productivity and wages and between firms' profits and wages in equilibrium. Second, the model predicts that wage differentials must be accompanied by differences in firm-level labour supply elasticities (not in market-level individual labour supply elasticities), where women get paid less if and only if they are the less elastic group from the firm's point of view. As we will see in Chapter 9, these differences are indeed found empirically. Third, the model predicts that the share of women in the workforce is lower for more productive firms, which can be tested empirically, too.

As we noted earlier, the driving force of the gender pay gap in this model is given by the difference in travel cost between high-travel-cost women and men and the resulting lower mobility of women on average. And we argued that one of the most convincing reasons for this difference is women's dominant role in housework, especially in rearing children. In the model, there are two variables that directly affect the magnitude of the gender pay gap: the share of high-travel-cost women among female workers and the travel cost of high-travel-cost women. Reducing one of these variables decreases as well the wage differential between men and women as the elasticity differential. Therefore, governments may wish to reduce one or both of these variables, for example, by subsidising or providing additional child care facilities.[26] Hence, this model highlights the role of gender-specific differences in

---

[25] Another objection that could be raised against this sort of reasoning is that equal pay legislation, which is present in many countries that, notwithstanding, experience significant gender pay gaps, should remove Robinsonian *wage* discrimination entirely. While this may be true in the literal sense, 'employers may try to separate the labour force more "objectively" by designing job amenities and job descriptions in such a way to produce self-selection of women into so-called "women's jobs". Working conditions for career jobs can be made incompatible for the lifestyle of many women, who are in charge of child rearing; part-time work can be paid less; seniority wage profiles make work interruptions more costly.' (Winter-Ebmer, 1995, p. 851) An interesting example of gender wage discrimination trough initial job assignments and promotions is discussed by Ransom and Oaxaca (2005; 2008).

[26] These remarks, though, are not intended as a normative recommendation to governments to actually pursue the sketched policies. Neither do we want to imply (nor do we actually think) that governments have the policy instruments for easily fine-tuning these variables. Nor do we think that these two variables of the model are the only influential determinants in reality and that our model in its present form is suited for answering normative questions. We rather see our model as a quite convincing exponent of qualitative pattern prediction in the sense propagated by von Hayek (1967; 1975), the core prediction being that lower gender differences in mobility should reduce the ability of employers to discriminate against women and thus lower actual discrimination if firms actually exercised their monopsony power. Concerning government policies, it just predicts qualitatively that policies that enhance women's mobility are likely to reduce the gender pay gap.

mobility patterns as one explanation for the gender pay gap and gives an argument why augmenting women's mobility is likely to reduce this gap.[27] Note that this argument is also able to provide an explanation for the narrowing of the gap over the last decades, viz. that women's mobility has partly caught up to men's.

Though we feel confident that this model is able to give a re-formulation of Robinsonian discrimination in line with the growing 'new' monopsony literature that is more convincing than its original formulation within the simple monopsony model with only one employer, the model is still highly stylised. For instance, workers' labour supply behaviour at the market level is modelled in a very rudimentary way just as a participation decision, whereas the amount of labour supplied by the individual worker is fixed. Similarly, we dealt with an environment with only two employers. Moreover, the model rests on the strong assumption of women being perfect substitutes to men, abstracting from other differences than those in travel cost likely to worsen women's labour market outcomes further. While we do not want to relax the latter assumption, the results derived earlier in Chapters 3 and 4 enable us to say something about potential generalisations and the obtained outcome when relaxing some of the other assumptions.

The crucial feature of the presented explanation of the gender pay gap is that equilibrium wages are lower in equilibrium for the group that faces higher travel cost (in segmented labour markets). Put differently, we need a negative comparative static effect of an increase in the travel cost on the equilibrium wage. In the short-run model presented in Chapter 3, we considered a labour market consisting of many employers and elastic individual labour supply, where the latter had two possible reasons: workers supply labour elastically (given participation) or workers differ in their reservation incomes. We found that the equilibrium wage falls if the travel cost rises and if either of the following conditions are met: competition is sufficiently fierce (that is, firms are distributed sufficiently densely in economic space and behave non-collusively) or individual labour supply is sufficiently elastic (i.e., log-linear or strictly log-convex). In the long-run model from Chapter 4, we additionally allowed for free entry and exit of firms and showed that the same conditions are sufficient for the existence of a negative comparative static effect of an increase in the travel cost on the long-run equilibrium wage. Note that sufficiently fierce competition means now that the fixed costs have to be sufficiently low, so that

---

It is not intended to give a quantifiable research lab for the politician to evaluate his or her policies in Lucas's (1980) sense nor to give normative recommendations.

[27] The model is also consistent with the persistence of a gender pay gap that originally might have been caused by traditional norms. Household optimisation would lead to more housework by women because women earning less than men may have lower opportunity cost when engaging in household production. If women's lower wages were the reason for high-travel-cost women's more pronounced affiliation to housework and thus for their higher travel cost, which in turn – as we have seen – results in a gender pay gap for all women due to Robinsonian discrimination, this could explain the persistence of women's more prominent role in household production even if the influence of traditional norms may have vanished. While traditional norms might have been the reason for this in the past, today household optimisation would have the same consequence. Hence, this would constitute some kind of a self-fulfilling feedback mechanism.

5.3 Conclusions

in the zero-profit equilibrium enough firms populate the labour market to generate the required strength of competition. Hence, in all these instances, our Robinsonian explanation of the gender pay gap resting on gender-specific differences in travel costs remains valid.

Of course, this discussion implicitly assumes that women and men have the same individual labour supply functions and therefore the same market-level labour supply elasticities. If women's market-level labour supply, however, is more elastic than men's, this also raises women's firm-level labour supply elasticity. Whether women's firm-level labour supply elasticity is lower than men's depends on whether the elasticity-reducing impact of higher female travel cost dominates over the elasticity-enhancing effect of more elastic market-level female labour supply. This is an empirical question. Since the gender differences in market-level labour supply elasticities typically found in the literature are not very large, this seems to be not too implausible to hold, so that our Robinsonian approach to discrimination might indeed have empirical relevance. This will be affirmed further in Chapter 9 where we shall investigate empirically whether women's labour supply to the firm is actually less elastic than men's.

We therefore conclude that our spatial monopsony variant of the Robinsonian explanation of the gender pay gap is a fairly robust outcome, not hinging on the restrictive assumptions concerning individual labour supply, the number of firms, the mode of competition, and the absence of competitive entry imposed in Section 5.2 merely for analytical convenience. In Chapter 6, we will combine the reasoning presented here with the constant long-run spatial monopsony model from Section 4.6 to deduce some regional implications for the gender pay gap. These implications will be tested empirically to access the model's success in pattern prediction. After that, we shall turn to a different strand of the 'new' monopsony literature, viz. equilibrium search models with wage posting. Investigating these models of dynamic monopsony will be of particular interest because the model by Burdett and Mortensen (1998) presented in Chapter 8 will enable us to investigate empirically whether women's labour supply to the firm is indeed less elastic than men's. Since this will turn out to be the case, we shall argue that much more tribute should be paid to Robinsonian discrimination as an alternative monopsonistic explanation of the gender pay gap.

Chapter 6
Spatial Monopsony and Regional Differences in the Gender Pay Gap[1]

While most of the empirical literature on the gender pay gap focusses on the variation of the gender pay gap between countries and its evolution over time, an aspect that has attracted far less attention is the regional variation of the gap *within* the same country. Though many studies use regional information as control variables in the estimations, only few explicitly deal with the gap's regional dimension.[2] However, to our knowledge, there has been made no attempt to systematically investigate regional differences in the gender pay gap and their evolution over time. What is more, there seems to be no *economic* theory around that readily explains why there should be such differences. We intend to remove both of these omissions.

In Chapter 5, we presented a spatial monopsony explanation of the gender pay gap, where women's lower average mobility causes firms to engage in third-degree wage discrimination *à la* Robinson. This spatial reasoning can be readily used to think about the regional dimension of the gender pay gap. In the following, we will employ the long-run spatial monopsony model with constant individual labour supply and HS conjectures from Section 4.6.1. Other than the short-run spatial dyopsony model employed in Chapter 5, this model allows for free entry of firms and therefore causes more profitable labour markets to be populated by more firms. This will turn out to be crucial below, as we will argue that economic hot spots, i.e., large metropolitan areas, have thicker labour markets giving rise to a more competitive environment. And this higher degree of competition, in turn, not only

---

[1] This chapter heavily draws on joint work with Marion König and Joachim Möller published as Hirsch *et al.* (2009a).

[2] Exceptions include Blien and Mederer (1998), who examine regional differences in the gender pay gap in Germany based on the wage curve approach, and McCall (1998), who deals with the relation between regional restructuring and gender wage differentials in the U.S. For the UK, Phimister (2005) studies differences in urban wage premia by gender, while Robinson (2005) analyses the effect of the national minimum wage on the gender pay gap across regions. For Canada, Olfert and Moebis (2006) examine the different impact of rural and urban environments on gender occupational segregation. The two studies that are closest to our investigation are Loureiro *et al.* (2004), who do not find regional differences in the gender pay gap in Brazil, and Busch and Holst (2008), who find lower gaps in cities than in rural areas for Germany in 2005.

pushes both female and male workers' wages but also constrains employers' ability to engage in Robinsonian discrimination.[3]

6.1 Theoretical Considerations

We now turn to the long-run spatial monopsony model with constant individual labour supply and HS conjectures as laid out in Section 4.6.1, where again the basic assumptions from Section 3.1 are assumed to hold. According to equation (4.34), the long-run equilibrium wage is given by

$$w_{HS} = \phi - \sqrt{\frac{ft}{D}}. \qquad (6.1)$$

Now, suppose we had two segmented labour markets, where the one labour market is more densely populated by workers, so that $D^1 > D^0$. Inspection of (6.1) reveals that the long-run equilibrium wage in the more densely populated labour market is higher, i.e., $w_{HS}^1 > w_{HS}^0$. Algebraically, we have $\partial w_{HS}/\partial D > 0$, which follows at once from partial differentiation of (6.1). Intuitively, the higher worker density makes the labour market more profitable for firms, so that more firms enter the market. This reduces the distance between firms and therefore increases the competition among them, so that workers' wage rises. Hence, the model predicts that workers earn higher wages in more densely populated labour markets.[4]

In the next step, we adopt the idea presented and developed in Chapter 5 and assume that women face higher (average) travel cost than men, *ceteris paribus*. The *ceteris paribus* clause in particular means that we assume men and women to be perfect substitutes in production and to exhibit the same labour supply behaviour (i.e., they just decide on whether to participate given some reservation income, see the discussion in Section 5.2). Assume further that employers are free to offer wages separately to men and women, so that they supply labour on segregated labour

---

[3] One could also argue that hot spots are trend-setters with more progressive environments and less discriminatory employers leading to less Beckerian discrimination. This kind of reasoning, however, suffers from several shortcomings (see the discussion in Section 5.1). In particular, Beckerian discrimination is costly for employers and should therefore be competed away in the long run if labour markets are sufficiently competitive. Furthermore, '[t]he attitudes which produce discriminatory behavior are taken as given. There is no consideration of whether the economic system fosters these attitudes.' (Madden, 1977b, p. 102) Put drastically, this reasoning arrives at the conclusion of less discrimination in economic hot spots by just assuming it. For this reason, we do not think that this sort of argument is able to contribute much to our (economic) understanding of potential regional variation in the gender pay gap.

[4] For a diagrammatic exposition of this argument, see Figure 4.21 and the discussion of the model's comparative statics in Section 4.6.1.

6.1 Theoretical Considerations

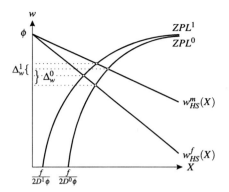

Fig. 6.1 The gender wage differentials Δ_w^1 and Δ_w^0 for segmented female and male labour markets with worker densities D^1 and D^0 with $D^1 > D^0$

markets.[5] Let t^f denote female and t^m male workers' travel cost per unit distance. Inspection of (6.1) reveals that the long-run equilibrium wage is lower for female than male workers, i.e., $w_{HS}^f < w_{HS}^m$. Algebraically, we have $\partial w_{HS}/\partial t < 0$, which follows at once from partial differentiation of (6.1). Intuitively, the higher travel cost reduces competition among firms because economic space – the source of firms' wage-setting power in this framework – becomes more relevant in the female labour market. The model thus predicts that women should earn less than men, i.e., we have a long-run equilibrium gender pay gap. Women's wage is lower because firms exploit the gender difference in the travel cost to exert Robinsonian discrimination.[6]

Finally, we are interested in the question whether the gender pay gap is higher or lower in more densely populated labour markets. Algebraically, this is readily answered by partially differentiating (6.1) to find $\partial^2 w_{HS}/\partial D \partial t > 0$. That is, the higher the worker density, the lower is the gender wage differential Δ_w. Diagrammatically, this can be seen by combining the two shifts from Figures 4.21 and 4.22 on page 86 to arrive at Figure 6.1: The wage differential in the more densely populated labour market Δ_w^1 is smaller than the one in the less densely populated Δ_w^0 because the WSC in the female labour market is steeper than its male counterpart. Furthermore, since wages are higher in more densely populated labour markets, this also implies that the gender pay gap $\Delta_{w\%}$ is lower in these markets, i.e., $\Delta_{w\%}^1 < \Delta_{w\%}^0$. We thus get another prediction from the model: The gender pay gap should be higher in less densely populated labour markets. Intuitively, more densely populated labour markets are more profitable ones. This causes competitive entry of firms and therefore constrains employers' monopsony power over both

---

[5] Note that we consider separate labour markets for women and men at this stage for expositional convenience. It is straightforward to extend the long-run spatial monopsony model with constant individual labour supply to the case of two groups of workers with different travel cost, which would be along the lines of Chapter 5. Whilst this would complicate the analysis, no additional insights are gained. Therefore, we shall not bother in the following to do so but just make use of the simplification of separate labour markets instead.

[6] For a diagrammatic exposition of this argument, see Figure 4.21 and the discussion of the model's comparative statics in Section 4.6.1.

their female and male workers and also limits their ability to engage in Robinsonian discrimination.

To sum up, our simple spatial oligopsony model delivers the following hypotheses:

(H1) We expect workers to earn higher wages in hot spots than in rural areas because the former have thicker labour markets with more competition among employers.
(H2) We conjecture female workers to earn lower wages, *ceteris paribus*, because of their higher average (indirect) travel cost.
(H3) Since we expect gender differences in the travel cost to have become less substantial over time (e.g., women have become more mobile relative to men due to more or better childcare facilities), we suspect the gender pay gap to decline over time as well.
(H4) We expect the gender pay gap to be less pronounced in hot spots than in rural areas because the more competitive environment in hot spots constrains employers' ability to engage in Robinsonian discrimination.

In the following empirical analysis, we will investigate to what extent these four hypotheses generated by the model are affirmed by the data and therefore check the model's success in pattern prediction.[7]

6.2 Empirical Specification

Empirically, the raw gender wage differential is of limited information as it neglects individual heterogeneity, such as gender differences in the human capital endowment. In order to deal with observed heterogeneity, two approaches have been extensively used in the literature. The first approach is to estimate a standard Mincerian (1974) earnings function controlling for individual characteristics reflecting the worker's productivity, such as education and experience, and including a female dummy as regressor. The coefficient of this dummy is then supposed to give the *ceteris paribus* gender pay gap that cannot be explained by differences in workers' productivity. A second, more sophisticated approach, pioneered by Blinder (1973) and Oaxaca (1973), estimates two separate earnings functions for

---

[7] Note that our model is highly stylised in some respects. For instance, workers' labour supply behaviour is modelled simplistically just as a '1–0 decision' with all workers having some reservation income and all workers participating in the equilibrium. It is, however, straightforward to extend the model, in a way presented in Section 4.6.2, to allow for varying participation of workers. While this would yield a positive relationship between workers' wages and their participation rate – and thus, as a corollary to the gender pay gap, an equilibrium gender participation rate differential –, the model's other predictions would remain unaffected. Therefore, we will not consider this extension in detail. Besides, note that the same qualitative results hold when considering GO instead of HS conjectures, as can be seen by considering the GO long-run equilibrium wage as given by equation (4.33).

6.2 Empirical Specification

female and male workers and then decomposes the gender pay gap into an explained part due to different endowments in workers' characteristics and an unexplained part. This well-known Oaxaca–Blinder decomposition and its extensions still serve as the backbone of the gender pay gap literature. In both approaches, the unexplained gender pay gap is typically attributed to discrimination (though gender differences in unobserved characteristics may also contribute to its explanation).

Using exact matching, Ñopo (2008) proposes another non-parametric approach to decompose the gender pay gap into an explained and an unexplained component.[8] The intuitive idea of this empirical strategy is to use male workers with otherwise identical personal characteristics as a comparison group for females. That is, one compares the earnings of a female worker to the earnings of male workers with the same observable characteristics. In analogy to the regression-based decomposition techniques, this approach allows to separate the endowment effect from the overall gender pay gap. The unexplained part is identified by taking the mean over the log gender wage differences of the matched female–male observations and is comparable to the unexplained part of the gender pay gap derived from an Oaxaca–Blinder decomposition based on female characteristics and evaluated at the male coefficients. Technically, the unexplained gender pay gap gained from this exact matching approach is the difference in expected log earnings for female and male workers with the same observable characteristic, i.e.,

$$\widehat{E}[\Delta_{w\%}] = \frac{1}{c} \sum_{x \in S} \left(\widehat{E}[\ln w_i | x, d_i = 1] - \widehat{E}[\ln w_j | x, d_j = 0] \right) \widehat{\Pr}[x | d_i = 1], \quad (6.2)$$

where x is a row vector of observed characteristics, d_i a dummy variable taking on the value one if individual i is female and zero otherwise, c the number of cells containing a given combination of covariates, and S the support of x.[9]

With highly differentiated characteristics, however, the number of cells containing a given combination of covariates becomes prohibitive. Consequently, finding exact matches gets hard, and exact matching turns out to be not viable anymore. To flee this curse of dimensionality, the matching literature has followed Rosenbaum and Rubin (1983) in using the propensity score as a one-dimensional measure of similarity between individuals. In the context of gender pay gaps, Frölich (2007) shows that propensity score matching can serve as a flexible semi-parametric approach to identify the unexplained part of the gap, where the appropriate propensity

---

[8] For details about the matching approach, see Imbens (2004), Angrist and Pischke (2009, pp. 68–91), or Imbens and Wooldridge (2009). Applications of Ñopo's exact matching approach include Djurdjevic and Radyakin (2007) for Switzerland and Black et al. (2008) for the U.S.

[9] In terms of the program evaluation literature, the idea is to find male 'statistical twins' to each female and to calculate the 'average treatment effect on the treated' (ATT) of being female. Of course, this would suggest an inappropriate causal interpretation of the 'treatment' sex. Notwithstanding, the basic principles of matching as a *statistical* approach to deal with heterogeneity in observable characteristics remain valid. For formal definitions of the different average treatment effects, see Imbens (2004) or Imbens and Wooldridge (2009).

score is individual i's fitted conditional probability of being female, i.e., $\widehat{\Pr}[d_i = 1|x_i]$.

The main advantage of this semi-parametric approach is its flexibility. Other than the regression-based decomposition techniques, no functional form is imposed, apart from the specification of the propensity score. But misspecification of the earnings equation could yield misleading results. In particular, using observations where the empirical distributions of females' and males' characteristics substantially differ in their supports S^f and S^m could give biased results if the underlying 'out-of-support' assumption is invalid. As shown by Black et al. (2008) and Ñopo (2008), common support problems yield systematically upward-biased estimates of the unexplained part of the gender pay gap. Using a flexible semi-parametric propensity score matching approach and restricting to observations with a common support $S = S^f \cap S^m$, on the other hand, ensures that only those female and male observations are matched that are actually comparable in terms of their observed characteristics.

In our empirical analysis, we arrive at individuals' propensity score by fitting a probit model for their probability of being female, i.e., $\widehat{\Pr}[d_i = 1|x_i] = \Phi(x_i\widehat{\beta})$ with the estimated column vector of coefficients $\widehat{\beta}$ and the c.d.f. of the standard normal distribution Φ.[10] As matching variables we use a large number of individual characteristics. We include actual on-the-job experience and its square as well as tenure and its square as regressors in the probit model. Furthermore, we add 13 dummies for occupation classes, four job position dummies, three dummies for pre-labour market education, seven establishment size dummies, a set of industry affiliation dummies, and a variable reporting the length of employment per year.[11] At this stage, it should be mentioned that lower gender pay gaps and higher wages in hot spots may feed back differently on female and male workers' decision where to live and work. This, in turn, would introduce an endogeneity problem. To alleviate this problem, we include a dummy for the type of region of first appearance in the labour market as additional matching variable. As a robustness check, we will also repeat the following analysis excluding those individuals that changed their type of region after their first appearance on the labour market.[12]

After fitting the propensity score, the next step is to choose a 'similarity distance' to match every female observation with comparable male observations based on the individual propensity score. For instance, n-nearest neighbour matching with replacement compares each female observation with its n nearest neighbours (in terms of their propensity score) among the male observations that lie in the common support S. For $n = 1$ we arrive at nearest neighbour matching with replacement.

---

[10] For details about binary response models, such as probit and logit models, see Wooldridge (2002, pp. 453–497), Davidson and MacKinnon (2004, pp. 451–465), and Cameron and Trivedi (2005, pp. 463–487).

[11] Note that we cannot control for the worker's marital status and number of children due to data constraints, see footnote 17 on page 120.

[12] Unfortunately, we cannot control for endogenous migration between different types of regions before individuals' labour market entrance as we do not have such pre-labour market information.

6.3 Data

The individual unexplained gender pay gap is then estimated as

$$\widehat{\Delta}_{w\%,i} = \ln w_i - \ln w_{j(i)}, \tag{6.3}$$

where $j(i)$ is the nearest male observation in the common support, i.e.,

$$j(i) = \underset{j \mid x_j \in S}{\arg\min} \left| \widehat{\Pr}[d_i = 1 \mid x_i, d_i = 1] - \widehat{\Pr}[d_j = 1 \mid x_j, d_j = 0] \right| \tag{6.4}$$

with $x_i \in S$. The expected unexplained gender pay gap in the sample is then estimated simply as

$$\widehat{E}[\Delta_{w\%}] = \frac{1}{I} \sum_{i=1}^{I} \widehat{\Delta}_{\%,i}, \tag{6.5}$$

where I denotes the total number of matched females.

Of course, this is not the only way to form female–male matches. In the following, we will use nearest neighbour matching without replacement and kernel matching. While the former uses every male observation only once and is therefore, arguably, the most restrictive procedure, kernel matching utilises all male observations within the common support for every female observation. It does so by attaching lower weights to more distant observations (in terms of their propensity score), where the weights follow from a kernel estimate of the characteristics distribution.[13] The corresponding standard errors and confidence intervals are computed using bootstrapping with 100 replications.[14] As a check of robustness, we will also apply the standard Oaxaca–Blinder decomposition technique.

To identify differences in the unexplained component of the gender pay gap between hot spots and rural areas, we will estimate $E[\Delta_{w\%}]$ for both types of regions separately. Comparing the resulting estimates, we will argue that they differ if their bootstrapped confidence intervals do not overlap. But before we will put this into practice, we have to describe our data set used.

6.3 Data

In the following, we shall use social security data from the Institute for Employment Research (*Institut für Arbeitsmarkt- und Berufsforschung*, IAB). Our data set is the Regional File of the IAB Employment Samples (IAB-REG) which is a 2 per cent random sample from the employment register of Germany's Federal Employment

---

[13] Since these two approaches can be regarded as the two 'extremes' of possible matching procedures, it may be interesting to consider a somewhere-in-between procedure as well. Therefore, we will also apply three-nearest neighbour matching with replacement, results of which are reported in Appendix Figure A.1 on page 229.
[14] For details about bootstrap methods, see, e.g., Cameron and Trivedi (2005, pp. 357–382).

Agency (*Bundesagentur für Arbeit*).[15] The German social security system requires firms to record the stock of workers at least at the beginning and the end of each year. Additionally, all changes in employment relationships within the year (e.g., hirings, quits, and dismissals) have to be reported with the exact information on the date when the change occurred. Therefore, the employment register traces detailed histories for each worker's time in covered employment as well as spells of unemployment for which the worker received unemployment benefits.[16] This large data set ranges from 1975 to 2004 and includes all workers, salaried employees, and trainees obliged to pay social security contributions. All in all, it covers more than 80 per cent of all those employed. Since they are not covered by social security, civil servants, family workers, and self-employed are not included. As misreporting leads to sanctions for the employer, the information on covered employment and earnings is highly reliable.

The data include, among others things, information for every employee on the daily gross wage, censored at the social security contribution ceiling, on several individual, and on some establishment characteristics. Characteristics contained are, among others, the worker's age, skill level, sex, job status, occupation, and nationality and the employer's industry, location at the district level, and establishment size.[17] Not included, however, is a variable with quantitative information on the hours worked. Although the data set comprises a qualitative variable distinguishing between full-time and two sorts of part-time work, this limits the information value of the daily gross wages contained in the data because we cannot infer workers' wage rate from them. Hence, we restrict our sample to individuals working full time in order to account for the problem of missing working hours information.[18]

In the following empirical analysis, we restrict our sample to individuals in western Germany who are employed full time on the 30th of June in each year. Additionally, we exclude part-time workers, home workers, trainees, and spells of minor employment. Since we argue that new social trends and especially changes in gender mobility patterns are first visible for entrants in the labour market and young workers, we restrict our sample to individuals between 25 and 34 years old. The lower bound ensures that most individuals have completed their education. Furthermore, the upper bound additionally alleviates a problem with the wage data,

---

[15] The data are briefly described in Bender *et al.* (2000) and in more detail in Bender *et al.* (1996).

[16] Episodes of unemployment during which the worker has no entitlement to unemployment benefits are not reported and thus cannot be distinguished from periods of non-participation in the labour market.

[17] Unfortunately, the data include information on the worker's marital status and number of children only due to notifications made in the case of changes in employment that are relevant according to benefit entitlement rules. Using this information would clearly introduce a severe selectivity problem. Consequently, we will not be able to use it in the following analysis.

[18] One might argue that higher daily earnings of male workers could be the consequence of gender differences in hours worked. Restricting to full-time employees again alleviates this potential problem. Moreover, this explanation would be at odds with differences in the gender pay gap between hot spots and rural areas because taking differences should eliminate this working hours effect (provided the gender distribution of working hours is sufficiently similar between full-time workers in the two types of regions).

6.3 Data

viz. daily gross wages are censored at the social security contribution ceiling. Since this censoring problem bites only for high-wage observations, we exclude high-skilled workers, i.e., workers with higher education (*Abitur*, which is the German equivalent to A-levels or graduation from high school) and a completed vocational training or with a university type of education. Together, the age restriction and the exclusion of high-skilled workers minimise the problem of censored wages as the number of top-coded observations in our sample is negligible.[19]

We are aware of possible job instability for female workers. Therefore, we construct a series of actual rather than potential experience on the job, where only periods of active employment are counted.[20] In a similar way, a measure of tenure is calculated as the total time period worked within the same firm.

Another limitation in the data set is that, despite a high precision for the earnings variable, information on personal characteristics might suffer from reporting errors. This could especially affect the skill variables. Several attempts have been made to correct the qualification information contained in IAB-REG, most notably the widely applied approach by Fitzenberger *et al.* (2006). Notwithstanding, we will follow a different route here: For most observations the data cover the complete training, employment, and unemployment history. Therefore, the individual skill level can be checked by taking all these spells into account. We apply the following procedure: Cases where the skill level is almost unambiguous according to the employment histories are used to fit a logit model for the conditional probability of having a certain skill level. In a next step, using the model's estimated coefficients, this probability is predicted for the 'uncertain' cases given the full set of information on the individual's employment history. Finally, we scan the whole employment history for each individual including the imputed skill level formed from the results of the logit estimations in order to check for consistency and to correct the qualifications accordingly.

Eventually, for the assignment of districts to rural areas and hot spots we use a classification scheme developed by the German Federal Office for Building and Regional Planning (*Bundesamt für Bauwesen und Raumordnung*, BBR). This scheme distinguishes between areas with large agglomerations, areas with features of conurbation, and areas of rural character, each of these again being subdivided into different groups. All in all, it differentiates between nine types of regions (districts) at the NUTS (*nomenclature des unités territoriales statistiques*) 3 level according to their population density and accessibility. Economic *hot spots* are defined as western Germany's eight biggest metropolitan areas: Cologne, Dortmund, Düsseldorf, Essen, Frankfurt, Hamburg, Munich, and Stuttgart. All hot spots are metropolitan core cities (BBR type 1). As *rural areas* we choose all districts with BBR types 7 to 9 (see Figure 6.2 on the following page).[21]

---

[19] In our sample, only 2.5 per cent of all observations contain censored wages. This number is slightly higher for men (3.3 per cent) than for women (0.9 per cent) and also for hot spots (4.3 per cent) than for rural areas (0.9 per cent).

[20] Note, however, that for observations prior to 1988 the measure of actual experience might be biased due to left censoring of employment spells in the data.

[21] BBR type 7 consists of rural districts in regions with intermediate agglomeration. BBR type 8 and 9 are made of urbanised and rural districts in regions of rural character.

122   6 Spatial Monopsony and Regional Differences in the Gender Pay Gap

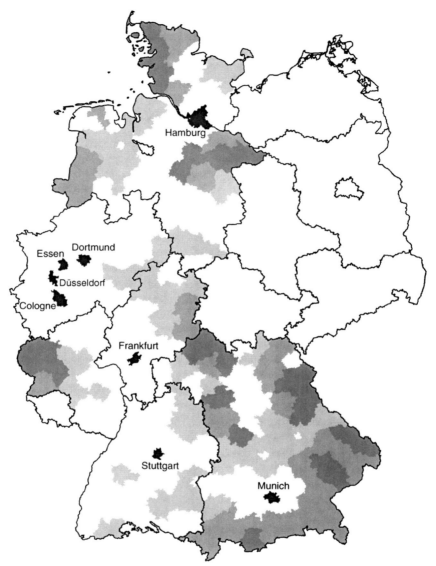

Notes: Hot spots are defined as the eight biggest metropolitan areas in western Germany coloured in black. The gray areas display the rural areas characterised by BBR types 7 to 9.

Fig. 6.2 Hot spots and rural areas

6.4 Descriptive Evidence

First of all, we present some descriptive evidence. The upper graph in Figure 6.3 shows a scatter plot of average gross daily wages of full-time employed young females and males of the 327 western German NUTS 3 regions in 2004 and their

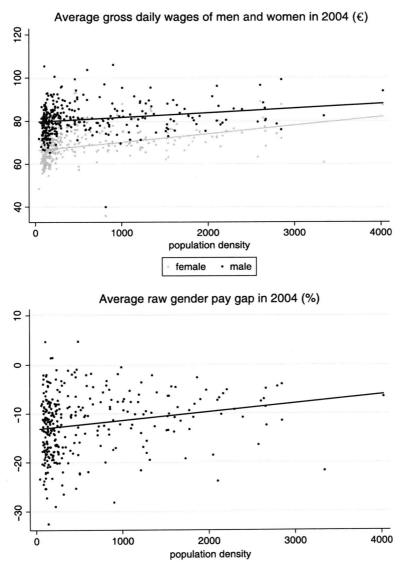

Fig. 6.3 Average wages and raw gender pay gaps at the NUTS 3 regional level by population density (the respective solid lines are trend lines from a univariate regression)

population density (measured as population per square kilometre) including trend lines. Three things are noteworthy: Firstly, the average wage is rising in the population density both for males and females. This is in line with our first hypothesis that workers earn higher wages in more densely populated labour markets. Second, the average wage is higher for males than for females and thus points at a gender pay gap, our second hypothesis. Third, the trend line for females appears to be steeper than that for males. This level effect points at a lower wage differential in hot spots than in rural areas and therefore, in particular, at a lower gender pay gap. In the lower graph of Figure 6.3, we see that the average raw gender pay gap is indeed decreasing (in absolute value) in the population density. Put differently, when not controlling for individual characteristics, the gap is more pronounced in rural areas than in cities. This is consistent with our fourth hypothesis that the gender pay gap should be lower in hot spots.

Figure 6.4 shows the evolution of the average raw gender pay gaps in hot spots and rural areas from 1975 to 2004. It is worth mentioning that both gaps are substantially declining over time by almost 16 percentage points. While women in rural areas (hot spots) earned on average about 38 per cent (25 per cent) less than men in 1975, this pay gap has narrowed to 22 per cent (9 per cent) in 2004. What is more, the difference in the gaps between hot spots and rural areas remained strikingly stable during this long period of time, oscillating around 13 percentage points. While the reduction in the gaps in both hot spots and rural areas is in line with our third hypothesis of declining gender pay gaps over time, the latter finding is consistent with our fourth hypothesis at the heart of our investigation, viz. that the gender pay gap should be lower in hot spots than in rural areas.

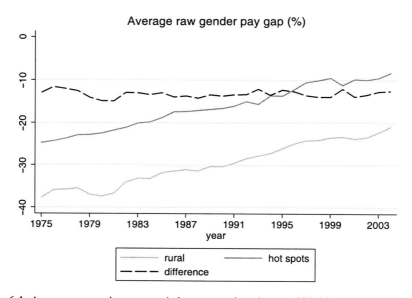

Fig. 6.4 Average raw gender pay gaps in hot spots and rural areas 1975–2004

6.5 Multivariate Evidence

While it is reassuring to see that there is supportive descriptive evidence to all our hypotheses, we now turn to our multivariate results. As laid out in detail in Section 6.2, we will in the following present estimates gained from a semi-parametric propensity score matching approach to the unexplained part of the gender pay gap as put forward by Frölich (2007). We use both nearest neighbour matching without replacement and kernel matching as the most and least restrictive methods in terms of the number of male observations used to create a 'synthetic' male comparison observation for each female observation in the common support of observed characteristics.[22] For each of the years 1975 to 2004 we estimate the unexplained gender pay gap in both hot spots and rural areas using nearest neighbour and kernel matching. The corresponding standard errors and confidence intervals are calculated using bootstrapping with 100 replications. The results obtained from nearest neighbour matching are shown in Figure 6.5 on the next page, those obtained from kernel matching in Figure 6.6 on the following page, where the thin dashed lines represent the respective 95 per cent confidence bands. Since the results of both approaches are very similar, we shall discuss them simultaneously.[23]

First of all, our second hypothesis is clearly confirmed. Young full-time employed females earn significantly less than males with the same (observed) characteristics. This even holds after controlling for experience, tenure, education, job position, occupation, establishment size, industry, length of employment, and region of first entrance in the labour market.[24] And this holds both in economic hot spots and rural areas.

Second, while this unexplained pay gap has narrowed considerably in both types of regions during our observation period, it is still of substantial size. In the mid-1970s, it was about 35 per cent (25 per cent) in rural areas (hot spots) and only 22 per cent (15 per cent) at the beginning of the new millennium. This gradual

---

[22] Since nearest neighbour matching uses male observations only once to form a comparison observation for females, there were clearly more female observations where no male could be matched than with the other matching methods. In this case, the results are only valid for the matched individuals. On the other hand, the resulting matched female–male observations were highly balanced with indistinguishable observed characteristics in nearly all cases, while this balancing property was satisfied to a lesser degree by the samples obtained from the less restrictive matching methods. Since results proved to be highly robust across specifications, we conclude that neither the absence of perfect balancing nor external validity seems to be a problem.

[23] Note that basically the same results are found when using three nearest neighbour matching with replacement, results of which are shown in Appendix Figure A.1 on page 229.

[24] Note that this unexplained pay gap may not only be due to discrimination but also due to differences in unobserved characteristics which we cannot control for. Therefore, this unexplained gap is likely to overestimate the impact of discrimination. Though one could argue that differences in unobservables would net out when taking differences between the two types of region if unobservables were equally distributed between hot spots and rural areas, we will not do so as this seems to be a far-fetched assumption in our eyes.

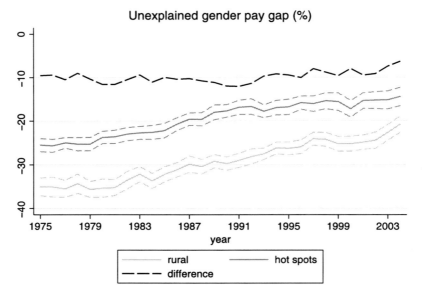

Fig. 6.5 Unexplained gender pay gaps in hot spots and rural areas 1975–2004 using nearest neighbour matching without replacement (the thin dashed lines represent the respective 95 per cent confidence bands)

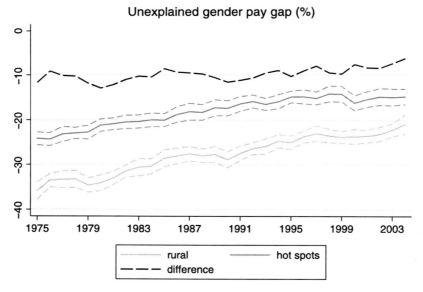

Fig. 6.6 Unexplained gender pay gaps in hot spots and rural areas 1975–2004 using kernel matching (the thin dashed lines represent the respective 95 per cent confidence bands)

6.5 Multivariate Evidence

decline is highly supportive to our third hypothesis. Moreover, this strikingly parallel development in both types of regions points at our next finding.

Third, and most importantly, there is a considerable difference between rural areas and hot spots. In each of the 30 years considered, the gender pay gap is smaller in hot spots than in rural areas. While this difference is statistically significant throughout, it is also economically significant: The unexplained part of the gender pay gap is about 10 percentage points lower in hot spots than in rural areas. What is more, this difference is remarkably stable over time (with a small decline in the point estimates in the last two years of observation) and therefore clearly affirms our fourth hypothesis.

Basically, the same picture arises when applying the standard Oaxaca–Blinder decomposition technique, results of which are shown in Figure 6.7. The same also holds when only those individuals are included in the analysis who stayed in the same regional type of first appearance in the labour market (see Appendix Figure A.2 on page 230). As argued above, this robustness check indicates that the endogeneity problem arising because individuals can choose to live and work in a hot spot is only of minor importance in this context.[25]

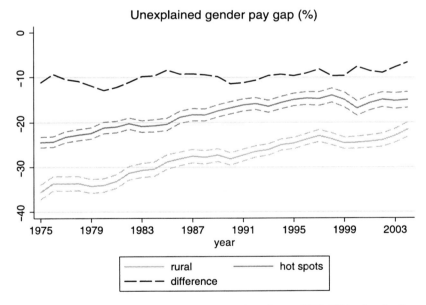

Fig. 6.7 Unexplained gender pay gaps in hot spots and rural areas 1975–2004 using the Oaxaca–Blinder decomposition (the thin dashed lines represent the respective 95 per cent confidence bands)

---

[25] Note that also a sample selection problem may arise due to the participation decisions of women. A possible solution would be to take these participation decisions explicitly into account by applying Heckman's (1976; 1979) two-stage procedure. Our data set, however, does not contain a personal characteristic that could serve as a reliable instrument for women's participation decision.

All in all, our very robust empirical findings strongly support the four hypotheses derived from our theoretical model. Firstly, workers' wages are higher in more densely populated areas. Second women earn significantly less than comparable men both in hot spots and rural areas. Third, the unexplained gender pay gap is decreasing over time in both types of regions. Fourth, the gap is significantly lower in hot spots than in rural areas. Strikingly, our main finding is that this hot spot–rural difference in the pay gap is almost constant over the entire period of 30 years without any sign of a catching-up process.

6.6 Conclusions

In this chapter, we have investigated regional differences in the gender pay gap between hot spots and rural areas for young full-time workers and their evolution over time using a large micro data set for western Germany ranging from 1975–2004. Our empirical results strongly support the hypotheses generated from a spatial monopsony model, the long-run model with constant individual labour supply from Section 4.6.1, where women are less mobile due to more domestic responsibilities. According to this model, hot spots have thick labour markets giving rise to a more competitive environment. This not only pushes wages in hot spots, but also constrains employers' ability to engage in monopsonistic Robinsonian discrimination. Other than under Beckerian discrimination due to distaste, firms do not forego profits when discriminating against women. Robinsonian discrimination is therefore more likely to survive in the long run and represents in our eyes a more convincing economic explanation of the gender pay gap and its regional dimension.

In our empirical analysis, we used a semi-parametric propensity score matching approach to identify the unexplained part of the gender pay gap. Other than the standard regression-based decomposition techniques, such as the Oaxaca–Blinder decomposition, this technique is more flexible in terms of the imposed functional form and does not rely on an 'out-of-support' assumption, i.e., it compares only female and male observations with characteristics in their common support.

Our main result is that the unexplained gender pay gap is about 10 percentage points larger in rural areas compared to hot spots. While the unexplained gap both in hot spots and rural areas gradually decreases over time, the hot spot–rural difference remains astonishingly stable. To the best of our knowledge, this analysis is the first to investigate and find such a stable difference over a long period of time. In the context

---

As argued by Olivetti and Petrongolo (2008), however, if non-participation is non-random and participating women therefore have more favourable characteristics, then differences in the gender pay gap may be explained by differences in the participation gap. In our sample, the participation rate of females is almost identical in hot spots and rural areas (69 vs. 70 per cent), as is the female full-time employment ratio (44 vs. 43 per cent). Therefore, it seems implausible that our results are driven by participation differences, whereas the initial sample selection problem is likely to net out when considering the hot spot–rural difference in the pay gaps.

6.6 Conclusions

of our model, the interpretation of these findings would be that the gender difference in mobility gradually shrank over time, leading to a decrease in the gender pay gaps, whereas the different competitive environments in hot spots and rural areas persisted. That is to say, labour markets of hot spots remained more competitive environments with more firms in them, limiting employers' ability to discriminate against women.

Other than the spatial monopsony explanation of the gender pay gap, which hinges on the negative comparative static effect of an increase in the travel cost on the equilibrium wage to be found in a large variety of cases (see the discussion in Section 5.3), we cannot readily conclude that the model's predictions about regional differences in the gender pay gap carry over to a larger class of spatial monopsony models. To find these effects, we would have to look at the cross derivative of the equilibrium wage with respect to the travel cost and the worker density. Given the mathematical complexity of the models with a supply effect considered in Chapter 4, this seems not to be feasible. Our best guess, however, is that the model's predictions will carry over to more general spatial monopsony models if the labour market under consideration is sufficiently competitive (in the sense discussed in Chapter 4). As we saw in Section 6.1, absent any supply effect, the gender pay gap is larger in more densely populated labour markets. If there were a supply effect to work in the other direction, then the outcome would be likely to depend on the relative strength of the competition effect and thus on the strength of competitive forces. Unfortunately, this educated guesswork seems to be all we can do.

Chapter 6 closes Part I. In Part I, we have dealt with 'new' monopsony models of spatial monopsony and their application to the gender pay gap. We extended the models of spatial monopsony proposed by Nakagome (1986) and Bhaskar and To (1999) in a way following Greenhut et al.'s (1987) analysis of spatial oligopoly. In these models presented in Chapters 3 and 4, workers are located at different places, while employers do not exist at each potential location on account of some fixed setup costs. Therefore, workers have to commute, facing some travel cost. Since employers and the jobs they offer are for this reason not perfect substitutes to workers, competition among employers is imperfect and employers possess some monopsony power. Allowing for elastic individual labour supply, we found that individual labour supply's convexity relative to an exponential and firms' likeliness to collude, i.e., their conjectural variations, are paramount for the model's outcomes; for they are the crucial determinants of competitive forces in the labour market.

In Chapter 5, we applied the spatial monopsony framework to the gender pay gap. Distinguishing groups of workers with different travel costs and thus different labour supply elasticities at the level of the firm, firms are able to profit from engaging in third-degree wage discrimination. Arguing that women have higher average travel cost than men due to more domestic responsibilities, we arrived at a Robinsonian explanation for the gender pay gap. In Chapter 6, we saw that this Robinsonian approach provides a framework to think about the regional dimension of the gender pay gap. Its main prediction is that the gender pay gap should be lower in more densely populated labour markets, i.e., in thick labour markets with more competition among employers. Our empirical investigation for western Germany strongly supported this view as we found a remarkably stable hot spot–rural gap in the gap for young workers over a period of 30 years.

In Part II, we will turn away from spatial to dynamic monopsony. In these models of equilibrium search with wage posting, workers' incomplete knowledge of the labour market will turn out to be the source of firms' monopsony power. Dynamic monopsony not only provides another sensible framework to think about monopsonistic labour markets, but its focus on the firm's in- and outflow of workers over time will also prove to be particularly useful in another respect. It will enable us to infer the labour supply elasticity at the level of the firm from transition data. And this, in turn, will equip us with a direct empirical approach to the main ingredient of Robinsonian discrimination, viz. to potential gender differences in firm-level labour supply elasticities.

Part II
Dynamic Monopsony

Chapter 7
Simple Dynamic Monopsony

The discussion of spatial monopsony in Part I descended from the simple static monopsony model, extending its argument to economic space with significant travel cost. The next step was to introduce spatial competition by considering equidistantly distributed firms in space setting wages under conditions of strategic interaction. In line with the spatial economics literature, e.g., Capozza and Van Order (1978) and Greenhut et al. (1987), we labelled this situation as the 'short run' as opposed to the 'long run' where firms' profits are driven to zero because of free entry. Apart from this labelling, however, there were no explicit dynamics considered, the reasoning was purely static. Things are different in models of equilibrium search theory with wage posting which explicitly take account of the labour market's dynamics. We therefore follow Boal and Ransom (1997) and Manning (2003a) in regarding these and related models as models of dynamic monopsony. Unsurprisingly, a good starting point for the following analysis of dynamic monopsony in this sense is a simple dynamic model of pure monopsony which we will set up now.[1]

In line with Chapter 2, consider a spaceless market for homogenous labour with a single non-discriminating firm that produces a homogenous commodity with a constant marginal revenue product from its labour input. Other than in Chapter 2, the monopsonist now wants to maximise her profits by choosing a wage profile over time. For simplicity, time is assumed to be discrete.[2] The firm's labour supply in period t with $t \in \mathbb{N}$ is represented by

$$L_t := L(w_t, L_{t-1}) \tag{7.1}$$

with $\partial L(w_t, L_{t-1})/\partial w_t > 0$ and $\partial L(w_t, L_{t-1})/\partial L_{t-1} > 0$ for all $(w_t, L_{t-1}) \gg 0$. Accordingly, we assume that the firm can raise its labour supply by increasing its wage and that its labour supply adjusts not instantaneously but sluggishly. This can

---

[1] For a textbook-like treatment of simple dynamic monopsony we refer to Boal and Ransom (1997) or Manning (2003a, pp. 32–34, 52/53).

[2] Analysing the following setting in continuous time would complicate matters without any gain of insights. While the general equilibrium version of this model will be set up in continuous time – again for analytical convenience –, we stick to discrete time at this stage. For a dynamic monopsony model in continuous time, see Baily (1975).

be justified, for instance, in terms of a partial-adjustment model or an adaptive expectations framework (cf. Boal, 1995; Boal and Ransom, 1997). The firm's profits in period t are thus given by

$$\Pi_t(w_t, L_{t-1}) = (\phi - w_t)L(w_t, L_{t-1}).^3 \tag{7.2}$$

Suppose that the firm discounts future profits with some discount factor ρ with $0 < \rho < 1$. Then the firm's problem is

$$\max_{\{w_t\}_{t=1}^{\infty}} \sum_{t=1}^{\infty} \rho^{t-1} \Pi_t(w_t, L_{t-1}) = \sum_{t=1}^{\infty} \rho^{t-1}(\phi - w_t)L(w_t, L_{t-1}) \tag{7.3}$$

given some $L_0 \geqslant 0$. Due to the recursive structure of problem (7.3), we can use standard dynamic programming techniques to investigate the firm's profit-maximising behaviour. The recursive restatement of the firm's problem yields the following Bellman equation

$$V(L_{t-1}) = \max_{w_t}\{(\phi - w_t)L(w_t, L_{t-1}) + \rho V(L_t)\}, \tag{7.4}$$

where L_{t-1} is the state variable, w_t the control variable, and V the value function solving this functional equation. Since the right-hand side of (7.4) is a contraction for all $0 < \rho < 1$, this unique fixed point solving the functional equation exists.[4] Hence, $V(L_{t-1})$ gives the maximum present value of future profits from period t onwards. The first-order condition of this problem is given by

$$[\phi - w_t + \rho V'(L_t)]\frac{\partial L(w_t, L_{t-1})}{\partial w_t} - L(w_t, L_{t-1}) \stackrel{!}{=} 0, \tag{7.5}$$

while application of the envelope theorem yields

$$V'(L_{t-1}) = [\phi - w_t + \rho V'(L_t)]\frac{\partial L(w_t, L_{t-1})}{\partial L_{t-1}}. \tag{7.6}$$

Now, consider a steady state where the firm's employment and wage are constant over time, i.e., $L_t = L$ and $w_t = w$ for all $t \in \mathbb{N}$. In a steady state, (7.6) can thus be rearranged to arrive at

$$V'(L) = (\phi - w)\frac{\partial L(w, L)/\partial L_{t-1}}{1 - \rho \partial L(w, L)/\partial L_{t-1}}. \tag{7.7}$$

---

[3] Note that we will abstract from any fixed costs in the discussion of dynamic monopsony because they would not play any role in gaining the following results.

[4] This claim follows at once from noting that the right-hand side of (7.4) satisfies Blackwell's sufficient conditions for a contraction (e.g., Stockey and Lucas, 1989, p. 54).

Combining (7.7) and (7.5) and rearranging terms give

$$E_m := \frac{\phi - w_m}{w_m} = \rho \frac{1 - \partial L(w_m, L_m)/\partial L_{t-1}}{e_{Lw}^{SR}(w_m, L_m)} + (1 - \rho) \frac{1}{e_{Lw}^{SR}(w_m, L_m)}, \quad (7.8)$$

where $e_{Lw}^{SR}(w, L) := [\partial L(w, L)/\partial w_t] w / L(w, L)$ is the short-run elasticity of the firm's labour supply. Furthermore, one can show that the long-run elasticity of the firm's labour supply is given by

$$e_{Lw}^{LR}(w, L) = \frac{e_{Lw}^{SR}(w, L)}{1 - \partial L(w, L)/\partial L_{t-1}}, \quad (7.9)$$

which can be seen most easily by considering inverse elasticities and which is demonstrated in Appendix B.1. Consequently, we have established the following:

Proposition 7.1 ('Exploitation' under Dynamic Monopsony). *In a steady state, the simple dynamic monopsonist sets her wage such that*

$$E_m = \rho \frac{1}{e_{Lw}^{LR}(w_m, L_m)} + (1 - \rho) \frac{1}{e_{Lw}^{SR}(w_m, L_m)}. \qquad \blacksquare$$

By virtue of Proposition 7.1 the percentage gap between workers' marginal revenue product and the simple dynamic monopsonist's wage – Pigou's (1932, pp. 813/814) 'exploitation' – is a weighted average of the inverse long-run and short-run labour supply elasticities, where the weight of the long-run elasticity is given by her discount factor. As a corollary to this result, we can conclude that the less the monopsonist discounts future profits the more the long-run elasticity determines her wage-setting behaviour. If discounting becomes negligible, then the long-run elasticity is the only determinant of the monopsony wage. Of course, this result is in line with simple intuition. If the monopsonist does not care about her future profits that much, it is more attractive to her to decrease present wages, for the costs of this – lower future labour supply and thus profits – are shifted to the future because her labour supply adjusts sluggishly.

In the following, it will be useful to consider a special case of simple dynamic monopsony which connects the firm's labour supply explicitly to its in- and outflow of workers. In particular, this specification will enable us to exploit the model's structure empirically.[5] Assume that every period t $R(w_t)$ recruits arrive at the firm, where this number is strictly increasing in the wage paid by the firm, i.e., $R'(w_t) > 0$ for all $w_t > 0$. Furthermore, assume that a fraction of the firm's existing employees decides to leave the firm at a separation rate $s(w_t)$ with $0 < s(w_t) < 1$, which is assumed to be strictly decreasing in the wage, so that $s'(w_t) < 0$ for all $w_t > 0$.

---

[5] This variant of the simple dynamic monopsony model is discussed, among others, by Card and Krueger (1995, pp. 373–379), Boal and Ransom (1997), and Manning (2003a, pp. 32–34, 52/53).

Therefore, the firm's labour supply in period t is given by

$$L_t := L(w_t, L_{t-1}) := R(w_t) + [1 - s(w_t)]L_{t-1} \qquad (7.10)$$

with

$$\frac{\partial L(w_t, L_{t-1})}{\partial w_t} = R'(w_t) - s'(w_t)L_{t-1} > 0 \qquad (7.11)$$

and

$$\frac{\partial L(w_t, L_{t-1})}{\partial L_{t-1}} = 1 - s(w_t) > 0 \qquad (7.12)$$

for all $(w_t, L_{t-1}) \gg 0$ given some initial value $L_0 \geqslant 0$. Hence, the firm's labour supply in period t is strictly increasing in the current wage paid and adjusts sluggishly because it is also strictly increasing in the previous period's labour supply. Therefore, the labour supply function (7.10) is just a special case of the more general function (7.1), so that all the results derived earlier remain valid for this specification.

Apart from relating the firm's dynamic labour supply to its in- and outflow of workers, which are observable and actually observed in several data sets, the model represents a (monopsonistic) view on the labour market that is in line with both intuition and observation (see, e.g., the quote by Samuelson in Section 1.1). In Chapter 8, we will demonstrate how this basic structure of dynamic monopsony can be extended to build up a dynamic general equilibrium model of oligopsony, the well-known equilibrium search model with wage posting by Burdett and Mortensen (1998). We will present a slightly simplified version following closely the presentations given by Manning (2003a) and Mortensen (2003). Making use of this model's structure, we will then be able to estimate the long-run labour supply elasticity at the level of the firm. This will be done within an approach put forward by Manning (2003a) where we exploit data on firms' in- and outflow of workers by methods of survival analysis.

Chapter 8
A General Equilibrium Model of Dynamic Monopsony

8.1 Some Introductory Remarks

Other than in Part I, the focus of equilibrium search theory with wage posting lies on search frictions in labour markets and how they give rise to wage-setting power on the side of firms and to wage dispersion both on the side of firms and workers. Put differently, it aims to answer the question 'Why are similar workers paid differently?,' which is the subtitle of a monograph by Mortensen (2003) assessing this strand of theory, and 'to explain both transitions in the labor market and the distribution of wages in the labor market in a coherent way.' (Mortensen, 2003, p. xi)[1]

The basic idea of this theory is quite easily grasped, although the models used to formalise this idea are technically quite demanding. Suppose a large labour market consisting of many firms and many workers. As well wages as other terms of employment are supposed to be posted by employers before they meet potential employees.[2] Assume that workers are totally identical. In particular, they are equally

---

[1] For a survey on alternative ways of modelling equilibrium wage dispersion, see Gaumont *et al.* (2006). Eckstein and van den Berg (2007) provide an overview on the empirical research that addresses labour market phenomena structurally utilising equilibrium search theory.

[2] A different approach is chosen by so-called search–matching–bargaining models where wages are determined bilaterally through a bargaining process after the worker and the employer have met instead of being set unilaterally by the employer. (For a survey, see Mortensen and Pissarides (1999) and Rogerson *et al.* (2005). Note that both approaches can be brought together as is done by Mortensen's (2000) synthesis.) For most jobs, however, wage posting seems to be more realistic. 'The idea that employers set the terms of employment while workers choose among available offers is consistent with how many labor economists view the wage setting process.' (Mortensen and Pissarides, 1999, p. 2607) Furthermore, Manning (2003a, pp. 14–16) stresses that monopsonistic wage posting does not necessarily imply that employers' shares of employment rents are large. Eventually, we argue that wage posting's explanatory power is superior in terms of simplicity: As Burdett and Mortensen's (1998) model can be thought of as a general equilibrium version of the special case of simple dynamic monopsony presented in Chapter 7, we are able to make use of this less complicated model or even the simple static monopsony model from Chapter 2 in many situations to gain clear-cut predictions, whilst we do not have such a simple model at hand when arguing within the search–matching–bargaining approach.

productive and have a common reservation wage. Similarly, jobs are identical except for the wage offered. Assume further that workers possess incomplete information on vacancies.

In such a labour market, workers do not know all wages offered, so they accept the highest wage offer received as long as it pays at least their reservation wage. By chance, some workers get only offers made by low-paying firms and find themselves employed at a low wage, whereas some workers receive and accept high wage offers. If on-the-job search takes place, then employed workers with low wages, however, are more likely to receive an offer which pays better than their current job and thus are more likely to change employers. As a consequence, firms can increase their labour supply by raising their wage: The higher the wage offered by a firm, the higher is its inflow of recruits and the lower its outflow of quitting workers, which implies that the firm's labour supply looks like the specification (7.10) discussed in Chapter 7. Since low-wage firms nonetheless survive due to workers' incomplete information, this setting gives rise to monopsony power, i.e., unlike perfect competition firms possess some discretion in setting wages.

The framework presented is formulated as a non-cooperative wage-posting game, played by firms in a labour market with significant search frictions (cf. Mortensen, 2003, p. 5). In equilibrium, a wage offer distribution emerges endogenously that is characterised both by lower wages than under perfect competition and wage dispersion. The first to model such a wage-setting game with homogenous agents was Diamond (1971), who derived the so-called Diamond paradox, that is, an equilibrium in pure strategies with all firms paying the collusive wage (i.e., workers' common reservation wage).[3] This conclusion, however, was reached under the assumption that only non-employed workers search for jobs, while employed workers stay with their employers. With off-the-job search only, there are no competitive forces that constrain employers' monopsony power.[4] As soon as on-the-job search takes place, however, workers have the opportunity of working their way up the wage distribution by changing employers, so that employers' monopsony power is 'constrained by competition with other similar employers over time.' (Mortensen and Pissarides, 1999, p. 2607)

In Burdett and Mortensen's (1998) model, the extent of wage dispersion is directly related to the degree of search frictions, being only absent if no on-the-job

---

[3] Actually, Diamond's (1971) model formulated a non-cooperative price-posting game at a commodity market characterised by incomplete information of consumers. Unsurprisingly, its results carry over to labour markets, just with the 'opposite sign.'

[4] To generate wage dispersion with off-the-job search only, a source of heterogeneity must be added. For instance, workers are supposed to differ in their opportunity costs of employment, resulting in different reservation wages, or firms in their production technologies. The former source of heterogeneity was first analysed by Butters (1977), MacMinn (1980), and Albrecht and Axell (1984), the latter by Reinganum (1979) and Montgomery (1991). Other than these models, however, the models incorporating on-the-job search, such as those by Mortensen (1990) and Burdett and Mortensen (1998), have the virtue of generating wage dispersion and monopsony power of employers even for homogenous workers and firms, the only source of both phenomena being search frictions.

8.2 The Model

search takes place (i.e., maximum search frictions) or if job offers arrive infinitely fast (i.e., no search frictions). The former corresponds to the Diamond paradox, whereas the latter results in a competitive outcome where all workers are employed at their common marginal revenue product of labour. In the next section, we shall discuss a slightly simplified version Burdett and Mortensen's (1998) model in detail.

8.2 The Model

8.2.1 The Basic Assumptions

The simple dynamic monopsony framework from Chapter 7 can be used to build up a slightly simplified version of the Burdett–Mortensen equilibrium search model with wage posting. In order to do so, the following basic assumptions are assumed to hold:

(B1) There is a continuum of homogenous workers with mass M. In particular, workers are equally productive and have the same opportunity cost of employment b (that is, the utility flow per instant when non-employed).

(B2) There is a continuum of homogenous firms with mass one. Each firm produces a homogenous good with a constant marginal revenue product of labour ϕ from its total labour input, where $\phi > b$ is assumed to hold.

(B3) Each firm pays a single wage to all its employees and sets its wage once-for-all to maximise its steady-state profits, which means that there is no discounting (i.e., the instantaneous discount rate ϱ is zero).

(B4) Workers are either employed or non-employed, searching for jobs both on the job and off the job. They receive job offers at an exogenous job offer arrival rate λ^e when employed and λ^n when non-employed. Job offers are drawn at random from the wage offer distribution F. When employed, workers supply a single unit of labour to their employer per instant. Finally, existing jobs break off at an exogenous job destruction rate δ.[5]

We shall now discuss these assumptions in some detail. Assumptions (B1) and (B2) tell us that we are considering a labour market with homogeneity on both sides of the market. Though this is obviously a strong restriction, this setting suffices to give significant monopsony power to employers just because there are substantial search frictions (see the discussion in Section 8.1). Assumption (B3) tells us

---

[5] Manning (2003a, p. 37) modifies this setting slightly by assuming that the job destruction rate is given by δ^n and that all workers, both employed and non-employed, leave the labour market at a rate δ^r, being replaced by an equal number of workers entering the labour market as non-employed. Consequently, the total number of workers in the labour market is not changed, while the model now allows for (wage-inelastic) transitions from and to non-participation. He then moves on defining $\delta := \delta^n + \delta^r$, so that the following results will also hold for this modification.

that employers are able to and also do commit themselves to a single wage. For this reason, their wage-setting behaviour will be guided by the long-run elasticity of their labour supplies (see Proposition 7.1).[6] Finally, assumption (B4) describes the matching technology which is given by random matching: Workers receive job offers from different firms at random, in particular regardless of firms' size. Therefore, a job offer is just a realisation of a random draw from the distribution of wages across employers F. Assume for the moment that this wage offer distribution is continuous, which simplifies the following analysis considerably. As we shall see later, this must be the case in equilibrium. Since we will set up the following model in continuous time, the rates at which job offers arrive λ^e and λ^n and the rate at which existing matches break off δ are parameters of (continuous) Poisson arrival processes.[7]

At this stage, it is of prime importance to note the inalienability of the random-matching assumption and its implication of diminishing returns to scale in the matching technology for recruiting new workers (cf., e.g., Manning, 2003a, p. 284). An alternative assumption would be balanced matching where workers are more likely to receive offers from larger firms. More specifically, balanced matching states that a firm's arrival rate at a given wage is proportional to its employment level (cf., e.g., Burdett and Vishwanath, 1988). 'However, as Manning himself acknowledges, if matching is balanced (which effectively amounts to constant returns to scale in the matching technology for recruiting new workers), all elements of monopsony disappear...' (Kuhn, 2004, p. 375) For instance, Burdett and Vishwanath show that under pure balanced matching employers no longer have monopsony power over their workers, yielding the competitive solution. Moreover, considering mixtures of random and balanced matching, Mortensen and Vishwanath (1994) demonstrate that the extent of monopsony power is gradually decreasing as balanced matching becomes more important. While Manning (2003a, pp. 286–292) presents some evidence supporting diminishing returns, Kuhn (2004), who offers several thoughtful criticisms against dynamic monopsony, gives several plausible reasons why the recruitment technology should inhibit non-diminishing or even increasing returns to scale. Essentially, Kuhn's (2004, p. 373) criticism against search models of dynamic monopsony states '(a) that heterogeneity in workers' ability does not play *enough* of a role, while (b) issues of scale (specifically, the absolute number of workers to a firm) play *too large* a role.'

Though there are instances where it seems implausible to impose diminishing returns, this needs not to invalidate the model's predictions as the descriptive realism or unrealism of an assumption is no guide to its usefulness. Whether the model's predictions hold is an empirical question, not one to be settled by comparing its assumptions to reality (cf. Friedman, 1953). From this and the discussion so far we

---

[6] One may wonder whether this sort of perfect pre-commitment is restrictive. Since we will restrict our analysis to a steady-state environment in the following, this assumption seems reasonable in our eyes. Besides, Coles (2001) demonstrates that even without pre-commitment by firms things are the same as in this model if discounting of future profits becomes negligible.

[7] For details, see Cahuc and Zylberberg (2004, pp. 801–803).

can conclude that the question whether there are indeed diminishing returns is far from settled as is the question whether random matching is a reasonable assumption to be drawn. Clearly, to give a definite answer to these questions more research is needed, which is not within the scope of this book. In spite of these *caveats*, we shall therefore stick to the very useful random-matching assumption in the following.

8.2.2 Workers' Reservation Wage

We now turn to workers' behaviour. Workers are assumed to maximise their expected discounted lifetime income, which means that workers are risk neutral.[8] For the sake of expositional convenience, suppose a discrete time setting first, where the length of each period is some $dt > 0$. Workers' discount factor ρ is then defined as $\rho := 1/(1 + \varrho\, dt)$, where ϱ denotes their instantaneous discount rate. Let V^n denote the value function of a non-employed worker and $V^e(w)$ the value function of a worker employed at some wage w. Then V^n solves the following Bellman equation

$$V^n = b\, dt + \rho \left(\lambda^n dt \int_{\underline{w}}^{\overline{w}} \max\{V^e(x), V^n\}\, dF(x) + (1 - \lambda^n dt) V^n \right), \quad (8.1)$$

where $\overline{w}$ ($\underline{w}$) denotes the supremum (infimum) of F's support. Intuitively, a non-employed worker receives an income $b\, dt$ at the current period. With probability $\lambda^n dt$ he or she receives an offer x for the next period from the wage offer distribution F which is accepted if and only if the value of being employed at that wage $V^e(x)$ is no smaller than the value of being non-employed V^n. Finally, with probability $1 - \lambda^n dt$ the worker does not receive a wage offer and stays non-employed.

Next, turn to a worker employed at some wage w whose value function $V^e(w)$ solves the Bellman equation

$$\begin{aligned}V^e(w) = w\, dt + \rho \Big(& \lambda^e dt \int_{\underline{w}}^{\overline{w}} \max\{V^e(x), V^e(w)\}\, dF(x) \\ & + \delta\, dt\, V^n + [1 - (\lambda^e + \delta)\, dt] V^e(w) \Big).\end{aligned} \quad (8.2)$$

Intuitively, an employed worker receives an income $w\, dt$ at the current period. With probability $\lambda^e dt$ he or she receives an offer x for the next period from the wage offer distribution F which is accepted if and only if the value of being employed at that wage $V^e(x)$ is no smaller than the value of being employed at the current wage $V^e(w)$. Next, with probability $\delta\, dt$ the worker loses his or her job and becomes

---

[8] Burdett and Coles (2003) investigate the equilibrium of the wage-posting game with liquidity-constrained risk averse workers allowing firms to post contracts where the wage paid varies with workers' tenure at the firm.

non-employed. Eventually, with probability $1 - (\lambda^e + \delta)\,dt$ the worker receives no offer and stays employed at wage w.

Rearranging terms in (8.1) and (8.2) and considering the limit $dt \to 0$, we arrive at the following two continuous-time Bellman equations

$$\varrho V^n = b + \lambda^n \int_{\underline{w}}^{\overline{w}} \max\{V^e(x) - V^n, 0\}\,dF(x), \tag{8.3}$$

$$\varrho V^e(w) = w + \lambda^e \int_{\underline{w}}^{\overline{w}} \max\{V^e(x) - V^e(w), 0\}\,dF(x) + \delta[V^e(w) - V^n]. \tag{8.4}$$

It is straightforward to show that the value functions V^e and V^n solving the functional equations (8.3) and (8.4) exist and are unique, where V^e is strictly increasing in w, while V^n is independent of w (cf. Mortensen and Neumann, 1988). Hence, there exists a unique reservation wage r with $V^e(w) \gtreqless V^n$ if and only if $w \gtreqless r$. Consequently, a non-employed worker accepts every job offering at least r. Furthermore, an employed worker accepts a job offering x if and only if $x \geq w$ because V^e's strict monotonicity implies $V^e(x) \geq V^e(w)$ if and only if $x \geq w$.

Setting $V^e(w) \stackrel{!}{=} V^n$ and letting $\varrho \to 0$, we find that workers' reservation wage is the unique fixed point of the equation

$$r = b + (\lambda^n - \lambda^e) \int_r^{\overline{w}} \frac{1 - F(x)}{\delta + \lambda^e[1 - F(x)]}\,dx.^9 \tag{8.5}$$

According to (8.5), workers' reservation wage r depends on whether on-the-job or off-the-job search is more prospective. If neither on-the-job nor off-the-job search is more effective, i.e., if $\lambda^e = \lambda^n$, then the workers' opportunity cost of employment b also gives their reservation wage, so that $r = b$. Intuitively, accepting a job does not harm nor promote their chance of receiving further job offers after accepting this job because job offers arrive at the same rate when employed and when non-employed. Therefore, a worker will be better off whenever the job offered to him or her gives a wage larger than b, so that he or she is willing to accept it. If job offer arrival rates differ between on- and off-the-job search, then we have $r > b$ if the job offer arrival

---

[9] For a derivation of (8.5), see Appendix B.2. The attentive reader may have realised that the notion of the reservation wage used here is slightly different from the notion of the reservation income used in Part I. Obviously, being non-employed and looking for a job is conceptually different from non-participation. For a discussion of this, see, e.g., Cahuc and Zylberberg (2004, pp. 115–118). Nevertheless, we follow the literature and refer to both thresholds as workers' reservation wage or income, respectively, because there is no danger of confusion. Note that there is still another slight difference of these thresholds: In Part I, workers decided to supply labour, i.e., to participate in the labour market, if and only if their income *exceeds* their reservation income, while here they take up a particular job instead of staying non-employed if and only if their wage is *no less* than their reservation wage. While the two reservation wages (incomes) differ conceptually in the sense laid out above, this latter difference is only for analytical convenience and has no deeper meaning.

8.2 The Model

rate when employed is larger than the job offer arrival rate when non-employed and $r < b$ if things are the other way round.

8.2.3 Firms' Steady-State Labour Supply

We now turn to firms' behaviour. The firm's decision in this model is to choose a single wage w that maximises its steady-state profits

$$\Pi(w|F,r) = (\phi - w)L(w|F,r), \tag{8.6}$$

where $L(w|F,r)$ is the firm's labour supply for the wage offer w given the distribution of wages across firms and the workers' reservation wage, which both emerge endogenously from the model. From this we see at once that offering a wage $w < r$ is a strictly dominated strategy for the firm because it would be unable to attract any workers and to make any profits. Therefore, $F(r) = 0$ must hold in equilibrium.

Let $N(t)$ denote the mass of non-employed workers at time t. Then the flow of workers into employment is given by $\lambda^n N(t)$ because non-employed workers receive job offers at rate λ^n and accept every job offer that pays at least r, where $\Pr(w > r) = 1 - F(r) = 1$. On the other hand, the flow of workers from employment into non-employment is $\delta[M - N(t)]$ since employed workers lose their jobs at rate δ. In a steady state, we therefore must have

$$\dot{N}(t) = \delta[M - N(t)] - \lambda^n N(t) \stackrel{!}{=} 0, \tag{8.7}$$

so that the steady-state mass of non-employed workers is given by

$$N = \frac{\delta}{\delta + \lambda^n} M \tag{8.8}$$

with non-employment rate $n = \delta/(\delta + \lambda^n)$.

Consider now the distribution of wages across workers, where we denote the corresponding c.d.f. by G. Then $G(w,t|F,r)$ denotes the share and $\Gamma(w,t|F,r) := [M - N(t)]G(w,t|F,r)$ the mass of workers receiving a wage no more than w at time t. Since non-employed workers receive (acceptable) job offers paying a wage no larger than w at rate $\lambda^n F(w)$, while workers employed at such a wage lose their jobs at rate δ and move to higher paying jobs at rate $\lambda^e[1 - F(w)]$, we have

$$\dot{\Gamma}(w,t|F,r) = \lambda^n F(w)N(t) - (\delta + \lambda^e[1 - F(w)])\Gamma(w,t|F,r). \tag{8.9}$$

In a steady state where $\dot{\Gamma}(w,t|F,r) \stackrel{!}{=} 0$, combining (8.8) and (8.9) therefore yields

$$G(w|F,r) = \frac{\Gamma(w|F,r)}{M - N} = \frac{\delta F(w)}{\delta + \lambda^e[1 - F(w)]}. \tag{8.10}$$

We are now in the position to derive the steady-state labour supply of a firm offering some wage w. Let $R(w|F,r)$ denote the firm's mass of recruits. Due to random matching, the firm recruits $\lambda^n N$ workers from non-employment and $\lambda^e(M-N)G(w|F,r)$ workers from employment.[10] Making use of (8.8) and (8.10), we arrive at

$$R(w|F,r) = \lambda^n N + \lambda^e(M-N)G(w|F,r) = \frac{\delta\lambda^n}{\delta+\lambda^n}\frac{\delta+\lambda^e}{\delta+\lambda^e[1-F(w)]}M. \quad (8.11)$$

Next, let $s(w|F,r)$ denote the separation rate of the firm's workers at wage w. Since existing matches break off at rate δ and workers employed at wage w receive higher-paying job offers at rate $\lambda^e[1-F(w)]$, we have

$$s(w|F,r) = \delta + \lambda^e[1-F(w)]. \quad (8.12)$$

In a steady state, the firm's mass of recruits $R(w|F,r)$ and its mass of separations $s(w|F,r)L(w|F,r)$ must be balanced. Therefore, the firm's steady-state labour supply at wage w is given by

$$L(w|F,r) = \frac{R(w|F,r)}{s(w|F,r)} = \frac{\delta\lambda^n}{\delta+\lambda^n}\frac{\delta+\lambda^e}{(\delta+\lambda^e[1-F(w)])^2}M, \quad (8.13)$$

which is (strictly) increasing in w given some (continuous) wage offer distribution F. In particular, L is always strictly increasing in w on the support of F. From the latter it follows at once that the only thing that matters for the firm's labour supply is its relative position in the wage offer distribution and not the absolute value of its wage offer. Of course, both the relative and the absolute position of its wage offer in the offer distribution coincide if F is continuous, which (at the moment) holds by assumption.

8.2.4 The Steady-State Equilibrium and Its Properties

In equilibrium, all firms must gain the same positive level of profits Π^*, for otherwise they would have an incentive to deviate from their wage offers. Therefore, we must have

$$\begin{aligned}\Pi(w|F,r) &= (\phi-w)L(w|F,r) \\ &= (\phi-w)\frac{\delta\lambda^n}{\delta+\lambda^n}\frac{\delta+\lambda^e}{(\delta+\lambda^e[1-F(w)])^2}M \\ &\stackrel{!}{=} \Pi^*\end{aligned} \quad (8.14)$$

---

[10] Note again that we have a unit mass of firms. If we had a continuum of firms with mass J instead, both expressions would be divided by J.

8.2 The Model

for all w in F's support. From this it is now straightforward to actually rule out that F is discontinuous, instead of just assuming this to be the case. Hence, there has to be wage dispersion though we have a situation with both homogenous firms and workers. F's continuity follows because it cannot be optimal for firms to offer wages such that F has a mass point. This can be seen as follows: Suppose F had a mass point at $w < \phi$. Then a firm offering a wage infinitesimally larger than w would be able to significantly increase its labour supply at the expense of those firms offering w because it would move up the wage offer distribution. Since profits per worker would decrease only infinitesimally, the firm's overall profits would rise, so that a mass point at w could not have been optimal. Trivially, a mass point at $w \geqslant \phi$ could not have been optimal either as this would yield no profits (or even losses), while deviating and offering some $r \leqslant w < \phi$ would yield strictly positive profits.

Next, note that the lowest-paying firm offers workers' reservation wage, so that $\underline{w} = r$. This must hold because only the relative position of the firm's wage offer in the wage offer distribution matters and offering r ensures that the firm is able to recruit at least some workers. From this and (8.14) it follows that

$$\begin{aligned}\Pi(w|F,r) &= (\phi - w)\frac{\delta\lambda^n}{\delta + \lambda^n}\frac{\delta + \lambda^e}{(\delta + \lambda^e[1 - F(w)])^2}M \\ &= (\phi - r)\frac{\delta\lambda^n}{\delta + \lambda^n}\frac{1}{\delta + \lambda^e}M \\ &= \Pi(r|F,r)\end{aligned} \quad (8.15)$$

for all w in F's support, where we again use that $F(r) = 0$ must hold in equilibrium. Next, define the market friction parameter ξ as the ratio of the job destruction rate and the job offer arrival rate when employed, $\xi := \delta/\lambda^e$. It is now straightforward to establish the following proposition:

Proposition 8.1 (The Steady-State Equilibrium). *In the steady-state equilibrium, the wage offer distribution is given by*

$$F(w) = (1 + \xi)\left(1 - \sqrt{\frac{\phi - w}{\phi - r}}\right), \quad (8.16)$$

while the distribution of wages across workers is

$$G(w) = \xi\left(\sqrt{\frac{\phi - r}{\phi - w}} - 1\right). \quad (8.17)$$

All wage offers satisfy

$$\underline{w} = r \leqslant w \leqslant \left(1 - \left(\frac{\xi}{1 + \xi}\right)^2\right)\phi + \left(\frac{\xi}{1 + \xi}\right)^2 r = \overline{w}, \quad (8.18)$$

while workers' expected wage is given by

$$E_G[w] = \frac{1}{1+\xi}\phi + \frac{\xi}{1+\xi}r. \tag{8.19}$$

Workers' uniform reservation wage is represented by

$$r = \frac{(\lambda^n - \lambda^e)\lambda^e}{(\delta + \lambda^e)^2 + (\lambda^n - \lambda^e)\lambda^e}\phi + \frac{(\delta + \lambda^e)^2}{(\delta + \lambda^e)^2 + (\lambda^n - \lambda^e)\lambda^e}b. \tag{8.20}$$

Proof. Rearranging (8.15) yields (8.16). Making use of (8.16), the distribution of wages across workers follows from (8.10). Furthermore, by setting $F(w) \stackrel{!}{=} 1$, we see that the highest wage offered $\overline{w}$ is given by

$$\overline{w} = \phi - \left(\frac{\xi}{1+\xi}\right)^2(\phi - r), \tag{8.21}$$

whilst the lowest wage offered is $\underline{w} = r$. For the derivation of workers' expected wage (8.19), see Appendix B.3. Inserting $\overline{w}$ according to (8.21) and $F(w)$ according to (8.16) into (8.5) and some tedious algebraic manipulations yield (8.20). For details concerning the latter, see Burdett and Mortensen (1998, p. 263). ∎

Together, equations (8.16) and (8.20) constitute the unique Bayesian–Nash steady-state equilibrium of firms' wage-posting game. Several observations follow from Proposition 8.1. Firstly, there is continuous wage dispersion across employers and workers, which can be seen from the continuous c.d.f.s of firms' and workers' wages (8.16) and (8.17), respectively, though we have a setting with entirely homogenous agents, i.e., identical firms and workers *ex ante*. Due to workers' imperfect information, firms are able to gain positive profits from both low- and high-pay strategies because some non-employed workers by chance end up with low-pay firms. Wage dispersion causes workers to make job-to-job transitions, where employed workers differ in their current wages and thus consider different wages as acceptable when making job-to-job moves. Workers are therefore heterogenous *ex post*.

Second, workers are more concentrated in higher-paying firms, which follows from inspecting (8.16) and (8.17) with $G(w) < F(w)$ for all $\underline{w} < w < \overline{w}$. The reason is that low-pay firms face higher separation rates and lower inflows of recruits giving rise to lower labour supply to these firms. Put differently, since labour supply at the level of the firm is strictly increasing in the wage offered, high-pay firms have larger workforces, so that we have a positive employer size–wage effect.[11]

Third, all wage offers are below workers' marginal revenue product and are therefore lower than under perfect competition. This holds because workers face

---

[11] Such an employer size–wage effect is a stylised fact of labour markets, see, e.g., Brown and Medoff (1989) and Oi and Idson (1999).

8.2 The Model

search frictions in the labour market. More precisely, the notion of search frictions is embodied in the market friction parameter ξ, where its level informs us how hard it is for employed workers to work their way up the wage distribution. As the market friction parameter rises, workers are relatively less likely to receive attractive outside options and are relatively more likely to lose their jobs; therefore, competitive forces among employers decrease. In response, both workers' reservation wage and their expected wage fall. Furthermore, both the wage offer distribution and the wage distribution across workers are 'pushed from above,' so that not only workers' expected wage but also wage dispersion is reduced. On the other hand, the lower are on-the-job search frictions, i.e., the lower is the market friction parameter, the more limited is firms' monopsony power. Hence, the market friction parameter is the essential parameter of this model when compared to pure off-the-job search models, for it tells us to which degree on-the-job search constrains employers' wage-setting power.

Fourth, consider what happens in the limit, i.e., when search frictions become very large or negligible. If $\xi \to \infty$, on-the-job search becomes totally ineffective, and employed workers become unable to receive attractive outside options. Competition among employers breaks down. Workers' opportunity cost of employment gives both their reservation wage and the only wage offered.[12] Put differently, F and G both become degenerated one-point distributions at point b. In the limit $\xi \to \infty$, we therefore arrive at Diamond's paradox. On the other hand, if $\xi \to 0$, outside options arrive infinitely fast for employed workers, leading to a situation of perfect competition. In response, workers' reservation wage rises to their marginal revenue product, and all firms offer the competitive wage.[13] 'This ... corresponds well with our notion of perfect competition as a market in which there is fierce competition among employers for workers and the high arrival rate of job offers means that the threat of workers leaving if they are paid a low wage is a very real one.' (Manning, 2003a, p. 43)

Last but not least, consider the ratio of the job offer rate when non-employed and the job destruction rate λ^n/δ. If $\lambda^n/\delta \to \infty$, i.e., if off-the-job search frictions disappear, then the number and the rate of (frictionally) non-employed approaches zero, which can be seen from (8.8). Non-employed workers immediately receive (acceptable) job offers. Workers' reservation wage again approaches their marginal revenue product and thus we get a competitive outcome without any frictional non-employed.[14] This is not surprising: The absence of any off-the-job search frictions makes on-the-job search and its pressure on firms' monopsony power irrelevant because every non-employed worker is able to find the best-paying job at once.

---

[12] Algebraically, we see from (8.20) and (8.21) that both $\underline{w} = r \to b$ and $\overline{w} \to b$ if $\xi = \delta/\lambda^e \to \infty$.

[13] More precisely, (8.20) and (8.21) yield $\underline{w} = r \to \phi$ and $\overline{w} \to \phi$ if $\xi = \delta/\lambda^e \to 0$.

[14] Algebraically, (8.20) and (8.21) give $\underline{w} = r \to \phi$ and $\overline{w} \to \phi$ if $\lambda^n/\delta \to \infty$.

8.3 Some Concluding Remarks

The essence of Burdett and Mortensen's model is beautifully captured by Manning (2003a, p. 29) who refers to it as a 'game of "snakes and ladders"':

> 'Workers are faced with a distribution of wages so that there are good jobs and bad jobs. They try to get themselves into the good jobs but their progress resembles a game of "snakes and ladders." Sometimes they meet a "snake" and suffer the misfortune of losing their job and sometimes they find a "ladder" and have the good fortune to move to a better job. From the perspective of employers, the frictions in labor markets give them some discretion in setting wages. If they lower wages, they find it more difficult to recruit and retain workers but the existing workers do not all leave immediately and they continue to be able to recruit some workers so that they retain some workers even in the long run. The wages that employers set are influenced by competition from other employers but this competition is neither so cutthroat as to enable workers to extract all the surplus from the employment relationship, nor so weak as to enable employers to extract all the rents.'

What the market friction parameter therefore tells us, is the proportion of the probability of finding a 'snake' to the probability of finding a 'ladder,' that is to say, how strong competitive forces really are.

In this model with homogenous agents, the level of wages, wage dispersion, and the extent of firms' monopsony power are solely determined by the degree of search frictions. Of course, heterogeneity among workers (e.g., differences in opportunity costs of employment) and among firms (e.g., differences in productivity levels) are other relevant sources of wage dispersion in reality. The framework considered so far can be readily extended to the case of heterogenous firms and/or workers (e.g., Burdett and Mortensen, 1998; van den Berg and Ridder, 1998; Bontemps et al., 1999; 2000) to capture the impact of heterogenous agents. Moreover, Postel-Vinay and Robin (2002a; 2002b) set up models where employers are allowed to respond to the outside offers received by their employees by making counteroffers, whereas Manning (2003a, pp. 56–79; 2004) allows for both free entry of firms and heterogeneity among workers. These heterogeneities being other relevant sources of wage dispersion, there is evidence that search frictions on their own remain an important but not the exclusive source of variation in observable wage offers.[15] For instance, van den Berg and Ridder (1998) structurally estimate a Burdett–Mortensen-like model with homogenous workers and heterogenous firms and report that search frictions explain about 20 per cent of this variation. For a model with both heterogenous workers and firms Postel-Vinay and Robin (2002b) find that search frictions explain even about 50 per cent of wage variability.[16]

---

[15] For surveys on the empirical evidence following from equilibrium search models with wage posting, see van den Berg (1999) and Eckstein and van den Berg (2007).

[16] One has to stress, however, that Postel-Vinay and Robin's (2002b) model differs in some respects from the type of models considered so far: It does not employ random matching as matching technology, it incorporates both different able workers and differences in opportunity costs of employment among them, and it allows for counteroffers of employers in response to outside offers made to their employees.

8.3 Some Concluding Remarks

In the following, we shall make use of the structure of the Burdett–Mortensen model to motivate a semi-structural approach proposed by Manning (2003a, pp. 96–104) that allows us to infer the labour supply elasticity at the level of the firm from its in- and outflow of workers. Basically, this is achieved by putting the model's structure on the model of simple dynamic monopsony presented in Chapter 7. Furthermore, we shall present a simple measure of on-the-job search frictions introduced by Manning (2003a, pp. 44–49), which allows us to say something about the extent of search frictions in the labour market. Both approaches will then be used (1) to investigate whether women's labour supply at the firm level is less elastic than men's, which aims at an answer whether Robinsonian wage discrimination is one potential source of the gender pay gap; and (2) to answer the related question whether women face higher on-the-job search frictions than men, so that gender differences in on-the-job search frictions may be one source of both the elasticity differential and the gender pay gap.

Chapter 9
Dynamic Monopsony and the Gender Pay Gap[1]

In the following, we shall turn away from pure theory. Instead, we will use the theory presented in Chapters 7 and 8 to assess whether the gender pay gap may be caused by (third-degree) Robinsonian wage discrimination as laid out in detail in Chapter 5. If firms are able to offer different wages to men and women, then – as should be clear from the discussion in Chapter 5 – differences in labour supply elasticities at the level of the firm give them the opportunity of increasing their profits by discriminating against women. Taking up the results from Chapter 7, the same holds for firms with monopsony power in a dynamic setting, where both the short- and the long-run elasticity of firm-level labour supply are crucial for firms' wage-setting behaviour. Additionally, if discounting becomes negligible, only the long-run elasticity matters, so that gender differences in the long-run firm-level labour supply elasticity may be the source of Robinsonian discrimination.

Again, we have to emphasise that the relevant elasticity differential to look at is the one at the level of the firm, not the one at the market level (for a more detailed discussion of this, see Chapter 5). While there is overwhelming empirical evidence that the labour supply elasticity at the level of the market is higher for women than for men (cf., e.g., Killingsworth and Heckman, 1986; Pencavel, 1986; Heckman, 1993; Blundell and MaCurdy, 1999), elasticity differentials at the level of the market and at the level of the firm may differ in signs (cf. Boal and Ransom, 1997). Reasons for this difference in firm-level labour supply elasticities may be, among others, gender differences in mobility costs or preferences over non-wage job characteristics (as explored in detail in Chapter 5) or differences in search frictions.

As laid out in Chapter 8, in the equilibrium search model with wage posting by Burdett and Mortensen, workers' outcomes are directly related to the search frictions faced by them. Suppose, similar to van den Berg and Ridder (1998), that there are segmented labour markets for different groups of workers. It is evident from the results presented in Proposition 8.1 that labour market outcomes will be worse for women if they face higher on-the-job search frictions than male workers, that is, if women's market friction parameter ξ^f is larger than men's ξ^m. While we argue at

---

[1] The following chapter extends joint work with Thorsten Schank and Claus Schnabel published as Hirsch *et al.* (2009*b*).

quite an intuitive level here, this can of course be shown by explicitly modelling firms' wage-setting decisions with two equally productive labour inputs with different market friction parameters. Barth and Dale-Olsen (1999), for example, show that in such an environment the group of workers with lower on-the-job search frictions achieves better outcomes and also has a higher labour supply elasticity at the level of the firm, so that the difference in on-the-job search frictions is the driving force of both differences in outcomes and elasticities. We thus again arrive at a Robinsonian explanation of the gender pay gap which is – other than in Chapter 5 – driven by gender differences in on-the-job search frictions.

But before concluding that this is a potential explanation of wage discrimination, we must ask ourselves what may cause ξ^f to be larger than ξ^m. There are several potential reasons for this, some of them being discussed by Bowlus (1997) and Barth and Dale-Olsen (1999). For simplicity, assume that job offer arrival rates when employed and when non-employed are the same, λ^f for women and λ^m for men. Obviously, $\xi^f > \xi^m$ requires $\lambda^f < \lambda^m$ and/or $\delta^f > \delta^m$, that is, women's job offer arrival rate has to be smaller and/or their job destruction rate has to be larger than men's. Reasons for such differences include, for instance, that women are more likely to quit their jobs due to family-related reasons or that their employment choices are traditionally more affected by their spouses than the other way round. This corresponds well with the observations by Bowlus (1997) that women have a greater tendency to exit jobs to non-participation and are less likely to make job-to-job transitions. Particularly the latter finding will be confirmed by our empirical analysis.

Having said this, two questions arise: (1) Is women's labour supply at the level of the firm less elastic than men's? If the answer to this first question is affirmative, then Robinsonian discrimination will be feasible because the necessary condition of differences in firm-level elasticities is satisfied.[2] (2) Do women face higher on-the-job search frictions than men? If the answer to this second question is affirmative, then Robinsonian discrimination may arise because of gender differences in on-the-job search frictions.

Both questions will be answered in the following from inspecting a large linked employer–employee data set for Germany. But before doing so, we shall derive a simple measure of on-the-job search frictions introduced by Manning (2003a, pp. 44–49) which is much more easier obtained from the data but also less informative than an estimate of the firm-level labour supply elasticity. This measure will

---

[2] It is important to stress 'that the presence of an upward sloping labor supply curve is necessary but not sufficient evidence of a monopsonistic outcome' (Hirsch and Schumacher, 1995, p. 444) because it provides employers with potential monopsony power, whereas it remains unclear whether they actually use it. They may, for example, be constrained by labour market institutions, such as minimum wages or collective bargaining, to make (full) use of their monopsony power. By the same token, gender differences in firm-level labour supply elasticities provide employers with different degrees of monopsony power over their male and female workers, while we cannot conclude from the existence of such differences that firms really engage in Robinsonian discrimination. Again, the institutional framework (e.g., equal pay legislation) may constrain employers' ability to exploit these differences.

allow us to answer the second question. To answer the first one, we shall derive a semi-structural approach proposed by Manning (2003a, pp. 96–104, 109/110), which utilises data on firms' in- and outflow of workers and the structure of a Burdett–Mortensen-like model to arrive at an estimate of the long-run firm-level labour supply elasticity.

9.1 A Simple Measure of On-the-Job Search Frictions

In Chapter 8, we extensively discussed the role of the market friction parameter $\xi := \delta/\lambda^e$ in the Burdett–Mortensen dynamic monopsony model. In particular, we found that in the steady-state equilibrium the worker's expected wage is strictly decreasing in this parameter. The higher is the market friction parameter, the less likely are employed workers to receive attractive outside offers, and the lower is the competition among employers. Put differently, it becomes harder to find a 'ladder' instead of a 'snake.' By the same token, Manning (2003a, p. 44) argues that the share of recruits hired from non-employment captures the extent of on-the-job search frictions and can be used as a proxy for the market friction parameter. For the higher is this share, the lower is workers' inter-employer mobility, and this decreased mobility is expected to raise employers' monopsony power.

In the following, let ζ denote the share of hires from non-employment. Within Burdett and Mortensen's model as laid out in Chapter 8 it follows that ζ is a strictly increasing function of the market friction parameter, where

$$\zeta(\xi) = \frac{1/\xi}{(1 + 1/\xi)\ln(1 + 1/\xi)} \tag{9.1}$$

with $\zeta'(\xi) > 0$ for all $\xi > 0$, a proof of which is given in Appendix B.4. The higher is the share of recruits hired from non-employment, the higher is the market friction parameter, and the higher are therefore workers' on-the-job search frictions. Hence, firms possess more monopsony power, being less constrained by inter-employer competition for workers, and workers' expected wage will fall if firms actually exercise their monopsony power.

Apart from just calculating the share of recruits from non-employment for different groups of workers at the labour market, one may also analyse the extent of search frictions for different groups multivariately by investigating the determinants of the probability that a recruit is hired from non-employment and controlling for person- as well as firm-specific characteristics. Consider that we have I_R transitions (indexed $i = 1, \ldots, I_R$) of M_R recruits (indexed $m = 1, \ldots, M_R$) being hired by J_R firms (indexed $j = 1, \ldots, J_R$). Let $x_i = (x_{i1}, \ldots, x_{ik})$ denote a row vector of k covariates observed for transition i, and let $\beta = (\beta_1, \ldots, \beta_k)^\top$ denote a column vector of k coefficients, which are the same for all transitions $i = 1, \ldots, I_R$. Similarly, let $z_{j(i)} = (z_{j(i)1}, \ldots, z_{j(i)l})$ denote a row vector of l covariates observed for firm $j(i)$, for which the worker $m(i)$ with spell i is working, and let $\gamma = (\gamma_1, \ldots, \gamma_l)^\top$

denote the corresponding column vector of l coefficients. Finally, let y_i denote a binary response taking on the value one if a recruit is hired from non-employment and zero otherwise. We now model the conditional probability that a recruit is hired from non-employment as

$$\Pr(y_i = 1 | x_i, z_{j(i)}) = \Phi(x_i \beta + z_{j(i)} \gamma), \quad (9.2)$$

where Φ again denotes the c.d.f. of the standard normal distribution. Estimates of (9.2) are done by fitting a probit model using maximum likelihood as the probit model utilises a standard normal link function.[3]

Manning (2003a pp. 47–49) uses this approach to assess group-specific differences in on-the-job search frictions for two data sets, the Current Population Survey for the U.S. and the Labour Force Survey for the UK. He finds that the probability of being hired from non-employment is higher for women, for young and old workers, for less-qualified workers, and for black men in the U.S. and for blacks generally in the UK, suggesting higher on-the-job search frictions and worse labour market outcomes for these groups. Moreover, he emphasises that these groups are typically those whose labour market outcomes are observed to be rather bad, which is in line with his findings as they suggest weaker competition among employers for these workers.

Hirsch and Schumacher (2005) employ the share of recruits hired from non-employment to investigate whether employers in the labour market for registered nurses in the U.S. possess more monopsony power than employers in other labour markets. They obtain similar results as Manning: The share of recruits from non-employment is larger for low-skilled workers and women. However, it is found to be substantially lower for registered nurses than for women or men in general, implying less monopsony power in this labour market segment. Furthermore, they do not find evidence for a negative relationship between registered nurses' share of hires from non-employment and their wages when considering 240 different labour market areas. All in all, they conclude that the market for registered nurses does not appear to be a prime example of a monopsonistic labour market, in contrast to what is often argued in the literature (see footnote 2 in Hirsch and Schumacher, 2005).[4] Nonetheless, Hirsch and Schumacher (2004) report a significantly negative relationship between less-educated female workers' share of hires from non-employment and their wages, suggesting worse labour market outcomes due to on-the-job search frictions and potential monopsonistic discrimination for this group.

In this section, we have derived a simple measure of search frictions put forward by Manning (2003a, pp. 44–49): the share of recruits hired from non-employment.

---

[3] Of course, we could also have chosen a logit model using the standard logistic c.d.f. Λ instead of Φ for modelling the probability that a recruit is hired from non-employment. For details about probit and logit models, see the references given in footnote 10 on page 118.

[4] Earlier studies investigating the labour market for registered nurses from a monopsonistic point of view include, among others, Link and Landon (1976), Adamache and Sloan (1982), Sullivan (1989), Hirsch and Schumacher (1995), and Staiger et al. (1999).

We demonstrated that this measure is strictly increasing in the market friction parameter and pointed out how to specify it empirically, viz. by fitting a probit model for the probability that a recruit is hired from non-employment. But before we will put this into practice, we shall derive a semi-structural estimation approach to the long-run labour supply elasticity at the level of the firm. Whereas this approach is much more demanding both technically and in terms of the data needed than the approach presented in this section, the framework employed is more general and its outcome is much more informative. While differences in the simple measure of on-the-job search frictions enable us only to say which group is likely to perform worse in the labour market on account of differences in on-the-job search frictions, differences in elasticities enable us to say even more within a less restrictive setting. Using the results from Proposition 7.1, we are not only able to say by how much the outcomes should differ under monopsonistic and competitive environments but also to compare the gender pay gap predicted by the model and the actual gap to assess the model's predictive plausibility.

9.2 A Semi-Structural Estimation Approach to the Firm-Level Labour Supply Elasticity

9.2.1 Combining Simple Dynamic Monopsony and the Burdett–Mortensen Model

Consider the special case of simple dynamic monopsony (7.10) where workers leave a firm paying wage w_t in period t at a strictly decreasing separation rate $s(w_t)$, while a strictly increasing number of recruits $R(w_t)$ arrives at that firm. So the firm's labour supply in period t is given by

$$L_t = L(w_t, L_{t-1}) = R(w_t) + [1 - s(w_t)]L_{t-1} \qquad (9.3)$$

with $t \in \mathbb{N}$ and some initial value $L_0 \geq 0$. The continuous-time analogue to this specification is represented by the differential equation

$$\dot{L}[w(t)] = R[w(t)] - s[w(t)]L[w(t)] \qquad (9.4)$$

with $t > 0$ and some initial value $L[w(0)] \geq 0$. Given a steady state with $\dot{L}[w(t)] = 0$ and $w(t) = w$ for all $t > 0$, the firm's hires $R(w)$ and separations $s(w)L(w)$ must be balanced, which gives a steady-state workforce of

$$L(w) = R(w)/s(w). \qquad (9.5)$$

Note that $L'(w) > 0$ for all $w > 0$, so that the firm's steady-state employment depends positively on the wage paid. Taking logs and differentiation of (9.5) yield

$$e_{Lw}^{LR}(w) = e_{Rw}(w) - e_{sw}(w), \qquad (9.6)$$

where $e_{Lw}^{LR}(w) := L'(w)w/L(w)$ denotes the long-run wage elasticity of the firm's labour supply, $e_{Rw}(w) := R'(w)w/R(w)$ the wage elasticity of its flow of recruits, and $e_{sw}(w) := s'(w)w/s(w)$ the wage elasticity of its separation rate.

This simple dynamic monopsony framework can be developed further by making use of the structure of the Burdett–Mortensen model of equilibrium search with wage posting as laid out in Chapter 8. Since existing matches break off at rate δ and employed workers receive job offers at rate λ^e which they accept if and only if they pay more than their current wage, the separation rate at wage w is given by

$$s(w) = \delta + \lambda^e [1 - F(w)], \qquad (9.7)$$

where F again denotes the wage offer distribution. The mass of recruits for a firm paying wage w is represented by

$$R(w) = \lambda^n N + \lambda^e \int_r^w L(x) \, dF(x), \qquad (9.8)$$

where N again denotes the steady-state mass of non-employed workers. (9.8) holds because non-employed workers receive acceptable job offers at rate λ^n, whereas only employed workers earning less than w are willing to accept the firm's offer.

Differentiation of both (9.7) and (9.8) and some rearrangement yield

$$e_{Rw}(w) = -e_{sw}(w) \Leftrightarrow e_{Lw}^{LR}(w) = -2e_{sw}(w) \qquad (9.9)$$

because we are in a steady state, so that (9.6) applies. Therefore, absolute values of the recruitment and the separation rate elasticity are the same. Roughly speaking, this holds since one firm's wage-related quit is another firm's wage-related hiring and since both hiring from and separations to non-employment are wage-inelastic.[5] Making use of this result, one is able to estimate the long-run labour supply elasticity at the level of the firm by simply estimating the separation rate elasticity and to investigate gender differences by separate estimations or including interactions. This can be done by using existing estimation procedures, such as

---

[5] It is important to note that the structure of the Burdett–Mortensen model is sufficient but not necessary for equation (9.9) to hold. Under spatial dyopsony as laid out in Chapter 5, for example, one firm's wage-related quit is also another (more precisely, *the* other) firm's wage-related hire, and transitions from and to non-employment are absent from the model (and thus wage-inelastic). The same holds under constant long-run spatial monopsony as laid out in Section 4.6.1. Therefore, we can conclude that the Burdett–Mortensen model is just one possible framework to motivate the equality (in absolute value) of the recruitment and the separation rate elasticity. But since this model is – other than spatial monopsony – dynamic by nature, it is the more natural candidate to motivate the result (9.9) which is gained from a dynamic monopsony specification; and we shall thus stick to this framework in the following.

hazard rate models, whereas we do not have such straightforward procedures for obtaining the recruitment elasticity.[6]

9.2.2 Introducing Stochastic Job-to-Job Transitions

This specification, however, is rather restrictive since it is assumed that workers change their jobs if and only if they are offered wages above their current wage and that transitions from and to non-employment are wage-inelastic. To overcome these restrictions, the first relaxation is to allow for stochastic transitions among employers. This is achieved by assuming that the probability of a worker to change his or her job depends positively on the ratio of the offered wage to the worker's current wage, so that workers are more likely to change jobs if offered a wage increase, but do not change jobs for sure.

Let $\varphi(x/w)$ denote the probability that a worker currently paid wage w quits and accepts a job offering wage x. Since φ is a probability, $0 \leqslant \varphi(x/w) \leqslant 1$ holds for all $x/w > 0$. Furthermore, assume that φ is continuously differentiable with $\varphi'(x/w) \geqslant 0$ for all $x/w > 0$, i.e., the probability that a worker changes his or her job weakly increases in the ratio of the offered to the current wage.[7] Let $\overline{w}$ denote the supremum of F's support, and let $\underline{w}$ denote its infimum. Using φ as defined above, the separation rate of a firm paying wage w is given by

$$s(w) = \delta + \lambda^e \int_{\underline{w}}^{\overline{w}} \varphi(x/w) \, dF(x). \tag{9.10}$$

Hence, some workers with current wage w might even accept a job offering a wage $x < w$. Similarly, the mass of recruits for a firm paying w is represented by

$$R(w) = \lambda^n N + \lambda^e \int_{\underline{w}}^{\overline{w}} \varphi(w/x) L(x) \, dF(x). \tag{9.11}$$

---

[6] There is a large empirical literature on quit rates, early influential papers including Parsons (1972) and Pencavel (1972). Though there are some papers considering gender differences in quit rates, e.g., Viscusi (1980), Blau and Kahn (1981), Weiss (1984), Meitzen (1986), Light and Ureta (1992), and Campbell (1993), much of this literature does not investigate whether there are gender differences in the wage responsiveness of quit rates. And even if papers do so, they do not link quit elasticity differentials to firm-level labour supply elasticity differentials and Robinsonian discrimination. On the other hand, there are – unsurprisingly, given the problems involved in identification – only very few papers around investigating recruit rates and their elasticities (e.g., Krueger, 1988; Holzer et al., 1991). And to the best of our knowledge, there has been made no attempt to analyse gender differences in the wage responsiveness of recruit rates.

[7] Obviously, the model considered so far is nested as a limiting case with $\varphi(x/w) = 0$ if $x/w < 1$ and $\varphi(x/w) = 1$ if $x/w \geqslant 1$.

Equations (9.10) and (9.11) can now be used to arrive at

$$\int_{\underline{w}}^{\overline{w}} e_{sw}(x) R(x)\, dF(x) = -\int_{\underline{w}}^{\overline{w}} e_{Rw}(x) R(x)\, dF(x), \tag{9.12}$$

which is Manning's (2003a) Proposition 4.3.[8] (9.12) says that absolute values of recruit-weighted recruitment and separation rate elasticities are the same. In particular, this means that for iso-elastic separation rate and recruitment functions absolute values of both elasticities are the same, so that (9.9) holds again.

9.2.3 Introducing Elastic Transitions from and to Non-Employment

The second relaxation is to allow additionally for wage-related transitions to and from non-employment. There are several reasons why these transitions should be influenced by wages. For instance, individuals paid low wages are more likely to leave the labour market due to the availability of transfer payments or because they are more productive in household production. By doing so, individuals are simply better off. On the other hand, a high wage offer may cause non-employed individuals to take up a job. In short, the volume of voluntary transitions to and from non-employment is likely to depend on wages.

Let $s^e(w)$ denote the separation rate to employment, $s^n(w)$ the separation rate to non-employment, and $\theta_s(w)$ the share of separations to employment, which is assumed to vary with the wage paid. Then the total separation rate is given by

$$s(w) = s^e(w) + s^n(w) \tag{9.13}$$

with

$$s^e(w) = \lambda^e \int_{\underline{w}}^{\overline{w}} \varphi(x/w)\, dF(x). \tag{9.14}$$

Moreover, we have $s^e(w) = \theta_s(w) s(w)$ and $s^n(w) = [1 - \theta_s(w)] s(w)$. Analogously, define $R^e(w)$ as the mass of recruits hired from employment, $R^n(w)$ as the mass of recruits hired from non-employment, and $\theta_R(w)$ as the share of recruits hired from employment. Therefore, we get

$$R(w) = R^e(w) + R^n(w) \tag{9.15}$$

with

$$R^e(w) = \lambda^e \int_{\underline{w}}^{\overline{w}} \varphi(w/x) L(x)\, dF(x), \tag{9.16}$$

$R^e(w) = \theta_R(w) R(w)$, and $R^n(w) = [1 - \theta_R(w)] R(w)$.

---

[8] A formal proof that (9.12) holds is given in Appendix B.5.

9.2 A Semi-Structural Estimation Approach to the Firm-Level Labour Supply Elasticity

Next, we define the corresponding elasticities. Let $e^e_{Rw}(w)$ and $e^n_{Rw}(w)$ denote the wage elasticities of the firm's mass of recruits hired from employment and non-employment, respectively, and let $e^e_{sw}(w)$ and $e^n_{sw}(w)$ denote the elasticities of its separation rates to employment and non-employment. The overall long-run wage elasticity of the firm's labour supply thus becomes

$$e^{LR}_{Lw}(w) = \theta_R(w)e^e_{Rw}(w) + [1-\theta_R(w)]e^n_{Rw}(w) - \theta_s(w)e^e_{sw}(w) - [1-\theta_s(w)]e^n_{sw}(w). \quad (9.17)$$

Hence, the long-run firm-level labour supply elasticity is a weighted average of the recruitment elasticities from employment and non-employment net of a weighted average of the separation rate elasticities to employment and non-employment, where weights are given by the share of recruits hired from employment and the share of separations to employment, respectively. In particular, this implies that we can infer e^{LR}_{Lw} from estimating these four elasticities separately.

In a next step, a relationship similar to (9.12) can be derived, which corresponds to Manning's (2003a) Proposition 4.4. Absolute values of a weighted average of the separation rate elasticity to employment and a weighted average of the recruitment elasticity from employment are the same, where the weights are the number of separations to employment for the former and the number of recruits hired from employment for the latter. We get

$$\int_{\underline{w}}^{\overline{w}} e^e_{sw}(x) s^e(x) L(x)\, dF(x) = -\int_{\underline{w}}^{\overline{w}} e^e_{Rw}(x) R^e(x)\, dF(x), \quad (9.18)$$

so that both elasticities are the same in absolute value if both the recruitment from employment and the separation rate to employment are iso-elastic functions.[9] In this case, (9.18) can be used to infer an estimate for e^e_{Rw} from the estimate of e^e_{sw}. In the case of non-constant elasticities, however, we would be confronted with the problem of obtaining the weights of the averages.

What is left is finding a procedure to estimate e^n_{Rw}. Consider the share of recruits hired from employment at wage w, which is $\theta_R(w) = R^e(w)/[R^e(w)+R^n(w)]$. Solving for $R^n(w)$ yields

$$R^n(w) = \frac{1-\theta_R(w)}{\theta_R(w)} R^e(w). \quad (9.19)$$

Taking logs and derivatives of both the left- and the right-hand side of (9.19) and some rearrangement give

$$e^n_{Rw}(w) = e^e_{Rw}(w) - \frac{\theta'_R(w)w}{\theta_R(w)[1-\theta_R(w)]}. \quad (9.20)$$

---

[9] A formal proof that (9.18) holds is given in appendix B.6.

Therefore, we may use this relationship, which is Manning's (2003a) Proposition 4.5, to estimate e_{Rw}^n indirectly through e_{Rw}^e, so that we do not have to estimate recruitment elasticities at all.

9.2.4 Procedure for Identifying the Long-Run Labour Supply Elasticity at the Level of the Firm

To sum up, the relationships in equations (9.17), (9.18), and (9.20) enable us to apply the following procedure for identifying the long-run firm-level labour supply elasticity: In the first step, we estimate the separation rate elasticity to employment e_{sw}^e, which also provides, in the second step, an estimate of the recruitment elasticity to employment e_{Rw}^e. Third, this estimate can be used to obtain an estimate of the recruitment elasticity from non-employment e_{Rw}^n if we additionally take into account the wage responsiveness of the share of recruits hired from employment. Fourth, we estimate the separation rate elasticity to non-employment e_{sw}^n. We thus have to infer some information on the firm's recruitment function. Finally, these four estimates can be combined to obtain an estimate for the long-run elasticity of the labour supply to the firm. Next, we shall demonstrate how this procedure can be put into action.

9.2.5 Empirical Specification

The results presented so far can now be used to estimate the long-run labour supply elasticity at the firm level. The following notation will be similar to the one employed in Section 9.1. Suppose there are M workers (indexed $m = 1, \ldots, M$) with I employment spells (indexed $i = 1, \ldots, I$) who work for J firms (indexed $j = 1, \ldots, J$). Let $x_i(t) = (x_{i1}(t), \ldots, x_{ik}(t))$ denote a row vector of k time-varying covariates observed for employment spell i at time t, where time corresponds to the time elapsed since the beginning of the spell, which is the worker's tenure with the firm. Next, let $\beta = (\beta_1, \ldots, \beta_k)^\top$ denote a column vector of k coefficients, which are the same for all spells i and constant over time. Analogously, $z_{j(i)}(t) = (z_{j(i)1}(t), \ldots, z_{j(i)l}(t))$ is a row vector of l time-varying covariates observed for firm $j(i)$ at time t, for which the worker $m(i)$ with spell i is working, while $\gamma = (\gamma_1, \ldots, \gamma_l)^\top$ denotes the corresponding vector of l coefficients. Finally, let $v_{j(i)}$ denote a firm-specific time-invariant constant.

We model the instantaneous separation rate to employment of the i-th spell at time t conditional on $x_i(t)$, $z_{j(i)}(t)$, and $v_{j(i)}^e$ as

$$s_i^e(t|x_i(t), z_{j(i)}(t), v_{j(i)}^e) = v_{j(i)}^e s_0^e(t) \exp(x_i(t)\beta^e + z_{j(i)}(t)\gamma^e). \qquad (9.21)$$

This gives a conditional hazard function with baseline hazard $s_0^e(t)$ and unobserved heterogeneity at the level of the firm $v_{j(i)}^e$, i.e., a mixed proportional hazard model

9.2 A Semi-Structural Estimation Approach to the Firm-Level Labour Supply Elasticity

with time-varying covariates.[10] By analogy, unobserved heterogeneity at the level of the worker can be taken into account by including a term $v^e_{m(i)}$ multiplicatively. Next, we model the conditional instantaneous separation rate to non-employment in the same manner as

$$s^n_i(t|x_i(t), z_{j(i)}(t), v^n_{j(i)}) = v^n_{j(i)} s^n_0(t) \exp(x_i(t)\beta^n + z_{j(i)}(t)\gamma^n). \quad (9.22)$$

In the following, let $s^\sigma_0(t) = 1$ for all $t > 0$ with $\sigma = e, n$, so that we get two exponential models with time-varying covariates. Moreover, we assume that $v^\sigma_{j(i)}$ follows a Gamma distribution with mean one and finite variance, i.e., $E[v^\sigma_{j(i)}] = 1$ and $\mathrm{Var}[v^\sigma_{j(i)}] < \infty$, as put forward by Abbring and van den Berg (2007). Therefore, we get two exponential models with shared gamma frailties, which can be thought of as gamma-distributed random effects reflecting unobserved heterogeneity at the level of the firm.

It is important to note that exponential models, such as ours or those employed by Manning, assume that there is no duration dependence, that is, the baseline hazard is assumed to be constant over time, which puts a severe restriction on the model. There are both reasons for and against including a time-varying baseline hazard, which corresponds to the question of whether or not to control for the worker's tenure. One might argue that tenure influences the separation rate. As Manning (2003a, p. 103) notes, one of the main hypotheses of the 'new' monopsony literature is that paying higher wages reduces the separations taking place and thus raises workers' tenure, so that including a time-varying baseline hazard may take away variation from the wage variable. According to this argument, excluding tenure provides the wage estimate that we are actually interested in. On the other hand, the existence of seniority wage schedules, for example, may require to control for tenure. For this reason, as a check of robustness, we will also estimate mixed proportional hazard models with time-varying baseline hazards. This will be implemented by fitting piecewise-constant exponential models, where $s^\sigma_0(t)$ is a step function in the worker's tenure.

Assuming that the instantaneous separation rates s^e_i and s^n_i are conditionally independent, Manning (2003a, p. 101) shows that they can be estimated separately: Two estimations are done, each of them considering two states. The separation rate to non-employment is estimated using the whole sample, where transitions to non-employment and censored spells (i.e., job-to-job transitions and stayers) are distinguished. The separation rate to employment is estimated using the sample of those employment spells not ending with a transition from employment to non-employment. In this case, transitions to other firms and stayers are distinguished. While such a two-step procedure is also employed here, our approach of modelling the separation rates according to (9.21) and (9.22) is less restrictive

---

[10] For details about mixed proportional hazard models, see van den Berg (2001), Cameron and Trivedi (2005, pp. 573–639), or Jenkins (2005).

than Manning's because the shared gamma frailties allow us to take account of unobserved heterogeneity at the level of the firm.

If $x_i(t)$ includes spell i's log wage at time t $\ln w_i(t)$ and β_w^σ denotes the respective coefficient, the wage elasticities of the conditional instantaneous separation rates are constant and obtained from (9.21) and (9.22) as

$$\frac{\partial \ln s_i^\sigma(t|x_i(t), z_{j(i)}(t), \upsilon_{j(i)}^\sigma)}{\partial \ln w_i(t)} = \beta_w^\sigma. \quad (9.23)$$

Making use of (9.23), $\widehat{\beta}_w^e$ provides an estimate for the separation rate elasticity to employment e_{sw}^e, while $\widehat{\beta}_w^n$ gives an estimate for the separation rate elasticity to non-employment e_{sw}^n. Since the mixed proportional hazard models estimate constant separation rate elasticities, we know from equation (9.18) that the absolute values of the separation rate elasticity to employment and the recruitment elasticity from employment are the same, so that $\widehat{e}_{sw}^e$ also provides an estimate for e_{Rw}^e. Thus, we do not have to estimate e_{Rw}^e on its own.

Finally, we model the share of recruits hired from employment θ_R as a standard logistic function Λ, where now $i = 1, \ldots, I_R$ transitions of M_R recruits are considered. Hence, the conditional probability that a recruit is hired from employment becomes

$$\Pr(y_i = 1|x_i, z_{j(i)}, \upsilon_{j(i)}) = \theta_{R,i}(x_i, z_{j(i)}, \upsilon_{j(i)}) = \frac{\exp(x_i\beta + z_{j(i)}\gamma + \upsilon_{j(i)})}{1 + \exp(x_i\beta + z_{j(i)}\gamma + \upsilon_{j(i)})}, \quad (9.24)$$

where the notation follows the same rules as in Section 9.1. Note that y_i is now a binary response taking on the value one if a recruit is hired from employment and zero otherwise. If x_i includes the worker's log wage $\ln w_i$ and β_w denotes the corresponding coefficient, β_w is given by

$$\beta_w = \frac{\partial \theta_{R,i}(x_i, z_{j(i)}, \upsilon_{j(i)})/\partial w_i}{\theta_{R,i}(x_i, z_{j(i)}, \upsilon_{j(i)})[1 - \theta_{R,i}(x_i, z_{j(i)}, \upsilon_{j(i)})]} w_i. \quad (9.25)$$

To get an estimate for β_w, we fit a logit model for the probability that a recruit is hired from employment since the logit model uses a standard logistic link function. Since the estimate $\widehat{\beta}_w$ from the logit model is the same for all spells $i = 1, \ldots, I_R$, we may drop the index i at θ_R, and (9.25) becomes exactly the second term on the right-hand side of equation (9.20). Therefore, we can obtain the estimate $\widehat{e}_{Rw}^n$ from $\widehat{e}_{Rw}^e$ by subtracting $\widehat{\beta}_w$ from the latter. Moreover, if we assume that the unobserved heterogeneity term $\upsilon_{j(i)}$ follows a normal distribution with mean zero and some finite variance, i.e., $\mathrm{E}[\upsilon_{j(i)}] = 0$ and $\mathrm{Var}[\upsilon_{j(i)}] < \infty$, we get a Gaussian random effects logit model.[11]

---

[11] For details about Gaussian random effects logit models, see Wooldridge (2002, pp. 490–492) or Cameron and Trivedi (2005, pp. 795/796).

9.2 A Semi-Structural Estimation Approach to the Firm-Level Labour Supply Elasticity

In a steady state, the share of recruits hired from employment and the share of separations to employment must be the same, so that we define $\theta := \theta_R = \theta_s$. To obtain an estimate for e_{Lw}^{LR} making use of (9.11), we have to estimate θ, for instance, by just calculating the share of recruits hired from employment from the data. Then we are able to estimate the long-run labour supply elasticity at the firm level as

$$\widehat{e}_{Lw}^{LR} = \widehat{\theta}\widehat{e}_{Rw}^{e} + (1 - \widehat{\theta})\widehat{e}_{Rw}^{n} - \widehat{\theta}\widehat{e}_{sw}^{e} - (1 - \widehat{\theta})\widehat{e}_{sw}^{n}$$
$$= -(1 + \widehat{\theta})\widehat{\beta}_{w}^{e} - (1 - \widehat{\theta})(\widehat{\beta}_{w}^{n} + \widehat{\beta}_{w}). \tag{9.26}$$

9.2.6 Related Empirical Literature

Manning (2003a pp. 100–105, 206–208) uses this procedure to estimate firm-level labour supply elasticities for two American and two British data sets: the Panel Study of Income Dynamics and the National Longitudinal Study of the Youth for the U.S. as well as the Labour Force Survey and the British Household Panel Study for the UK. He fits exponential hazard models and estimates separation rate elasticities separately for men and women. Since he uses data sets based on supply-side individual- or household-level surveys, he is not able to control adequately for firm-specific determinants of transition behaviour. For all four data sets estimated separation rate elasticities are negative, low in absolute value and statistically significant at the 1 per cent level. The resulting overall long-run labour supply elasticities are quite low, ranging from 0.7 to 1.4. Investigating the gender-specific separation rate elasticities, there is no evidence that women supply labour less elastically than men at the level of the firm.[12]

Ransom and Oaxaca (2008), on the other hand, do find gender differences in elasticities, but they use the restrictive specification with deterministic transition behaviour across firms and wage-inelastic transitions from and to non-employment, so that equation (9.9) applies. Using data from a U.S. chain of regional grocery stores, they fit a probit model for the probability that a separation takes place. Again no firm-specific controls are added. Estimated firm-level labour supply elasticities are around 2.7 for male and 1.5 for female workers (depending on specification), implying that firms have significant monopsony power. Moreover, the noticeable difference in elasticities could give employers the opportunity of engaging in

---

[12] Note that these gender differences are found in an early (spatial monopsony) study by Madden (1977a), who uses U.S. data from the National Longitudinal Survey of Labor Force Behavior. Apart from finding lower firm-level labour supply elasticities for female workers, Madden also finds in her spatial monopsony approach that women are less inclined to commute for wage-related reasons, which is in line with our Robinsonian spatial monopsony explanation of the gender pay gap presented in Chapter 5.

Robinsonian discrimination, and the observed industry pay gaps are close to those predicted by simple dynamic monopsony.[13]

Finally, using a Norwegian linked employer–employee data set and a specification similar in spirit to the one used by Ransom and Oaxaca, Barth and Dale-Olsen (2009) find a similar pattern for low- and high-educated workers: Both low- and high-educated females supply labour less elastically than males at the level of the firm, where this elasticity differential is more pronounced for low-educated workers. Comparing their estimates to the observed gender pay gaps, Barth and Dale-Olsen also find that a large part of these gaps is predicted by dynamic monopsony.[14]

9.3 Data

Before we will investigate gender differences in on-the-job search frictions and long-run firm-level labour supply elasticities, we have to describe the data we are going to use: The data set utilised in subsequent empirical analyses is the German LIAB, i.e., the Linked Employer–Employee Data Set of the Institute for Employment Research (*Institut für Arbeitsmarkt- und Berufsforschung*, IAB) of the German Federal Employment Agency (*Bundesagentur für Arbeit*). The LIAB is created by linking the process-produced person-specific data of the IAB with the IAB Establishment Panel (cf. Alda *et al.*, 2005). Using the LIAB, we are therefore able to control both for worker and establishment characteristics.

The employee history used for constructing the LIAB is based on the integrated notification procedure for the health, pension, and unemployment insurances.[15] This procedure requires all employers to report all information of their employees if covered by the social security system, where misreporting is legally sanctioned. Notifications are compulsory at the beginning and the end of employment. Additionally, an annual report must be made for each employee employed on the 31st December of the year. As a consequence, only those workers, salaried employees, and trainees who are covered by social security are included. Thus, among others, civil servants, self-employed, those in marginal employment, students enrolled in higher education, and family workers are not included. All in all, approximately 80 per cent of all people employed in western Germany are part of the employee history.

---

[13] It is interesting to note that the employer under consideration was actually found guilty of engaging in discriminatory practices during the observation period. This is a particularly reassuring piece of information which is not easy to arrive at when considering survey-based or administrative data sets.

[14] In line with these findings of Ransom and Oaxaca (2008) and Barth and Dale-Olsen (2009), Green *et al.* (1996) report more pronounced employer size–wage effects for female than male workers pointing at less elastic female labour supply at the firm level.

[15] Details are given by Alda *et al.* (2005) and Bender *et al.* (2000).

9.3 Data

The data include, among others things, information for every employee on the daily gross wage, censored at the social security contribution ceiling, on the employee's occupation and occupational status, on industry, and on the start and end of each employee notification. Furthermore, individual characteristics, such as age, schooling, training, sex, and nationality are contained.[16] Finally, an establishment number is included which is used to link the employee history and the IAB Establishment Panel.

The employer side of our data set is given by the IAB Establishment Panel, a random sample of establishments (not companies) from the comprehensive Employment Statistics drawn according to the principle of optimal stratification.[17] Strata are defined over plant sizes and industries, where all in all ten plant sizes and 16 industries are considered. Since the survey is based on the Employment Statistics aggregated via the establishment number as of the 30th June of a year, it only includes establishments which employ at least one employee covered by social security. Every year since 1993 (1996) the IAB Establishment Panel has surveyed the same establishments from all industries in western (eastern) Germany. Response rates of units which have been interviewed repeatedly exceed 80 per cent. The IAB Establishment Panel is created to serve the needs of the Federal Employment Agency, so that the focus on employment-related topics is predominant. Questions deal, among other things, with the number of employees, the working week for full-time workers, the establishment's commitment to collective agreements, the existence of a works council, the establishment's performance and export share, and its technological status.

Linking both the IAB Establishment Panel and the employee history through the establishment number gives the LIAB.[18] We will use version 2 of the LIAB longitudinal model, which is based on a balanced panel of establishments participating in the IAB Establishment Panel in each year between 2000 and 2002 and provides information on all workers which have been employed by any of these establishments for at least one day. This data set enables us to use the available flow information of individuals to analyse the separation rates as discussed in Section 9.2, viz. the separation rates to employment and to non-employment, where employment refers to employment at another establishment. Due to the inclusion of establishment data, we are able to control as well for person-specific characteristics as for characteristics of the establishment the employee is working for or is entering. Therefore, the labour market's demand and supply side can be taken into consideration (e.g., Abowd and

---

[16] Due to notifications made in the case of changes which are relevant according to benefit entitlement rules, there is also information on the employee's marital status and the number of children. However, these variables contain much measurement error and are very fragmentary (cf. Alda, 2005, p. 21), so that we will not be able to use them.

[17] Details about the IAB Establishment Panel are given by Kölling (2000).

[18] Details about the different LIAB models and their versions are given by Alda (2005).

Kramarz, 1999). In the following, we restrict our analysis to western Germany[19] and to full-time employees[20].

A shortcoming of the LIAB is that daily gross wages are censored at the social security contribution ceiling, viz. €143.95 in 2000, €146.02 in 2001, and €147.95 in 2002. Obviously, using the wage data without any correction would give biased estimates. However, any imputation of the censored values cannot completely remedy this problem since it would introduce, by construction, some measurement error. And this would cause inconsistent estimates of the impact of the wage if included as an regressor. Therefore, we carry out our analysis only for those workers whose wages were always below the ceiling during the period of observation, which reduces the whole (recruitment) sample for men by 21.8 (17.0) and for women by 8.0 (7.4) per cent.[21] This leaves us – after dropping establishments (and their employees) with missing values in any of the covariates in any of the years – with information on 402,105 employees working for 3,560 establishments.

The wages analysed here are influenced by various actors and institutions in the German system of wage determination. In Germany, collective bargaining between unions and employers, which predominantly takes place at the sectoral and regional level but may also occur at the firm level, still plays a major role. In our period of observation, about 48 per cent of establishments in western Germany were bound by collective agreements with unions (cf. Schnabel *et al.*, 2006). This means they were not allowed to pay wages below the minimum set in the union contract, but they could pay higher wages, which many of them did. The 52 per cent of establishments not bound by collective agreements were free to set wages of their own (although in some sectors, such as construction, government extension decrees stipulated that the union-set minimum wages were generally binding for the whole industry). Since large establishments are more likely to be engaged in collective bargaining, almost 93 per cent of the employees in our sample are covered by collective agreements. The main sources of wage variation are thus sectoral (and to a lesser degree regional) differences in collectively agreed minimum wages as well as premia above this minimum that were individually paid by establishments.

The sample averages of the wage and the other covariates are displayed in Appendix Tables B.1 on page 237 and B.2 on page 239. It can be seen that wages of men are on average 13 per cent larger than those of female employees in the

---

[19] We exclude observations from eastern Germany because the semi-structural approach we make use of assumes steady-state conditions. These are more likely to be found in western than in eastern Germany that still experiences the long transition from a socialist to a capitalist economy.

[20] Since there is no detailed information on the number of hours worked, we exclude employees working part-time (at any time in the observation period). Moreover, apprentices and a small number of employees experiencing recalls are excluded. In addition, we keep only individuals which were on the 1st January 2000 between 16 and 55 years old, where the upper bound should ensure that transitions into non-employment are not due to (early) retirement. Finally, notifications which start and end at the same day and benefit notifications which correspond to employment notifications at the same time are deleted.

[21] This exclusion restriction reduces the average observed wage from €103.89 (including the censored values) to €94.80 (see also Appendix Table B.1 on page 237).

9.3 Data

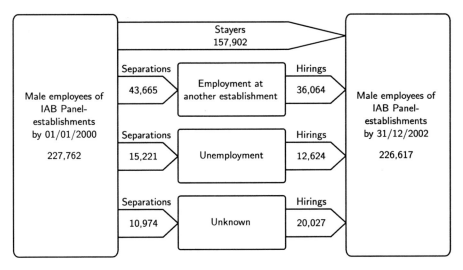

Fig. 9.1 Transitions of men

regression sample.[22] This number hardly changes when estimating a standard earnings function (see Appendix Table B.3 on page 242). Just 26 per cent of all employees in our sample are women (whereas the average share of women in employment subject to social security was around 43 per cent in western Germany in 2000). The lower share of female employment in our sample is to a large extent due to the fact that we have excluded part-time workers.

Figures 9.1 and 9.2 on the next page display the transitions of male and female employees between the 1st January 2000 and the 31st December 2002. First of all, it appears that the stock of workers reduces only very slightly between the beginning and the end of the observation period, which reassures the steady-state assumption at the heart of our semi-structural approach. About two out of three male and female employees stay in the establishment where they worked at the beginning of 2000.[23] The majority of separations and hirings taking place are job-to-job moves. The remaining separations end either in unemployment or are not recorded in the data any more ('unknown'). The latter either implies that the person has changed to

---

[22] Using the LIAB, Gartner and Stephan (2004) report an unconditional gender pay gap for Germany between 20 and 27 per cent. Our (unconditional) figure is lower because more observations of men than of women fall on the ceiling and are consequently dropped, thereby automatically reducing the endowment effect in the working sample between men and women. For long-time evidence with IAB data, see, e.g., Fitzenberger and Wunderlich (2002). For an overview on empirical studies of the pay gap in Germany, see Maier (2007). For (international) surveys on the gender pay gap, see also the references given in footnote 2 on page 95.

[23] Separations are ignored if the employee is recalled by the same establishment within 120 days.

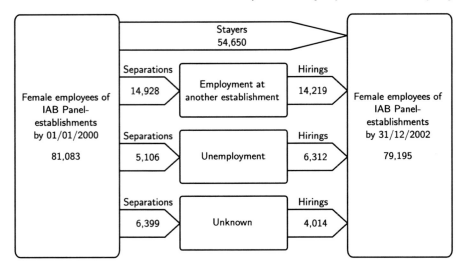

Fig. 9.2 Transitions of women

non-employment without receiving benefits from the unemployment office or that the person has become, for instance, a self-employed not included in the employee history. While our data set does not enable us to disaggregate this category of unknown destination, information from other data sets suggests that the majority of employees in this category has moved to non-employment.[24] For this reason and in order to be consistent with our theoretical considerations in Section 9.2, in subsequent analyses we combine the transitions into unemployment and into 'unknown' to separations into non-employment. Similarly, hirings from unemployment and hirings from 'unknown' are combined to hirings from non-employment.

9.4 Gender Differences in Search Frictions

In this section, we will investigate whether there are gender differences in the simple monopsony power measure derived in Section 9.1. We will do so by fitting a probit model for the probability that a recruit is hired from non-employment. The following estimations use data of 68,715 male and 24,545 female recruits of IAB Panel-establishments, where 32,651 male and 10,326 female recruits are hired from non-employment. From this we see that the share of recruits hired from non-employment is larger for men with $\zeta^m = 0.475$ than for women with $\zeta^f = 0.421$.

---

[24] See, for example, Bartelheimer and Wieck (2005) for a transition matrix between employment and non-employment, based on the German Socio-Economic Panel, which allows stratification of the 'unknown' into detailed categories.

9.4 Gender Differences in Search Frictions

This would indicate higher search frictions for men. These results are, of course, only descriptive by nature. For this reason, a multivariate analysis might clarify whether these results endure, *ceteris paribus*.

First, we include person-specific variables. Since we are looking for a gender difference in the probability of being hired from non-employment, we include a male dummy as regressor. The relative share of a particular group that is hired from employment depends on the ratio of employed to non-employed within this group, which again depends on differences in search frictions between different groups. Taking non-Germans as an example, search frictions for this group may be higher due to language barriers not fully reflected in formal qualification and/or due to discrimination, giving rise to higher unemployment for these workers. Non-employment rates also vary according to age, qualification, and occupation as do search frictions (see, for instance, van den Berg and Ridder, 1998; Postel-Vinay and Robin, 2002b; Manning, 2003a, pp. 44–49). Note that the group of non-employed also includes those in the educational system, so that the probability of being hired from non-employment should be higher for young workers and those with an academic degree.

To control for all the effects mentioned, several control variable are included as regressors. Firstly, we include a set of age dummies. Second, we also add a set of dummy variables that indicate the worker's formal education. We distinguish six different groups: workers with neither apprenticeship nor *Abitur* (which is the German equivalent to A-levels or graduation from high school), those with only apprenticeship, those with only *Abitur*, those with both, workers with a technical college degree, and finally those with a university degree. Third, we include a set of dummy variables indicating the worker's occupation. We distinguish eleven groups of occupations: basic and qualified manual occupations, engineers/technicians, basic and qualified service occupations, semi-professionals and professionals, basic and qualified business occupations, and, eventually, managers. Fourth, we add a non-German dummy and, finally, a set of year dummies to control for potential cyclical influences.

The estimates of this model presented in the second column of Table 9.1 on the following page display that hiring from non-employment varies significantly according to nationality, age, and qualification. Younger workers, those with low formal education, and those with occupations requiring less skills tend to have a higher probability of being hired from non-employment. This points at higher on-the-job search frictions and worse labour market outcomes for these groups. However, we do not find gender differences. The marginal effect of the male dummy is near zero and statistically insignificant at conventional levels.

Next, establishment controls are included. Ten sectoral dummies control for differences among sectors since we expect establishments of different sectors to resort differently to non-employed workers.[25] On account of asymmetric information

---

[25] Sectors are (1) agriculture, hunting, and forestry (including fishing), (2) mining, quarrying, electricity, gas, and water supply, (3) manufacturing, (4) trade and repair, (5) construction,

Table 9.1 Determinants of the probability of being hired from non-employment[a]

Regressors	Sample without censored observations			Sample with all observations	
Models	without establishment controls	with establishment controls	with person frailties	with establishment frailties	
Male (dummy)	0.000 (0.010)	0.008 (0.008)	−0.030 (0.009)	−0.018 (0.007)	
Non-German (dummy)	0.095 (0.019)	0.096 (0.018)	0.117 (0.019)	0.119 (0.019)	
Age under 21 years (ref. group)	—	—	—	—	
Age 21–25 years (dummy)	−0.210 (0.014)	−0.225 (0.018)	−0.197 (0.013)	−0.211 (0.017)	
Age 26–30 years (dummy)	−0.241 (0.022)	−0.263 (0.015)	−0.224 (0.021)	−0.247 (0.014)	
Age 31–35 years (dummy)	−0.270 (0.028)	−0.299 (0.015)	−0.266 (0.027)	−0.294 (0.014)	
Age 36–40 years (dummy)	−0.259 (0.029)	−0.291 (0.015)	−0.268 (0.027)	−0.298 (0.014)	
Age 41–45 years (dummy)	−0.264 (0.026)	−0.289 (0.015)	−0.268 (0.024)	−0.292 (0.014)	
Age 46–50 years (dummy)	−0.280 (0.026)	−0.307 (0.015)	−0.280 (0.022)	−0.304 (0.013)	
Age 51–55 years (dummy)	−0.261 (0.043)	−0.305 (0.019)	−0.266 (0.035)	−0.303 (0.015)	
Age 56–58 years (dummy)	−0.320 (0.020)	−0.353 (0.020)	−0.310 (0.017)	−0.336 (0.018)	
No apprenticeship, no Abitur (ref. group)	—	—	—	—	
Apprenticeship, no Abitur (dummy)	−0.133 (0.035)	−0.083 (0.020)	−0.127 (0.034)	−0.079 (0.019)	
No apprenticeship, with Abitur (dummy)	0.064 (0.034)	0.144 (0.026)	0.048 (0.034)	0.127 (0.026)	
Apprenticeship and Abitur (dummy)	−0.099 (0.034)	−0.029 (0.021)	−0.104 (0.031)	−0.036 (0.018)	
Technical college degree (dummy)	−0.039 (0.035)	0.032 (0.025)	−0.087 (0.030)	−0.010 (0.024)	
University degree (dummy)	0.069 (0.040)	0.129 (0.030)	−0.016 (0.034)	0.054 (0.025)	
Basic manual occupation (ref. group)	—	—	—	—	
Qualified manual occupation (dummy)	−0.047 (0.033)	−0.044 (0.031)	−0.037 (0.036)	−0.039 (0.032)	
Engineer or technician (dummy)	−0.185 (0.057)	−0.125 (0.018)	−0.210 (0.061)	−0.155 (0.019)	
Basic service occupation (dummy)	−0.040 (0.034)	−0.045 (0.025)	−0.040 (0.034)	−0.050 (0.023)	

9.4 Gender Differences in Search Frictions

Qualified service occupation (dummy)	−0.053 (0.049)	−0.053 (0.041)	−0.072 (0.050)	−0.074 (0.036)
Semi-professional (dummy)	−0.139 (0.056)	−0.161 (0.035)	−0.148 (0.057)	−0.176 (0.030)
Professional (dummy)	−0.083 (0.056)	−0.075 (0.039)	−0.143 (0.058)	−0.147 (0.033)
Basic business occupation (dummy)	−0.118 (0.055)	−0.052 (0.022)	−0.153 (0.058)	−0.087 (0.022)
Qualified business occupation (dummy)	−0.184 (0.058)	−0.119 (0.016)	−0.218 (0.063)	−0.150 (0.017)
Manager (dummy)	−0.162 (0.056)	−0.154 (0.030)	−0.210 (0.058)	−0.189 (0.026)
Coll. agreement at sect. level (dummy)		−0.051 (0.019)		−0.054 (0.018)
Coll. agreement at firm level (dummy)		0.209 (0.063)		0.213 (0.064)
Works council (dummy)		−0.123 (0.023)		−0.132 (0.023)
Proportion of female workers		−0.106 (0.056)		−0.113 (0.055)
Proportion of qualified workers		−0.298 (0.070)		−0.270 (0.066)
Good economic performance (dummy)		0.031 (0.025)		0.029 (0.024)
Bad economic performance (dummy)		−0.019 (0.024)		−0.030 (0.025)
New production technology (dummy)		0.030 (0.047)		0.026 (0.047)
Ten sectoral dummies	—	($p < 0.001$)	—	($p < 0.001$)
Year 2000 (ref. group)				
Year 2001 (dummy)	−0.130 (0.085)	−0.097 (0.046)	−0.117 (0.080)	−0.088 (0.043)
Year 2002 (dummy)	−0.109 (0.080)	−0.071 (0.034)	−0.088 (0.075)	−0.055 (0.032)
Constant	1.119 (0.125)	2.003 (0.350)	1.169 (0.125)	2.081 (0.356)
Observations	93,260	93,260	109,266	109,266
Hires from non-employment	42,977	42,977	46,462	46,462
Log likelihood	−60,392.529	−55,836.306	−69,127.713	−63,981.536
McFadden-R^2	0.0616	0.1324	0.0722	0.1413

[a] The data set used is version 2 of the LIAB longitudinal model. The regressand of the probit models is a binary response taking on the value one if the individual is hired from non-employment and zero otherwise. Reported estimates are marginal effects evaluated at the sample average of the other regressors. Standard errors (adjusted for intra-establishment correlations) are given in parentheses. Only transitions in 2000–2002 are considered.

on workers' productivity, firms are likely to prefer recruiting from employment (through poaching). We therefore expect that establishments with a high share of qualified workers and new production technology tend to recruit less often from non-employment. Therefore, we include the share of qualified workers and a dummy indicating new production technology as regressors. Moreover, poaching will be easier if (in addition to higher wages) working conditions are more attractive. This is usually reflected by establishments being covered by a collective agreement or having a works council, so that these variables should be negatively related to recruiting from non-employment. This argument also holds for firms with good economic performance, but these firms may also have to rely on non-employed workers to urgently fill vacancies. Additionally to the corresponding dummy variables, we also include the proportion of female workers in the workforce because the impact of gender is our main focus.

The results reported in the third column of Table 9.1 show that there are noticeable differences among sectors and that the existence of a works council has a significantly negative impact on the hiring probability, whereas this does not generally apply for the coverage by a collective agreement. As an (unreported) likelihood ratio test indicates, the model's fit is significantly improved by the inclusion of the establishment controls. Again, however, we do not find gender differences. The estimated marginal effect of the male dummy is still near zero and statistically insignificant.

Is this really a startling finding? Actually, we do not think so. The sample we are using excludes those recruits with censored wage observations. As discussed in Section 9.3, this reduces the size of the recruitment sample for men by 17.0 and for women by 7.4 per cent. As a consequence, more male observations with high wages are excluded than are female. And workers with high wages are arguably those with low on-the-job search frictions as they are the most successful ones in terms of their labour market outcomes. Hence, we argue that it is more sensible to look at the whole sample including the recruits with censored wage observations.

Including also the censored observations gives us a sample of 82,756 male and 26,510 female recruits of IAB Panel-establishments, where 35,705 male and 10,757 female recruits are hired from non-employment. From this we see that the share of recruits hired from non-employment is still larger for men with $\zeta^m = 0.431$ than for women with $\zeta^f = 0.406$. Interestingly, both shares are reduced which means that high-wage recruits with censored wage observations are more likely to come from employment. This is in line with our dynamic monopsony view of the labour market where workers move their way up the wage distribution via job-to-job moves.

Turning to the multivariate results, which are reported in the third and fourth column of Table 9.1, we now find gender differences: Male workers' probability of being hired from non-employment is 3.0 percentage points lower than females' if no establishment controls are added and 1.8 percentage points lower if they are

---

(6) transport, storage, and communication, (7) financial intermediation, (8) business activities, (9) other activities, and (10) non-profit organisations and public administration.

added, where the former (latter) marginal effect is statistically significant at the 1 (5) per cent level. Besides, note that the positive marginal effect for foreign workers is now higher. Since foreign workers have lower wages on average and therefore are less likely to have a censored wage observation compared to German workers, their search frictions are understated when dropping those recruits with censored wage observations.[26] By the same token, the more pronounced negative marginal effects for workers with high skills and formal education are consistent with our argument.

We therefore conclude that there is (multivariate) evidence that women have a higher probability of being hired from non-employment. As argued in Section 9.1, this points at higher on-the-job search frictions for female workers and therefore provides an explanation for worse labour market outcomes for women than men, *ceteris paribus*. Therefore, gender differences in on-the-job search frictions may be one potential explanation of the gender pay gap. While it is interesting to know that on-the-job search frictions are higher for women than men, this gender difference in on-the-job search frictions found here does not easily translate into a gender difference in wages. Moreover, our simple measure of monopsony power is built on the Burdett–Mortensen model and thus imposes quite a restrictive setting (see the discussion in Section 9.2). Both these drawbacks will be absent in the following empirical analysis which uses the flexible semi-structural approach developed in Section 9.2 to investigate gender differences in labour supply elasticities at the level of the firm.

9.5 Estimates of the Gender Difference in Long-Run Firm-Level Labour Supply Elasticities

We will now apply the semi-structural estimation procedure developed in Section 9.2 to estimate the long-run labour supply elasticity at the level of the firm separately for men and women. We fit exponential proportional hazard models for the instantaneous separation rates to employment and non-employment to obtain the corresponding separation rate elasticities.[27] We further estimate a logit model for the probability that a recruit is hired from employment, where the estimated coefficient for the log wage links the separation rate elasticity to employment and the recruitment elasticity from non-employment. Separately for men and women, we estimate four models: without establishment controls, with establishment controls, with establishment controls and person-specific frailties (random effects), and with establishment controls and establishment-specific frailties (random effects).

---

[26] In line with this, excluding recruits with censored wage observations in any of the years 2000–2002 reduces the recruitment sample for Germans by 15.7 and for non-Germans by 6.7 per cent.

[27] Previous empirical analyses for Germany on job-to-job moves as well as on transitions into unemployment include Bergemann and Mertens (2004), Wolff (2004), and Bachmann (2005), while Winkelmann and Zimmermann (1998) and Korpi and Mertens (2003) investigate the determinants of job mobility and stability.

9.5.1 Transition to Employment

First of all, we estimate the separation rate elasticity to employment. This is done by fitting an exponential proportional hazard model for the instantaneous separation rate to employment, using a sample of 788,520 observations of 270,282 male workers and 265,970 observations of 94,123 female workers at IAB Panel-establishments, where 43,665 of men's and 14,928 of women's observations end with a transition to another establishment.[28] The effect we are mainly interested in is the effect of the wage on the separation rate to employment, so the log daily gross wage is included as a regressor. Theory implies that this effect should be negative: The higher is the wage paid, the lower should be the separation rate. Since we argue that Robinsonian discrimination could be part of the explanation of the gender pay gap, we expect women to be less wage-elastic than men.

First, we include only person-specific controls. There are several other variables than the wage which may influence the separation rate to employment, so that controlling for these factors is necessary to get a reliable estimate for the separation rate elasticity of men and women. For instance, the transition behaviour of German and non-German workers may differ. Next, we expect the worker's age to play an important role. If we think of labour markets as characterised by important search frictions as in the theoretical model from Section 9.2, one would conjecture that older workers are more likely to be found at better-paying jobs. This simply reflects their longer search activity, giving rise to better jobs on average. Therefore, we expect workers to change jobs more often when they are young, while the extent of job changes reduces as workers get older.[29] To control for these age effects, we add a set of age dummies as regressors.[30] A different story applies to the worker's formal education. We expect higher degrees of formal education to reflect higher productivity both in terms of signalling productivity and of higher investments in (general) human capital (cf., e.g., Spence, 1973; Becker, 1993; Weiss, 1995). And we conjecture that workers with higher formal qualification face less severe search frictions. Hence, their separation rate should be higher. Similarly, workers in occupations which need more skills should exhibit lower search frictions and therefore have

---

[28] Note that only those employment spells are considered which do not end in non-employment, so that there are only spells ending with a transition to another establishment or spells being censored without such a transition. For example, the number of 270,282 male workers is obtained by adding up 157,902 stayers, 43,665 separations to employment, and 68,715 hirings (see Figure 9.1 on page 167).

[29] This is also in line with empirical observation as reported in the references given in footnote 27 on the preceding page. Besides, our own empirical findings from Section 9.4 where we found lower search frictions for older workers point at the same direction.

[30] One might also argue that tenure could influence the separation rate. As discussed in Section 9.2.5, we will first do all the estimations without controlling for tenure and shall then repeat them with controlling for tenure as a robustness check.

9.5 Estimates of the Gender Difference in Long-Run Firm-Level Labour Supply Elasticities

a higher separation rate to employment as well.[31] To control for formal education and occupation, we include a set of six education and ten occupation dummies as regressors.[32] Finally, we add a set of year dummies to control for potential cyclical influences.

Estimation results for this model without establishment controls are reported for men and women in the second columns of Table 9.2 on the next page and Table 9.3 on page 178, respectively. As expected, women are less wage-elastic than men, their elasticity being estimated only as -1.012 compared to -1.594 for men, where the difference between these estimates is statistically significant at the 1 per cent level. All in all, controls' coefficients have the expected signs. Younger workers, workers with higher formal education, and those in occupations requiring more skills tend to have higher separation rates. Separation rates are significantly lower for non-German male workers and do not differ significantly for non-German female workers.

In a next step, we include establishment controls, estimates of which are reported in the third columns of Tables 9.2 and 9.3. We now take into account that separation rates for workers of establishments belonging to different sectors may differ. Hence, we include a set of ten sectoral dummies.[33] Since workers of different qualification as well as male and female workers differ in transition behaviour, it is likely that working for establishments with different proportions of qualified and female workers in the workforce makes a difference, in particular if occupational segregation plays a role. Therefore, we include the shares of qualified and female workers as regressors. Following the collective voice argument given by Freeman and Medoff (1984), the representation of workers' interests either by a works council or by a union (via collective agreements at the sectoral or the firm level) may improve morale and thus reduce the separation rate to employment.[34] Finally, we expect the separation rate to be lower in establishments with good economic

---

[31] Note that these hypotheses are in line with our empirical results from Section 9.4. Other studies finding higher search frictions for less qualified workers and workers in occupations requiring less skills include, for instance, van den Berg and Ridder (1998), Postel-Vinay and Robin (2002b), and Manning (2003a, pp. 44–49).

[32] For details about these control variables, see Section 9.4.

[33] See footnote 25 on page 172 for a list of the different sectors.

[34] For details on the German system of codetermination (at the workplace), see Addison et al. (2004a). For a survey on the empirical evidence on the economic consequences of works councils, see Addison et al. (2004b). Empirical studies finding that the presence of a works council reduces separations and labour turnover include, among others, Frick and Sadowski (1995), Addison et al. (2001), and Frick and Möller (2003). Boockmann and Steffes (2008) and Hirsch et al. (2009c) present further evidence that both the separation rate to employment and non-employment are reduced if there exists a works council. For evidence on the impact of unions on separations and labour turnover, see additionally Freeman (1980), Delery et al. (2000), and Addison and Belfield (2004).

Table 9.2 Determinants of males' instantaneous separation rate to employment[a]

Regressors	Models without establishment controls	with establishment controls	with person frailties	with establishment frailties
Log daily gross wage (in €)	−1.594 (0.183)	−1.516 (0.163)	−1.865 (0.029)	−1.461 (0.028)
Non-German (dummy)	−0.156 (0.062)	−0.174 (0.059)	−0.196 (0.020)	−0.171 (0.018)
Age under 21 years (ref. group)	—	—	—	—
Age 21–25 years (dummy)	−0.488 (0.204)	−0.514 (0.185)	−0.668 (0.076)	−0.369 (0.062)
Age 26–30 years (dummy)	−0.705 (0.206)	−0.744 (0.190)	−0.928 (0.076)	−0.562 (0.061)
Age 31–35 years (dummy)	−0.744 (0.207)	−0.785 (0.192)	−0.965 (0.075)	−0.602 (0.061)
Age 36–40 years (dummy)	−0.896 (0.208)	−0.926 (0.195)	−1.113 (0.076)	−0.769 (0.062)
Age 41–45 years (dummy)	−0.965 (0.206)	−0.995 (0.195)	−1.184 (0.076)	−0.860 (0.062)
Age 46–50 years (dummy)	−1.022 (0.205)	−1.047 (0.194)	−1.240 (0.076)	−0.898 (0.062)
Age 51–55 years (dummy)	−0.914 (0.212)	−0.929 (0.203)	−1.113 (0.077)	−0.785 (0.063)
Age 56–58 years (dummy)	−0.888 (0.220)	−0.893 (0.211)	−1.082 (0.088)	−0.689 (0.075)
No apprenticeship, no Abitur (ref. group)	—	—	—	—
Apprenticeship, no Abitur (dummy)	0.011 (0.066)	−0.033 (0.066)	−0.021 (0.017)	0.100 (0.016)
No apprenticeship, with Abitur (dummy)	0.716 (0.130)	0.699 (0.134)	0.979 (0.058)	0.596 (0.046)
Apprenticeship and Abitur (dummy)	0.392 (0.085)	0.284 (0.076)	0.382 (0.033)	0.439 (0.029)
Technical college degree (dummy)	0.729 (0.134)	0.672 (0.134)	0.864 (0.036)	0.734 (0.030)
University degree (dummy)	1.094 (0.129)	1.031 (0.150)	1.354 (0.036)	1.040 (0.030)
Basic manual occupation (ref. group)	—	—	—	—
Qualified manual occupation (dummy)	0.132 (0.079)	0.088 (0.082)	0.106 (0.016)	0.095 (0.016)
Engineer or technician (dummy)	0.604 (0.106)	0.559 (0.114)	0.674 (0.022)	0.411 (0.021)
Basic service occupation (dummy)	−0.179 (0.093)	−0.162 (0.097)	−0.178 (0.022)	−0.089 (0.022)
Qualified service occupation (dummy)	−0.256 (0.140)	−0.249 (0.185)	−0.233 (0.051)	0.095 (0.051)
Semi-professional (dummy)	−0.126 (0.108)	0.121 (0.138)	0.168 (0.047)	0.226 (0.048)
Professional (dummy)	0.398 (0.138)	0.525 (0.128)	0.615 (0.058)	0.712 (0.050)
Basic business occupation (dummy)	0.440 (0.113)	0.387 (0.123)	0.439 (0.039)	0.290 (0.037)

9.5 Estimates of the Gender Difference in Long-Run Firm-Level Labour Supply Elasticities

Qualified business occupation (dummy)	0.358 (0.104)	0.342 (0.103)	0.406 (0.024)	0.247 (0.023)
Manager (dummy)	0.875 (0.176)	0.890 (0.219)	1.154 (0.053)	0.792 (0.045)
Coll. agreement at sect. level (dummy)		−0.056 (0.135)	−0.067 (0.022)	−0.105 (0.040)
Coll. agreement at firm level (dummy)		−0.046 (0.223)	−0.070 (0.027)	−0.019 (0.049)
Works council (dummy)		−0.181 (0.114)	−0.244 (0.024)	0.047 (0.045)
Proportion of female workers		0.168 (0.361)	0.241 (0.037)	0.273 (0.086)
Proportion of qualified workers		0.304 (0.265)	0.412 (0.024)	0.553 (0.043)
Good economic performance (dummy)		−0.123 (0.140)	−0.136 (0.013)	−0.004 (0.017)
Bad economic performance (dummy)		0.307 (0.165)	0.342 (0.014)	0.372 (0.018)
New production technology (dummy)		−0.158 (0.133)	−0.171 (0.012)	−0.198 (0.018)
Ten sectoral dummies		($p < 0.001$)	($p < 0.001$)	($p < 0.001$)
Year 2000 (ref. group)				
Year 2001 (dummy)	0.109 (0.135)	0.110 (0.133)	0.214 (0.012)	0.271 (0.012)
Year 2002 (dummy)	−0.160 (0.145)	−0.202 (0.150)	−0.022 (0.014)	0.183 (0.013)
Constant	−0.778 (0.725)	−0.732 (0.704)	1.056 (0.180)	−0.703 (0.269)
Frailty variance			1.405 (0.051)	1.179 (0.038)
Observations	788,520	788,520	788,520	788,520
Subjects	270,282	270,282	270,282	270,282
Transitions	43,665	43,665	43,665	43,665
Log likelihood	−96,865.069	−94,697.179	−94,080.125	−68,238.099
McFadden-R^2	0.0646	0.0855	0.0915	0.3410

[a] The data set used is version 2 of the LIAB longitudinal model. The regressand of the exponential proportional hazard models is a binary response taking on the value one if the individual changes from an IAB Panel-establishment to another establishment and zero otherwise. Standard errors (adjusted for intra-establishment correlations in the non-frailty models) are given in parentheses. Only spells ending or beginning in 2000–2002 which do not end with a transition to non-employment are considered.

Table 9.3 Determinants of females' instantaneous separation rate to employment[a]

Regressors	Models without establishment controls	with establishment controls	with person frailties	with establishment frailties
Log daily gross wage (in €)	−1.012 (0.131)	−1.027 (0.103)	−1.270 (0.042)	−1.171 (0.038)
Non-German (dummy)	0.054 (0.059)	0.028 (0.057)	0.028 (0.041)	−0.035 (0.037)
Age under 21 years (ref. group)	–	–	–	–
Age 21–25 years (dummy)	−0.410 (0.099)	−0.418 (0.099)	−0.424 (0.092)	−0.185 (0.080)
Age 26–30 years (dummy)	−0.486 (0.100)	−0.498 (0.099)	−0.496 (0.092)	−0.217 (0.080)
Age 31–35 years (dummy)	−0.668 (0.102)	−0.682 (0.102)	−0.698 (0.093)	−0.418 (0.081)
Age 36–40 years (dummy)	−0.981 (0.103)	−0.988 (0.104)	−1.027 (0.094)	−0.729 (0.082)
Age 41–45 years (dummy)	−1.157 (0.110)	−1.157 (0.115)	−1.219 (0.094)	−0.905 (0.083)
Age 46–50 years (dummy)	−1.230 (0.119)	−1.226 (0.123)	−1.302 (0.095)	−1.009 (0.083)
Age 51–55 years (dummy)	−1.207 (0.121)	−1.197 (0.126)	−1.277 (0.097)	−0.983 (0.085)
Age 56–58 years (dummy)	−1.103 (0.155)	−1.089 (0.157)	−1.201 (0.128)	−0.878 (0.116)
No apprenticeship, no Abitur (ref. group)	–	–	–	–
Apprenticeship, no Abitur (dummy)	0.060 (0.068)	0.050 (0.064)	0.058 (0.032)	0.098 (0.030)
No apprenticeship, with Abitur (dummy)	0.637 (0.109)	0.616 (0.109)	0.709 (0.080)	0.433 (0.067)
Apprenticeship and Abitur (dummy)	0.347 (0.084)	0.293 (0.096)	0.337 (0.045)	0.336 (0.041)
Technical college degree (dummy)	0.649 (0.109)	0.617 (0.102)	0.695 (0.064)	0.618 (0.056)
University degree (dummy)	0.936 (0.102)	0.939 (0.097)	1.083 (0.057)	0.944 (0.049)
Basic manual occupation (ref. group)	–	–	–	–
Qualified manual occupation (dummy)	0.004 (0.113)	0.076 (0.118)	0.096 (0.055)	0.082 (0.057)
Engineer or technician (dummy)	0.562 (0.136)	0.589 (0.142)	0.692 (0.055)	0.423 (0.053)
Basic service occupation (dummy)	0.007 (0.124)	0.183 (0.123)	0.196 (0.058)	0.102 (0.058)
Qualified service occupation (dummy)	0.116 (0.117)	0.398 (0.131)	0.484 (0.061)	0.377 (0.062)
Semi-professional (dummy)	0.024 (0.116)	0.394 (0.139)	0.492 (0.055)	0.477 (0.057)
Professional (dummy)	0.586 (0.128)	0.815 (0.139)	0.970 (0.084)	0.803 (0.074)
Basic business occupation (dummy)	0.347 (0.121)	0.469 (0.123)	0.535 (0.046)	0.312 (0.046)

9.5 Estimates of the Gender Difference in Long-Run Firm-Level Labour Supply Elasticities

Qualified business occupation (dummy)	0.413 (0.123)	0.493 (0.108)	0.589 (0.040)	0.356 (0.040)
Manager (dummy)	0.690 (0.148)	0.672 (0.170)	0.841 (0.096)	0.664 (0.087)
Coll. agreement at sect. level (dummy)		−0.160 (0.099)	−0.164 (0.033)	−0.158 (0.050)
Coll. agreement at firm level (dummy)		−0.148 (0.133)	−0.160 (0.044)	−0.034 (0.067)
Works council (dummy)		−0.015 (0.093)	−0.035 (0.037)	0.095 (0.058)
Proportion of female workers		0.008 (0.201)	−0.009 (0.055)	−0.139 (0.098)
Proportion of qualified workers		0.192 (0.194)	0.251 (0.045)	0.306 (0.072)
Good economic performance (dummy)		−0.007 (0.133)	−0.016 (0.024)	0.054 (0.030)
Bad economic performance (dummy)		0.383 (0.127)	0.410 (0.026)	0.252 (0.034)
New production technology (dummy)		−0.061 (0.076)	−0.058 (0.022)	−0.022 (0.030)
Ten sectoral dummies		($p = 0.039$)	($p < 0.001$)	($p < 0.001$)
Year 2000 (ref. group)				
Year 2001 (dummy)	0.047 (0.090)	0.044 (0.091)	0.150 (0.033)	0.142 (0.020)
Year 2002 (dummy)	−0.161 (0.097)	−0.187 (0.103)	−0.007 (0.024)	0.037 (0.022)
Constant	−3.710 (0.529)	−3.174 (0.518)	−1.749 (0.287)	−2.336 (0.355)
Frailty variance			1.489 (0.093)	1.018 (0.043)
Observations	265,970	265,970	265,970	265,970
Subjects	94,123	94,123	94,123	94,123
Transitions	14,928	14,928	14,928	14,928
Log likelihood	−35,725.623	−35,250.456	−35,048.146	−30,057.185
McFadden-R^2	0.0618	0.0743	0.0796	0.2107

[a] The data set used is version 2 of the LIAB longitudinal model. The regressand of the exponential proportional hazard models is a binary response taking on the value one if the individual changes from an IAB Panel-establishment to another establishment and zero otherwise. Standard errors (adjusted for intra-establishment correlations in the non-frailty models) are given in parentheses. Only spells ending or beginning in 2000–2002 which do not end with a transition to non-employment are considered.

performance and new production technology as these establishments may be more attractive employers.[35]

As (unreported) likelihood ratio tests reveal, the models with establishment controls fit the data significantly better. The coefficients of the establishment controls usually have the expected signs, although most of them are not significant. Industry affiliation, however, plays a highly significant role. Adding establishment characteristics to the models leaves both the estimated separation elasticities and the size of the (significant) difference between female and male workers nearly unchanged. With an elasticity of -1.027, women are still less wage-elastic than men whose elasticity is estimated as -1.516.

In a next step, person-specific frailties are included to take account of unobserved heterogeneity at the level of the worker. This yields the estimates presented in the fourth columns of Tables 9.2 and 9.3. Though adding person-specific frailties increases the overall fit of the model significantly, the magnitudes and signs of nearly all coefficients do not change much. What does change noticeably in magnitude, however, are the estimated separation rate elasticities which are now -1.270 for female and -1.865 for male workers.

While it would be desirable to include both person- and establishment-specific frailties in the estimations, there is no established procedure for this sort of estimation, which would have to take account of the joint distribution of the random terms.[36] The last specification therefore includes establishment- rather than person-specific frailties to take account of unobserved heterogeneity at the level of the establishment. This is particularly interesting because this specification allows us to take into account (at least to some extent) occupational segregation, which is argued to be an important determinant of the gender pay gap.[37] Estimates are presented in the fifth columns of Tables 9.2 and 9.3. While the impact of most covariates remains unaltered, the gender difference in separation rate elasticities is reduced markedly, though it is still significant at the 1 per cent level. The estimated separation rate elasticity is still lower for women than for men, being estimated as -1.171 and -1.461, respectively. Furthermore, the considerable changes in the models' log-likelihood

---

[35] One might expect that establishment size, i.e., the establishment's total number of employees, is another influential variable. However, models of (dynamic) monopsony, such as the Burdett–Mortensen model, imply that establishment size can (only) be extended by paying higher wages, so that establishment size variables should not matter. (An exception is the generalised model of monopsony proposed by Manning (2006) where firms are also able to raise their labour supply by increasing their expenditures on recruitment.) In order to check this hypothesis, we added establishment size and its square as regressors to the models. As expected, our results were robust to this change in specification.

[36] To our knowledge, the paper by Horny et al. (2009) is the only one hitherto modelling and estimating the joint distribution of two correlated frailty terms utilising linked employer–employee data.

[37] The role of occupational segregation and its relation to the gender pay gap in monopsonistic labour markets is discussed in detail by Usui (2006; 2009). For empirical analyses of occupational segregation with the LIAB, see Beblo et al. (2008) and Heinze (2009).

9.5 Estimates of the Gender Difference in Long-Run Firm-Level Labour Supply Elasticities   181

imply that unobserved heterogeneity at the level of the establishment plays a more important role than unobserved heterogeneity at the level of the worker.

9.5.2 *Transition to Non-Employment*

After estimating the separation rate elasticity to employment, we now turn to the separation rate elasticity to non-employment. Estimation is done by fitting exponential proportional hazard models for the instantaneous separation rate to non-employment separately for men and women. The following estimates use a sample of 834,867 observations of 296,477 male workers and 287,428 observations of 105,628 female workers at IAB Panel-establishments, where 26,195 transitions of men and 11,505 transitions of women to non-employment take place. Spells ending with a transition from an IAB Panel-establishment to another establishment are included as censored since no transition to non-employment takes place.

Again, we begin with including only person-specific controls. In analogy to the discussion in Section 9.5.1, prime-age workers should find themselves in better matches and thus should have a lower separation rate to non-employment. In contrast, workers close to retirement may have an incentive to leave jobs due to generous early-retirement options and welfare payments for old unemployed.[38] The quality and value of a match may also be higher for those workers who have more formal education and those in occupations which require more skills. In particular, employers are less likely to lay off these workers. However, some groups of workers also have outside options that increase the likelihood of moving into our category of non-employment. For instance, workers with *Abitur* are entitled to attend university, and employees with technical college or university degrees, managers, and professionals are more likely to become self-employed.

As can be seen from the second columns of Table 9.4 on the following page and Table 9.5 on page 184, estimated coefficients tend to have the expected signs and are for the most part significant. The estimated separation rate elasticities of men and women differ significantly at the 1 per cent level. Women's transitions to non-employment are less wage-elastic than men's with estimated elasticities of −2.107 and −2.982, respectively.

Including the same establishment controls as above in Section 9.5.1 gives the models presented in the third columns of Tables 9.4 and 9.5. Since our data do not allow us to distinguish voluntary from involuntary separations (i.e., between quits and layoffs), it is important to control for factors that influence establishments' layoff behaviour. This alleviates the problem that the negative correlation between wages and the separation rate may not just be a supply-side response but also demand-driven. A case in point is establishments' profitability: Establishments

---

[38] Details about (early) retirement and social security in Germany are given by Börsch-Supan and Schnabel (1998; 1999) and Trampusch (2005).

Table 9.4 Determinants of males' instantaneous separation rate to non-employment[a]

Regressors	Models without establishment controls	with establishment controls	with person frailties	with establishment frailties
Log daily gross wage (in €)	−2.982 (0.139)	−2.676 (0.109)	−3.702 (0.032)	−2.724 (0.024)
Non-German (dummy)	0.291 (0.047)	0.288 (0.043)	0.337 (0.021)	0.241 (0.018)
Age under 21 years (ref. group)	–	–	–	–
Age 21–25 years (dummy)	−0.328 (0.203)	−0.328 (0.172)	−0.901 (0.059)	−0.415 (0.042)
Age 26–30 years (dummy)	−0.664 (0.228)	−0.690 (0.200)	−1.404 (0.059)	−0.810 (0.042)
Age 31–35 years (dummy)	−0.775 (0.239)	−0.822 (0.214)	−1.549 (0.059)	−0.949 (0.043)
Age 36–40 years (dummy)	−0.970 (0.246)	−1.024 (0.222)	−1.743 (0.059)	−1.127 (0.043)
Age 41–45 years (dummy)	−1.097 (0.250)	−1.153 (0.229)	−1.888 (0.060)	−1.263 (0.044)
Age 46–50 years (dummy)	−1.115 (0.263)	−1.169 (0.238)	−1.910 (0.061)	−1.273 (0.045)
Age 51–55 years (dummy)	−0.747 (0.281)	−0.783 (0.244)	−1.446 (0.061)	−0.873 (0.045)
Age 56–58 years (dummy)	−0.001 (0.371)	−0.040 (0.347)	−0.564 (0.071)	−0.130 (0.054)
No apprenticeship, no Abitur (ref. group)	–	–	–	–
Apprenticeship, no Abitur (dummy)	−0.248 (0.051)	−0.208 (0.050)	−0.184 (0.019)	−0.131 (0.018)
No apprenticeship, with Abitur (dummy)	0.382 (0.338)	0.761 (0.260)	1.516 (0.056)	1.156 (0.042)
Apprenticeship and Abitur (dummy)	0.173 (0.087)	0.225 (0.091)	0.358 (0.047)	0.336 (0.041)
Technical college degree (dummy)	0.509 (0.088)	0.511 (0.090)	0.709 (0.054)	0.562 (0.049)
University degree (dummy)	1.248 (0.121)	1.258 (0.106)	1.736 (0.046)	1.338 (0.040)
Basic manual occupation (ref. group)	–	–	–	–
Qualified manual occupation (dummy)	−0.247 (0.072)	−0.255 (0.056)	−0.257 (0.021)	−0.274 (0.021)
Engineer or technician (dummy)	0.005 (0.097)	−0.049 (0.097)	0.137 (0.035)	0.052 (0.033)
Basic service occupation (dummy)	−0.279 (0.088)	−0.260 (0.088)	−0.239 (0.026)	−0.134 (0.025)
Qualified service occupation (dummy)	−0.524 (0.123)	−0.518 (0.155)	−0.458 (0.070)	−0.049 (0.069)
Semi-professional (dummy)	−0.349 (0.092)	−0.514 (0.151)	−0.373 (0.064)	−0.174 (0.061)
Professional (dummy)	0.217 (0.185)	0.142 (0.184)	0.633 (0.068)	0.552 (0.060)
Basic business occupation (dummy)	0.117 (0.106)	0.213 (0.093)	0.306 (0.051)	0.285 (0.046)

9.5 Estimates of the Gender Difference in Long-Run Firm-Level Labour Supply Elasticities

Qualified business occupation (dummy)	−0.171 (0.095)	−0.198 (0.083)	−0.014 (0.034)	−0.088 (0.032)
Manager (dummy)	0.471 (0.146)	0.373 (0.136)	0.730 (0.073)	0.526 (0.067)
Coll. agreement at sect. level (dummy)		0.025 (0.070)	0.015 (0.027)	−0.078 (0.038)
Coll. agreement at firm level (dummy)		−0.283 (0.166)	−0.176 (0.036)	−0.087 (0.051)
Works council (dummy)		−0.334 (0.118)	−0.465 (0.027)	−0.280 (0.042)
Proportion of female workers		−0.433 (0.195)	−0.519 (0.046)	−0.349 (0.082)
Proportion of qualified workers		−0.328 (0.213)	−0.128 (0.029)	−0.082 (0.047)
Good economic performance (dummy)		−0.037 (0.060)	−0.043 (0.019)	0.047 (0.023)
Bad economic performance (dummy)		0.296 (0.093)	0.320 (0.019)	0.159 (0.024)
New production technology (dummy)		−0.214 (0.087)	−0.176 (0.016)	−0.124 (0.021)
Ten sectoral dummies		($p < 0.001$)	($p < 0.001$)	($p < 0.001$)
Year 2000 (ref. group)				
Year 2001 (dummy)	−0.043 (0.046)	−0.030 (0.045)	0.085 (0.016)	0.001 (0.015)
Year 2002 (dummy)	0.165 (0.045)	0.151 (0.036)	0.388 (0.017)	0.217 (0.016)
Constant	5.055 (0.548)	4.620 (0.467)	9.703 (0.168)	4.830 (0.211)
Frailty variance			1.786 (0.053)	0.565 (0.024)
Observations	834,867	834,867	834,867	834,867
Subjects	296,477	296,477	296,477	296,477
Transitions	26,195	26,195	26,195	26,195
Log likelihood	−84,090.789	−82,614.361	−80,846.485	−77,825.631
McFadden-R^2	0.1814	0.1958	0.2130	0.2424

[a] The data set used is version 2 of the LIAB longitudinal model. The regressand of the exponential proportional hazard models is a binary response taking on the value one if the individual changes from an IAB Panel-establishment to non-employment and zero otherwise. Standard errors (adjusted for intra-establishment correlations in the non-frailty models) are given in parentheses. Only spells ending or beginning in 2000–2002 are considered.

Table 9.5 Determinants of females' instantaneous separation rate to non-employment[a]

Regressors	Models without establishment controls	with establishment controls	with person frailties	with establishment frailties
Log daily gross wage (in €)	−2.107 (0.067)	−2.112 (0.068)	−2.980 (0.045)	−2.256 (0.032)
Non-German (dummy)	0.404 (0.047)	0.382 (0.047)	0.461 (0.041)	0.325 (0.032)
Age under 21 years (ref. group)	–	–	–	–
Age 21–25 years (dummy)	−0.695 (0.101)	−0.686 (0.106)	−0.876 (0.081)	−0.612 (0.059)
Age 26–30 years (dummy)	−0.715 (0.103)	−0.706 (0.108)	−0.842 (0.081)	−0.607 (0.059)
Age 31–35 years (dummy)	−0.809 (0.103)	−0.813 (0.108)	−0.900 (0.082)	−0.708 (0.059)
Age 36–40 years (dummy)	−1.268 (0.105)	−1.274 (0.114)	−1.410 (0.083)	−1.168 (0.061)
Age 41–45 years (dummy)	−1.563 (0.111)	−1.564 (0.119)	−1.761 (0.085)	−1.466 (0.064)
Age 46–50 years (dummy)	−1.627 (0.115)	−1.628 (0.123)	−1.831 (0.085)	−1.534 (0.064)
Age 51–55 years (dummy)	−1.375 (0.118)	−1.381 (0.119)	−1.544 (0.087)	−1.265 (0.066)
Age 56–58 years (dummy)	−0.937 (0.142)	−0.949 (0.142)	−1.051 (0.116)	−0.804 (0.093)
No apprenticeship, no Abitur (ref. group)	–	–	–	–
Apprenticeship, no Abitur (dummy)	−0.095 (0.064)	−0.065 (0.052)	−0.026 (0.036)	−0.035 (0.030)
No apprenticeship, with Abitur (dummy)	0.746 (0.151)	0.795 (0.131)	1.355 (0.083)	0.955 (0.059)
Apprenticeship and Abitur (dummy)	0.240 (0.078)	0.264 (0.068)	0.370 (0.056)	0.296 (0.047)
Technical college degree (dummy)	0.628 (0.091)	0.592 (0.086)	0.756 (0.082)	0.601 (0.067)
University degree (dummy)	1.120 (0.094)	1.091 (0.089)	1.499 (0.068)	1.107 (0.053)
Basic manual occupation (ref. group)	–	–	–	–
Qualified manual occupation (dummy)	−0.238 (0.094)	−0.206 (0.108)	−0.259 (0.060)	−0.282 (0.058)
Engineer or technician (dummy)	0.017 (0.086)	−0.097 (0.098)	−0.025 (0.070)	−0.047 (0.061)
Basic service occupation (dummy)	−0.265 (0.135)	−0.233 (0.174)	−0.293 (0.062)	−0.276 (0.056)
Qualified service occupation (dummy)	−0.320 (0.091)	−0.190 (0.151)	−0.132 (0.072)	−0.060 (0.066)
Semi-professional (dummy)	−0.137 (0.098)	−0.002 (0.155)	0.096 (0.060)	0.074 (0.056)
Professional (dummy)	0.503 (0.137)	0.573 (0.169)	1.067 (0.094)	0.646 (0.073)
Basic business occupation (dummy)	−0.127 (0.078)	−0.035 (0.086)	−0.021 (0.054)	−0.065 (0.049)

9.5 Estimates of the Gender Difference in Long-Run Firm-Level Labour Supply Elasticities

Qualified business occupation (dummy)	−0.127 (0.081)	−0.132 (0.087)	−0.041 (0.046)	−0.171 (0.041)
Manager (dummy)	0.350 (0.131)	0.374 (0.138)	0.666 (0.116)	0.413 (0.096)
Coll. agreement at sect. level (dummy)		0.011 (0.062)	0.003 (0.040)	−0.090 (0.047)
Coll. agreement at firm level (dummy)		−0.055 (0.114)	−0.050 (0.054)	−0.043 (0.066)
Works council (dummy)		−0.128 (0.076)	−0.148 (0.043)	0.016 (0.050)
Proportion of female workers		−0.907 (0.223)	−1.023 (0.063)	−0.761 (0.084)
Proportion of qualified workers		−0.272 (0.184)	−0.209 (0.052)	0.030 (0.066)
Good economic performance (dummy)		−0.094 (0.050)	−0.096 (0.030)	−0.085 (0.033)
Bad economic performance (dummy)		0.176 (0.058)	0.205 (0.032)	0.142 (0.035)
New production technology (dummy)		−0.094 (0.067)	−0.101 (0.025)	−0.038 (0.030)
Ten sectoral dummies		($p < 0.001$)	($p < 0.001$)	($p < 0.001$)
Year 2000 (ref. group)				
Year 2001 (dummy)	0.128 (0.041)	0.126 (0.040)	0.283 (0.025)	0.143 (0.023)
Year 2002 (dummy)	0.311 (0.042)	0.299 (0.040)	0.604 (0.027)	0.334 (0.024)
Constant	1.122 (0.301)	1.804 (0.544)	6.111 (0.312)	2.360 (0.264)
Frailty variance			2.868 (0.122)	0.394 (0.024)
Observations	287,428	287,428	287,428	287,428
Subjects	105,628	105,628	105,628	105,628
Transitions	11,505	11,505	11,505	11,505
Log likelihood	−36,356.345	−36,071.276	−35,470.457	−34,998.391
McFadden-R^2	0.1268	0.1336	0.1481	0.1594

[a] The data set used is version 2 of the LIAB longitudinal model. The regressand of the exponential proportional hazard models is a binary response taking on the value one if the individual changes from an IAB Panel-establishment to non-employment and zero otherwise. Standard errors (adjusted for intra-establishment correlations in the non-frailty models) are given in parentheses. Only spells ending or beginning in 2000–2002 are considered.

with bad economic performance should lay off workers more often, so that the separation rate should be higher. We also include a set of ten sectoral dummies because establishments belonging to different sectors may differ in layoff behaviour. The existence of a works council or of collective agreements may reduce the separation rate to non-employment as establishments find it more difficult to lay off employees.[39] Taking account of segregation, we also include the proportions of female and qualified workers in the workforce as regressors because establishments with different shares of these groups may differ in layoff behaviour as well. In our eyes, the effect of new production technology is unclear because on the one hand it may reflect capital–labour substitution, whereas on the other hand the higher training costs associated with new production technology make layoffs more costly.

Performing a likelihood ratio test (not reported here), we find that the models with establishment controls fit the data evidently better, while the impact of person-specific controls is not changed. Most coefficients of the establishment controls have the expected sign (though not all of them are statistically significant). For example, firms with bad economic performance have significantly higher separation rates to non-employment, and there are differences between sectors. The estimated separation rate elasticity to non-employment is still significantly higher for men than for women. The difference in elasticities, however, is reduced with elasticities estimated as -2.112 for women and -2.676 for men.

Adding person-specific frailties gives the models reported in the fourth columns of Tables 9.4 and 9.5. While there are only minor changes for most of the covariates' impacts, separation rate elasticities are estimated markedly higher, estimates being -2.980 for women and -3.702 for men. The relative gender difference in elasticities, however, does not change much. Besides, the models' fit to the data is improved significantly, as the increases in the log likelihood indicate.

Again, adding establishment- instead of person-specific frailties is particularly interesting in order to take account of unobserved heterogeneity at the level of the establishment. The resulting estimates, reported in the fifth columns of Tables 9.4 and 9.5, show that the gender-specific separation rate elasticities do not change much compared to the models with establishment controls and without frailties. Estimated elasticities are -2.256 for women and -2.724 for men, so that the elasticity of women's separation rate to non-employment remains markedly lower than men's.

Given that our sample is based on a balanced panel of establishments, it is ruled out that transitions into non-employment are driven by plant closings. Nevertheless, downsizing can still exist. In these establishments, separations of workers to non-employment are to a large extent due to a fall in labour demand, rather than being a supply-side response. A negative coefficient of the log wage for transitions to non-employment would appear if a low wage was a signal of low productivity and

---

[39] As argued by Agell (2002, p. 22), works councils and collective agreements – like other labour market institutions – 'serve an important function of social insurance' against labour market risks. For empirical evidence on this insurance effect in the case of works councils, see Hirsch *et al.* (2009c), who find that the existence of a works council decreases the separation rate to non-employment, *ceteris paribus*.

9.5 Estimates of the Gender Difference in Long-Run Firm-Level Labour Supply Elasticities   187

therefore of a high probability of mass layoffs. To inspect the robustness of our results, we have repeated the empirical analysis excluding those 259 plants with a workforce of at least ten employees that experienced an employment reduction by at least 25 per cent between 2000 and 2002. However, the obtained wage elasticities are hardly affected, so that we conclude that the estimated supply elasticities are not driven by downsizing effects.[40]

9.5.3 Hiring from Employment

Finally, we fit a logit model for the probability that a recruit is hired from employment, where the estimated coefficient of the log wage links the separation rate elasticity to employment and the recruitment elasticity from non-employment. The following estimations use data of 68,715 male and 24,545 female recruits of IAB Panel-establishments, where 36,064 male and 14,219 female recruits are hired from employment.

First, we include person-specific variables. We expect the probability that a recruit comes from employment (and thus the share of recruits hired from employment) to rise with the wage offered. That is to say, high-wage firms poach more effectively, which is what theory predicts. One implication of this is that the recruitment elasticity from employment is higher than that from non-employment, which can be seen from equation (9.20). The relative share of a particular group that is hired from employment depends on the ratio of employed to non-employed within this group, which again depends on differences in search frictions between different groups. As we have shown in Section 9.1, the share of recruits hired from non-employment can serve as a simple measure of on-the-job search frictions and the degree of competition among employers within a labour market. Our own empirical investigation from Section 9.4 showed that search frictions vary according to age, qualification, education, sex, and nationality. Therefore, all the person-specific variables included in the exponential models in Sections 9.5.1 and 9.5.2 are also included here.

The estimates of the models presented in the second columns of Table 9.6 on the next page and Table 9.7 on page 190 display that hiring from employment varies significantly according to nationality, age, and qualification. The estimated coefficients of the log daily gross wage for female and male recruits are 1.277 and 1.475, respectively. This gender difference, however, is not statistically significant at conventional levels.

Next, all the establishment controls used in the exponential models are included.[41] The results reported in the third columns of Tables 9.6 and 9.7 show that there are noticeable differences among sectors and that the existence of a works

---

[40] The key results of this check of robustness are presented in Appendix Table B.4 on page 243.

[41] For a discussion of their likely impact, see Section 9.4.

Table 9.6 Determinants of males' probability of being hired from employment[a]

Regressors	Models without establishment controls	with establishment controls	with person random effects	with establishment random effects
Log daily gross wage (in €)	1.277 (0.747)	1.899 (0.156)	1.993 (0.041)	2.174 (0.047)
Non-German (dummy)	−0.382 (0.097)	−0.395 (0.076)	−0.417 (0.029)	−0.364 (0.031)
Age under 21 years (ref. group)	—	—	—	—
Age 21–25 years (dummy)	0.609 (0.084)	0.741 (0.109)	0.784 (0.075)	0.855 (0.075)
Age 26–30 years (dummy)	0.642 (0.096)	0.820 (0.098)	0.870 (0.075)	0.942 (0.075)
Age 31–35 years (dummy)	0.790 (0.111)	0.988 (0.098)	1.048 (0.075)	1.113 (0.075)
Age 36–40 years (dummy)	0.736 (0.119)	0.923 (0.102)	0.980 (0.076)	1.037 (0.076)
Age 41–45 years (dummy)	0.756 (0.134)	0.893 (0.108)	0.948 (0.077)	1.017 (0.078)
Age 46–50 years (dummy)	0.830 (0.145)	0.998 (0.115)	1.058 (0.079)	1.095 (0.081)
Age 51–55 years (dummy)	0.619 (0.173)	0.939 (0.133)	0.994 (0.082)	1.132 (0.085)
Age 56–58 years (dummy)	1.206 (0.178)	1.521 (0.205)	1.611 (0.150)	1.750 (0.161)
No apprenticeship, no Abitur (ref. group)	—	—	—	—
Apprenticeship, no Abitur (dummy)	0.363 (0.104)	0.145 (0.074)	0.153 (0.026)	0.150 (0.030)
No apprenticeship, with Abitur (dummy)	−0.241 (0.115)	−0.530 (0.111)	−0.584 (0.071)	−0.492 (0.073)
Apprenticeship and Abitur (dummy)	0.063 (0.111)	−0.212 (0.089)	−0.225 (0.053)	−0.119 (0.056)
Technical college degree (dummy)	−0.227 (0.171)	−0.616 (0.106)	−0.646 (0.055)	−0.578 (0.058)
University degree (dummy)	−0.707 (0.181)	−1.153 (0.134)	−1.214 (0.054)	−0.992 (0.058)
Basic manual occupation (ref. group)	—	—	—	—
Qualified manual occupation (dummy)	0.094 (0.106)	0.048 (0.116)	0.050 (0.027)	0.085 (0.031)
Engineer or technician (dummy)	0.589 (0.438)	0.028 (0.080)	0.032 (0.041)	−0.122 (0.045)
Basic service occupation (dummy)	0.281 (0.127)	0.169 (0.099)	0.182 (0.034)	0.054 (0.041)
Qualified service occupation (dummy)	0.228 (0.213)	−0.148 (0.177)	−0.155 (0.088)	−0.340 (0.096)
Semi-professional (dummy)	0.528 (0.334)	0.242 (0.161)	0.255 (0.076)	0.112 (0.085)
Professional (dummy)	0.277 (0.362)	−0.168 (0.171)	−0.179 (0.085)	−0.310 (0.092)
Basic business occupation (dummy)	0.338 (0.306)	−0.210 (0.105)	−0.224 (0.064)	−0.400 (0.071)

9.5 Estimates of the Gender Difference in Long-Run Firm-Level Labour Supply Elasticities

Qualified business occupation (dummy)	0.577 (0.389)	0.042 (0.041)	−0.153 (0.044)
Manager (dummy)	0.432 (0.447)	−0.010 (0.085)	−0.215 (0.093)
Coll. agreement at sect. level (dummy)	0.102 (0.086)	0.108 (0.036)	0.127 (0.059)
Coll. agreement at firm level (dummy)	−1.401 (0.331)	−1.477 (0.044)	−0.894 (0.069)
Works council (dummy)	0.356 (0.103)	0.378 (0.036)	0.201 (0.064)
Proportion of female workers	0.917 (0.257)	0.972 (0.060)	0.909 (0.117)
Proportion of qualified workers	1.239 (0.329)	1.313 (0.039)	0.823 (0.070)
Good economic performance (dummy)	−0.244 (0.106)	−0.259 (0.024)	−0.168 (0.034)
Bad economic performance (dummy)	0.071 (0.108)	0.074 (0.029)	−0.051 (0.039)
New production technology (dummy)	−0.229 (0.240)	−0.241 (0.023)	−0.625 (0.035)
Ten sectoral dummies	($p < 0.001$)	($p < 0.001$)	($p < 0.001$)
Year 2000 (ref. group)	—	—	—
Year 2001 (dummy)	0.748 (0.424)	0.526 (0.022)	0.435 (0.023)
Year 2002 (dummy)	0.566 (0.431)	0.248 (0.025)	0.168 (0.027)
Constant	−6.921 (2.763)	−10.799 (0.231)	−10.585 (0.351)
Standard deviation of random effects		0.524 (0.022)	0.925 (0.024)
Proportion of random-effects variance in total variance		0.077 (0.006)	0.207 (0.009)
Observations	68,715	68,715	68,715
Hires from employment	36,064	36,064	36,064
Log likelihood	−43,628.020	−39,090.808	−35,186.031
McFadden-R^2	0.0824	0.1778	0.2599

[a] The data set used is version 2 of the LIAB longitudinal model. The regressand of the logit models is a binary response taking on the value one if the individual is hired from employment and zero otherwise. Standard errors (adjusted for intra-establishment correlations in the non-random effects models) are given in parentheses. Only transitions in 2000–2002 are considered.

Table 9.7 Determinants of females' probability of being hired from employment[a]

Regressors	Models without establishment controls	with establishment controls	with person random effects	with establishment random effects
Log daily gross wage (in €)	1.475 (0.292)	1.410 (0.144)	1.601 (0.057)	1.554 (0.056)
Non-German (dummy)	−0.508 (0.079)	−0.526 (0.077)	−0.611 (0.058)	−0.553 (0.056)
Age under 21 years (ref. group)	–	–	–	–
Age 21–25 years (dummy)	1.107 (0.112)	1.128 (0.109)	1.288 (0.105)	1.206 (0.097)
Age 26–30 years (dummy)	1.167 (0.123)	1.203 (0.117)	1.377 (0.105)	1.267 (0.098)
Age 31–35 years (dummy)	0.996 (0.124)	1.079 (0.116)	1.233 (0.105)	1.155 (0.098)
Age 36–40 years (dummy)	0.877 (0.127)	0.975 (0.121)	1.116 (0.106)	1.042 (0.100)
Age 41–45 years (dummy)	0.919 (0.124)	0.998 (0.123)	1.145 (0.109)	1.012 (0.103)
Age 46–50 years (dummy)	1.045 (0.129)	1.145 (0.127)	1.316 (0.113)	1.148 (0.106)
Age 51–55 years (dummy)	1.147 (0.166)	1.273 (0.154)	1.463 (0.124)	1.278 (0.118)
Age 56–58 years (dummy)	1.306 (0.278)	1.476 (0.281)	1.696 (0.255)	1.351 (0.245)
No apprenticeship, no Abitur (ref. group)	–	–	–	–
Apprenticeship, no Abitur (dummy)	0.200 (0.104)	0.128 (0.082)	0.146 (0.053)	0.128 (0.053)
No apprenticeship, with Abitur (dummy)	−0.480 (0.129)	−0.607 (0.120)	−0.720 (0.110)	−0.649 (0.105)
Apprenticeship and Abitur (dummy)	0.008 (0.100)	−0.162 (0.090)	−0.184 (0.076)	−0.135 (0.074)
Technical college degree (dummy)	0.457 (0.128)	−0.494 (0.121)	−0.562 (0.101)	−0.545 (0.098)
University degree (dummy)	−0.972 (0.124)	−1.021 (0.114)	−1.161 (0.085)	−1.071 (0.083)
Basic manual occupation (ref. group)	–	–	–	–
Qualified manual occupation (dummy)	0.151 (0.122)	0.077 (0.129)	0.076 (0.087)	0.235 (0.096)
Engineer or technician (dummy)	0.386 (0.363)	0.248 (0.179)	0.274 (0.090)	0.167 (0.094)
Basic service occupation (dummy)	0.227 (0.184)	0.122 (0.136)	0.122 (0.086)	0.147 (0.094)
Qualified service occupation (dummy)	0.265 (0.317)	0.081 (0.156)	0.086 (0.094)	−0.058 (0.099)
Semi-professional (dummy)	0.497 (0.352)	0.358 (0.166)	0.398 (0.083)	0.416 (0.090)
Professional (dummy)	0.054 (0.364)	−0.131 (0.180)	−0.159 (0.117)	−0.212 (0.118)
Basic business occupation (dummy)	0.653 (0.305)	0.398 (0.156)	0.445 (0.076)	0.330 (0.082)

9.5 Estimates of the Gender Difference in Long-Run Firm-Level Labour Supply Elasticities 191

Qualified business occupation (dummy)	0.669 (0.354)	0.426 (0.167)	0.478 (0.063)	0.339 (0.067)
Manager (dummy)	0.317 (0.381)	0.195 (0.223)	0.218 (0.134)	0.173 (0.134)
Coll. agreement at sect. level (dummy)		0.108 (0.102)	0.124 (0.057)	0.178 (0.071)
Coll. agreement at firm level (dummy)		−0.483 (0.262)	−0.547 (0.071)	−0.114 (0.091)
Works council (dummy)		0.141 (0.103)	0.168 (0.059)	0.077 (0.076)
Proportion of female workers		0.634 (0.261)	0.737 (0.088)	0.318 (0.125)
Proportion of qualified workers		0.818 (0.207)	0.933 (0.072)	0.473 (0.098)
Good economic performance (dummy)		−0.011 (0.126)	−0.010 (0.043)	0.072 (0.052)
Bad economic performance (dummy)		0.096 (0.127)	0.108 (0.052)	0.097 (0.062)
New production technology (dummy)		−0.073 (0.100)	−0.080 (0.039)	−0.166 (0.048)
Ten sectoral dummies		($p < 0.001$)	($p < 0.001$)	($p < 0.001$)
Year 2000 (ref. group)	—	—	—	—
Year 2001 (dummy)	0.351 (0.164)	0.327 (0.111)	0.368 (0.038)	0.264 (0.037)
Year 2002 (dummy)	0.364 (0.154)	0.350 (0.092)	0.398 (0.042)	0.334 (0.041)
Constant	−7.573 (0.951)	−8.633 (0.978)	−9.806 (0.422)	−8.451 (0.475)
Standard deviation of random effects			0.832 (0.037)	0.710 (0.028)
Proportion of random-effects variance in total variance			0.174 (0.013)	0.133 (0.009)
Observations	24,545	24,545	24,545	24,545
Hires from employment	14,219	14,219	14,219	14,219
Log likelihood	−14,969.390	−14,548.229	−14,521.447	−13,767.716
McFadden-R^2	0.1038	0.1290	0.1306	0.1757

[a] The data set used is version 2 of the LIAB longitudinal model. The regressand of the logit models is a binary response taking on the value one if the individual is hired from employment and zero otherwise. Standard errors (adjusted for intra-establishment correlations in the non-random effects models) are given in parentheses. Only transitions in 2000–2002 are considered.

council has a significantly positive impact on the hiring probability, whereas this does not apply for the coverage by a collective agreement. The estimated coefficient of the log daily wage reduces slightly for women, whereas it is markedly increased for men. The difference between female and male workers is now statistically significant at the 5 per cent level, estimated coefficients of log wage being 1.410 for women and 1.899 for men, respectively.

Including person-specific random effects to take account of unobserved heterogeneity at the level of the worker results only in minor changes, as can be seen from the fourth columns of Tables 9.6 and 9.7. In particular, the models' overall fit remains nearly unchanged. Finally, the inclusion of establishment-specific random effects, estimation results of which being presented in the fifth columns of Tables 9.6 and 9.7, leaves the sign and the magnitude of most coefficients unchanged. The coefficient of the log wage, however, changes to 1.554 for women and 2.174 for men, where the difference is now statistically significant at the 1 per cent level. Furthermore, the changes in the log likelihood indicate that the models' overall fit is significantly improved.

9.5.4 Estimates of the Long-Run Firm-Level Labour Supply Elasticities

Combining the results from Tables 9.2–9.7, we can now use equation (9.26) to obtain estimates for the long-run labour supply elasticity at the firm level separately for female and male workers. Table 9.8 on page 194 presents the results for the four specifications estimated. The share of recruits from employment is obtained by calculating the group-specific sample average.[42]

Table 9.8 makes clear that firm-level labour supply elasticities are rather low and that there are differences between male and female workers. Estimated elasticities for female workers range from 1.865 to 2.585, whereas those of men range from 2.489 to 3.655.[43] While there is consensus that females' labour supply is more

---

[42] In a steady state, assumed here, the share of recruits hired from employment must be equal to the share of separations to employment, i.e., $\theta^\sigma := \theta^\sigma_R = \theta^\sigma_s$ with $\sigma = f, m$. For female workers there are 14,928 separations to employment and 11,505 to non-employment, while there are 14,219 female recruits from employment and 10,326 from non-employment. So $\theta^f_s = 0.565$ and $\theta^f_R = 0.579$. For male workers, however, shares do differ substantially. There are 43,665 separations to employment and 26,195 to non-employment compared to 36,064 recruits from employment and 32,651 recruits from non-employment. Therefore, $\theta^m_s = 0.625$ and $\theta^m_R = 0.525$. Nonetheless, the implied differences in labour supply elasticities are less than 0.1 in all specifications. For the following calculations we used θ^σ_R, which gives lower labour supply elasticities compared to using θ^σ_s and slightly smaller gender differentials.

[43] Note that we also estimated the simple specification with wage-inelastic transitions to and from non-employment used by Ransom and Oaxaca (2008), where the labour supply elasticities are just given by the double absolute value of the respective estimated separation rate elasticity to employment. Estimated labour supply elasticities for male workers are then 3.032 with establishment

9.5 Estimates of the Gender Difference in Long-Run Firm-Level Labour Supply Elasticities

elastic than males' in terms of market supply (cf., e.g., Killingsworth and Heckman, 1986; Pencavel, 1986; Heckman, 1993; Blundell and MaCurdy, 1999), we find that female labour supply to the firm is less elastic than that of men.

In a model of dynamic monopsony, the long-run labour supply elasticity at the level of the firm is intimately related to the firm's wage-setting power, which in turn enables us to use the estimated labour supply elasticities for calculating implied gender pay gaps. This stems from Proposition 7.1 in Chapter 7 which states that the percentage gap between workers' wage and their marginal revenue product of labour under simple dynamic monopsony is given by the inverse of their long-run firm-level labour supply elasticity, i.e.,

$$E_m^\sigma := \frac{\phi - w^\sigma}{w^\sigma} = \frac{1}{e_{Lw}^\sigma} \qquad (9.27)$$

with $\sigma = f, m$, provided that the firm maximises its steady-state profits and discounts future profits at a negligible rate. Since this was assumed in the Burdett–Mortensen model in Chapter 8 and thus throughout the semi-structural approach applied here, it is appropriate to make use of this result in the discussion of our estimation results.[44] Assuming that men and women have the same marginal revenue product of labour, which is plausible since we have controlled for many of workers' characteristics, these gender pay gaps are calculated as

$$\Delta_{\%w}^f := \frac{w^m - w^f}{w^f} = \frac{e_{Lw}^m - e_{Lw}^f}{e_{Lw}^f(e_{Lw}^m + 1)} \qquad (9.28)$$

and

$$\Delta_{\%w}^m := \frac{w^f - w^m}{w^m} = \frac{e_{Lw}^f - e_{Lw}^m}{e_{Lw}^m(e_{Lw}^f + 1)} \qquad (9.29)$$

from the perspective of men and women, respectively, where both expressions follow at once from equation (9.27).

As the inverse of the elasticities presented in Table 9.8 gives the percentage gap of workers' marginal revenue product and their wages under dynamic monopsony, our estimates imply substantial, though not implausibly high market power on the firms' side. Given these firm-level labour supply elasticities, female workers would earn 38.7–53.6 per cent more were they paid their marginal products, whereas the gap is only 27.4–40.2 per cent for male workers. For example, in the specification with establishment frailties (random effects) these numbers are 46.6 per cent for

---

controls, 3.730 with person, and 2.922 with establishment frailties (random effects), which are clearly larger than the numbers reported in Table 9.8. On the other hand, the corresponding estimates for females' labour supply elasticity are 2.054, 2.540, and 2.342, respectively, which are all quite close to the estimates presented in Table 9.8. Consequently, this simple specification would imply larger gender pay gaps than those gained from the less restrictive approach chosen here.

[44] Note that we dropped the superscript 'LR' at e_{Lw} for notational convenience.

Table 9.8 Estimates of the long-run firm-level elasticity of female and male labour supplies when tenure is not controlled for[a]

Parameters	Models without establishment controls		with establishment controls		with all controls and person frailties/RE		with all controls and establishment frailties/RE	
	male workers	female workers	male workers	female workers	male workers	female workers	male workers	female workers
Estimated wage elasticity of the separation rate to employment ($\hat{\beta}_w^e$)	−1.594 (0.183)	−1.012 (0.131)	−1.516 (0.163)	−1.027 (0.103)	−1.865 (0.029)	−1.270 (0.042)	−1.461 (0.028)	−1.171 (0.038)
Estimated wage elasticity of the separation rate to non-employment ($\hat{\beta}_w^n$)	−2.982 (0.139)	−2.107 (0.067)	−2.676 (0.109)	−2.112 (0.068)	−3.702 (0.032)	−2.980 (0.045)	−2.724 (0.024)	−2.256 (0.032)
Estimated coefficient of the log wage in a logit model for the probability that a recruit is hired from employment ($\hat{\beta}_w$)	1.277 (0.747)	1.475 (0.292)	1.899 (0.156)	1.410 (0.144)	1.993 (0.041)	1.601 (0.057)	2.174 (0.047)	1.554 (0.056)
Share of recruits from employment ($\hat{\theta}$)	0.525	0.579	0.525	0.579	0.525	0.579	0.525	0.579

9.5 Estimates of the Gender Difference in Long-Run Firm-Level Labour Supply Elasticities

Estimated long-run firm-level labour supply elasticity ($\widehat{e}_{Lw}^{LR}$)[b]	3.242	1.865	2.681	1.917	3.655	2.585	2.489	2.145
Implied 'exploitation' ($\widehat{E}_m$)[c]	0.308	0.536	0.373	0.522	0.274	0.387	0.402	0.466
Implied gender pay gaps ($\widehat{\Delta}_{\%w}$)[d]	0.174	−0.148	0.108	−0.098	0.089	−0.082	0.046	−0.044

[a] Estimated coefficients are taken from Tables 9.2–9.7. Standard errors (adjusted for intra-establishment correlations in the non-frailty/random effects models) are given in parentheses.
[b] Estimated firm-level labour supply elasticities are obtained according to equation (9.26).
[c] The implied percentage gap between workers' marginal revenue product and their wages is calculated according to equation (9.27).
[d] Implied gender pay gaps are calculated according to equation (9.28) for male and (9.29) for female workers, respectively.

Table 9.9 Estimates of the long-run firm-level elasticity of female and male labour supplies when tenure is controlled for[a]

Parameters	Models without establishment controls		with establishment controls		with all controls and person frailties/RE		with all controls and establishment frailties/RE	
	male workers	female workers	male workers	female workers	male workers	female workers	male workers	female workers
Estimated wage elasticity of the separation rate to employment ($\hat{\beta}_w^e$)	−1.372 (0.221)	−0.802 (0.118)	−1.301 (0.179)	−0.815 (0.096)	−1.485 (0.029)	−0.877 (0.037)	−1.229 (0.028)	−0.939 (0.038)
Estimated wage elasticity of the separation rate to non-employment ($\hat{\beta}_w^n$)	−2.337 (0.195)	−1.625 (0.074)	−2.126 (0.127)	−1.629 (0.070)	−2.778 (0.033)	−1.887 (0.042)	−2.119 (0.026)	−1.689 (0.033)
Estimated coefficient of the log wage in a logit model for the probability that a recruit is hired from employment ($\hat{\beta}_w$)	1.277 (0.747)	1.475 (0.292)	1.899 (0.156)	1.410 (0.144)	1.993 (0.041)	1.601 (0.057)	2.174 (0.047)	1.554 (0.056)
Share of recruits from employment ($\hat{\theta}$)	0.525	0.579	0.525	0.579	0.525	0.579	0.525	0.579

9.5 Estimates of the Gender Difference in Long-Run Firm-Level Labour Supply Elasticities

Estimated long-run firm-level labour supply elasticity ($\widehat{e}_{Lw}^{LR}$)[b]	2.596	1.330	2.092	1.380	2.637	1.505	1.848	1.541
Implied 'exploitation' ($\widehat{E}_m$)[c]	0.385	0.752	0.478	0.725	0.379	0.664	0.541	0.649
Implied gender pay gaps ($\widehat{\Delta}_{\%w}$)[d]	0.265	−0.209	0.167	−0.143	0.207	−0.171	0.070	−0.065

[a] Estimated coefficients are taken from estimations similar to those presented in Tables 9.2–9.7 not reported in detail. In the piecewise-constant proportional hazard models, 24 intervals of tenure are considered: no more than 30, 30–59, 60–89, 90–119, 120–149, 150–179, 180–209, 210–239, 240–269, 270–299, 300–329, 330–359, 360–719, 720–1079, 1080–1439, 1440–1799, 1800–2159, 2160–2519, 2520–2879, 2880–3239, 3240–3599, 3600–5399, 5400–7199, and at least 7200 days. Standard errors (adjusted for intra-establishment correlations in the non-frailty/random effects models) are given in parentheses.
[b] Estimated firm-level labour supply elasticities are obtained according to equation (9.26).
[c] The implied percentage gap between workers' marginal revenue product and their wages is calculated according to equation (9.27).
[d] Implied gender pay gaps are calculated according to equation (9.28) for male and (9.29) for female workers, respectively.

female workers and 40.2 per cent for male workers, so that men earn only 71.3 per cent and women only 68.2 per cent of their marginal revenue product.

These differences in firms' wage-setting power in turn imply gender pay gaps.[45] When controlling for both workers' and establishments' characteristics but not allowing for unobserved heterogeneity at the level of the worker or establishment, the estimates suggest that women earn 9.8 per cent less than men or, put the other way round, that men earn 10.8 per cent more than women, *ceteris paribus*. These numbers are not implausible: Note that the actual unexplained gender pay gap in our sample obtained from an Oaxaca–Blinder decomposition is estimated as 11.4 or 14.3 per cent, respectively, depending on the reference group (see Appendix Table B.3 on page 242).[46]

When allowing for unobserved heterogeneity at the level of the worker or the establishment by incorporating person- or establishment-specific frailties (random effects), the implied gender pay gaps are substantially reduced in magnitude, although their size is still of economic relevance: Our estimates suggest that women earn 8.2 (4.4) per cent less than men or, put the other way round, that men earn 8.9 (4.6) per cent more than women when taking account of unobserved heterogeneity at the level of the worker (establishment). These findings give rise to the following interpretation: At least one third of the gender pay gap in our sample is explained by a model of dynamic monopsony focussing on gender differences in firm-level labour supply elasticities. Up to two thirds are due to other reasons not investigated here, such as discrimination due to distaste, occupational segregation, or unobserved productivity differences.

As a robustness check, we repeated the whole analysis relaxing the assumption of a constant baseline hazard, i.e., by controlling for the worker's tenure in the hazard rate models. This was implemented by fitting piecewise-constant exponential models. The key results of this analysis are presented in Table 9.9 on page 196. The estimated labour supply elasticities are generally lower (ranging from 1.848 to 2.596 for male workers and from 1.330 to 1.541 for female workers), whereas the implied gender pay gaps are larger (ranging from 7.0 to 26.5 per cent for men and from −6.5 to −20.9 per cent for women).[47] While both the wage-setting power of firms and the gender pay gaps implied by these numbers appear to be implausibly high, our main findings concerning gender-specific differences in firm-level labour supply elasticities still hold. We therefore conclude that they are pretty robust to specification.

---

[45] One should stress at this stage of the discussion that we do not know whether firms actually exercise their market power. Therefore, the implied wage-setting power of firms and gender pay gaps refer to firms' *potential* monopsony power, which might be constrained by institutional factors, such as collective bargaining or worker codetermination.

[46] For a short introduction to the Oaxaca–Blinder decomposition, see Section 6.2.

[47] Note that these results are in line with the expectation that the inclusion of the worker's tenure as another control variable sponges up some of the wage effect giving rise to lower separation rate elasticities and overstating of firms' monopsony power over their workers.

9.6 Conclusions

In this chapter, we have investigated gender differences in on-the-job search frictions and labour supply elasticities at the level of the firm. Using the Burdett–Mortensen model of equilibrium search theory with wage posting as laid out in Chapter 8, we showed that the share of recruits hired from non-employment can serve as a simple measure of on-the-job search frictions faced by workers. Since on-the-job search frictions are the obstacle to competition in this dynamic monopsony model, the share of recruits hired from non-employment is also a proxy of firms' monopsony power over their workers. While descriptive evidence suggested that women do not exhibit higher on-the-job search frictions than men, our multivariate analysis showed that women are significantly more likely to be hired from non-employment. Accordingly, firms' monopsony power over their female workers should be higher, so that the gender difference in on-the-job search frictions could be one explanation of the gender pay gap found in the data.[48]

Next, we estimated labour supply elasticities within a semi-structural approach resting on a dynamic model of 'new' monopsony similar to the Burdett–Mortensen model. Unlike Burdett and Mortensen, we allowed for stochastic transitions between firms and wage-elastic transitions from and to non-employment, in such a way following Manning (2003a). Estimations were carried out by methods of survival analysis, and we made use of the German linked employer–employee data set LIAB for the years 2000–2002. All in all, estimated elasticities range from 1.9 to 3.7, depending on specification, where women's elasticity is always lower than men's. Although we have not been able to test for the semi-structural approach chosen, our results should enable us to draw some cautious conclusions concerning the relevance and implications of these gender differences in labour supply to the firm.

One important general insight is that estimated labour supply elasticities are far from the conventional textbook case of being perfectly elastic. This implies that the 'new' monopsony approach is not rejected by the data, for its main feature is upward-sloping labour supply to the firm (see Sections 1.1 and 1.2). Since the estimated elasticities are rather small in size, 'new' monopsony models would suggest that firms possess substantial (potential) monopsony power.

Moreover, we found that – in contrast to labour supply at the level of the market – labour supply to the firm is less elastic for women than for men. Since this means

---

[48] Other potential explanations are different preferences over non-wage job characteristics and a higher degree of immobility of women, as put forward in Chapter 5. Manning (2003a, pp. 47–49, 199–208) presents some evidence for the U.S. and the UK that women are less driven by pecuniary considerations than men when changing jobs and that they face higher on-the-job search frictions. For Germany, an analysis by Arntz (2005) shows that unemployed women are less inclined to leave local labour markets with an unfavourable labour demand situation than men, which points in the same direction. Also for Germany, Heinze (2009) provides evidence that women select themselves into establishments offering attractive working conditions but lower pay, while Pollmann-Schult (2009) identifies (limited) gender differences in job values, with men placing a higher value on extrinsic rewards, such as high pay.

that women's labour supply curve to the firm is steeper than men's, our findings are consistent with those of Green *et al.* (1996) who report larger employer size–wage effects for women than for men. Furthermore, our results confirm and extend the three other attempts made to investigate women's and men's labour supply elasticities at the level of the firm, namely the studies by Manning (2003*a*, pp. 100–105, 206–208), Ransom and Oaxaca (2008), and Barth and Dale-Olsen (2009), because our analysis is built on less restrictive assumptions than the latter two and explicitly controls for establishment characteristics.

Since in a model of (dynamic) monopsony the labour supply elasticity at the level of the firm is intimately related to firms' wage-setting power, we were able to use the estimated labour supply elasticities for calculating implied gender pay gaps. Depending on specification, women earn 4.4–14.8% less than men, *ceteris paribus*. Therefore, at least one third of the observed gender pay gap can be explained in terms of different labour supply elasticities at the firm level. These findings are consistent with the notion of wage discrimination put forward by Robinson (1969). Therefore, our results affirm our theoretical considerations from Chapter 5 that differences in firm-level labour supply elasticities and thus Robinsonian wage discrimination may contribute to the explanation of the persisting empirical regularity of the gender pay gap.

Chapter 10
Concluding Remarks

This book has dealt with models of 'new' monopsony and their application to the empirical regularity of the gender pay gap. Other than perfect competition, these models give rise to upward-sloping labour supply at the level of the firm and therefore equip firms with some monopsony power over their workers due to workers' mobility costs, heterogenous preferences, or incomplete knowledge. In contrast to models of 'classic' monopsony, however, no concentration on the demand side is needed to sustain monopsonistic outcomes, and firms may possess some monopsony power even in labour markets consisting of many employers.

In Part I, we focussed on the role of mobility costs in models of spatial monopsony. Enriching a model of simple static spaceless monopsony, discussed in Chapter 2, we built up a model of spatial monopsony – both in the strict sense of a single employer in economic space and in the wider sense of a spatial oligopsony model. We considered homogenous economic space where workers face significant travel cost to commute to their employers. In the short run considered in Chapter 3, the number of firms is fixed, and the travel cost turns out to be the obstacle to competition and the source of firms' monopsony power. Other things being equal, workers prefer an employer nearby over a more distant one because the lower travel cost involved earns them a higher income. If one firm cuts its wage by some amount, not all its employees suddenly turn to one of its competitors. Firms are therefore anything but passive wage takers. Instead, they play an active role and set wages such that their profits are maximised in equilibrium. In their wage-setting decisions, they are constrained by three forces: the number of competitors in the market, their likely wage-setting behaviour embodied in the conjectural variations, and workers' labour supply behaviour. A general insight was that the more firms collude the lower is the equilibrium wage. We also found that competitive entry and a decrease in the travel cost are equivalent in an economic way as both cause economic space to be less significant either because the distance between firms reduces directly or because the same distance becomes less costly. Furthermore, both these changes do not necessarily lead to a rise in the equilibrium wage. Our general conclusion was that competitive entry or a decrease in the travel cost only has a positive effect on workers' equilibrium wage if the labour market is sufficiently competitive, i.e., if (1) there are many non-collusive firms, (2) workers' labour supply is very elastic, or (3) firms conjecture aggressive wage-setting behaviour. On the other hand, the effect is negative if competitive forces are weak, particularly if firms act in concert because of (tacitly) collusive behaviour and workers' labour supply is not 'extremely elastic.'

In the long run considered in Chapter 4, we analysed the model's zero-profit equilibrium. This was done by adding a zero-profit condition to the model and allowing for free entry and costless relocation of firms. Accordingly, firms' fixed costs and the implied economies of scale prevent them from being set up everywhere in economic space. To survive, i.e., to cover their fixed costs, firms need a profit, and workers' partial immobility equips them with the monopsony power to earn it. Because of free entry, however, covering their fixed costs is all firms can achieve in equilibrium. The number of firms therefore becomes an endogenous outcome of the model. If the labour market becomes more profitable because, for instance, there are more workers around and competitive forces are strong enough in the sense given in the last paragraph, then this causes more firms to survive and thus yields a more competitive environment with a higher equilibrium wage. Moreover, if the travel cost rises, this reduces workers' labour supply and thus the labour market's profitability. While this causes competitive exit, at the same time workers' immobility increases as does firms' monopsony power over them. Both of these forces put downwards pressure on the wage provided competitive forces are not very weak. Finally, we saw that the model may give rise to several outcomes that have attracted the label 'perverse' in the literature (though they follow gradually from a spatial reasoning). If competitive forces are very weak in the sense given above, spatial competitors pay a lower wage than a spatial monopsonist, there may be a negative relationship between workers' marginal revenue product and their equilibrium wage, and the comparative static results discussed so far revolve. Note also that all the things said are easily relabelled to embrace the case of heterogenous preferences over non-wage job characteristics instead of mobility costs. Economic space then becomes the job characteristic space, and the travel cost now refers to the utility loss that follows from taking up a job 'distanced' from the worker's preferred one.

The negative relationship between workers' travel cost and their equilibrium wage under spatial monopsony offers a starting point for the analysis of the gender pay gap carried out in Chapter 5. If firms are able to segment the labour market by sex and women face higher travel cost than men, e.g., higher indirect costs of commuting due to more domestic responsibilities, this will offer employers the opportunity of increasing their profits via third-degree wage discrimination. By analogy, the same holds if women are more tied to their employers than men because of their preferences over non-wage job characteristics. Women get paid lower wages because they are less likely to leave their employer to take up a job at another firm. Since women's labour supply at the level of the firm is for this reason less elastic than men's, this gives a spatial monopsony re-formulation of Robinsonian discrimination. While this sort of discrimination may occur only if there is a gender difference in labour supply elasticities at the level of the firm (not the market), this framework also provides a rationale why decreasing women's opportunity costs of travelling (e.g., due to better or more child care facilities) is likely to reduce the gender pay gap.

10 Concluding Remarks

In Chapter 6, we used this spatial monopsony reasoning to think about the regional dimension of the gender pay gap. According to spatial monopsony, more densely populated labour markets are thicker labour markets with a more competitive environment. This not only pushes both female and male workers' wages, but also constrains employers' ability to engage in Robinsonian discrimination. Utilising a large social security data set for western Germany ranging from 1975–2004, the IAB-REG, and a semi-parametric propensity score matching approach, we found that the unexplained part of the gender pay gap of young workers is around 10 percentage points smaller in hot spots, i.e., large metropolitan areas, than in rural areas. While the gap both in hot spots and rural areas gradually decreased over time, this hot spot–rural difference remained astonishingly stable over the entire period of 30 years. The former finding is in line with decreasing gender mobility differences over time, yielding lower Robinsonian discrimination in our spatial monopsony model. The latter result is consistent with a time-invariant hot spot–rural difference in competitive environments that effectively constrains the ability of employers to discriminate against women. Therefore, our spatial monopsony re-formulation of Robinsonian discrimination provides a theoretical framework to think about the regional dimension of the gender pay gap that is in line with empirical observation.

In Part II, we turned to models of dynamic monopsony that highlight search frictions as another source of firms' monopsony power. We started from a simple model of dynamic monopsony, laid out in Chapter 7, and enriched this setting in Chapter 8 by building up a general equilibrium model of dynamic monopsony, the Burdett–Mortensen model of equilibrium search with wage posting. In this model, job searchers only have incomplete knowledge on the labour market and the vacancies offered to them. By chance, some of them end up with low-paying and some with high-paying jobs. Since workers also search on the job, they try to work their way up the wage distribution by making job-to-job moves. While this inter-employer mobility of workers constrains the monopsony power of firms, both low- and high-pay firms are able to survive in the labour market. In this model, both workers' expected wage and the level of wage dispersion in the labour market depend on the extent of on-the-job search frictions.

In Chapter 9, we exploited the focus of dynamic monopsony on firms' in- and outflow of workers empirically in a way following Manning (2003*a*). We first derived a simple measure of on-the-job search frictions, the share of recruits hired from non-employment. Intuitively, this measure tells us how likely firms are to poach workers and therefore allows us to assess the extent of inter-employer competition and on-the-job search frictions. Next, we used simple dynamic monopsony and the structure of equilibrium search with wage posting to derive a semi-structural estimation approach to the long-run firm-level labour supply elasticity. Roughly speaking, this approach allows us to infer the elasticity from the wage responsiveness of firms' separations to employment and non-employment and the composition of their inflow of recruits using methods of survival analysis. Using both approaches to investigate gender differences in search frictions and firm-level labour supply elasticities, we utilised a large linked employer–employee data set for western Germany, the LIAB, consisting of a balanced panel of establishments in 2000–2002 and all their employees if covered by the social security system. We found evidence that women face higher on-the-job search frictions than men and that they supply labour less elastically at the level of the firm, where both male and female labour supply are far from being infinitely elastic. Plugged into the model of simple dynamic monopsony, the pronounced gender elasticity differentials proved to predict at least a third of the unexplained gender pay gap found in the data.

Both these findings are clearly supportive to Robinsonian discrimination. Taking all our results together, we conclude that a monopsonistic Robinsonian explanation of gender discrimination in the labour market clearly contributes to our economic understanding of the gender pay gap. Roughly speaking, this reasoning highlights that women earn lower wages if they are less driven by pecuniary considerations than men. If firms are aware of this, Robinsonian discrimination allows them to increase their profits and is therefore likely to survive in the long run.

In contrast, under Beckerian discrimination, which is typically utilised to explain discrimination in the labour market, firms trade off their profits with their taste for discrimination. Assuming a distaste for women on employers' side, this framework finds that employers are willing to pay for discrimination. In competitive markets, however, this sort of costly discrimination should be competed away. And even under imperfect competition, we end up with discriminating firms being less profitable. What is more, this line of argument leaves out why firms have such a distaste. Put drastically, discrimination is the result from firms' assumed discriminatory preferences and therefore is basically assumed itself. 'We ... claim, however, that no significant behavior has been illuminated by assumptions on differences in tastes. Instead, they ... have been a convenient crutch to lean on when the analysis has bogged down. They give the appearance of considered judgement, yet really have only been *ad hoc* arguments that disguise analytical failures.' (Stigler and Becker, 1977, p. 89) Given these shortcomings of Beckerian discrimination and given the empirical support to Robinsonian discrimination found, we cannot help but consider the latter a more convincing and less *ad hoc* explanation of the gender pay gap.[1]

What is more, from a political point of view, it seems hard to figure out what should be done against something mushy like a distaste parameter in an employer's utility function. The incentives of Robinsonian discriminators, on the other hand, are comparably easily be dealt with. If they cannot earn a profit from discrimination, firms will stop it. At the level of workers, one may try to reduce gender differences in mobility, for instance, by providing or subsidising additional childcare facilities. In short, facilitating work–life balance for women seems to be paramount. At the level of the market, one may try to remove obstacles to competition. More competition among employers decreases their monopsony power over their workers and thus

---

[1] As has been argued by Schlicht (1982, p. 82), Robinsonian discrimination 'has less difficulties in explaining persistent discrimination, thereby enforcing the argument of the other approaches: Discrimination might lead, through habit formation, to a taste for discrimination...' In this respect, Robinsonian discrimination might even serve as an explanation for Beckerian discrimination due to distaste.

10 Concluding Remarks

is also likely to reduce their ability to discriminate against women. For example, increasing the level of transparency on the labour market may contribute to reduce the impact of search frictions and removing hindrances to mobility may decrease firms' monopsony power in economic space.

All in all, we conclude that we have succeeded in generalising the spatial monopsony models by Nakagome (1986) and Bhaskar and To (1999) and applying 'new' monopsony to the gender pay gap. Our spatial monopsony re-formulation of Robinsonian discrimination has proved to be successful in pattern prediction and a valuable framework to think about the regional dimension of the gender pay gap. It also gives an intuitively appealing explanation of gender discrimination readily from common economic reasoning without the need to impose any *ad hoc* assumptions concerning employers' taste for discrimination. Last but not least, empirical evidence strongly supported that women supply labour less elastically at the firm level, so that Robinsonian discrimination may be feasible to firms.

Nevertheless, there is much more research needed. While Chapter 6 presented – to the best of our knowledge – the first systematic investigation of regional differences in the gender pay gap over a long period of time, this finding should also be investigated with data sets from other countries. Whereas our spatial monopsony explanation of the gender pay gap highlighted the role of women's mobility and the likely impact of mobility-enhancing policies, one should not implement half-baked policies. Systematic research of potential policy instruments and careful normative analyses are needed for such policies to be effective and welfare-improving. Whilst we found gender differences in firm-level labour supply elasticities, '[i]t does not follow that differences in supply elasticities necessarily generate differences in wages. Before concluding that monopsony is important, one should measure outcomes.' (Hirsch and Schumacher, 2005, p. 987) Future research should try to take wage outcomes explicitly into account and investigate whether the gender pay gap is reduced if one controls for firms' monopsony power. We also could not investigate whether women with more domestic responsibilities, in particular married women with children at home, supply labour less elastically than single women due to data restrictions. It would affirm our theoretical argument for Robinsonian discrimination further if this were found empirically. Seizing on these suggestions, the strong case of monopsonistic Robinsonian discrimination of women could be made even stronger.

Appendix A
Appendix: Spatial Monopsony

A.1 Proof of Remark 3.2

Consider the individual labour supply function

$$l(z) := \exp[\tan(z - \pi/2)] \tag{A.1}$$

and its restriction $l|_{(r,\phi)}$ with $\phi = \pi$ and $r = \inf\{z|l(z) > 0\} = 0$, where the latter holds because

$$\lim_{z \searrow 0} \exp[\tan(z - \pi/2)] = \lim_{\vartheta \to -\infty} \exp(\vartheta) = 0. \tag{A.2}$$

Obviously, $l(z) > 0$ for all $0 < z < \pi$ as $\exp \vartheta > 0$ for all $\vartheta \in \mathbb{R}$. Furthermore,

$$l'(z) = \frac{\exp[\tan(z - \pi/2)]}{\cos^2(z - \pi/2)} > 0 \tag{A.3}$$

for all $0 < z < \pi$ because $\cos \vartheta > 0$ for all $-\pi/2 < \vartheta < \pi/2$. Next, the logarithm of $l(z)$ is given by

$$\ell(z) = \tan(z - \pi/2), \tag{A.4}$$

so that

$$\ell''(z) = \frac{2\sin(z - \pi/2)}{\cos^3(z - \pi/2)} \gtreqless 0 \tag{A.5}$$

if $z \gtreqless \pi/2$ because $\cos \vartheta > 0$ for all $-\pi/2 < \vartheta < \pi/2$ and $\sin \vartheta \gtreqless 0$ if $(-\pi/2, \pi/2) \ni \vartheta \gtreqless 0$. Hence, $l|_{(0,\pi)}$ is strictly log-concave for all $0 < z < \pi/2$ and strictly log-convex for all $\pi/2 < z < \pi$ and therefore does not fit into any of Definitions 3.1–3.3. ∎

A.2 Proof of Example 3.5

Consider the individual labour supply function

$$l(z) := \left(\frac{\gamma}{\beta}(z-\alpha)\right)^{1/\gamma} \tag{A.6}$$

with constants $\alpha, \beta > 0$ and $-1 < \gamma \neq 0$. Note that for $\gamma > 0$ individual labour supply is only positive if $z > \alpha$, so that $r = \inf\{z | l(z) > 0\} = \alpha$ in this case. On the other hand, for $-1 < \gamma < 0$ we have $l(z) > 0$ for all $z < \alpha$ and $l(z) \to 0$ if $z \to -\infty$, so that $r = \inf\{z | l(z) > 0\} = -\infty$. Since $l(z) > 0$ holds only if $z < \alpha$ in this case, α can be thought of as an upper ceiling that incomes must not exceed. In particular, imposing $\alpha > \phi$ guarantees that $l(z) > 0$ holds for all relevant cases, i.e., for all $r < z < \phi$.[1]

Moreover, the restriction $\gamma > -1$ is needed to rule out implausible results (cf. Greenhut, 1978; Greenhut et al., 1987, pp. 57/367), which we will demonstrate next. Consider only workers with $x = 0$, i.e., individuals who live at the location of their employer, so that $z = w$. Using the inverse labour supply function

$$w(l) = \alpha + \frac{\beta l^\gamma}{\gamma}, \tag{A.7}$$

the employer's employment cost for l units of labour is given by

$$lw(l) = \alpha l + \frac{\beta l^{\gamma+1}}{\gamma}. \tag{A.8}$$

Hence, the marginal labour cost faced by the employer is

$$\frac{dlw(l)}{dl} = \alpha + \frac{\beta(\gamma+1)l^\gamma}{\gamma} \tag{A.9}$$

with derivative

$$\frac{d^2 lw(l)}{dl^2} = \beta(\gamma+1)l^{\gamma-1} \gtreqless 0 \tag{A.10}$$

if and only if $\gamma \gtreqless -1$. Hence, $\gamma > -1$ has to hold in order to avoid the implausible case of non-increasing marginal labour cost for this group of workers.

---

[1] As argued above in footnote 7 on page 19, firms always choose a wage smaller than workers' marginal revenue product in all relevant cases. Hence, $\phi > w \geqslant z(w, x)$ holds for all $(w, x) \in Z$, so that postulating $\alpha > \phi$ makes this upper ceiling irrelevant in all economically interesting situations.

A.2 Proof of Example 3.5

Next, note that individual labour supply is strictly increasing because

$$l'(z) = \frac{1}{\beta} \left(\frac{\gamma}{\beta}(z-\alpha) \right)^{1/\gamma - 1} > 0 \qquad (A.11)$$

for all z with $l(z) > 0$. Taking a look at the second derivative of l, we find

$$l''(z) = \frac{1-\gamma}{\beta^2} \left(\frac{\gamma}{\beta}(z-\alpha) \right)^{1/\gamma - 2} \gtreqless 0 \qquad (A.12)$$

if $\gamma \lesseqgtr 1$ for all z with $l(z) > 0$. Hence, l is strictly convex if $\gamma < 1$, strictly concave if $\gamma > 1$, and linear if $\gamma = 1$.

Moreover, consider l's convexity relative to an exponential. Since

$$\ell(z) = \frac{1}{\gamma} \ln \left(\frac{\gamma}{\beta}(z-\alpha) \right), \qquad (A.13)$$

we get

$$\ell''(z) = -\frac{1}{\gamma(z-\alpha)^2} \gtreqless 0 \qquad (A.14)$$

if $\gamma \lesseqgtr 0$. Thus, we find that l is strictly log-convex if $\gamma < 0$ and strictly log-concave if $\gamma > 0$.

Next, consider what happens if $\gamma \to 0$. To do so, we have to slightly modify $l(z)$ in order to be able to apply de l'Hôpital's rule (see the discussion in footnote 15 on page 25). Therefore, consider now

$$l(z) := \left(\frac{\gamma}{\beta}(z-\alpha) + 1 \right)^{1/\gamma}. \qquad (A.15)$$

By looking at the corresponding indirect individual labour supply function, we find

$$\lim_{\gamma \to 0} z(l) = \alpha + \beta \lim_{\gamma \to 0} \frac{l^\gamma - 1}{\gamma} \qquad (A.16)$$

$$= \alpha + \beta \lim_{\gamma \to 0} \frac{\exp(\gamma \ln l) - 1}{\gamma} \qquad (A.17)$$

$$= \alpha + \beta \lim_{\gamma \to 0} l^\gamma \ln l \qquad (A.18)$$

$$= \alpha + \beta \ln l, \qquad (A.19)$$

where the third equality follows from applying de l'Hôpital's rule. Hence, individual labour supply converges pointwise to exponential labour supply if $\gamma \to 0$, which is given by

$$\lim_{\gamma \to 0} l(z) = \exp \left(\frac{1}{\beta}(z-\alpha) \right). \qquad (A.20)$$

In a next step, consider l's elasticity, which is

$$\varepsilon(z) := \frac{l'(z)z}{l(z)} = \frac{\frac{1}{\beta}\left(\frac{\gamma}{\beta}(z-\alpha)\right)^{1/\gamma-1} z}{\left(\frac{\gamma}{\beta}(z-\alpha)\right)^{1/\gamma}} = \frac{1}{\gamma}\frac{z}{z-\alpha}. \quad (A.21)$$

This becomes a constant, viz. $1/\gamma$, for all z with $l(z) > 0$ if $\alpha \to 0$. Obviously, $\gamma > 0$ must hold in this case to get a positive elasticity which is not surprising as the iso-elastic labour supply function from Example 3.4 on page 24 is less convex than an exponential.

Eventually, l becomes a constant function if $\gamma \to \infty$; for

$$\lim_{\gamma \to \infty} \left(\frac{\gamma}{\beta}(z-\alpha)\right)^{1/\gamma} = 1, \quad (A.22)$$

so that $l(z) \to 1$ for all $z \in \mathbb{R}$ if $\gamma \to \infty$. Accordingly, l converges pointwise to the limiting function $\widehat{1}$.[2] This limiting function corresponds to constant individual labour supply as discussed in Example 3.6, although there exists no $r = \inf\{z|l(z) > 0\}$ as $l(z) = 1$ for all $z \in \overline{\mathbb{R}} := \mathbb{R} \cup \{-\infty, \infty\}$. ■

A.3 Proof of Proposition 3.3

The short-run equilibrium wage is implicitly given by

$$w_i = \frac{e_i(w_i, X)}{1 + e_i(w_i, X)} \phi \Leftrightarrow \phi - w_i \frac{1 + e_i(w_i, X)}{e_i(w_i, X)} = 0 \quad (A.23)$$

with $i \in \{Lö, HS, GO\}$.

(a) Changes in the Fixed Costs f and the Worker Density D

Since

$$e_i(w_i, X) = \frac{w_i \left[\int_0^X l'(w_i - tx)\,dx + v_i l(w_i - tX)\right]}{\int_0^X l(w_i - tx)\,dx}, \quad (A.24)$$

we have

$$\frac{\partial e_i(w_i, X)}{\partial f} = \frac{\partial e_i(w_i, X)}{\partial D} = 0. \quad (A.25)$$

---

[2] $\widehat{1}$ denotes the constant function with value 1 for the entire domain, i.e., $\widehat{1} : \mathbb{R} \to \mathbb{R}$ with $\widehat{1}(z) = 1$ for all $z \in \mathbb{R}$.

A.3 Proof of Proposition 3.3

Hence, implicit differentiation of (A.23) with respect to f or D obviously yields

$$\frac{\partial w_i}{\partial f} = \frac{\partial w_i}{\partial D} = 0. \tag{A.26}$$

(b) Changes in the Marginal Revenue Product of Labour ϕ

To prove $\partial w_i/\partial \phi > 0$ first note that implicit differentiation of (A.23) with respect to ϕ gives

$$1 - \left(\frac{\partial w_i}{\partial \phi}\frac{1 + e_i(w_i, X)}{e_i(w_i, X)} - \frac{w_i}{e_i^2(w_i, X)}\frac{\partial e_i(w_i, X)}{\partial w_i}\frac{\partial w_i}{\partial \phi}\right) = 0, \tag{A.27}$$

so that

$$\frac{\partial w_i}{\partial \phi} = \left(\frac{1 + e_i(w_i, X)}{e_i(w_i, X)} - \frac{w_i}{e_i^2(w_i, X)}\frac{\partial e_i(w_i, X)}{\partial w_i}\right)^{-1}. \tag{A.28}$$

Next, note that

$$\frac{1 + e_i(w_i, X)}{e_i(w_i, X)} - \frac{w_i}{e_i^2(w_i, X)}\frac{\partial e_i(w_i, X)}{\partial w_i} = -\frac{\partial}{\partial w_i}\left(\phi - w_i\frac{1 + e_i(w_i, X)}{e_i(w_i, X)}\right). \tag{A.29}$$

Since

$$\frac{\partial \Pi_i(w_i, X)}{\partial w_i} \gtreqless 0 \Leftrightarrow \phi - w_i\frac{1 + e_i(w_i, X)}{e_i(w_i, X)} \gtreqless 0 \tag{A.30}$$

and since we are considering profit-maximising wage setting where $\partial \Pi_i(w_i, X)/\partial w_i$ must be strictly decreasing in the wage, we must have

$$\frac{\partial}{\partial w_i}\left(\phi - w_i\frac{1 + e_i(w_i, X)}{e_i(w_i, X)}\right) < 0 \tag{A.31}$$

in the optimum.[3] Hence, it follows from (A.28), (A.29), and (A.31) that

$$\frac{\partial w_i}{\partial \phi} = \left(\frac{1 + e_i(w_i, X)}{e_i(w_i, X)} - \frac{w_i}{e_i^2(w_i, X)}\frac{\partial e_i(w_i, X)}{\partial w_i}\right)^{-1} > 0 \tag{A.32}$$

for all $0 < X < X_M$ and $i \in \{Lö, HS, GO\}$.

---

[3] Note that this proof requires Π_i to be continuously differentiable, i.e., $\Pi_i \in \mathcal{C}$, which immediately follows from our assumption that l is smooth. In particular, l's smoothness implies Π_i's smoothness, so that $\Pi_i \in \mathcal{C}^\infty$ as well.

(c)–(e) Changes in the Travel Cost t

Finally, implicit differentiation of (A.23) with respect to t gives

$$-\frac{\partial w_i}{\partial t}\frac{1+e_i(w_i,X)}{e_i(w_i,X)} + \frac{w_i}{e_i^2(w_i,X)}\left(\frac{\partial e_i(w_i,X)}{\partial w_i}\frac{\partial w_i}{\partial t} + \frac{\partial e_i(w_i,X)}{\partial t}\right) = 0, \quad \text{(A.33)}$$

so that

$$\frac{\partial w_i}{\partial t} = \frac{w_i}{e_i^2(w_i,X)}\frac{\partial e_i(w_i,X)}{\partial t}\left(\frac{1+e_i(w_i,X)}{e_i(w_i,X)} - \frac{w_i}{e_i^2(w_i,X)}\frac{\partial e_i(w_i,X)}{\partial w_i}\right)^{-1} \quad \text{(A.34)}$$

$$= \frac{w_i}{e_i^2(w_i,X)}\frac{\partial e_i(w_i,X)}{\partial t}\frac{\partial w_i}{\partial \phi}. \quad \text{(A.35)}$$

From the discussion above we know $\partial w_i/\partial \phi > 0$. Thus, it follows that

$$\operatorname{sgn}\frac{\partial w_i}{\partial t} = \operatorname{sgn}\frac{\partial e_i(w_i,X)}{\partial t}. \quad \text{(A.36)}$$

According to (3.10), the aggregate labour supply elasticity is given by

$$e_i(w_i,X) = \frac{w_i\left[\int_0^X l'(w_i-tx)\,dx + v_i l(w_i-tX)\right]}{\int_0^X l(w_i-tx)\,dx}. \quad \text{(A.37)}$$

Substitution of the variable of integration with $\vartheta := w_i - tx$ yields

$$\int_0^X l'(w_i-tx)\,dx = -\frac{1}{t}\int_{w_i}^{w_i-tX} l'(\vartheta)\,d\vartheta \quad \text{(A.38)}$$

$$= \frac{1}{t}\int_{w_i-tX}^{w_i} l'(\vartheta)\,d\vartheta \quad \text{(A.39)}$$

$$= \frac{l(w_i) - l(w_i-tX)}{t}, \quad \text{(A.40)}$$

which follows directly from the fundamental theorem of calculus. Inserting this into (A.37), we get

$$e_i(w_i,X) = \frac{w_i[l(w_i) - (1-v_i t)l(w_i-tX)]}{t\int_0^X l(w_i-tx)\,dx}. \quad \text{(A.41)}$$

For notational convenience we shall drop from now on the index i at w. Furthermore, define $\Theta := \int_0^X l(w-tx)\,dx$ and $\Psi := \int_0^X l'(w-tx)x\,dx$ for notational brevity in the following expressions. Note that $\partial\Theta/\partial t = -\Psi$.

A.3 Proof of Proposition 3.3

(d) Löschian Competition

Consider the case of Löschian competition with $v_{Lö} = 0$ first, so that (A.41) gives

$$e_{Lö}(w, X) = \frac{w[l(w) - l(w - tX)]}{t \int_0^X l(w - tx)\, dx} = \frac{w[l(w) - l(w - tX)]}{t\Theta}. \tag{A.42}$$

Differentiation of (A.42) with respect to t yields

$$\frac{\partial e_{Lö}(w, X)}{\partial t} = \frac{w[l'(w - tX)Xt\Theta - [l(w) - l(w - tX)](\Theta - t\Psi)]}{t^2\Theta^2}. \tag{A.43}$$

Note that

$$\Psi := \int_0^X l'(w - tx) x\, dx = -\frac{1}{t}\int_0^X \frac{\partial l(w - tx)}{\partial x} x\, dx \tag{A.44}$$

$$= -\frac{1}{t}\left(l(w - tx)x \Big|_0^X - \int_0^X l(w - tx)\, dx \right) \tag{A.45}$$

$$= \frac{\Theta - l(w - tX)X}{t}, \tag{A.46}$$

where the first equality holds due to the chain rule and the second equality due to integration by parts. Inserting this into (A.43) and some straightforward algebraic simplifications give

$$\frac{\partial e_{Lö}(w, X)}{\partial t} = \frac{wX[l'(w - tX)t\Theta - [l(w) - l(w - tX)]l(w - tX)]}{t^2\Theta^2}. \tag{A.47}$$

At first sight, it seems hard to say anything clear-cut about the sign of (A.47). This changes, however, when manipulating (A.47) in the right way.

Applying Taylor's theorem by using a second-order Taylor series yields

$$l(w) - l(w - tX) = tXl'(w - tX) + \frac{t^2X^2}{2}l''(w - \vartheta tX) \tag{A.48}$$

with $0 < \vartheta < 1$, where the last term on the right-hand side of (A.48) is the Lagrange form of the remainder term. Inserting (A.48) into (A.47) gives

$$\frac{\partial e_{Lö}(w, X)}{\partial t} = \frac{wXl'(w - tX)}{t\Theta^2}\left(\Theta - Xl(w - tX) - \frac{tX^2 l''(w - \vartheta tX)l(w - tX)}{2l'(w - tX)} \right). \tag{A.49}$$

Note that $l'(z) > 0$ for all $r < z < \phi$ implies

$$\Theta - Xl(w - tX) = \int_0^X [l(w - tx) - l(w - tX)]\, dx > 0 \tag{A.50}$$

for all $0 < X < X_M$. Hence, (A.49) is obviously positive if individual labour supply is concave, i.e., $l''(z) \leqslant 0$ for all $r < z < \phi$. Furthermore, (A.49) is also positive if individual labour supply is strictly convex, i.e., if $l''(z) > 0$ for all $r < z < \phi$ but not too convex. Next, we will show that convexity relative to an exponential is the relevant criterion to look at when deciding on the sign of (A.49).

Assume now that individual labour supply is strictly convex, i.e., $l''(z) > 0$ for all $r < z < \phi$, so that we cannot see at once whether the term in parentheses on the right-hand side of (A.49) is positive. Return for the moment to equation (A.47). Applying Taylor's theorem by using a third-order Taylor series yields

$$l(w) - l(w - tX) = tXl'(w - tX) + \frac{t^2 X^2}{2} l''(w - tX) + \frac{t^3 X^3}{6} l'''(w - \vartheta tX) \quad \text{(A.51)}$$

with $0 < \vartheta < 1$, where again the last term on the right-hand side of (A.51) is the Lagrange form of the remainder term. Inserting (A.51) into (A.47) gives

$$\frac{\partial e_{L\ddot{o}}(w, tX)}{\partial t} = \frac{wXl'(w - tX)}{t\Theta^2} \left(\Theta - Xl(w - tX) - \frac{tX^2 l''(w - tX) l(w - tX)}{2l'(w - tX)} \right.$$
$$\left. - \frac{t^2 X^3 l'''(w - \vartheta tX) l(w - tX)}{6 l'(w - tX)} \right). \quad \text{(A.52)}$$

Next, define the function ψ as

$$\psi(X) := \Theta := \int_0^X l(w - tx) \, dx. \quad \text{(A.53)}$$

Obviously, $\psi(0) = 0$, $\psi'(X) = l(w - tX)$, $\psi''(X) = -tl'(w - tX)$, and $\psi'''(X) = t^2 l''(w - tX)$ hold for all $0 < X < X_M$. Applying Taylor's theorem by using a third-order Taylor series yields

$$\psi(0) = \psi(X) - X\psi'(X) + \frac{X^2}{2} \psi''(X) - \frac{X^3}{6} \psi'''(\chi X) = 0 \quad \text{(A.54)}$$

with $0 < \chi < 1$. Therefore,

$$\Theta - Xl(w - tX) = \frac{tX^2}{2} l'(w - tX) + \frac{t^2 X^3}{6} l''(w - \chi tX). \quad \text{(A.55)}$$

Inserting (A.55) into (A.52) and rearranging terms, we get

$$\frac{\partial e_{L\ddot{o}}(w, X)}{\partial t} = \frac{wX^3 l'(w - tX)}{2\Theta^2} \left(\Xi - \frac{tX}{3} \Upsilon \right) \quad \text{(A.56)}$$

A.3 Proof of Proposition 3.3

with
$$\Xi := l'(w - tX) - \frac{l''(w - tX)l(w - tX)}{l'(w - tX)} \quad \text{(A.57)}$$

and
$$\Upsilon := \frac{l'''(w - \vartheta tX)l(w - tX)}{l'(w - tX)} - l''(w - \chi tX). \quad \text{(A.58)}$$

Note that from the definition of individual labour supply's convexity relative to an exponential the sign of Ξ follows immediately:

$$\forall r < z < \phi : \ell''(z) \lesseqgtr 0$$

$$\Leftrightarrow \forall r < z < \phi : l''(z) \lesseqgtr \frac{l'(z)^2}{l(z)} \quad \text{(A.59)}$$

$$\Leftrightarrow \forall (w, X) \in Z : l'(w - tX) \gtreqless \frac{l''(w - tX)l(w - tX)}{l'(w - tX)} \quad \text{(A.60)}$$

$$\Leftrightarrow \forall (w, X) \in Z : \Xi \gtreqless 0 \quad \text{(A.61)}$$

Now, take a closer look at Υ. It holds that

$$\Upsilon \gtreqless 0 \Leftrightarrow \frac{l'''(w - \vartheta tX)l(w - tX)}{l'(w - tX)} \gtreqless l''(w - \chi tX) \quad \text{(A.62)}$$

$$\Leftrightarrow \frac{l'''(w - \chi tX)}{l''(w - \vartheta tX)} \gtreqless \frac{l'(w - tX)}{l(w - tX)}. \quad \text{(A.63)}$$

If individual labour supply is an exponential, i.e., $l(z) := \alpha \exp(\beta z)$, then $\Xi = 0$ holds. Furthermore, $\vartheta = \chi$ must hold by construction. Since

$$\frac{l'''(w - \vartheta tX)}{l''(w - \vartheta tX)} = \frac{\alpha \beta^3 \gamma^{\beta(w - \vartheta tX)}}{\alpha \beta^2 \gamma^{\beta(w - \vartheta tX)}} = \beta = \frac{\alpha \beta \gamma^{\beta(w - tX)}}{\alpha \gamma^{\beta(w - tX)}} = \frac{l'(w - tX)}{l(w - tX)}, \quad \text{(A.64)}$$

$\Upsilon = 0$ holds if individual labour supply is log-linear. Furthermore, it obviously holds that $\Upsilon \lesseqgtr 0$ for all $(w, X) \in Z$ if and only if $\ell''(z) \lesseqgtr 0$ for all $r < z < \phi$.

Now, it follows directly from (A.56) that for individual labour supply that is less (more) convex than an exponential $\partial e_{L\ddot{o}}(w, X)/\partial t$ is positive (negative). Hence, we have shown that

$$\forall r < z < \phi : \ell''(z) \lesseqgtr 0 \Rightarrow \forall (w, X) \in Z : \frac{\partial e_{L\ddot{o}}(w, X)}{\partial t} \gtreqless 0. \quad \text{(A.65)}$$

Therefore, we have

$$\forall r < z < \phi : \ell''(z) \lesseqgtr 0 \Rightarrow \forall 0 < X < X_M : \frac{\partial w_{L\ddot{o}}}{\partial t} \gtreqless 0 \quad \text{(A.66)}$$

without the need to impose additional assumptions on l.

(c) Greenhut–Ohta Competition

Next, consider the case of GO competition with $v_{GO} = 1/t$. Making use of (A.37), we have

$$\frac{\partial e_{GO}(w, X)}{\partial t} = \frac{\partial e_{L\ddot{o}}(w, X)}{\partial t} + \frac{\partial}{\partial t} \frac{wl(w - tX)}{t\Theta} \tag{A.67}$$

with

$$\frac{\partial}{\partial t} \frac{wl(w - tX)}{t\Theta} = -\frac{w[l'(w - tX)Xt\Theta + l(w - tX)(\Theta - t\Psi)]}{t^2\Theta^2} \tag{A.68}$$

$$= -\frac{wX[l'(w - tX)t\Theta + l(w - tX)^2]}{t^2\Theta^2}, \tag{A.69}$$

where we again used the result from (A.46). Adding this to (A.47) and rearranging terms give

$$\frac{\partial e_{GO}(w, X)}{\partial t} = -\frac{wXl(w)l(w - tX)}{t^2\Theta^2} < 0, \tag{A.70}$$

so that

$$\frac{\partial w_{GO}}{\partial t} < 0 \tag{A.71}$$

for all $0 < X < X_M$ no matter the convexity of individual labour supply.

(e) Hotelling–Smithies Competition

Eventually, consider the case of HS competition with $v_{HS} = 1/2t$. According to (A.37), we have

$$\frac{\partial e_{HS}(w, X)}{\partial t} = \frac{\partial e_{L\ddot{o}}(w, X)}{\partial t} + \frac{\partial}{\partial t} \frac{wl(w - tX)}{2t\Theta} \tag{A.72}$$

with

$$\frac{\partial}{\partial t} \frac{wl(w - tX)}{2t\Theta} = -\frac{wX[l'(w - tX)t\Theta + l(w - tX)^2]}{2t^2\Theta^2}, \tag{A.73}$$

which follows from the GO case, *mutatis mutandis*. Adding this to (A.47) and doing some simplifications, we get

$$\frac{\partial e_{HS}(w, X)}{\partial t} = \frac{wX[l'(w - tX)t\Theta - [2l(w) - l(w - tX)]l(w - tX)]}{2t^2\Theta^2}. \tag{A.74}$$

By basically the same reasoning as in the Löschian case, one can show that $\partial e_{HS}/\partial t$ is negative if individual labour supply is strictly log-convex or log-linear. Furthermore, if individual labour supply is strictly log-concave,

$$\frac{\partial w_{HS}}{\partial t} \gtreqless 0 \tag{A.75}$$

holds for all $0 < X < X_M$ depending on the level of X. From the discussion of the Löschian case we know that $\partial e_{HS}(w, X)/\partial t$ must be positive for high X because (A.72) implies $\partial e_{HS}(w, X)/\partial t \to \partial e_{Lö}(w, X)/\partial t$ if $X \to X_M$ due to $l(w - tX) \to 0$. Consider now the limiting case $X \to 0$. After applying de l'Hôpital's and the Leibniz rule and some straightforward simplifications, we find

$$\lim_{X \to 0} \frac{\partial e_{HS}(w, X)}{\partial t} = \lim_{X \to 0} -\frac{w[2l(w) - l(w - tX)]}{4t^2 \int_0^X l(w - tx)\,dx} = -\infty. \tag{A.76}$$

Therefore, we have

$$\frac{\partial w_{HS}}{\partial t} \begin{cases} < 0 \text{ if } \ell''(z) > 0 \text{ of } \ell''(z) = 0 \text{ for all } r < z < \phi \\ < 0 \text{ if } \ell''(z) < 0 \text{ for all } r < z < \phi \text{ and } X \text{ sufficiently small} \\ > 0 \text{ if } \ell''(z) < 0 \text{ for all } r < z < \phi \text{ and } X \text{ sufficiently high} \end{cases} \tag{A.77}$$

for all $0 < X < X_M$. ∎

A.4 Proof of Proposition 3.5

(a) Greenhut–Ohta Competition

According to (A.41), the aggregate labour supply elasticity under GO competition with $v_{GO} = 1/t$ is given by

$$e_{GO}(w, X) = \frac{wl(w)}{t \int_0^X l(w - tx)\,dx}. \tag{A.78}$$

(Note that we again suppress the index at w for notational convenience.) Applying the Leibniz rule, partial differentiation of (A.78) with respect to X yields

$$\frac{\partial e_{GO}(w, X)}{\partial X} = \frac{-wl(w)l(w - tX)}{t \left(\int_0^X l(w - tx)\,dx\right)^2} < 0 \tag{A.79}$$

for all $(w, X) \in Z$, so that competitive entry unambiguously increases the aggregate labour supply elasticity and wage under GO competition no matter the convexity of individual labour supply.

(b) Hotelling–Smithies Competition

Things are more intricate under HS competition. If individual labour supply is strictly log-convex or log-linear, then the supply effect is nonnegative (which follows directly from the proof of Proposition 3.4). Since there is a positive competition effect under HS competition (on account of $v_{HS} = 1/2t > 0$), competitive entry then increases the aggregate labour supply elasticity. However, if individual labour supply is strictly log-concave, the supply and the competition effect work in different directions. Applying the Leibniz rule, partial differentiation of (A.42) with respect to X yields

$$\frac{\partial e_i(w, X)}{\partial X} = \frac{w}{t\left(\int_0^X l(w-tx)\,dx\right)^2}\left(\overbrace{[(1-v_it)l(w-tX) - l(w)]l(w-tX)}^{=:\Psi} \right.$$
$$\left. + \underbrace{(1-v_it)tl'(w-tX)\int_0^X l(w-tx)\,dx}_{=:\Theta}\right). \quad (A.80)$$

If $0 < v_i < 1/t$, so that conjectural variations are 'somewhere in-between' Löschian and GO competition (e.g., $v_{HS} = 1/2t$ under HS competition), $\Psi < 0$ and $\Theta > 0$ obviously hold. If $X \to 0$, $\int_0^X l(w-tx)\,dx \to 0$ and thus $\Theta \to 0$, while $\Psi < 0$ still holds. Therefore, $\partial e_i(w, X)/\partial X \to -\infty$ if $X \to 0$. On the other hand, if $X \to X_M$, $l(w-tX) \to 0$ and thus $\Psi \to 0$, whereas $\Theta > 0$ still holds. Hence, $\partial e_i(w, X)/\partial X$ is positive (negative) for sufficiently small (large) X.

Furthermore, the larger is X, the larger is $\Psi + \Theta$, so that $\partial e_{HS}(w, X)/\partial X$ is positive (negative) for all X larger (smaller) than some unique market radius X^*. To see this, note that

$$\frac{\partial \Psi}{\partial X} + \frac{\partial \Theta}{\partial X} = [l(w) - (1-v_it)l(w-tX)]tl'(w-tX)$$
$$- (1-v_it)t^2 l''(w-tX)\int_0^X l(w-tx)\,dx, \quad (A.81)$$

which is obviously positive if l is concave (i.e., $l''(z) \leqslant 0$ for all $r < z < \phi$). Now, suppose l is strictly convex but less convex than an exponential (i.e., $l''(z) > 0$ and $\ell'''(z) < 0$ for all $r < z < \phi$). Then we have

$$\frac{\partial \Psi}{\partial X} = [l(w) - 2(1-v_it)l(w-tX)]tl'(w-tX) > 0 \quad (A.82)$$

for all $1/2t \leqslant v_i < 1/t$ (in particular, under HS competition with $v_{HS} = 1/2t$) and for all $0 < v_i < 1/2t$ provided X is large enough. Next, define $\psi(X) := \int_0^X l(w-tx)\,dx$ with $\psi'(X) = l(w-tX)$, $\psi''(X) = -tl'(w-tX)$, and $\psi'''(X) = t^2 l''(w-tX)$ for all $0 < X < X_M$. It is straightforward to show that ψ' is strictly

A.4 Proof of Proposition 3.5

log-concave.[4] Making use of Prékopa's (1973) Theorem 6, which tells us that the integral of a strictly log-concave function is strictly log-concave itself, we know that ψ is strictly log-concave, too. We can now use l's and ψ's strict log-concavity to establish $\partial\Theta/\partial X > 0$ if l is convex but less convex than an exponential: We have

$$\frac{\partial \Theta}{\partial X} = (1 - v_i t) t \left(l'(w - tX) l(w - tX) - t l''(w - tX) \int_0^X l(w - tx)\, dx \right)$$
(A.83)

which is positive if

$$l'(w - tX) l(w - tX) - \frac{t l'(w - tX)^2}{l(w - tX)} \int_0^X l(w - tx)\, dx > 0 \qquad (A.84)$$

because $l''(w - tX) < l'(w - tX)^2 / l(w - tX)$ due to l's strict log-concavity (see Remark 3.1). Obviously, the inequality (A.84) holds if and only if

$$\frac{t l'(w - tX) \int_0^X l(w - tx)\, dx}{l(w - tX)} < 1. \qquad (A.85)$$

Since ψ is strictly log-concave, Remark 3.1 tells us that $\psi''(X)\psi(X)/\psi'(X)^2 < 1$ for all $0 < X < X_M$, so that (A.85) holds. We therefore have shown that $\partial\Theta/\partial X > 0$ holds if l is strictly log-concave.

All in all, we have

$$\frac{\partial e_{HS}(w, X)}{\partial X} \begin{cases} < 0 \text{ if } \ell''(z) > 0 \text{ of } \ell''(z) = 0 \text{ for all } r < z < \phi \\ < 0 \text{ if } \ell''(z) < 0 \text{ for all } r < z < \phi \text{ and } X < X^* \\ > 0 \text{ if } \ell''(z) < 0 \text{ for all } r < z < \phi \text{ and } X > X^* \end{cases} \qquad (A.86)$$

for a unique X^* with $0 < X^* < X_M$. Hence, competitive entry (a decrease in X) raises HS competitors' wage if individual labour is strictly log-convex or log-linear. On the other hand, if individual labour supply is strictly log-concave, then their wage rises (falls) in response to competitive entry if $X < X^*$ ($X > X^*$), which completes the proof of Proposition 3.5. ∎

---

[4] Just note that

$$\frac{d^2 \ln \psi'(X)}{dX^2} = \frac{\partial \ln l(w - tX)}{\partial X^2} = \frac{t^2 [l''(w - tX) l(w - tX) - l'(w - tX)^2]}{l(w - tX)^2} < 0,$$

where $l''(w - tX) l(w - tX) < l'(w - tX)^2$ for all $0 < X < X_M$ is equivalent to l's strict log-concavity (see Remark 3.1).

A.5 The Slope of the Zero-Profit Locus in the Löschian Long-Run Equilibrium

Under Löschian competition, firms set their wage according to equation (3.35), where $e_{L\ddot{o}}(w_{L\ddot{o}}, X) = w_{L\ddot{o}} \int_0^X l'(w_{L\ddot{o}} - tx)\, dx \Big/ \int_0^X l(w_{L\ddot{o}} - tx)\, dx$, which follows from (3.10). Therefore, we get

$$w_{L\ddot{o}} = \frac{e_{L\ddot{o}}(w_{L\ddot{o}}, X)}{1 + e_{L\ddot{o}}(w_{L\ddot{o}}, X)} \phi \tag{A.87}$$

$$\Leftrightarrow \phi - w_{L\ddot{o}} \left(\frac{\int_0^X l(w_{L\ddot{o}} - tx)\, dx}{w_{L\ddot{o}} \int_0^X l'(w_{L\ddot{o}} - tx)\, dx} + 1 \right) = 0 \tag{A.88}$$

$$\Leftrightarrow \phi - w_{L\ddot{o}} - \frac{\int_0^X l(w_{L\ddot{o}} - tx)\, dx}{\int_0^X l'(w_{L\ddot{o}} - tx)\, dx} = 0 \tag{A.89}$$

$$\Leftrightarrow 2D(\phi - w_{L\ddot{o}}) \int_0^X l'(w_{L\ddot{o}} - tx)\, dx - 2D \int_0^X l(w_{L\ddot{o}} - tx)\, dx = 0 \tag{A.90}$$

$$\Leftrightarrow \frac{\partial \Pi(w_{L\ddot{o}}, X)}{\partial w} = 0 \tag{A.91}$$

for all $0 < X < X_M$. In particular, $\partial \Pi(w_{L\ddot{o}}, X_{L\ddot{o}})/\partial w = 0$, so that the slope of the zero-profit locus in the (X, w)-plane approaches infinity at the Löschian long-run equilibrium wage, where $X_{L\ddot{o}}$ denotes the long-run equilibrium market radius under Löschian competition.

A.6 Proof of Lemma 4.1

(a) The Sign of $\partial W_i(w, X)/\partial w$

To prove that $\partial W_i(w, X)/\partial w < 0$ for all $(w, X) \in Z$ that satisfy (4.4), note that the sign of the partial derivative of firms' perceived profits Π_i with respect to the wage is given by

$$\operatorname{sgn} \frac{\partial \Pi_i(w, X)}{\partial w} = \operatorname{sgn}\left\{ (\phi - w) \frac{\partial L_i(w, X)}{\partial w} - L_i(w, X) \right\} \tag{A.92}$$

$$= \operatorname{sgn}\left\{ (\phi - w) \frac{\partial L_i(w, X)}{\partial w} \frac{w}{L_i(w, X)} - w \right\} \tag{A.93}$$

$$= \operatorname{sgn}\{(\phi - w)e_i(w, X) - w\} \tag{A.94}$$

$$= \operatorname{sgn} W_i(w, X). \tag{A.95}$$

A.6 Proof of Lemma 4.1

In the optimum where perceived profits are maximised by setting the wage optimally given some market radius X, the first-order condition requires $\partial \Pi_i(w, X)/\partial w = W_i(w, X) = 0$. Furthermore, we assume that the corresponding second-order condition holds, i.e., $\partial^2 \Pi_i(w, X)/\partial w^2 < 0$ for all $(w, X) \in Z$ that maximise perceived profits.[5] Since firms' perceived profits must be strictly concave with respect to the wage in the optimum for the second-order condition to hold, we must have $\partial \Pi_i(w, X)/\partial w > 0$ for all wages slightly below the maximand of profits and $\partial \Pi_i(w, X)/\partial w < 0$ for all wages slightly above. Therefore, $W_i(w, X)$ must be positive slightly below this maximand and negative slightly above and thus strictly decreasing in the wage for all $(w, X) \in Z$ that maximise Π_i. Since perceived profits are strictly concave in all optima by assumption, this implies $\partial W_i(w, X)/\partial w < 0$ for all $(w, X) \in Z$ that maximise perceived profits.

(b)–(d) The Sign of $\partial W_i(w, X)/\partial X$

By virtue of the wage-setting condition (4.4), we get

$$\frac{\partial W_i(w, X)}{\partial X} = (\phi - w)\frac{\partial e_i(w, X)}{\partial X}, \tag{A.96}$$

so that according to part (a) of this lemma and (4.5)

$$\operatorname{sgn} w_i'(X) = \operatorname{sgn} \frac{\partial W_i(w, X)}{\partial X} = \operatorname{sgn} \frac{\partial e_i(w, X)}{\partial X}. \tag{A.97}$$

Therefore, the sign of the slope of the wage-setting curve $w_i(\cdot)$ in the (X, w)-plane solely depends on the sign of $\partial e_i(w, X)/\partial X$.

(b) Strictly Log-Convex Individual Labour Supply

From equation (3.38) and the proof of Proposition 3.5 in Appendix A.4 we know that $\partial e_i(w, X)/\partial X < 0$ for all $(w, X) \in Z$ and all $i \in \{L\ddot{o}, HS, GO\}$ if individual labour supply is strictly log-convex.

---

[5] Generally, $\partial^2 \Pi_i(w, X)/\partial w^2 < 0$ for all $(w, X) \in Z$ that maximise perceived profits given some $0 < X < X_M$ is not required to hold in all optima. In particular, if $\partial^j \Pi_i(w, X)/\partial w^j = 0$ for all $j = 1, \ldots, k-1$ and some $k \in \mathbb{N}$ with $k/2 \in \mathbb{N}$, then $\partial^k \Pi_i(w, X)/\partial w^k < 0$ suffices for an optimum in (w, X). This is easily seen from an example: Consider the real function ψ with $\psi(x) := -x^4$ which obviously has a global maximum at 0 though $\psi''(0) = 0$. This holds because $\psi'(0) = \psi''(0) = \psi'''(0) = 0$ and $\psi^{(4)}(0) = -24 < 0$.

(c) Strictly Log-Concave Individual Labour Supply

According to equation (3.38) and the proof of Proposition 3.5 in Appendix A.4, we have $\partial e_{GO}(w, X)/\partial X > 0$ and $\partial e_{L\ddot{o}}(w, X)/\partial X < 0$ for all $(w, X) \in Z$ if individual labour supply is strictly log-concave. Furthermore, we have $\partial e_{HS}(w, X)/\partial X < 0$ if $X < X^*$ and $\partial e_{HS}(w, X)/\partial X > 0$ if $X > X^*$ for some unique $0 < X^* < X_M$.

(d) Log-Linear Individual Labour Supply

Finally, with log-linear individual labour supply, the supply effect is zero, while the competition effect under competitive entry, i.e., for a falling market radius, is strictly increasing in v. Since $v_{GO} > v_{HS} > v_{L\ddot{o}} = 0$ holds, we have $\partial e_{GO}(w, X)/\partial X < \partial e_{HS}(w, X)/\partial X < \partial e_{L\ddot{o}}(w, X)/\partial X = 0$ and thus $\partial W_{GO}(w, X)/\partial X < \partial W_{HS}(w, X)/\partial X < \partial W_{L\ddot{o}}(w, X)/\partial X = 0$ for all $(w, X) \in Z$ that satisfy (4.4). ∎

A.7 Proof of Lemma 4.3

The Effect on the Position of the Zero-Profit Locus

Consider the zero-profit condition

$$\Pi(w, X) = 2D(\phi - w) \int_0^X l(w - tx)\, dx - f \stackrel{!}{=} 0. \tag{A.98}$$

To compute the comparative static effect of changes in the market conditions – viz. an increase in f, D, ϕ, or t – on the ZPL's position, we first have to compute the partial derivatives of $\Pi(w, X)$, which gives

$$\frac{\partial \Pi(w, X)}{\partial X} = 2D(\phi - w)l(w - tX) > 0, \tag{A.99}$$

$$\frac{\partial \Pi(w, X)}{\partial f} = -1 < 0, \tag{A.100}$$

$$\frac{\partial \Pi(w, X)}{\partial D} = 2(\phi - w) \int_0^X l(w - tx)\, dx > 0, \tag{A.101}$$

$$\frac{\partial \Pi(w, X)}{\partial \phi} = 2D \int_0^X l(w - tx)\, dx > 0, \tag{A.102}$$

$$\frac{\partial \Pi(w, X)}{\partial t} = -2D(\phi - w) \int_0^X l'(w - tx)x\, dx < 0, \tag{A.103}$$

A.7 Proof of Lemma 4.3

respectively. Hence, repeated application of the implicit function theorem, which is applicable here because $\partial \Pi(w, X)/\partial X > 0$ for all $(w, X) \in Z$, yields

$$\frac{\partial X(w)}{\partial f} = -\frac{\partial \Pi(w, X)/\partial f}{\partial \Pi(w, X)/\partial X} = \frac{1}{2D(\phi - w)l(w - tX)} > 0, \qquad (A.104)$$

$$\frac{\partial X(w)}{\partial D} = -\frac{\partial \Pi(w, X)/\partial D}{\partial \Pi(w, X)/\partial X} = -\frac{\int_0^X l(w - tx)\,dx}{Dl(w - tX)} < 0, \qquad (A.105)$$

$$\frac{\partial X(w)}{\partial \phi} = -\frac{\partial \Pi(w, X)/\partial \phi}{\partial \Pi(w, X)/\partial X} = -\frac{\int_0^X l(w - tx)\,dx}{(\phi - w)l(w - tX)} < 0, \qquad (A.106)$$

$$\frac{\partial X(w)}{\partial t} = -\frac{\partial \Pi(w, X)/\partial t}{\partial \Pi(w, X)/\partial X} = \frac{\int_0^X l'(w - tx)x\,dx}{l(w - tX)} > 0, \qquad (A.107)$$

respectively, where these results hold independently of the convexity of individual labour supply and the mode of competition for all $(w, X) \in Z$. A positive (negative) partial derivative indicates that an increase in the respective parameter raises (reduces) $X(w)$ for all relevant w, so that the ZPL is shifted to the right (left) in the (X, w)-plane.

The Effect on the Position of the Wage-Setting Curve

Next, consider the wage-setting condition

$$W_i(w, X) = (\phi - w)e_i(w, X) - w \stackrel{!}{=} 0 \qquad (A.108)$$

with $i \in \{Lö, HS, GO\}$, where we dropped the index i at w for notational convenience. To compute the comparative static effect of changes in the market conditions – viz. an increase in f, D, ϕ, or t – on the WSC's position, we first have to compute the partial derivatives of $W_i(w, X)$.

Partial Derivative of W_i with Respect to w

The partial derivative of W_i with respect to w is given by

$$\frac{\partial W_i(w, X)}{\partial w} = (\phi - w)\frac{\partial e_i(w, X)}{\partial w} - e_i(w, X) < 0 \qquad (A.109)$$

because $\partial^2 \Pi(w, X)/\partial w^2 < 0$ is assumed to hold for all $(w, X) \in Z$ that satisfy (A.108) and all i with $0 \leqslant v_i \leqslant 1/t$ (see the discussion in Appendix A.6).

Partial Derivative of W_i with Respect to f

Partial differentiation of (A.108) with respect to f and making use of (A.25) give

$$\frac{\partial W_i(w, X)}{\partial f} = (\phi - w)\frac{\partial e_i(w, X)}{\partial f} = 0. \quad \text{(A.110)}$$

Partial Derivative of W_i with Respect to D

Partial differentiation of (A.108) with respect to D and making use of (A.25) give

$$\frac{\partial W_i(w, X)}{\partial D} = (\phi - w)\frac{\partial e_i(w, X)}{\partial D} = 0. \quad \text{(A.111)}$$

Partial Derivative of W_i with Respect to ϕ

Partial differentiation of (A.108) with respect to ϕ gives

$$\frac{\partial W_i(w, X)}{\partial \phi} = e_i(w, X) > 0. \quad \text{(A.112)}$$

Partial Derivatives of W_i with respect to t

Partial differentiation of (A.108) with respect to t yields

$$\frac{\partial W_i(w, X)}{\partial t} = (\phi - w)\frac{\partial e_i(w, X)}{\partial t}, \quad \text{(A.113)}$$

so that

$$\operatorname{sgn} \frac{\partial W_i(w, X)}{\partial t} = \operatorname{sgn} \frac{\partial e_i(w, X)}{\partial t}. \quad \text{(A.114)}$$

From the discussion in Appendix A.3 we know that

$$\forall r < z < \phi : \ell''(z) \lesseqgtr 0 \Rightarrow \forall (w, X) \in Z : \frac{\partial e_{L\ddot{o}}(w, X)}{\partial t} \gtreqless 0 \quad \text{(A.115)}$$

under Löschian competition,

$$\frac{\partial e_{GO}(w, X)}{\partial t} < 0 \quad \text{(A.116)}$$

A.7 Proof of Lemma 4.3

for all $(w, X) \in Z$ under GO competition, and

$$\frac{\partial e_{HS}(w, X)}{\partial t} \begin{cases} < 0 \text{ if } \ell''(z) > 0 \text{ or } \ell''(z) = 0 \text{ for all } r < z < \phi \\ < 0 \text{ if } \ell''(z) < 0 \text{ for all } r < z < \phi \text{ and } X \text{ small} \\ > 0 \text{ if } \ell''(z) < 0 \text{ for all } r < z < \phi \text{ and } X \text{ large} \end{cases} \quad (A.117)$$

for all $(w, X) \in Z$ under HS competition. Therefore, we get

$$\frac{\partial W_i(w, X)}{\partial t} \begin{cases} < 0 \text{ if } i = GO \text{ no matter } l\text{'s convexity} \\ \gtreqless 0 \text{ if } i = L\ddot{o} \text{ and } \ell''(z) \lesseqgtr 0 \text{ for all } r < z < \phi \\ < 0 \text{ if } i = HS \text{ and } \ell''(z) > 0 \text{ or } \ell''(z) = 0 \text{ for all } r < z < \phi \\ < 0 \text{ if } i = HS, \ell''(z) < 0 \text{ for all } r < z < \phi, \text{ and } X \text{ small} \\ > 0 \text{ if } i = HS, \ell''(z) < 0 \text{ for all } r < z < \phi, \text{ and } X \text{ large} \end{cases} \quad (A.118)$$

Applying the Implicit Function Theorem

Repeated application of the implicit function theorem, which is applicable due to $\partial W_i(w, X)/\partial w < 0$ for all $(w, X) \in Z$ that satisfy (A.108) and all i with $0 \leq v_i \leq 1/t$, yields

$$\frac{\partial w_i(X)}{\partial f} = -\frac{\partial W_i(w, X)/\partial f}{\partial W_i(w, X)/\partial w} = 0, \quad (A.119)$$

$$\frac{\partial w_i(X)}{\partial D} = -\frac{\partial W_i(w, X)/\partial D}{\partial W_i(w, X)/\partial w} = 0, \quad (A.120)$$

$$\frac{\partial w_i(X)}{\partial \phi} = -\frac{\partial W_i(w, X)/\partial w}{\partial W_i(w, X)/\partial \phi} > 0, \quad (A.121)$$

where these results hold independently of the convexity of individual labour supply and the mode of competition. There are no such clear-cut results if t changes:

$$\frac{\partial w_i(X)}{\partial t} = -\frac{\partial W_i(w, X)/\partial t}{\partial W_i(w, X)/\partial w} \quad (A.122)$$

$$\begin{cases} < 0 \text{ if } i = GO \text{ no matter } l\text{'s convexity} \\ \gtreqless 0 \text{ if } i = L\ddot{o} \text{ and } \ell''(z) \lesseqgtr 0 \text{ for all } r < z < \phi \\ < 0 \text{ if } i = HS \text{ and } \ell''(z) > 0 \text{ or } \ell''(z) = 0 \text{ for all } r < z < \phi \\ < 0 \text{ if } i = HS, \ell''(z) < 0 \text{ for all } r < z < \phi, \text{ and } X \text{ small} \\ > 0 \text{ if } i = HS, \ell''(z) < 0 \text{ for all } r < z < \phi, \text{ and } X \text{ large} \end{cases} \quad (A.123)$$

A positive (negative) partial derivative indicates that an increase in the respective parameter raises (reduces) $w_i(X)$ for all relevant X, so that the WSC is shifted upwards (downwards) in the (X, w)-plane. ∎

A.8 Comparative Statics under Linear Spatial Monopsony

Löschian Competition

The long-run equilibrium wage under Löschian competition is implicitly given by

$$(2w_{Lö} - \phi - \alpha)(\phi - w_{Lö})^2 = \frac{f\beta t}{4D}. \quad (A.124)$$

Firstly, note that $w_{Lö} < (2\phi + \alpha)/3 = w_M$ holds for all $f < f_{max}$ due to the upward-sloping WSC with $w(X) \to w_M$ if $X \to X_M$. Second, note that $\phi > w_{Lö}$ must be satisfied for the zero-profit condition to hold. Implicit differentiation of (A.124) with respect to f, D, t, β, or α gives, respectively,

$$\frac{\partial w_{Lö}}{\partial f} = \frac{\beta t}{8D(2\phi + \alpha - 3w_{Lö})(\phi - w_{Lö})} > 0, \quad (A.125)$$

$$\frac{\partial w_{Lö}}{\partial D} = -\frac{f\beta t}{8D^2(2\phi + \alpha - 3w_{Lö})(\phi - w_{Lö})} < 0, \quad (A.126)$$

$$\frac{\partial w_{Lö}}{\partial t} = \frac{f\beta}{8D(2\phi + \alpha - 3w_{Lö})(\phi - w_{Lö})} > 0, \quad (A.127)$$

$$\frac{\partial w_{Lö}}{\partial \beta} = \frac{ft}{8D(2\phi + \alpha - 3w_{Lö})(\phi - w_{Lö})} > 0, \quad (A.128)$$

$$\frac{\partial w_{Lö}}{\partial \alpha} = \frac{\phi - w_{Lö}}{2(2\phi + \alpha - 3w_{Lö})} > 0, \quad (A.129)$$

where a positive (negative) derivative indicates a positive (negative) comparative static effect of the respective parameter on the long-run equilibrium wage. Finally, implicit differentiation of (A.124) with respect to ϕ yields

$$\frac{\partial w_{Lö}}{\partial \phi} = \frac{3\phi + 2\alpha - 5w_{Lö}}{2(2\phi + \alpha - 3w_{Lö})} \gtreqless 0 \quad (A.130)$$

if $w_{Lö} \lesseqgtr (3\phi + 2\alpha)/5$ and thus if $X_{Lö} \gtreqless X^* := 2(\phi - \alpha)/5t$ because $w_{Lö}(X) = (\phi + \alpha)/2 + tX/4$. Since $0 < 2(\phi - \alpha)/5t < 2(\phi - \alpha)/3t = X_M$, an increase in ϕ causes the $w_{Lö}$ to rise if competition is strong (i.e., market areas are small with $X_{Lö} < 2(\phi - \alpha)/5t$) and to fall if competition is weak (i.e., market areas are large with $X_{Lö} > 2(\phi - \alpha)/5t$).

A.9 The Implicit Solution for the Long-Run Hotelling–Smithies Equilibrium Wage

Greenhut–Ohta Competition

The long-run equilibrium wage under GO competition is implicitly given by

$$(w_{GO} - \alpha)(\phi - w_{GO})^2 = \frac{f\beta t}{2D}. \tag{A.131}$$

Firstly, note that $w_{GO} > (\phi + 2\alpha)/3 > \alpha$ holds for all $f < f_{max}$ on account of the downward-sloping WSC with $w_{GO}(X) \to (2\phi + \alpha)/3 = w_M > (\phi + 2\alpha)/3$ if $X \to X_M$ and $\phi > \alpha$. Hence, $\phi + 2\alpha - 3w_{GO} < 0$ must hold. Second, note that $\phi > w_{GO}$ must be satisfied for the zero-profit condition to hold. Implicit differentiation of (A.131) with respect to f, D, t, β, α, or ϕ yields, respectively,

$$\frac{\partial w_{GO}}{\partial f} = \frac{\beta t}{2D(\phi + 2\alpha - 3w_{GO})(\phi - w_{GO})} < 0, \tag{A.132}$$

$$\frac{\partial w_{GO}}{\partial D} = -\frac{f\beta t}{2D^2(\phi + 2\alpha - 3w_{GO})(\phi - w_{GO})} > 0, \tag{A.133}$$

$$\frac{\partial w_{GO}}{\partial t} = \frac{f\beta}{2D(\phi + 2\alpha - 3w_{GO})(\phi - w_{GO})} < 0, \tag{A.134}$$

$$\frac{\partial w_{GO}}{\partial \beta} = \frac{ft}{2D(\phi + 2\alpha - 3w_{GO})(\phi - w_{GO})} < 0, \tag{A.135}$$

$$\frac{\partial w_{GO}}{\partial \alpha} = \frac{\phi - w_{GO}}{\phi + 2\alpha - 3w_{GO}} < 0, \tag{A.136}$$

$$\frac{\partial w_{GO}}{\partial \phi} = -\frac{2(w_{GO} - \alpha)}{\phi + 2\alpha - 3w_{GO}} > 0, \tag{A.137}$$

where a positive (negative) derivative indicates a positive (negative) comparative static effect of the respective parameter on the long-run equilibrium wage.

A.9 The Implicit Solution for the Long-Run Hotelling–Smithies Equilibrium Wage in the Linear Model

The zero-profit and the wage-setting conditions are given by

$$\Pi(w, X) = \frac{2DX}{\beta}\left(w - \frac{tX}{2} - \alpha\right)(\phi - w) - f \stackrel{!}{=} 0, \tag{A.138}$$

$$W(w, X) = X\left(\phi - 2w + \frac{tX}{2} + \alpha\right) + \frac{1}{2t}(w - tX - \alpha)(\phi - w) \stackrel{!}{=} 0. \tag{A.139}$$

Solving (A.138) for X yields the roots

$$X(w) = \frac{1}{t}\left(w - \alpha \pm \sqrt{(w-\alpha)^2 - \frac{f\beta t}{D(\phi - w)}}\right),\qquad (A.140)$$

which define the ZPL. Economic relevance requires the last term in parentheses to be negative since we are interested in the part of the ZPL left to the straight line $w = \alpha + tX$ where individual labour supply is positive. Consequently, the relevant root is

$$X(w) = \frac{1}{t}\left(w - \alpha - \sqrt{(w-\alpha)^2 - \frac{f\beta t}{D(\phi - w)}}\right).\qquad (A.141)$$

Inserting (A.141) into (A.139) and some tedious algebraic manipulations yield

$$(2(w_{HS} - \alpha) + \Theta)(\phi - w_{HS})^2 = \frac{f\beta t}{D} \qquad (A.142)$$

with $\Theta := w_{HS} - \phi \pm \sqrt{(\phi + 2\alpha - 3w_{HS})^2 - 4(\phi - w_{HS})(w_{HS} - \alpha)}$.

A.10 Proof of Corollary 5.3

The equilibrium labour supply elasticity of men to firm i is given by

$$\widehat{e}_i^m = \frac{\partial L_i^m(\widehat{w}_i^m, \widehat{w}_j^m)}{\partial w_i^m} \frac{\widehat{w}_i^m}{L_i^m(\widehat{w}_i^m, \widehat{w}_j^m)} = \frac{\frac{2}{3}\phi_i + \frac{1}{3}\phi_j - \underline{t}}{\frac{1}{3}\phi_i - \frac{1}{3}\phi_j + \underline{t}} \qquad (A.143)$$

with $i = 0, 1$ and $j \neq i$, which follows from (5.5) and (5.12). Analogously, for women we have

$$\widehat{e}_i^f = \frac{\partial L_i^f(\widehat{w}_i^f, \widehat{w}_j^f)}{\partial w_i^f} \frac{\widehat{w}_i^f}{L_i^f(\widehat{w}_i^f, \widehat{w}_j^f)} = \frac{\frac{2}{3}\phi_i + \frac{1}{3}\phi_j - \frac{\bar{t}\underline{t}}{\eta\underline{t}+(1-\eta)\bar{t}}}{\frac{1}{3}\phi_i - \frac{1}{3}\phi_j + \frac{\bar{t}\underline{t}}{\eta\underline{t}+(1-\eta)\bar{t}}}, \qquad (A.144)$$

which follows from (5.6) and (5.13). Subtracting (A.144) from (A.143) yields

$$\Delta_{e,i} = \frac{\phi_i}{\left(\frac{1}{3}\phi_i - \frac{1}{3}\phi_j + \underline{t}\right)\left(\frac{1}{3}\phi_i - \frac{1}{3}\phi_j + \frac{\bar{t}\underline{t}}{\eta\underline{t}+(1-\eta)\bar{t}}\right)}\Delta_w > 0, \qquad (A.145)$$

where $\Delta_w = \eta\underline{t}(\bar{t} - \underline{t})/[\eta\underline{t} + (1-\eta)\bar{t}]$. Since the ratio in (A.145) is positive (due to $|\phi_0 - \phi_1| < 3\underline{t}$), $\Delta_{e,i} \propto \Delta_w$ holds. Finally, $\Delta_{e,i}$ is strictly increasing in both $\bar{t}$ and η, which follows directly from partial differentiation of (A.145) with

A.11 Appendix to Chapter 6

$$\frac{\partial \Delta_{e,i}}{\partial \bar{t}} = \frac{\phi_i \eta \underline{t}^2}{\left(\frac{1}{3}\phi_i - \frac{1}{3}\phi_j + \frac{\bar{t}\underline{t}}{\eta \underline{t} + (1-\eta)\bar{t}}\right)^2 \left(\eta \underline{t} + (1-\eta)\bar{t}\right)^2} > 0 \qquad (A.146)$$

and

$$\frac{\partial \Delta_{e,i}}{\partial \eta} = \frac{\phi_i \bar{t}\underline{t}(\bar{t}-\underline{t})}{\left(\frac{1}{3}\phi_i - \frac{1}{3}\phi_j + \frac{\bar{t}\underline{t}}{\eta \underline{t} + (1-\eta)\bar{t}}\right)^2 \left(\eta \underline{t} + (1-\eta)\bar{t}\right)^2} > 0, \qquad (A.147)$$

respectively. ∎

A.11 Appendix to Chapter 6

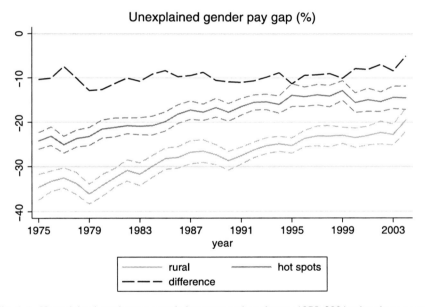

Fig. A.1 Unexplained gender pay gaps in hot spots and rural areas 1975–2004 using three-nearest neighbour matching with replacement (the thin dashed lines represent the respective 95 per cent confidence bands)

A Appendix: Spatial Monopsony

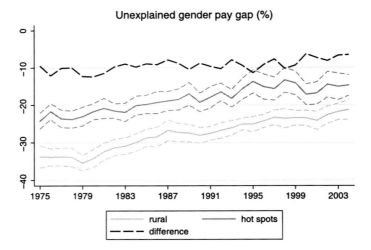

Fig. A.2 Unexplained gender pay gaps using only individuals without change of regional type of first appearance in the labour market and nearest neighbour matching without replacement (the thin dashed lines represent the respective 95 per cent confidence bands)

Appendix B
Appendix: Dynamic Monopsony

B.1 The Relation between the Firm's Short- and Long-Run Labour Supply Elasticity

As noted in Chapter 7, the relation between the firm's short- and long-run labour supply elasticity is most easily seen when considering inverse elasticities. We thus apply the inverse function theorem on $L_t = L(w_t, L_{t-1})$ to get

$$w_t = w(L_t, L_{t-1}), \tag{B.1}$$

where $w(L_t, L_{t-1})$ is the wage needed in period t to gain a labour supply of L_t given the previous period's labour supply L_{t-1}. Obviously, we have $\partial w(L_t, L_{t-1})/\partial L_t > 0$ and $\partial w(L_t, L_{t-1})/\partial L_{t-1} < 0$ for all $(L_t, L_{t-1}) \gg 0$. That is, to achieve an increase in employment, the firm must raise its wage, whereas the higher is employment in the previous period the lower is the wage needed in the current period to accomplish a certain level of employment.

Next, define the short-run and the lagged inverse labour supply elasticity as

$$e_{wL}^{SR}(L_t, L_{t-1}) := \frac{\partial w(L_t, L_{t-1})}{\partial L_t} \frac{L_t}{w(L_t, L_{t-1})} \tag{B.2}$$

and

$$e_{wL}^{\ell}(L_t, L_{t-1}) := \frac{\partial w(L_t, L_{t-1})}{\partial L_{t-1}} \frac{L_{t-1}}{w(L_t, L_{t-1})}, \tag{B.3}$$

respectively. Now, consider a steady state with $L_t = L$ and $w_t = w$ for all $t \in \mathbb{N}$. Adding up the two elasticities then yields

$$e_{wL}^{SR}(L, L) + e_{wL}^{\ell}(L, L) = \frac{\partial w(L, L)}{\partial L_t} \frac{L}{w(L, L)} + \frac{\partial w(L, L)}{\partial L_{t-1}} \frac{L}{w(L, L)} \tag{B.4}$$

$$= \left(\frac{\partial w(L, L)}{\partial L_t} + \frac{\partial w(L, L)}{\partial L_{t-1}} \right) \frac{L}{w(L, L)} \tag{B.5}$$

$$= e_{wL}^{LR}(L, L), \tag{B.6}$$

which is the inverse long-run labour supply elasticity of the firm. This holds because it takes into account both the direct effect of current employment and the indirect effect of past employment on the sensitiveness of the current wage. In terms of direct elasticities, we have thus demonstrated that

$$e_{Lw}^{LR}(L, L) = \frac{e_{Lw}^{SR}(L, L)}{1 - \partial L(w, L)/\partial L_{t-1}} \qquad (B.7)$$

because the implicit function theorem implies

$$e_{wL}^{\ell}(L, L) = e_{wL}^{SR}(L, L) \frac{\partial w(L, L)/\partial L_{t-1}}{\partial w(L, L)/\partial L_t} = -e_{wL}^{SR}(L, L) \frac{\partial L(w, L)}{\partial L_{t-1}}. \qquad (B.8)$$

B.2 Workers' Optimal Reservation Wage

From $V^e(r) = V^n$ workers' optimal reservation wage is implicitly given by

$$r = b + (\lambda^n - \lambda^e) \int_r^{\overline{w}} [V^e(x) - V^n] dF(x), \qquad (B.9)$$

where $\underline{w} = r$ because no worker offered a wage lower than r is willing to accept this offer, so that it is a strictly dominated strategy for firms to offer a wage less than r. Due to integration by parts, we get

$$\int_r^{\overline{w}} [V^e(x) - V^n] dF(x) = V^e(x)[1 - F(x)]\Big|_r^{\overline{w}} + \int_r^{\overline{w}} V^e(x) dF(x) \qquad (B.10)$$

$$= \int_r^{\overline{w}} \frac{dV^e(x)}{dx} [1 - F(x)] dx. \qquad (B.11)$$

Implicit differentiation of (8.4) with respect to w yields

$$\frac{dV^e(w)}{dw} = \frac{1}{\varrho + \delta + \lambda^e[1 - F(w)]}, \qquad (B.12)$$

so that we arrive at

$$r = b + (\lambda^n - \lambda^e) \int_r^{\overline{w}} \frac{1 - F(x)}{\varrho + \delta + \lambda^e[1 - F(x)]} dx. \qquad (B.13)$$

Letting $\varrho \to 0$ in (B.13) yields (8.5).

B.3 Proof of Proposition 8.1: Workers' Expected Wage[1]

Workers' expected wage $E_G[w]$ must equal the ratio of the expected total payroll $E_F[wL(w|F,r)]$ and the expected total employment $E_F[L(w|F,r)] = M - N = M\lambda^n/(\delta + \lambda^n)$, where the last equality follows from (8.8). Thus, we get

$$E_G[w] = \frac{E_F[wL(w|F,r)]}{M-N} \tag{B.14}$$

$$= \phi \underbrace{\left(1 - \frac{E_F[L(w|F,r)]}{M-N}\right)}_{=0} + \frac{E_F[wL(w|F,r)]}{M-N} \tag{B.15}$$

So

$$E_G[w] = \phi - \frac{\delta + \lambda^n}{\lambda^n} \frac{E_F[(\phi - w)L(w|F,r)]}{M} \tag{B.16}$$

$$= \phi - \frac{\delta + \lambda^n}{\lambda^n} \frac{\Pi^*}{M}. \tag{B.17}$$

The last equality holds because steady-state profits are the same for all firms as given by (8.15). Inserting (8.15) into (B.17) yields

$$E_G[w] = \frac{\lambda^e}{\delta + \lambda^e}\phi + \frac{\delta}{\delta + \lambda^e}r = \frac{1}{1+\xi}\phi + \frac{\xi}{1+\xi}r \tag{B.18}$$

with the market friction parameter $\xi := \delta/\lambda^e$. ∎

B.4 Proof of Equation (9.1)[2]

As already noted several times, the steady-state workforce of a firm offering some wage w depends only on the firm's relative position in the wage offer distribution $F(w)$. Its number of recruits can therefore be expressed as

$$R[F(w)|F,r] = \lambda^n N + \lambda^e (M-N) G[F(w)], \tag{B.19}$$

where the first term on the right-hand side represents the recruits from non-employment and the second term the recruits from employment. The latter holds as the fraction of workers employed at position $F(w)$ is given by $G[F(w)]$, while $M - N$ gives the total number of employed workers. Next, we make use of (8.8),

---

[1] The following proof is along the lines of Manning (2003a, p. 54).
[2] This proof relies on the proof given by Manning (2003a, p. 55).

(8.10), and $F(r) = 0$ to rewrite (B.19) as

$$R[F(w)|F,r] = \frac{\delta + \lambda^e}{\delta + \lambda^n} \frac{\lambda^n \delta}{\delta + \lambda^e[1 - F(w)]} M. \qquad \text{(B.20)}$$

Since wages are distributed across firms according to F, i.e., $w \sim F$, $\vartheta := F(w)$ is uniformly distributed on the interval $[0, 1]$, i.e., $\vartheta \sim \widehat{1}|_{[0,1]}$, which is readily proven via a univariate probability integral transformation (e.g., Mittelhammer, 1996, pp. 348/349). Hence, the total flow of recruits $\mathcal{R}$ in the economy is given by

$$\mathcal{R} = \int_0^1 R[F(w)|F,r] \, dF(w), \qquad \text{(B.21)}$$

that is, the mass of firms, which is one, times the average number of recruits per firm. Inserting (B.20) into (B.21) yields

$$\mathcal{R} = \frac{\delta + \lambda^e}{\delta + \lambda^n} \lambda^n M \int_0^1 \frac{1}{1 + \lambda^e/\delta[1 - F(w)]} \, dF(w) \qquad \text{(B.22)}$$

$$= \frac{\delta + \lambda^e}{\delta + \lambda^n} \frac{\lambda^n \delta}{\lambda^e} M \ln(1 + \lambda^e/\delta). \qquad \text{(B.23)}$$

As the number of recruits from non-employment is given by $\lambda^n N = \delta \lambda^n M/(\delta + \lambda^n)$, the share of recruits from non-employment is

$$\zeta := \frac{\lambda^n N}{\mathcal{R}} = \frac{\lambda^e}{\delta + \lambda^e} \frac{1}{\ln(1 + \lambda^e/\delta)}. \qquad \text{(B.24)}$$

Consider now the market friction parameter $\xi := \delta/\lambda^e$. ζ is thus a strictly increasing function of ξ with

$$\zeta(\xi) = \frac{1/\xi}{(1 + 1/\xi)\ln(1 + 1/\xi)} \qquad \text{(B.25)}$$

and

$$\zeta'(\xi) = \frac{1/\xi - \ln(1 + 1/\xi)}{[(1 + \xi)\ln(1 + 1/\xi)]^2} > 0 \qquad \text{(B.26)}$$

for all $\xi > 0$. The latter holds because

$$\exp x := \sum_{i=0}^{\infty} \frac{x^i}{i!}, \qquad \text{(B.27)}$$

so that we have $1 + x \nearrow \exp x$ if $x \searrow 0$ and thus $\ln(1 + x) \nearrow x$ if $x \searrow 0$ and the nominator of (B.26) is positive for all $\xi > 0$. ∎

B.5   Proof of Equation (9.12)[3]

The separation rate of a firm paying some wage w is given by

$$s(w) = \delta + \lambda^e \int_w^{\overline{w}} \varphi(x/w)\,dF(x) \tag{B.28}$$

with derivative

$$s'(w) = -\lambda^e \int_w^{\overline{w}} \frac{\varphi'(x/w)x}{w^2}\,dF(x). \tag{B.29}$$

The firm's number of recruits is

$$R(w) = \lambda^n N + \lambda^e \int_w^{\overline{w}} \varphi(w/x) L(x)\,dF(x) \tag{B.30}$$

with derivative

$$R'(w) = \lambda^e \int_w^{\overline{w}} \frac{\varphi'(w/x) L(x)}{x}\,dF(x). \tag{B.31}$$

Making use of (B.29) and (B.31) and the fact that in a steady state we have $L(w) = R(w)/s(w)$, the following line of argument holds

$$\int_w^{\overline{w}} e_{sw}(x) R(x)\,dF(x) = \int_w^{\overline{w}} \frac{s'(x)x}{s(x)} R(x)\,dF(x) \tag{B.32}$$

$$= \int_w^{\overline{w}} s'(x) x L(x)\,dF(x) \tag{B.33}$$

$$= \int_w^{\overline{w}} \left(-\lambda^e \int_x^{\overline{w}} \frac{\varphi(z/x)z}{x^2}\,dF(z)\right) x L(x)\,dF(x) \tag{B.34}$$

$$= -\lambda^e \int_w^{\overline{w}}\int_x^{\overline{w}} \frac{\varphi'(z/x) z L(x)}{x}\,dF(z)\,dF(x) \tag{B.35}$$

$$= -\int_w^{\overline{w}} R'(x) x\,dF(x) \tag{B.36}$$

$$= -\int_w^{\overline{w}} e_{Rw}(x) R(x)\,dF(x), \tag{B.37}$$

which establishes the claim. ∎

---

[3] This proof closely follows the proof given by Manning (2003a, p. 109).

B.6 Proof of Equation (9.17)[4]

The separation rate to employment of a firm paying some wage w is given by

$$s^e(w) = \lambda^e \int_{\underline{w}}^{\overline{w}} \varphi(x/w) \, dF(x) \tag{B.38}$$

with derivative

$$\frac{ds^e(w)}{dw} = -\lambda^e \int_{\underline{w}}^{\overline{w}} \frac{\varphi'(x/w)x}{w^2} \, dF(x). \tag{B.39}$$

The firm's number of recruits from employment is

$$R^e(w) = \lambda^e \int_{\underline{w}}^{\overline{w}} \varphi(w/x) L(x) \, dF(x) \tag{B.40}$$

with derivative

$$\frac{dR^e(w)}{dw} = \lambda^e \int_{\underline{w}}^{\overline{w}} \frac{\varphi'(w/x) L(x)}{x} \, dF(x). \tag{B.41}$$

Therefore, the following line of argument holds

$$\int_{\underline{w}}^{\overline{w}} e^e_{sw}(x) s^e(x) L(x) \, dF(x) = \int_{\underline{w}}^{\overline{w}} \frac{ds^e(x)}{dx} \frac{x}{s^e(x)} s^e(x) L(x) \, dF(x) \tag{B.42}$$

$$= \int_{\underline{w}}^{\overline{w}} \left(-\lambda^e \int_{x}^{\overline{w}} \frac{\varphi'(z/x)z}{x^2} \, dF(z) \right) x L(x) \, dF(x) \tag{B.43}$$

$$= -\lambda^e \int_{\underline{w}}^{\overline{w}} \int_{x}^{\overline{w}} \frac{\varphi'(z/x) z L(x)}{x} \, dF(z) \, dF(x) \tag{B.44}$$

$$= -\int_{\underline{w}}^{\overline{w}} \frac{dR^e(x)}{dx} x \, dF(x) \tag{B.45}$$

$$= -\int_{\underline{w}}^{\overline{w}} e^e_{Rw}(x) R^e(x) \, dF(x), \tag{B.46}$$

which establishes the claim. ■

B.7 Appendix to Chapter 9

---

[4] This proof is along the lines of Manning (2003a, pp. 109/110).

Table B.1 Descriptive statistics for the whole sample (sample averages)[a]

Variables	without censored observations			with all observations		
Sample	all	men	women	all	men	women
Daily wage (in €)	94.802	97.780	86.453	103.892	107.761	90.666
Log of daily wage	4.522	4.557	4.418	4.628	4.675	4.467
Censored wage observation (dummy)	0.000	0.000	0.000	0.142	0.167	0.057
Worker with a censored wage observation in any of the years 2000–2002 (dummy)	0.000	0.000	0.000	0.187	0.218	0.080
Male (dummy)	0.744	1.000	0.000	0.774	1.000	0.000
Non-German (dummy)	0.102	0.112	0.073	0.090	0.095	0.070
Tenure (number of years)	10.825	11.058	10.151	11.076	11.350	10.140
Age under 21 years (dummy)	0.004	0.003	0.007	0.003	0.003	0.006
Age 21–25 years (dummy)	0.062	0.054	0.086	0.051	0.043	0.080
Age 26–30 years (dummy)	0.131	0.125	0.148	0.116	0.108	0.145
Age 31–35 years (dummy)	0.183	0.189	0.166	0.180	0.183	0.170
Age 36–40 years (dummy)	0.187	0.197	0.161	0.193	0.202	0.165
Age 41–45 years (dummy)	0.165	0.168	0.156	0.172	0.176	0.159
Age 46–50 years (dummy)	0.147	0.143	0.157	0.154	0.152	0.157
Age 51–55 years (dummy)	0.106	0.106	0.106	0.113	0.116	0.105
Age 56–58 years (dummy)	0.015	0.015	0.014	0.016	0.017	0.014
No apprenticeship, no Abitur (dummy)	0.189	0.184	0.201	0.159	0.150	0.189
Apprenticeship, no Abitur (dummy)	0.707	0.727	0.649	0.661	0.671	0.627
No apprenticeship, with Abitur (dummy)	0.008	0.007	0.013	0.009	0.008	0.013
Apprenticeship and Abitur (dummy)	0.044	0.032	0.079	0.049	0.039	0.083
Technical college degree (dummy)	0.025	0.025	0.023	0.054	0.061	0.030
University degree (dummy)	0.028	0.026	0.034	0.069	0.072	0.058

(Continued)

Table B.1 (Continued)

Sample Variables	without censored observations			with all observations		
	all	men	women	all	men	women
Basic manual occupation (dummy)	0.308	0.354	0.175	0.259	0.288	0.162
Qualified manual occupation (dummy)	0.204	0.257	0.049	0.181	0.221	0.045
Engineer or technician (dummy)	0.081	0.094	0.043	0.132	0.157	0.048
Basic service occupation (dummy)	0.095	0.111	0.048	0.080	0.090	0.045
Qualified service occupation (dummy)	0.027	0.018	0.055	0.023	0.015	0.051
Semi-professional (dummy)	0.053	0.022	0.144	0.047	0.020	0.137
Professional (dummy)	0.009	0.008	0.014	0.020	0.019	0.024
Basic business occupation (dummy)	0.041	0.019	0.104	0.042	0.023	0.107
Qualified business occupation (dummy)	0.174	0.110	0.358	0.192	0.141	0.365
Manager (dummy)	0.008	0.008	0.009	0.022	0.025	0.014
Coll. agreement at sect. level (dummy)	0.810	0.810	0.809	0.817	0.818	0.812
Coll. agreement at firm level (dummy)	0.117	0.125	0.096	0.113	0.118	0.096
Works council (dummy)	0.935	0.939	0.923	0.942	0.946	0.927
Proportion of female workers	0.299	0.230	0.500	0.293	0.235	0.492
Proportion of qualified workers	0.710	0.701	0.736	0.721	0.715	0.742
Good economic performance (dummy)	0.320	0.343	0.254	0.328	0.348	0.261
Bad economic performance (dummy)	0.224	0.244	0.167	0.230	0.248	0.170
New production technology (dummy)	0.745	0.743	0.753	0.759	0.759	0.759
Year 2000 (dummy)	0.326	0.325	0.328	0.324	0.323	0.327
Year 2001 (dummy)	0.350	0.354	0.339	0.354	0.358	0.341
Year 2002 (dummy)	0.324	0.321	0.332	0.321	0.318	0.332
Observations	1,122,295	834,867	287,428	1,379,795	1,067,492	312,303
Subjects	402,105	296,477	105,628	475,636	364,764	110,872
Separations to employment	58,593	43,665	14,928	71,860	55,672	16,188
Separations to non-employment	37,700	26,195	11,505	41,850	29,597	12,253

[a] The data set used is version 2 of the LIAB longitudinal model, 2000–2002.

B.7 Appendix to Chapter 9

Table B.2 Descriptive statistics for the recruitment sample (sample averages)[a]

Variables \ Sample	without censored observations			with all observations		
	all	men	women	all	men	women
Daily wage (in €)	85.156	87.703	78.027	93.639	97.066	82.942
Log of daily wage	4.386	4.419	4.292	4.487	4.533	4.345
Censored wage observations	0.000	0.000	0.000	0.106	0.124	0.048
Worker with a censored wage observation in any of the years 2000–2002 (dummy)	0.000	0.000	0.000	0.146	0.170	0.074
Male (dummy)	0.737	1.000	0.000	0.757	1.000	0.000
Non-German (dummy)	0.124	0.134	0.095	0.113	0.120	0.092
Age under 21 years (dummy)	0.026	0.022	0.037	0.022	0.018	0.034
Age 21–25 years (dummy)	0.139	0.132	0.158	0.120	0.111	0.149
Age 26–30 years (dummy)	0.197	0.193	0.209	0.184	0.177	0.208
Age 31–35 years (dummy)	0.210	0.215	0.194	0.219	0.225	0.201
Age 36–40 years (dummy)	0.162	0.165	0.153	0.174	0.179	0.158
Age 41–45 years (dummy)	0.117	0.119	0.109	0.124	0.128	0.111
Age 46–50 years (dummy)	0.087	0.087	0.087	0.090	0.091	0.087
Age 51–55 years (dummy)	0.057	0.061	0.048	0.060	0.064	0.048
Age 56–58 years (dummy)	0.006	0.006	0.005	0.006	0.006	0.005
No apprenticeship, no Abitur (dummy)	0.195	0.204	0.169	0.170	0.174	0.158
Apprenticeship, no Abitur (dummy)	0.606	0.618	0.572	0.563	0.568	0.548
No apprenticeship, with Abitur (dummy)	0.024	0.022	0.031	0.023	0.020	0.030
Apprenticeship and Abitur (dummy)	0.062	0.046	0.104	0.066	0.053	0.108
Technical college degree (dummy)	0.044	0.047	0.037	0.064	0.071	0.042
University degree (dummy)	0.070	0.063	0.087	0.114	0.113	0.114
Basic manual occupation (dummy)	0.306	0.357	0.165	0.267	0.303	0.154
Qualified manual occupation (dummy)	0.169	0.215	0.042	0.153	0.189	0.039

(*Continued*)

Table B.2 (Continued)

Variables	Sample						
	without censored observations			with all observations			
	all	men	women		all	men	women
Engineer or technician (dummy)	0.092	0.105	0.056		0.121	0.141	0.042
Basic service occupation (dummy)	0.096	0.111	0.053		0.083	0.094	0.049
Qualified service occupation (dummy)	0.024	0.012	0.058		0.021	0.011	0.114
Semi-professional (dummy)	0.048	0.019	0.127		0.043	0.018	0.120
Professional (dummy)	0.021	0.017	0.033		0.034	0.030	0.047
Basic business occupation (dummy)	0.041	0.025	0.086		0.043	0.094	0.088
Qualified business occupation (dummy)	0.187	0.125	0.362		0.205	0.153	0.367
Manager (dummy)	0.015	0.014	0.018		0.030	0.032	0.023
Coll. agreement at sect. level (dummy)	0.699	0.683	0.744		0.716	0.704	0.753
Coll. agreement at firm level (dummy)	0.188	0.211	0.125		0.178	0.196	0.121
Works council (dummy)	0.875	0.875	0.874		0.887	0.890	0.881
Proportion of female workers	0.315	0.253	0.490		0.315	0.260	0.487
Proportion of qualified workers	0.660	0.640	0.715		0.675	0.660	0.722
Good economic performance (dummy)	0.395	0.421	0.321		0.402	0.426	0.327
Bad economic performance (dummy)	0.164	0.172	0.144		0.172	0.179	0.148
New production technology (dummy)	0.777	0.783	0.760		0.786	0.793	0.766
Year 2000 (dummy)	0.464	0.485	0.405		0.467	0.485	0.409
Year 2001 (dummy)	0.306	0.293	0.340		0.311	0.301	0.342
Year 2002 (dummy)	0.230	0.222	0.255		0.222	0.214	0.249
Observations	93,260	68,715	24,545		109,266	82,756	26,510
Hired from non-employment (dummy)	0.461	0.475	0.421		0.425	0.431	0.406

[a] The data set used is version 2 of the LIAB longitudinal model, 2000–2002.

Table B.3 Wage regressions[a]

Regressors	Groups	all	men	women
Male (dummy)		0.121 (0.004)	—	—
Non-German (dummy)		0.004 (0.004)	0.004 (0.004)	-0.000 (0.006)
Age (number of years)		0.028 (0.001)	0.025 (0.001)	0.034 (0.001)
Age squared (divided by 100)		-0.031 (0.001)	-0.028 (0.002)	-0.038 (0.002)
Tenure (number of years)		0.011 (0.001)	0.011 (0.002)	0.012 (0.001)
Tenure squared (divided by 100)		-0.026 (0.004)	-0.027 (0.005)	-0.026 (0.003)
No apprenticeship, no Abitur (ref. group)		—	—	—
Apprenticeship, no Abitur (dummy)		0.080 (0.005)	0.078 (0.006)	0.075 (0.006)
No apprenticeship, with Abitur (dummy)		-0.006 (0.023)	-0.020 (0.024)	-0.015 (0.023)
Apprenticeship and Abitur (dummy)		0.120 (0.008)	0.104 (0.009)	0.133 (0.007)
Technical college degree (dummy)		0.211 (0.007)	0.204 (0.008)	0.223 (0.008)
University degree (dummy)		0.235 (0.009)	0.225 (0.011)	0.256 (0.009)
Basic manual occupation (ref. group)		—	—	—
Qualified manual occupation (dummy)		0.062 (0.006)	0.065 (0.006)	0.005 (0.019)
Engineer or technician (dummy)		0.209 (0.007)	0.212 (0.007)	0.203 (0.013)
Basic service occupation (dummy)		0.002 (0.008)	0.005 (0.008)	0.031 (0.013)
Qualified service occupation (dummy)		0.126 (0.015)	0.082 (0.016)	0.172 (0.017)
Semi-professional (dummy)		0.264 (0.013)	0.231 (0.017)	0.283 (0.013)
Professional (dummy)		0.217 (0.016)	0.194 (0.020)	0.255 (0.019)
Basic business occupation (dummy)		0.103 (0.009)	0.080 (0.012)	0.123 (0.014)
Qualified business occupation (dummy)		0.179 (0.007)	0.173 (0.007)	0.195 (0.012)
Manager (dummy)		0.294 (0.013)	0.279 (0.013)	0.339 (0.016)
Log of establishment size (number of employees)		0.032 (0.005)	0.031 (0.005)	0.038 (0.004)
Coll. agreement at sect. level (dummy)		0.021 (0.009)	0.015 (0.010)	0.034 (0.011)
Coll. agreement at firm level (dummy)		0.064 (0.028)	0.068 (0.029)	0.047 (0.023)
Works council (dummy)		0.084 (0.013)	0.072 (0.014)	0.111 (0.016)

(Continued)

Table B.3 (Continued)

Regressors	Groups	all	men	women
Proportion of female workers		−0.163 (0.022)	−0.139 (0.026)	−0.170 (0.024)
Proportion of qualified workers		0.087 (0.019)	0.082 (0.021)	0.100 (0.017)
Good economic performance (dummy)		0.020 (0.007)	0.021 (0.008)	0.021 (0.007)
Bad economic performance (dummy)		−0.008 (0.008)	−0.007 (0.008)	−0.001 (0.009)
New production technology (dummy)		−0.005 (0.009)	−0.005 (0.010)	−0.007 (0.008)
Ten sectoral dummies		($p < 0.001$)	($p < 0.001$)	($p < 0.001$)
Year 2000 (ref. group)		—	—	—
Year 2001 (dummy)		0.024 (0.002)	0.024 (0.002)	0.023 (0.002)
Year 2002 (dummy)		0.037 (0.002)	0.036 (0.003)	0.039 (0.002)
Constant		3.117 (0.069)	3.316 (0.084)	2.887 (0.058)
Unexplained log wage gap obtained from an Oaxaca–Blinder decomposition		—	0.1432	0.1141
Observations		1,122,295	834,867	287,428
R^2		0.4289	0.3937	0.4180

[a] The data set used is version 2 of the LIAB longitudinal model, 2000–2002. The regressand is log daily gross wage. Estimation is done by ordinary least squares, robust standard errors are given in parentheses (adjusted for intra-establishment correlation).

B.7 Appendix to Chapter 9

Table B.4 Estimates of the long-run firm-level elasticity of female and male labour supplies when tenure is not controlled for and downsizing establishments are excluded[a]

Exponential Models Parameters	without establishment controls male workers	without establishment controls female workers	with establishment controls male workers	with establishment controls female workers	with all controls and person frailties/RE male workers	with all controls and person frailties/RE female workers	with all controls and establishment frailties/RE male workers	with all controls and establishment frailties/RE female workers
Estimated wage elasticity of the separation rate to employment ($\widehat{\beta}_w^e$)	−1.639 (0.165)	−1.203 (0.082)	−1.473 (0.138)	−1.151 (0.093)	−1.854 (0.036)	−1.458 (0.049)	−1.626 (0.032)	−1.340 (0.042)
Estimated wage elasticity of the separation rate to non-employment ($\widehat{\beta}_w^n$)	−2.820 (0.134)	−2.031 (0.065)	−2.625 (0.115)	−2.096 (0.071)	−3.829 (0.037)	−2.981 (0.049)	−2.813 (0.026)	−2.314 (0.034)
Estimated coefficient of the log wage in a logit model for the probability that a recruit is hired from employment ($\widehat{\beta}_w$)	1.062 (0.756)	1.400 (0.301)	1.866 (0.150)	1.388 (0.144)	1.962 (0.043)	1.575 (0.060)	2.183 (0.050)	1.544 (0.058)
Share of recruits from employment ($\widehat{\theta}$)	0.534	0.585	0.534	0.585	0.534	0.585	0.534	0.585

(*Continued*)

Table B.4 (Continued)

Exponential Models	without establishment controls		with establishment controls		with all controls and person frailties/RE		with all controls and establishment frailties/RE	
Parameters	male workers	female workers	male workers	female workers	male workers	female workers	male workers	female workers
Estimated long-run firm-level labour supply elasticity $(\widehat{e}_{Lw}^{LR})^b$	3.333	2.169	2.613	2.118	3.714	2.894	2.788	2.443
Implied 'exploitation' $(\widehat{E}_m)^c$	0.300	0.461	0.383	0.472	0.269	0.351	0.359	0.409
Implied gender pay gaps $(\widehat{\Delta}_{\mathscr{G}_W})^d$	0.124	−0.110	0.065	−0.061	0.060	−0.057	0.037	−0.036

[a] Estimated coefficients are taken from estimations similar to those presented in Tables 9.2–9.7 not reported in detail. Downsizing establishments are excluded from the sample, where establishments with a workforce of at least ten employees are regarded as downsizing if they experienced an employment reduction by at least 25 per cent between 2000 and 2002.
[b] Estimated long-run firm-level labour supply elasticities are obtained according to equation (9.26).
[c] The implied percentage gap between workers' marginal revenue product and their wages is calculated according to equation (9.27).
[d] Implied gender pay gaps are calculated according to equation (9.28) for male and (9.29) for female workers, respectively.

References

ABBRING, J.H. and VAN DEN BERG, G.J. (2007), 'The unobserved heterogeneity distribution in duration analysis', *Biometrika*, **94**(1):87–99.
ABOWD, J.M. and KRAMARZ, F. (1999), 'The analysis of labor markets using matched employer–employee data,' *in* O.C. Ashenfelter and D.E. Card (eds.), 'Handbook of Labor Economics,' vol. 3B, pp. 2629–2710, Amsterdam: Elsevier.
ADAMACHE, K.W. and SLOAN, F.A. (1982), 'Unions and hospitals: Some unresolved issues,' *Journal of Health Economics*, **1**(1):81–108.
ADDISON, J.T. and BELFIELD, C.R. (2004), 'Union voice,' *Journal of Labor Research*, **25**(4):563–597.
ADDISON, J.T., BELLMANN, L., SCHNABEL, C., and WAGNER, J. (2004*a*), 'The reform of the German Works Constitution Act: A critical assessment,' *Industrial Relations*, **43**(2):392–420.
ADDISON, J.T., SCHNABEL, C., and WAGNER, J. (2001), 'Works councils in Germany: Their effects on establishment performance,' *Oxford Economic Papers*, **53**(4):659–694.
—— (2004*b*), 'The course of research into the economic consequences of German works councils,' *British Journal of Industrial Relations*, **42**(2):255–281.
AGELL, J. (2002), 'On the determinants of labour market institutions: Rent seeking vs. social insurance,' *German Economic Review*, **3**(2):107–135.
ALBRECHT, J.W. and AXELL, B. (1984), 'An equilibrium model of search unemployment,' *Journal of Political Economy*, **92**(5):824–840.
ALDA, H. (2005), Datenbeschreibung der Version 2.0 des LIAB-Längsschnittmodells, Forschungsdatenzentrum des Instituts für Arbeitsmarkt- und Berufsforschung, Nuremberg, Datenreport Nr. 7/2005.
ALDA, H., BENDER, S., and GARTNER, H. (2005), 'The linked employer-employee dataset created from the IAB establishment panel and the process-produced data of the IAB (LIAB),' *Schmollers Jahrbuch (Journal of Applied Social Science Studies)*, **125**(2):327–336.
ALTONJI, J.G. and BLANK, R.M. (1999), 'Race and gender in the labor market,' *in* O.C. Ashenfelter and D.E. Card (eds.), 'Handbook of Labor Economics,' vol. 3C, pp. 3143–3259, Amsterdam: Elsevier.
ANGRIST, J.D. and PISCHKE, J.S. (2009), *Mostly Harmless Econometrics: An Empiricist's Companion*, Princeton, NJ: Princeton University Press.
ARNTZ, M. (2005), The Geographical Mobility of Unemployed Workers: Evidence from West Germany, Centre for European Economic Research, Mannheim, ZEW Discussion Paper No. 05-34.
ARROW, K.J. (1972), 'Models of job discrimination,' *in* A.H. Pascal (ed.), 'Racial Discrimination in Economic Life,' pp. 83–102, Lexington, MA: D.C. Heath.
BACHMANN, R. (2005), Labour Market Dynamics in Germany: Hirings, Separations, and Job-to-Job Transitions over the Business Cycle, Department of Economics, Humboldt-Universität zu Berlin, SFB 649 Discussion Paper 2005-045.

BAGNOLI, M. and BERGSTROM, T. (2005), 'Log-concave probability and its applications,' *Economic Theory*, **26**(2):445–469.
BAILY, M.N. (1975), 'Dynamic monopsony and structural change,' *American Economic Review*, **65**(3):338–349.
BARTELHEIMER, P. and WIECK, M. (2005), 'Arbeitslosigkeit und Unterbeschäftigung,' *in* Soziologisches Forschungsinstitut, Institut für Arbeitsmarkt- und Berufsforschung, Institut für Sozialwissenschaftliche Forschung, and Internationales Institut für empirische Sozialökonomie (eds.), 'Berichterstattung zur sozioökonomischen Entwicklung in Deutschland – Arbeit und Lebensweisen. Erster Bericht,' pp. 271–302, Wiesbaden: VS Verlag für Sozialwissenschaften.
BARTH, E. and DALE-OLSEN, H. (1999), Monopsonistic Discrimination and the Gender Wage Gap, National Bureau of Economic Research, Cambridge, MA, NBER Working Paper No. 7197.
——— (2009), 'Monopsonistic discrimination, worker turnover, and the gender wage gap,' *Labour Economics*, **16**(5):589–597.
BEBLO, M., HEINZE, A., and WOLF, E. (2008), 'Entwicklung der beruflichen Segregation von Männern und Frauen zwischen 1996 und 2005 – Eine Bestandsaufnahme auf betrieblicher Ebene,' *Zeitschrift für ArbeitsmarktForschung (Journal of Labour Market Research)*, **41**(2/3):181–198.
BECK, P.M. (1993), Monopsony in the Market for Public School Teachers in Missouri: The Static and Dynamic Impact On Salaries and Employment, Ph.D. thesis, University of Missouri.
BECKER, G.S. (1971), *The Economics of Discrimination*, Chicago, IL: University of Chicago Press, 2nd edn.
——— (1993), *Human Capital: A Theoretical and Empirical Analysis with Special Reference to Education*, Chicago, IL: University of Chicago Press.
BECKMANN, M.J. (1976), 'Spatial price policies revisited,' *Bell Journal of Economics*, **7**(2):619–630.
BENDER, S., HAAS, A., and KLOSE, C. (2000), 'The IAB employment subsample 1975–95,' *Schmollers Jahrbuch (Journal of Applied Social Science Studies)*, **120**(4):649–662.
BENDER, S., HILZENDEGEN, J., ROHWER, G., and RUDOLPH, H. (1996), *Die IAB-Beschäftigtenstichprobe 1975–1990*, Beiträge zur Arbeitsmarkt- und Berufsforschung Nr. 197, Nuremberg: Institut für Arbeitsmarkt- und Berufsforschung.
BENSON, B.L. (1980), 'Löschian competition under alternative demand conditions,' *American Economic Review*, **70**(5):1098–1105.
——— (1984), 'On the ability of spatial competitors to price discriminate,' *Journal of Industrial Economics*, **33**(2):251–255.
——— (1988), 'The Economics of Imperfect Competition: A Spatial Approach (book review),' *Journal of Economic Literature*, **26**(1):93–94.
——— (1989), 'Spatial Price Theory of Imperfect Competition (book review),' *Annals of Regional Science*, **23**(3):247/248.
BERGEMANN, A. and MERTENS, A. (2004), Job Stability Trends, Layoffs, and Transitions to Unemployment: An Empirical Analysis for West Germany, Institute for the Study of Labor, IZA Discussion Paper No. 1368, Bonn.
BHASKAR, V., MANNING, A., and TO, T. (2002), 'Oligopsony and monopsonistic competition in labor markets,' *Journal of Economic Perspectives*, **16**(2):155–174.
BHASKAR, V. and TO, T. (1999), 'Minimum wages for Ronald McDonald monopsonies: A theory of monopsonistic competition,' *Economic Journal*, **109**(455):190–203.
——— (2003), 'Oligopsony and the distribution of wages,' *European Economic Review*, **47**(2):371–399.
BINMORE, K.G., RUBINSTEIN, A., and WOLINSKY, A. (1986), 'The Nash bargaining solution in economic modelling,' *Rand Journal of Economics*, **17**(2):176–188.
BLACK, D.A. (1995), 'Discrimination in an equilibrium search model,' *Journal of Labor Economics*, **13**(2):309–334.
BLACK, D.A., HAVILAND, A.M., SANDERS, S.G., and TAYLOR, L.J. (2008), 'Gender wage disparities among the highly educated,' *Journal of Human Resources*,' **43**(3):630–659.

References

BLAIR, R.D. and HARRISON, J.L. (1993), *Monopsony: Antitrust Law and Economics*, Princeton, NJ: Princeton University Press.

BLANCHFLOWER, D.G., OSWALD, A.J., and SANFEY, P. (1996), 'Wages, profits, and rent-sharing,' *Quarterly Journal of Economics*, **111**(1):227–251.

BLAU, F.D. and KAHN, L.M. (1981), 'Race and sex differences in quits by young workers,' *Industrial and Labor Relations Review*, **34**(4):563–577.

——— (2000), 'Gender differences in pay,' *Journal of Economic Perspectives*, **14**(4):75–99.

——— (2003), 'Understanding international differences in the gender pay gap,' *Journal of Labor Economics*, **21**(1):106–144.

BLIEN, U. and MEDERER, A. (1998), 'Regional determinants of gender specific wages – an empirical analysis,' *in* F. Haslinger and O. Stönner-Venkatarama (eds.), 'Aspects of the Distribution of Income,' pp. 273–295, Marburg: Metropolis.

BLINDER, A.S. (1973), 'Wage discrimination: Reduced form and structural estimates,' *Journal of Human Resources*, **8**(4):435–455.

BLUNDELL, R. and MACURDY, T.R. (1999), 'Labor supply: A review of alternative approaches,' *in* O.C. Ashenfelter and D.E. Card (eds.), 'Handbook of Labor Economics,' vol. 3A, pp. 1559–1695, Amsterdam: Elsevier.

BOAL, W.M. (1995), 'Testing for employer monopsony in turn-of-the-century coal mining,' *Rand Journal of Economics*, **26**(3):519–536.

BOAL, W.M. and RANSOM, M.R. (1997), 'Monopsony in the labor market,' *Journal of Economic Literature*, **35**(1):86–112.

BONTEMPS, C., ROBIN, J.M., and VAN DEN BERG, G.J. (1999), 'An empirical equilibrium job search model with search on the job and heterogeneous workers and firms,' *International Economic Review*, **40**(4):1039–1074.

——— (2000), 'Equilibrium search with continuous productivity dispersion: Theory and nonparametric estimation,' *International Economic Review*, **41**(2):305–358.

BOOCKMANN, B. and STEFFES, S. (2008), Workers, Firms, or Institutions: What Determines Job Duration for Male Employees in Germany?, Centre for European Economic Research, Mannheim, ZEW Discussion Paper 08-116.

BOOTH, A.L. (1995), *The Economics of the Trade Union*, Cambridge: Cambridge University Press.

BOOTH, A.L. and COLES, M.G. (2007), 'A microfoundation for increasing returns in human capital accumulation and the under-participation trap,' *European Economic Review*, **51**(7):1661–1681.

BÖRSCH-SUPAN, A. and SCHNABEL, R. (1998), 'Social security and declining labor-force participation in Germany,' *American Economic Review (Papers and Proceedings)*, **88**(2):173–178.

——— (1999), 'Social security and retirement in Germany,' *in* J. Gruber and D.A. Wise (eds.), 'Social Security and Retirement around the World,' pp. 135–180, Chicago, IL: University of Chicago Press.

BOWLEY, A.L. (1924), *The Mathematical Groundwork of Economics: An Introductory Treatise*, Oxford: Oxford University Press.

——— (1928), 'Bilateral monopoly,' *Economic Journal*, **38**(152):651–659.

BOWLUS, A.J. (1997), 'A search interpretation of male–female wage differentials,' *Journal of Labor Economics*, **15**(4):625–657.

BOWLUS, A.J. and ECKSTEIN, Z. (2002), 'Discrimination and skill differences in an equilibrium search model,' *International Economic Review*, **43**(4):1309–1345.

BOYD, L.W. (1993), The Economics of the Coal Company Town: Institutional Relationships, Monopsony, and Distributional Conflicts in American Coal Towns, Ph.D. thesis, West Virginia University.

BOYD, S. and VANDENBERGHE, L. (2004), *Convex Optimization*, Cambridge: Cambridge University Press.

BOYER, M. and MOREAUX, M. (1983a), 'Conjectures, rationality, and duopoly theory,' *International Journal of Industrial Organization*, **1**(1):23–41.

——— (1983b), 'Consistent versus non-consistent conjectures in duopoly theory: Some examples,' *Journal of Industrial Economics*, **32**(1):97–110.
BRADFIELD, M. (1990), 'Long-run equilibrium under pure monopsony,' *Canadian Journal of Economics*, **23**(3):700–704.
BRAKMAN, S. and HEIJDRA, B.J. (eds.) (2004), *The Monopolistic Competition Revolution in Retrorespect*, Cambridge: Cambridge University Press.
BRANDNER, J.A. and ZHANG, A. (1990), 'Market conduct in the airline industry: An empirical investigation,' *Rand Journal of Economics*, **21**(4):567–583.
BRESNAHAN, T.F. (1981), 'Duopoly models with consistent conjectures,' *American Economic Review*, **71**(5):934–945.
BROWN, C.C. and MEDOFF, J.L. (1989), 'The employer size–wage effect,' *Journal of Political Economy*, **97**(5):1027–1059.
BROWN, R.W. (1993), 'An estimate of the rent generated by a premium college football player,' *Economic Inquiry*, **31**(4):671–684.
BURDETT, K. and COLES, M.G. (2003), 'Equilibrium wage–tenure contracts,' *Econometrica*, **71**(5):1377–1404.
BURDETT, K. and MORTENSEN, D.T. (1998), 'Wage differentials, employer size, and unemployment,' *International Economic Review*, **39**(2):257–273.
BURDETT, K. and VISHWANATH, T. (1988), 'Balanced matching and labor market equilibrium,' *Journal of Political Economy*, **96**(5):1048–1065.
BUSCH, A. and HOLST, E. (2008), '"Gender Pay Gap": In Großstädten geringer als auf dem Land,' *DIW Wochenbericht*, **75**(33):462–468.
BUTTERS, G.R. (1977), 'Distributions of sales and advertising prices,' *Review of Economic Studies*, **44**(3):465–491.
CABRAL, L.M.B. (1995), 'Conjectural variations as a reduced form,' *Economics Letters*, **49**(4):397–402.
CAHUC, P. and ZYLBERBERG, A. (2004), *Labor Economics*, Cambridge, MA: MIT Press.
CAMERON, A.C. and TRIVEDI, P.K. (2005), *Microeconometrics: Methods and Applications*, Cambridge: Cambridge University Press.
CAMPBELL, C.M. (1993), 'Do firms pay efficiency wages? Evidence with data at the firm level,' *Journal of Labor Economics*, **11**(3):442–470.
CAPOZZA, D.R. and ATTARAN, K. (1976), 'Pricing in urban areas under free entry,' *Journal of Regional Science*, **16**(2):167–182.
CAPOZZA, D.R. and VAN ORDER, R. (1977a), 'Pricing under spatial competition and spatial monopoly,' *Econometrica*, **45**(6):1329–1338.
——— (1977b), 'A simple model of spatial pricing under free entry,' *Southern Economic Journal*, **44**(2):361–367.
——— (1978), 'A generalized model of spatial competition,' *American Economic Review*, **68**(5):896–908.
——— (1989), 'Spatial competition with consistent conjectures,' *Journal of Regional Science*, **29**(1):1–13.
CARD, D.E. and KRUEGER, A.B. (1995), *Myth and Measurement: The New Economics of the Minimum Wage*, Princeton, NJ: Princeton University Press.
CARDWELL, L.A. and ROSENZWEIG, M.R. (1980), 'Economic mobility, monopsonistic discrimination and sex differences in wages,' *Southern Economic Journal*, **46**(4):1102–1117.
CHAMBERLIN, E.H. (1933), *The Theory of Monopolistic Competition*, Cambridge, MA: Havard University Press.
——— (1962), *The Theory of Monopolistic Competition: A Re-orientation of the Theory of Value*, Cambridge, MA: Harvard University Press, 8th edn.
COLES, M.G. (2001), 'Equilibrium wage dispersion, firm size and growth,' *Review of Economic Dynamics*, **4**(1):159–187.
COURNOT, A.A. (1838), *Recherches sur les principes mathématiques de la théorie des richesses*, Paris: Chez L. Hachette.

References

DAVIDSON, R. and MACKINNON, J.G. (2004), *Econometric Theory and Methods*, Oxford: Oxford University Press.

DELERY, J.E., GUPTA, N., SHAW, J.D., and GANSTER, M.L. (2000), 'Unionization, compensation, and voice effects on quits and retention,' *Industrial Relations*, 39(4):625–645.

DIAMOND, P.A. (1971), 'A model of price adjustment,' *Journal of Economic Theory*, 3(2):156–168.

DIXIT, A.K. (1988), 'Anti-dumping and counterveiling duties under oligopoly,' *European Economic Review*, 32(1):55–68.

DIXIT, A.K. and STIGLITZ, J.E. (1977), 'Monopolistic competition and optimum product diversity,' *American Economic Review*, 67(3):297–308.

DJURDJEVIC, D. and RADYAKIN, S. (2007), 'Decomposition of the gender wage gap using matching: An application from Switzerland,' *Swiss Journal of Economics and Statistics*, 143(4):365–396.

DOCKNER, E.J. (1992), 'A dynamic theory of conjectural variations,' *Journal of Industrial Economics*, 40(4):377–395.

ECKSTEIN, Z. and VAN DEN BERG, G.J. (2007), 'Empirical labor search: A survey,' *Journal of Econometrics*, 136(2):531–564.

EDGEWORTH, F.Y. (1881), *Mathematical Psychics: An Essay on the Application of Mathematics to the Moral Sciences*, London: Kegan Paul.

ERICKSON, C.L. and MITCHELL, D.J. (2007), 'Monopsony as a metaphor for the emerging post-union labour market,' *International Labour Review*, 146(3/4):163–187.

EUCKEN, W. (1950), *Die Grundlagen der Nationalökonomie*, Berlin: Springer, 7th edn.

EUROPEAN COMMISSION (2006), *The Gender Pay Gap – Origins and Policy Responses: A Comparative Review of 30 European Countries*, Luxembourg: European Commission.

FALCH, T. (2008), The Elasticity of Labor Supply at the Establishment Level, Industrial Relations Section, Princeton University, Working Paper No. 536.

FALCH, T. and STRØM, B. (2007), 'Wage bargaining and monopsony,' *Economics Letters*, 94(2):202–207.

FARBER, H.S. (1986), 'The analysis of union behavior,' in R. Layard and O.C. Ashenfelter (eds.), 'Handbook of Labor Economics,' vol. 2, pp. 1039–1089, Amsterdam: Elsevier.

FELLNER, W.J. (1949), *Competition Among the Few*, New York: A.A. Knopf.

FIGUIÈRES, C., JEAN-MARIE, A., QUÉROU, N., and TIDBALL, M. (2004), *Theory of Conjectural Variations*, Singapore: World Scientific.

FITZENBERGER, B., OSIKOMINU, A., and VÖLTER, R. (2006), 'Imputation rules to improve the education variable in the IAB employment subsample,' *Schmollers Jahrbuch (Journal of Applied Social Science Studies)*, 126(3):405–436.

FITZENBERGER, B. and WUNDERLICH, G. (2002), 'Gender wage differentials in West Germany: A cohort analysis,' *German Economic Review*, 3(4):379–414.

FLINN, C.J. and HECKMAN, J.J. (1983), 'Are unemployment and out of the labor force behaviorally distinct labor force states?' *Journal of Labor Economics*, 1(1):28–42.

FREEMAN, R.B. (1980), 'The exit-voice tradeoff in the labor market: Unionism, job tenure, quits and separations,' *Quarterly Journal of Economics*, 94(4):643–673.

FREEMAN, R.B. and MEDOFF, J.L. (1984), *What Do Unions Do?*, New York: Basic Books.

FRICK, B. and MÖLLER, I. (2003), 'Mandated works councils and firm performance: Labor productivity and personnel turnover in German establishments,' *Schmollers Jahrbuch (Journal of Applied Social Science Studies)*, 123(3):423–454.

FRICK, B. and SADOWSKI, D. (1995), 'Works councils, unions, and firm performance,' in F. Buttler, W. Franz, R. Schettkat, and D. Soskice (eds.), 'Institutional Frameworks and Labor Market Performance,' pp. 46–81, London: Routledge.

FRIEDMAN, J.W. (1971), 'A non-cooperative equilibrium for supergames,' *Review of Economic Studies*, 38(1):1–12.

——— (1983), *Oligopoly Theory*, Cambridge: Cambridge University Press.

FRIEDMAN, M. (1953), 'The methodology of positive economics,' in M. Friedman (ed.), 'Essays in Positive Economics,' pp. 3–43, Chicago, IL: University of Chicago Press.

FRÖLICH, M. (2007), 'Propensity score matching without conditional independence assumption – with an application to the gender wage gap in the United Kingdom,' *Econometrics Journal*, **10**(2):359–407.

GARTNER, H. and STEPHAN, G. (2004), How Collective Contracts and Works Councils Reduce the Gender Wage Gap, Institut für Arbeitsmarkt- und Berufsforschung, Nuremberg, IAB Discussion Paper No. 7/2004.

GAUMONT, D., SCHINDLER, M., and WRIGHT, R.D. (2006), 'Alternative theories of wage dispersion,' *European Economic Review*, **50**(4):831–848.

GIOCOLI, N. (2003), 'Conjecturizing Cournot: The conjectural variations approach to duopoly theory,' *History of Political Economy*, **35**(2):175–204.

—— (2005), 'The escape from conjectural variations: The consistency condition in duopoly theory from Bowley to Fellner,' *Cambridge Journal of Economics*, **29**(4):601–618.

GORDON, N.M. and MORTON, T.E. (1974), 'A low mobility model of wage discrimination – with special reference to sex differentials,' *Journal of Economic Theory*, **7**(3):241–253.

GREEN, F., MACHIN, S., and MANNING, A. (1996), 'The employer size–wage effect: Can dynamic monopsony provide an explanation?' *Oxford Economic Papers*, **48**(3):433–455.

GREENHUT, J.G. and GREENHUT, M.L. (1975), 'Spatial price discrimination, competition and locational effects,' *Economica*, **42**(168):401–419.

—— (1977), 'Nonlinearity of delivered price schedules and predatory pricing,' *Econometrica*, **45**(8):1871–1875.

GREENHUT, M.L. (1978), 'Impacts of distance on microeconomic theory,' *Manchester School*, **46**(1):17–40.

GREENHUT, M.L., HWANG, M.J., and OHTA, H. (1975), 'Observations on the shape and relevance of the spatial demand function,' *Econometrica*, **43**(4):669–682.

GREENHUT, M.L. and NORMAN, G. (1992), 'Conjectural variations and location theory,' *Journal of Economic Surveys*, **6**(4):299–320.

GREENHUT, M.L., NORMAN, G., and GREENHUT, J.G. (1995), 'A short- and long-run theory of price under conditions of imperfect competition,' *Aoyama Journal of Economics*, **46**(4):34–68.

GREENHUT, M.L., NORMAN, G., and HUNG, C. (1987), *The Economics of Imperfect Competition: A Spatial Approach*, Cambridge: Cambridge University Press.

GREENHUT, M.L. and OHTA, H. (1973), 'Spatial configurations and competitive equilibrium,' *Weltwirtschaftliches Archiv (Review of World Economics)*, **109**(1):87–104.

—— (1975), 'Discriminatory and nondiscriminatory spatial prices and outputs under varying market conditions,' *Weltwirtschaftliches Archiv (Review of World Economics)*, **111**(2):310–332.

GROSHEN, E.L. (1991), 'Five reasons why wages vary among employers,' *Industrial Relations*, **30**(3):350–381.

HARROD, R.F. (1934*a*), 'Doctrines of imperfect competition,' *Quarterly Journal of Economics*, **48**(3):442–470.

—— (1934*b*), 'The equilibrium of duopoly,' *Economic Journal*, **44**(174):335–337.

HECKMAN, J.J. (1976), 'The common structure of statistical models of truncation, sample selection and limited dependent variables and a simple estimator for such models,' *Annals of Economic and Social Measurement*, **5**(4):475–492.

—— (1979), 'Sample selection bias as a specification error,' *Econometrica*, **47**(1):153–161.

—— (1993), 'What has been learned about labor supply in the past twenty years?' *American Economic Review (Papers and Proceedings)*, **83**(2):116–121.

HEINZE, A. (2009), Earnings of Men and Women in Firms with a Female Dominated Workforce: What Drives the Impact of Sex Segregation in Wages?, Centre for European Economic Research, Mannheim, ZEW Discussion Paper No. 09-012.

HERSCH, J. and STRATTON, L.S. (1997), 'Housework, fixed effects, and wages of married women,' *Journal of Human Resources*, **32**(2):285–307.

HICKS, J.R. (1963), *The Theory of Wages*, London: Macmillan, 2nd edn.

HILDRETH, A.K.G. and OSWALD, A.J. (1997), 'Rent-sharing and wages: Evidence from company and establishment panels,' *Journal of Labor Economics*, **15**(2):318–337.

References

HINZ, T. and GARTNER, H. (2005), 'Geschlechtsspezifische Lohnunterschiede in Branchen,' *Zeitschrift für Soziologie*, **34**(1):22–39.

HIRSCH, B.T. and SCHUMACHER, E.J. (1995), 'Monopsony power and relative wages in the labor market for nurses,' *Journal of Health Economics*, **14**(4):443–476.

——— (2004), Classic Monopsony or New Monopsony? Searching for Evidence in Nursing Labor Markets, Institute for the Study of Labor, Bonn, IZA Discussion Paper No. 1154.

——— (2005), 'Classic or new monopsony? Searching for evidence in nursing labor markets,' *Journal of Health Economics*, **24**(5):969–989.

HIRSCH, B. (2009), 'The gender pay gap under duopsony: Joan Robinson meets Harold Hotelling,' *Scottish Journal of Political Economy*, **56**(5):543–558.

HIRSCH, B., KÖNIG, M., and MÖLLER, J. (2009a), Is There a Gap in the Gap? Regional Differences in the Gender Pay Gap, Institute for the Study of Labor, Bonn, IZA Discussion Paper No. 4231.

HIRSCH, B., SCHANK, T., and SCHNABEL, C. (2009b), 'Differences in labor supply to monopsonistic firms and the gender pay gap: An empirical analysis using linked employer–employee data from Germany,' *Journal of Labor Economics*, forthcoming.

——— (2009c), Works Councils and Separations: Voice, Monopoly, and Insurance Effects, Institute for the Study of Labor, Bonn, IZA Discussion Paper No. 4126.

HOLZER, H.J., KATZ, L.F., and KRUEGER, A.B. (1991), 'Job queues and wages,' *Quarterly Journal of Economics*, **106**(3):739–768.

HORNY, G., MENDES, R., and VAN DEN BERG, G.J. (2009), Job Durations with Worker and Firm Specific Effects: MCMC Estimation with Longitudinal Employer–Employee Data, Institute for the Study of Labor, Bonn, IZA Discussion Paper No. 3992.

HOTELLING, H. (1929), 'Stability in competition,' *Economic Journal*, **39**(153):41–57.

IMBENS, G.W. (2004), 'Nonparametric estimation of average treatment effects under exogeneity: A review,' *Review of Economics and Statistics*, **86**(1):4–29.

IMBENS, G.W. and WOOLDRIDGE, J.M. (2009), 'Recent developments in the econometrics of program evaluation,' *Journal of Economic Literature*, **47**(1):5–86.

IVALDI, M., JULLIEN, B., REY, P., SEABRIGHT, P., and TIROLE, J. (2007), 'The economics of tacit collusion in merger analysis,' *in* V. Ghosal and J. Stennek (eds.), 'The Political Economy of Antitrust,' pp. 217–239, Amsterdam: Elsevier.

JENKINS, S.P. (2005), Survival Analysis, Institute for Social and Economic Research, University of Essex, unpublished manuscript.

KAAS, L. and MADDEN, P. (2004), 'A new model of equilibrium involuntary unemployment,' *Economic Theory*, **23**(3):507–527.

——— (2008), Minimum Wages and Welfare in a Hotelling Duopsony, Institute for the Study of Labor, Bonn, IZA Discussion Paper No. 3434.

KAHN, R.F. (1937), 'The problem of duopoly,' *Economic Journal*, **47**(185):1–20.

KAMIEN, M.I. and SCHWARTZ, N.L. (1983), 'Conjectural variations,' *Canadian Journal of Economics*, **16**(2):191–211.

KIEFER, N.M. and NEUMANN, G.M. (1993), 'Wage dispersion with homogeneity: The empirical equilibrium search model,' *in* H. Bunzel, P. Jensen, and N. Westergård-Nielsen (eds.), 'Panel Data and Labour Market Dynamics,' pp. 57–74, Amsterdam: Elsevier.

KILLINGSWORTH, M.R. and HECKMAN, J.J. (1986), 'Female labor supply: A survey,' *in* O.C. Ashenfelter and R. Layard (eds.), 'Handbook of Labor Economics,' vol. 1, pp. 103–204, Amsterdam: Elsevier.

KÖLLING, A. (2000), 'The IAB-establishment panel,' *Schmollers Jahrbuch (Journal of Applied Social Science Studies)*, **120**(2):291–300.

KORPI, T. and MERTENS, A. (2003), 'Training systems and labor mobility: A comparison between Germany and Sweden,' *Scandinavian Journal of Economics*, **105**(4):597–617.

KRUEGER, A.B. (1988), 'The determinants of queues for federal jobs,' *Industrial and Labor Relations Review*, **41**(4):567–581.

KRUEGER, A.O. (1963), 'The economics of discrimination,' *Journal of Political Economy*, **71**(5):481–486.

KUHN, P.J. (2004), 'Is monopsony the right way to model labor markets? A review of Alan Manning's Monopsony in Motion,' *International Journal of the Economics of Business*, **11**(3):369–378.

LEONTIEF, W. (1936), 'Stackelberg on monopolistic competition,' *Journal of Political Economy*, **44**(4):554–559.

LIDDELL, H.G., SCOTT, R., and JONES, H.S. (1996), *Greek–English Lexicon*, Oxford: Oxford University Press, 9th edn.

LIGHT, A.L. and URETA, M. (1992), 'Panel estimates of male and female job turnover behavior: Can female nonquitters be identified?' *Journal of Labor Economics*, **10**(2):156–181.

LINK, C.R. and LANDON, J.H. (1976), 'Market structure, nonpecuniary factors and professional salaries: Registered nurses,' *Journal of Economics and Business*, **28**(2):151–155.

LÖFGREN, K.G. (1985), 'The pricing of pulpwood and spatial price discrimination: Theory and practice,' *European Review of Agricultural Economics*, **12**(2):283–293.

——— (1986), 'The spatial monopsony: A theoretical analysis,' *Journal of Regional Science*, **26**(4):707–730.

——— (1992), 'Spatial monopsony and monopoly pricing in a stochastic environment,' *Journal of Regional Science*, **32**(2):155–168.

LÖSCH, A. (1944), *Die räumliche Ordnung der Wirtschaft*, Jena: Fischer, 2nd edn.

LOUREIRO, P.R.A., CARNEIRO, F.G., and SACHSIDA, A. (2004), 'Race and gender discrimination in the labor market: An urban and rural sector analysis for Brazil,' *Journal of Economic Studies*, **31**(2):129–143.

LUCAS, R.E. (1980), 'Methods and problems of business cycle theory,' *Journal of Money, Credit and Banking*, **12**(4):696–715.

LUIZER, J.C. and THORNTON, R.J. (1986), 'Concentration in the labor market for public school teachers,' *Industrial and Labor Relations Review*, **39**(4):573–584.

MACHLUP, F. (1952), *The Economics of Sellers' Competition: Model Analysis of Sellers' Conduct*, Baltimore, MD: The Johns Hopkins Press.

MACMINN, R.D. (1980), 'Job search and the labor dropout problem reconsidered,' *Quarterly Journal of Economics*, **95**(1):69–87.

MADDEN, J.F. (1973), *The Economics of Sex Discrimination*, Lexington, MA: D.C. Heath.

——— (1977a), 'An empirical analysis of the spatial elasticity of labor supply,' *Papers in Regional Science*, **39**(1):157–171.

——— (1977b), 'A spatial theory of sex discrimination,' *Journal of Regional Science*, **17**(3):369–380.

MAIER, F. (2007), The Persistence of the Gender Wage Gap in Germany, Harriet Taylor Mill–Institut für Ökonomie und Geschlechterforschung, Berlin, Discussion Paper 01-2007.

MANNING, A. (2003a), *Monopsony in Motion: Imperfect Competition in Labor Markets*, Princeton, NJ: Princeton University Press.

——— (2003b), 'The real thin theory: Monopsony in modern labour markets,' *Labour Economics*, **10**(2):105–131.

——— (2004), 'Monopsony and the efficiency of labour market interventions,' *Labour Economics*, **11**(2):145–163.

——— (2006), 'A generalised model of monopsony,' *Economic Journal*, **116**(508):84–100.

MARSHALL, A. (1920), *Principles of Economics: An Introductory Volume*, London: Macmillan, 8th edn.

MCCALL, L. (1998), 'Spatial routes to gender wage (in)equality: Regional restructuring and wage differentials by gender and education,' *Economic Geography*, **74**(4):379–404.

MCCORMICK, R.E. and TOLLISON, R.D. (2001), 'Why do black basketball players work more for less money?' *Journal of Economic Behavior and Organization*, **44**(2):201–219.

MEITZEN, M.E. (1986), 'Differences in male and female job-quitting bahavior,' *Journal of Labor Economics*, **4**(2):151–167.

MILLS, E.S. and LAV, M.R. (1964), 'A model of market areas with free entry,' *Journal of Political Economy*, **72**(3):278–288.

References

MINCER, J. (1974), *Schooling, Experience, and Earnings*, New York: National Bureau of Economic Research.
MITTELHAMMER, R.C. (1996), *Mathematical Statistics for Economics and Business*, New York: Springer.
MONTGOMERY, J.D. (1991), 'Equilibrium wage dispersion and interindustry wage differentials,' *Quarterly Journal of Economics*, **106**(1):163–179.
MORTENSEN, D.T. (1990), 'Equilibrium wage distributions: A synthesis,' *in* J. Hartog, G. Ridder, and J. Theeuwes (eds.), 'Panel Data and Labor Market Studies,' pp. 279–296, Amsterdam: Elsevier.
―――― (2000), 'Equilibrium unemployment with wage posting: Burdett–Mortensen meet Pissarides,' *in* H. Bunzel, B.J. Christensen, P. Jensen, N.M. Kiefer, and D.T. Mortensen (eds.), 'Panel Data and Structural Labor Market Models,' pp. 281–292, Amsterdam: Elsevier.
―――― (2003), *Wage Dispersion: Why Are Similar Workers Paid Differently?*, Cambridge, MA: MIT Press.
MORTENSEN, D.T. and NEUMANN, G.R. (1988), 'Estimating structural models of unemployment and job duration,' *in* W.A. Barnett, E.R. Bernt, and H. White (eds.), 'Dynamic Econometric Modeling, Proceedings of the Third International Symposium in Economic Theory and Econometrics,' pp. 335–355, Cambridge: Cambridge University Press.
MORTENSEN, D.T. and PISSARIDES, C.A. (1999), 'New developments in models of search in the labor market,' *in* O.C. Ashenfelter and D.E. Card (eds.), 'Handbook of Labor Economics,' vol. 3B, pp. 2567–2627, Amsterdam: Elsevier.
MORTENSEN, D.T. and VISHWANATH, T. (1994), 'Personal contacts and earnings: It is who you know!' *Labour Economics*, **1**(2):187–201.
NAKAGOME, M. (1986), 'The spatial labour market and spatial competition,' *Regional Studies*, **20**(4):307–312.
NASH, J.F. (1953), 'Two-person cooperative games,' *Econometrica*, **21**(1):128–140.
NAYLOR, R.A. (1994), 'Pay discrimination and imperfect competition in the labor market,' *Journal of Economics (Zeitschrift für Nationalökonomie)*, **60**(2):177–188.
―――― (1996), 'Discrimination as collusion in imperfectly competitive labour markets,' *Labour*, **10**(2):447–455.
―――― (2003), 'Economic models of union behaviour,' *in* J.T. Addison and C. Schnabel (eds.), 'International Handbook of Trade Unions,' pp. 44–85, Cheltenham: Edward Elgar.
ÑOPO, H. (2008), 'Matching as a tool to decompose wage gaps,' *Review of Economics and Statistics*, **90**(2):290–299.
OAXACA, R.L. (1973), 'Male–female wage differentials in urban labor markets,' *International Economic Review*, **14**(3):693–709.
OECD (2002), 'Women at work: Who are they and how are they faring?' *in* OECD (ed.), 'OECD Employment Outlook,' pp. 61–128, Paris: OECD.
OHTA, H. (1980), 'Spatial competition, concentration, and welfare,' *Regional Science and Urban Economics*, **10**(1):3–16.
―――― (1988), *Spatial Price Theory of Imperfect Competition*, College Station, TX: Texas A&M University Press.
OI, W.Y. and IDSON, T.L. (1999), 'Firm size and wages,' *in* O.C. Ashenfelter and D.E. Card (eds.), 'Handbook of Labor Economics,' vol. 3B, pp. 2165–2214, Amsterdam: Elsevier.
OLFERT, R.M. and MOEBIS, D.M. (2006), 'The spatial economy of gender-based occupational segregation,' *Review of Regional Studies*, **36**(1):44–62.
OLIVETTI, C. and PETRONGOLO, B. (2008), 'Unequal pay of unequal employment? A cross-country analysis of gender gaps,' *Journal of Labor Economics*, **26**(4):621–654.
PARSONS, D.O. (1972), 'Specific human capital: An application to quit rates and layoff rates,' *Journal of Political Economy*, **80**(6):1120–1143.
PENCAVEL, J.H. (1972), 'Wages, specific training, and labor turnover in U.S. manufactoring industries,' *International Economic Review*, **13**(1):53–64.
―――― (1986), 'Labor supply of men: A survey,' *in* O.C. Ashenfelter and R. Layard (eds.), 'Handbook of Labor Economics,' vol. 1, pp. 3–102, Amsterdam: Elsevier.

PERRY, M.K. (1982), 'Oligopoly and consistent conjectural variations,' *Bell Journal of Economics*, **13**(1):197–205.

PHIMISTER, E. (2005), 'Urban effects on participation and wages: Are there gender differences?' *Journal of Urban Economics*, **58**(3):513–536.

PIGOU, A.C. (1908), 'Equilibrium under bilateral monopoly,' *Economic Journal*, **18**(70):205–220.

——— (1932), *The Economics of Welfare*, London: Macmillan, 4th edn.

PISSARIDES, C.A. (2000), *Equilibrium Unemployment Theory*, Cambridge, MA: MIT Press, 2nd edn.

POLLMANN-SCHULT, M. (2009), 'Geschlechterunterschiede in den Arbeitswerten: eine Analyse für die alten Bundesländer 1980–2000,' *Zeitschrift für ArbeitsmarktForschung (Journal of Labour Market Research)*, **42**(2):140–154.

POPPER, K.R. (2005), *Die Logik der Forschung*, Tübingen: Mohr Siebeck, 11th edn.

POSTEL-VINAY, F. and ROBIN, J.M. (2002a), 'The distribution of earnings in an equilibrium search model with state-dependent offers and counteroffers,' *International Economic Review*, **43**(4):989–1016.

——— (2002b), 'Equilibrium wage dispersion with worker and employer heterogeneity,' *Econometrica*, **70**(6):2295–2350.

PRÉKOPA, A. (1973), 'On logarithmic concave measures and functions,' *Acta Scientiarum Mathematicarum*, **34**(2):335–343.

RANSOM, M.R. and OAXACA, R.L. (2005), 'Intrafirm mobility and sex differences in pay,' *Industrial and Labor Relations Review*, **58**(2):219–237.

——— (2008), New Market Power Models and Sex Differences in Pay, Industrial Relations Section, Princeton University, Working Paper No. 540.

REINGANUM, J.F. (1979), 'A simple model of equilibrium price dispersion,' *Journal of Political Economy*, **87**(4):851–858.

ROBINSON, H. (2005), 'Regional evidence on the effect of the national minimum wage on the gender pay gap,' *Regional Studies*, **39**(7):855–872.

ROBINSON, J.V. (1933), *The Economics of Imperfect Competition*, London: Macmillan.

——— (1969), *The Economics of Imperfect Competition*, London: Macmillan, 2nd edn.

ROGERSON, R., SHIMER, R., and WRIGHT, R.D. (2005), 'Search-theoretic models of the labor market: A survey,' *Journal of Economic Literature*, **43**(4):959–988.

ROSEN, S. (1974), 'Hedonic prices and implicit markets: Product differentiation in pure competition,' *Journal of Political Economy*, **82**(1):34–55.

——— (1986), 'The theory of equalizing differences,' in O.C. Ashenfelter and R. Layard (eds.), 'Handbook of Labor Economics,' vol. 1, pp. 641–692, Amsterdam: Elsevier.

ROSENBAUM, P.R. and RUBIN, D.B. (1983), 'The central role of the propensity score in observational studies of causal effects,' *Biometrika*, **70**(1):41–55.

RUBINSTEIN, A. (1982), 'Perfect equilibrium in a bargaining model,' *Econometrica*, **50**(1):97–109.

SALOP, S.C. (1979a), 'A model of the natural rate of unemployment,' *American Economic Review*, **69**(1):117–125.

——— (1979b), 'Monopolistic competition with outside goods,' *Bell Journal of Economics*, **10**(1):141–156.

SAMUELSON, P.A. (1951), *Economics: An Introductory Analysis*, New York: McGraw-Hill, 2nd edn.

SCHLICHT, E. (1978), 'Labour turnover, wage structure, and natural unemployment,' *Zeitschrift für die Gesamte Staatswissenschaft (Journal of Institutional and Theoretical Economics)*, **134**(2):337–364.

——— (1982), 'A Robinsonian approach to discrimination,' *Zeitschrift für die Gesamte Staatswissenschaft (Journal of Institutional and Theoretical Economics)*, **138**(1):64–83.

SCHNABEL, C., ZAGELMEYER, S., and KOHAUT, S. (2006), 'Collective bargaining stucture and its determinants: An empirical analysis with British and German establishment data,' *European Journal of Industrial Relations*, **12**(2):165–188.

SCULLY, G.W. (1974), 'Pay and performance in major league baseball,' *American Economic Review*, **64**(6):915–30.
SHAPIRO, C. and STIGLITZ, J.E. (1984), 'Equilibrium unemployment as a worker discipline device,' *American Economic Review*, **74**(3):433–444.
SMITHIES, A.F. (1941), 'Optimum location in spatial competition,' *Journal of Political Economy*, **49**(3):423–439.
SPENCE, A.M. (1973), 'Job market signaling,' *Quarterly Journal of Economics*, **87**(3):355–374.
SRAFFA, P. (1926), 'The laws of returns under competitive conditions,' *Economic Journal*, **36**(144):535–550.
STAIGER, D., SPETZ, J., and PHIBBS, C. (1999), Is There Monopsony in the Labor Market? Evidence from a Natural Experiment, National Bureau of Economic Research, Working Paper No. 7258, Cambridge, MA.
STATISTISCHES BUNDESAMT (2005), *Leben und Arbeiten in Deutschland*, Wiesbaden: Statistisches Bundesamt.
STERN, N. (1972), 'The optimal size of market areas,' *Journal of Economic Theory*, **4**(1):154–173.
STEVENS, B.H. and RYDELL, C.P. (1966), 'Spatial demand theory and monopoly price policy,' *Papers of the Regional Science Association*, **17**(1):195–204.
STIGLER, G.J. (1940), 'Notes on the theory of duopoly,' *Journal of Political Economy*, **48**(4):521–541.
STIGLER, G.J. and BECKER, G.S. (1977), 'De gustibus non est disputandum,' *American Economic Review*, **67**(2):76–90.
STIGLITZ, J.E. (1973), 'Approaches to the economics of discrimination,' *American Economic Review (Papers and Proceedings)*, **63**(2):287–295.
—— (1975), 'The theory of "screening," education, and the distribution of income,' *American Economic Review*, **65**(3):283–300.
STOCKEY, N.L. and LUCAS, R.E. (1989), *Recursive Methods in Economic Dynamics*, Cambridge, MA: Harvard University Press.
SULLIVAN, D.S. (1989), 'Monopsony power in the market for nurses,' *Journal of Law and Economics*, **32**(2):S135–S178.
THORNTON, R.J. (2004), 'Retrospectives: How Joan Robinson and B. L. Hallward named monopsony,' *Journal of Economic Perspectives*, **18**(2):257–261.
TIROLE, J. (1988), *The Theory of Industrial Organization*, Cambridge, MA: MIT Press.
TO, T. (2009), 'Monopsonistic competition in formal and informal labour markets,' *in* R. Kanbur and J. Svejnar (eds.), 'Labour Markets and Economic Development,' pp. 139–156, London: Routledge.
TRAMPUSCH, C. (2005), 'Institutional resettlement: The case of early retirement in Germany,' *in* W. Streeck and K. Thelen (eds.), 'Beyond Continuity: Institutional Change in Advanced Political Economies,' pp. 203–228, Oxford: Oxford University Press.
USUI, E. (2006), Gender Occupational Segregation in an Equilibrium Search Model, Wayne State University, Detroit, MI, mimeo.
—— (2009), 'Wages, non-wage characteristics, and predominantly male jobs,' *Labour Economics*, **16**(1):52–63.
VAN DEN BERG, G.J. (1999), 'Empirical inference with equilibrium search models of the labour market,' *Economic Journal*, **109**(456):F283–F306.
—— (2001), 'Duration models: Specification, identification and multiple durations,' *in* J.J. Heckman and E.E. Leamer (eds.), 'Handbook of Econometrics,' vol. 5, pp. 3381–3460, Amsterdam: Elsevier.
VAN DEN BERG, G.J. and RIDDER, G. (1998), 'An empirical equilibrium search model of the labor market,' *Econometrica*, **66**(5):1183–1221.
VEENDORP, E.C.H. (1981), 'Instability in competition: Two variations on a Hotelling theme,' *Atlantic Economic Journal*, **9**(2):30–34.
VISCUSI, W.K. (1980), 'Sex differences in worker quitting,' *Review of Economics and Statistics*, **62**(3):388–398.

VON HAYEK, F.A. (1967), 'The theory of complex phenomena,' *in* F.A. von Hayek (ed.), 'Studies in Philosophy, Politics and Economics,' pp. 22–42, Chicago, IL: University of Chicago Press.

——— (1975), 'The pretence of knowledge,' *Swedish Journal of Economics*, **77**(4):433–442.

VON STACKELBERG, H. (1934), *Marktform und Gleichgewicht*, Vienna: Julius Springer.

——— (1943), *Grundzüge der theoretischen Volkswirtschaft*, Stuttgart: Kohlhammer.

WEICHSELBAUMER, D. and WINTER-EBMER, R. (2005), 'A meta-analysis of the international gender wage gap,' *Journal of Economic Surveys*, **19**(3):479–511.

WEISS, A. (1984), 'Determinants of quit behavior,' *Journal of Labor Economics*, **2**(3):371–387.

——— (1995), 'Human capital vs. signalling explanations of wages,' *Journal of Economic Perspectives*, **9**(4):133–154.

WINKELMANN, R. and ZIMMERMANN, K.F. (1998), 'Is job stability declining in Germany? Evidence from count data models,' *Applied Economics*, **30**(11):1413–1420.

WINTER-EBMER, R. (1995), 'Sex discrimination and competition in product and labour markets,' *Applied Economics*, **27**(9):849–857.

WOLFF, J. (2004), The Duration of New Job Matches in East and West Germany, Department of Economics, University of Munich, Discussion paper 2004-10.

WOOLDRIDGE, J.M. (2002), *Econometric Analysis of Cross Section and Panel Data*, Cambridge, MA: MIT Press.

YELLEN, J.L. (1984), 'Efficiency wage models of unemployment,' *American Economic Review (Papers and Proceedings)*, **74**(2):200–205.

Index

Beckerian discrimination, 96–98, 108–109, 114n, 198, 204–205
Burdett–Mortensen model, 97n, 106n, 137–148, 156–160
    and Robinsonian discrimination, 151–152
    basic assumptions of, 139–141
    objections to, 140–141
    with stochastic transitions among employers, 157–158
    with wage-elastic transitions to and from non-employment, 158–160

comparative statics
    Burdett–Mortensen model, 147
    dynamic monopsony, 135
    simple static monopsony, 13–14
    spatial monopsony
        constant model, 85–87, 91–92
        constant model allowing for varying participation, 89–90
        dyopsony model, 105–106
        linear model, 76–82
        long-run model, 60–70
        short-run model, 38–45
competition effect, 37–38, 43–44, 56n, 60n, 64–65, 79, 82–83, 92, 129
competitive wage
    Burdett–Mortensen model, 147
    simple static monopsony, 13–14
    spatial monopsony
        constant model, 84–85
        linear model, 74, 78
        long-run model, 54–55
        pure spatial monopsony, 20
        short-run model, 44–45
conjectural variations, 31–35
    and firm-level labour supply elasticity, 35–38
    consistency of, 34n

Diamond paradox, 138, 147
dynamic monopsony, 133–136

earnings function, 116–117, 166–167, 241, 242
economic space, 14–16
    one- vs. two-dimensional, 15–16, 19n, 71n
employer size–wage effect, 104–105, 146
equilibrium
    Burdett–Mortensen model, 144–147
    dynamic monopsony, 135
    simple static monopsony, 12–14, 73n
    spatial monopsony
        constant model, 85–86, 91–92
        constant model allowing for varying participation, 89
        dyopsony model, 103–108
        linear model, 75–76, 78–80
        long-run model, 36, 49, 55–60
        pure spatial monopsony, 19–20, 28–29, 72–73
        short-run model, 35–38
    stability of, 35, 60–61, 103–104

firm-level labour supply
    elasticity of, 13, 20–21, 29, 30n, 35–38, 41–44, 135, 155–156, 159
    and conjectural variations, 35–38
    and market-level supply's convexity relative to an exponential, 28
    estimate of, 192–198, 243, 244
    estimation of, 1n, 155–163
    long-run vs. short-run elasticity, 135, 151
    relation to monopsony power, 1, 4–5, 13–14, 19–20, 35, 135, 193
    vs. market-level supply elasticity, 20–21, 28, 30, 106
    vs. market-level supply, 11, 19, 30

257

gender difference
  in employer size–wage effect, 107, 164n, 199
  in firm-level labour supply elasticities, 97, 106–107, 110–111, 151–152, 163–164, 192–198, 205, 243, 244
    and implied gender pay gap, 193–198, 243, 244
  in market-level labour supply elasticities, 97, 151, 192–193
  in search frictions, 151–154, 168–173
  in separation rate elasticities, 157n, 163–164, 174–187, 243, 244
  in travel costs, 99, 114–116, 151
gender difference in
  employer size–wage effect, 200
gender pay gap
  and discrimination, 96, 117, 125n, 193–198, 205
  evolution over time, 95–96, 110, 116, 124–127, 229, 230
  in Germany, 95–96, 123–127, 166–167, 198, 229, 230, 237, 238, 241, 242
  raw, 95, 116, 123–124, 166–167, 237, 238
  regional variation in, 113, 115–116, 118, 123–124, 126–127, 229, 230
  unexplained, 95–96, 116–119, 125–127, 166–167, 198, 229, 230, 241, 242

horizontal job differentiation, 5
  vs. vertical job differentiation, 5n
Hotelling model, 31, 98n, 104n

labour demand, 12
Leibniz rule, 20n
Lerner index, 13
Linked Employer–Employee Data Set of the IAB (LIAB), 164–168
Lösch–Mills–Lav model, 31, 61n, 83n

market friction parameter, 145–148
  proxy of, 153–154
market-level labour supply
  as c.d.f. of workers' reservation incomes, 18, 26–27, 71, 77–78, 82, 87–88
  as workers' common supply curve, 16–18, 71, 77–78, 82, 88
  convexity relative to an exponential of, 21–28
  elasticity of, 20

  and convexity relative to an exponential, 26–28
  vs. firm-level supply elasticity, 20–21, 28, 30, 106
  vs. firm-level supply, 11, 19, 30
matching (statistical)
  exact matching, 117
  propensity score matching, 117–119, 125–127, 229, 230
matching technology
  balanced matching, 140
  random matching, 139–141
monopsony
  'classic' vs. 'new' monopsony, 1n, 4–6, 14
  empirical evidence on, 1n, 163–164, 192–200, 243, 244
  etymology of, 4
  history of, 3–6
  simple static monopsony, 11–14, 73n
  vs. bilateral monopoly, 2n
  vs. perfect competition, 1–3
  welfare implications of, 13
monopsony power
  actual vs. potential, 152n, 198n, 205
  degree of, 12–14, 19–20, 29–30, 35–45, 57–60, 62–70, 76–82, 85–87, 89–92, 104, 135, 145–148, 193
  estimate of, 193–198, 243, 244
  regional variation in, 114
  sources of
    demand-side concentration, 4, 14
    heterogenous preferences, 4–6, 14, 82n, 202
    search frictions, 4–6, 137–139, 145–148
    travel cost, 4–6, 14, 39–40, 45, 67–70, 76–77, 79, 81, 85–87, 91, 104

Oaxaca–Blinder decomposition, 116–117, 127, 166–167, 198, 241, 242
occupational segregation, 96, 109n, 113n, 175, 180, 186, 198

perfect competition
  vs. monopsony, 1–3

recruitment elasticity, 155–160
  estimation of, 156–160, 162
Regional File of the IAB Employment Samples (IAB-REG), 119–122
reservation income, 17–18, 26–27, 71, 77–78, 82, 87–88
  vs. reservation wage, 142n

Index

reservation wage, 138, 141–143, 145–147
   vs. reservation income, 142n
Robinsonian discrimination, 96–98, 105–107, 110–111, 114–115, 151–152, 193, 204–205
   and equal pay legislation, 109n
   and gender difference in market- vs. firm-level labour supply elasticities, 97, 106, 111, 151
   empirical evidence on, 163–164, 173, 193–200, 205, 243, 244
   policy implications of, 109–110, 204–205
   regional variation in, 115–116, 129
   vs. Beckerian discrimination, 96–98, 108–109, 204–205
   vs. first-degree wage discrimination, 100n

Salop model, 82, 92
search frictions, 4–6, 137–139, 145–148
   group-specific differences in, 153–154, 169–173
   measure of, 153–154
separation rate
   determinants of, 174–187
   elasticity of, 155–159
      estimate of, 174–187, 243, 244
      estimation of, 156–157, 162
   empiricial specification of, 160–162
spatial monopsony
   and Robinsonian discrimination, 105–107, 110–111, 114–115
   regional variation in, 115–116, 129
   basic assumptions of, 15–19
   constant model, 82–92
      allowing for varying participation, 87–90, 91n
   dyopsony model, 98n, 98–108
      basic assumptions of, 98–100, 102
      'dyopsony' vs. 'duopsony', 7n

linear model, 70–82
long-run model, 36, 49–70
pure spatial monopsony, 19–21, 28–29, 37–38, 72–73
   vs. spaceless monopsony, 29–30
short-run model, 15–45
   vs. pure spatial and spaceless monopsony, 37–38, 42–45, 54–55, 59–60, 65, 69, 72–74, 76–79
supply effect, 37, 43–44, 60n, 64–65, 82–85, 92, 129

'unfairness', 13

vertical job differentiation, 5n

wage dispersion, 104–105, 137–139, 145–148
   sources of, 104, 137–139, 148
wage posting, 137–140
   vs. bargaining, 137n
wage-setting curve
   changes in the position of, 61–62, 85–86
   curvature of, 52–55, 73–75, 84, 88–91
wages
   and employer characteristics, 104–105
   and profits, 104–105
   regional variation in, 114, 123–124
worker heterogeneity
   in reservation incomes, 18, 26–27, 71, 77–78, 82, 87–88

zero-profit locus
   changes in the position of, 54–55, 61–62, 72, 85–86
   curvature of, 50–52, 54–55, 72, 84–85, 89

Breinigsville, PA USA
25 March 2010
234871BV00004B/19/P